THE ENGLISH TEACHER

Books by Joseph Mersand, Ph.D.

Chaucer's Romance Vocabulary (1937, 1969)

The American Drama Since 1930 (1949, 1969)

Spelling Your Way To Success (1958)

English Grammar and Composition (1958, 1969)

Guide to Play Selection (1958, 1975)

Attitudes Toward English Teaching (1961)

Index to Plays—With Suggestions for Teaching (1966)

The American Drama, 1930-1940 (1969)

The Play's the Thing (1969)

Teaching Drama in Secondary Schools (1969)

Traditions in American Literature (1969)

In addition there are numerous anthologies, collections,
and edited editions of classic works.

Joseph Mersand

The
English Teacher
BASIC TRADITIONS
and
SUCCESSFUL INNOVATIONS

National University Publications
KENNIKAT PRESS   //   1977
Port Washington, N. Y.   //   London

The author and publisher wish to express their deep appreciation to the editors, periodicals, and organizations for their permission to reprint the chapters which originally appeared in these publications.

"The Emerging Curriculum in English" from the *Report of the Fourteenth Annual English Conference* of the Metropolitan Detroit Bureau of School Studies, March 1964. Also from *The English Review*, May 1964, New York City Association of Teachers of English.

"The Aims of English Instruction" from *High Points*, January 1965, published by the Board of Education of the City of New York. Also in revised form from *The Principal*, October 1972, published by the Yeshiva English Principals of the Board of Jewish Education, Inc.

"Individualizing Instruction in Large and Small Classes," from the *Bulletin of the National Association of Secondary–School Principals*, March 1960. Copyright: Washington, D. C.

"The Role of the Department Head in Providing for Individualizing of Instruction" from *The High School Journal*, April 1959.

"English for the Bright Student" from *The Principal*, September/October/November 1970.

"English for the Slow Learner," from *High Points*, May 1966.

"Reading for the Superior Student in a Comprehensive High School" from *The Reading Teacher*, May 1963. Reprinted with permission of the International Reading Association.

"The Paperback in High School" from the *Proceedings of the College Reading Association*, Volume III, Summer 1962. Reprinted by permission of the College Reading Association. Also in revised form in the *Florida English Journal*, May 1967, published by the Florida Council of Teachers of English.

"How to Teach Library Skills" from *The Principal*, February 1971.

"Contemporary Plays for the English Classroom" from the *Journal of English Teaching Techniques*, Winter 1971–1972.

"How Can We Help Students Enjoy Literature?" from *Illinois English Bulletin*, October 1959, published by the Illinois Association of Teachers of English.

"Selection of Adult Books for School-Age Readers" from *Perspectives in Reading No. 10*. Reprinted with permission of the International Reading Association.

"What Has Happened to Written Composition in the Past Fifty Years?" from *The English Journal*, April 1961. Reprinted with the permission of the National Council of Teachers of English and Joseph Mersand.

"Why Teach Listening?" from *The English Journal*, May 1951. Reprinted with the permission of the National Council of Teachers of English and Joseph Mersand.

"Developing Competence in Listening in Secondary Schools" from *The Speech Teacher*, November 1958, published by the Speech Communication Association.

"Teaching the Use of Television" from the *Journal of English Teaching Techniques*, Spring 1973. Also in revised form in *The Principal*, October/November 1973.

"How to Plan a Lesson" from *High Points*, June 1965.

"How to Teach by the Unit Method" from *High Points*, April 1965.

"How to Test and Evaluate" from *The English Review*, May 1967.

"How to Plan a Curriculum" from *High Points*, March 1965.

"Articulating Our Efforts in the Teaching of English" from *The English Review*, May 1963.

"Correlation and Integration in English" from *The Leaflet*, February 1969, published by the New England Association of Teachers of English.

"Creative Supervision in the Secondary School," from the *Bulletin of the National Association of Secondary-School Principals*, December 1959. Copyright: Washington, D. C.

"The Principal and His Influence on the English Program" from *The English Record*, published by the New York State English Council.

"The High School English Chairman Looks at the Humanities Approach for All Students" from *The Humanities Journal*, Fall 1965, published by the National Association for Humanities Education.

"Persistent Problems of English Department Heads and Some Solutions" from *The Leaflet*, May 1972.

Manufactured in the United States of America

Published by
Kennikat Press Corp.
Port Washington, N. Y./London

Library of Congress Cataloging in Publication Data

Mersand, Joseph E 1907–
The English teacher.

    Bibliography: p.
    Includes index.
    1. English philology—Study and teaching (Secondary)
I. Title.
PE65.M4   428'.007   76-54168
ISBN 0-8046-9170-3 (hard cover)
ISBN 0-8046-9175-4 (paper)

CONTENTS

PART FOUR
TEACHING THE ART OF LISTENING

PART FIVE
LIGHTENING THE BURDEN OF THE ENGLISH TEACHER

PART SIX
THE ENGLISH TEACHER AND CURRICULUM IMPROVEMENT

PART SEVEN
THE HIGH SCHOOL ENGLISH CHAIRMAN:
PERSISTENT PROBLEMS

FOREWORD

The English Teacher represents forty years of teaching experience on the secondary, college and graduate school levels. Since 1943 I have supervised English teachers in my own high schools and for a period of several years in all the summer schools and evening high schools of New York City. The privilege of serving on the Executive Committee of the National Council of Teachers of English over a five-year period and the opportunities of addressing thousands of English teachers in more than half of the United States have given me insight into many of the problems of our colleagues in their daily tasks as teachers of English.

The twenty-six chapters that follow either have been presented as addresses before groups of English teachers or as lectures to my graduate students in methods classes over the past twenty years at the following institutions: Cornell, Teachers College of Columbia University, Syracuse, New York University, North Texas State, University of Colorado, Hunter College, Yeshiva, York College, Johns Hopkins, Hofstra and Fairleigh Dickinson. Most were subsequently printed in professional journals, where they were exposed to a larger audience. It would be no exaggeration to state that the book represents not only the fruits of my own thinking and practice as a teacher and supervisor but also the judgments of those many students and readers who have commented on individual chapters as they first appeared in print.

The arrangement of the chapters needs some explanation. The book begins with two introductory chapters on the Emerging Curriculum in English and the Aims of English Instruction, both topics that have interested all writers of methods books in secondary English for the past seventy-five years.

Part Two: Individualization of Instruction includes four chapters showing how many teachers can individualize instruction for the average, the bright, and the slow student. To many teachers this is the most difficult of daily tasks, and hence I have placed it first among the practical chapters in the book.

Part Three: Reading, Writing, and Literature contains seven chapters discussing ways of teaching both reading and writing skills and the appreciation of literature, with additional observations on the impact of the paperback revolution upon classroom procedures.

Part Four: Teaching the Art of Listening contains three chapters of practical suggestions in the area of listening, a topic which has interested me for the past two decades. Now that there are more than fifteen hundred professional articles on the subject in print, no one need defend the need to teach this important skill in our secondary schools and colleges.

Part Five: Lightening the Burden of the English Teacher shows how the English teacher, already overburdened with many non-teaching chores, may plan for more effective instruction. We shall never have enough time to do all the things expected of us. We therefore must learn how to make the best use of the limited time that we have. Many successful procedures are indicated in this section.

Part Six: The English Teacher and Curriculum Improvement shows in its three chapters how every teacher can prepare to participate in curriculum improvement, an ongoing process in these days of change. I have long felt that more classroom teachers would be interested in improving the curriculum if they knew how to go about it; in these chapters I have tried to point out practical procedures.

Part Seven: The High School English Chairman: Persistent Problems demonstrates some ways in which I personally have tried to assist in the past three decades the hundreds of teachers who have come under my supervision and what I have learned from them. Supervision, to be successful, must be a two-way street. Both teachers and supervisors may find valuable suggestions here.

Each chapter in the book, with few exceptions, is followed by copious footnotes with the sources of the many quotations and a reading list for those who wish to pursue any topic further. The references consist of the best in books, pamphlets, and magazine articles—all culled from a much larger list.

Although the twenty-six chapters now assembled in book form originally appeared over a period of several years, I sincerely believe that the principles and practices described have permanent values relevant to our own times. Most of the problems that faced me when I began my teaching career are still with us, many of them in more intensive form. It would be foolhardy to assume that this book has all the solutions. I trust, however, that this book will encourage our teachers and supervisors of English of today to face their problems with greater expertise and confidence than I had and to look toward the future with greater hope.

Users of this book will soon notice that I like to take a scholarly and historical approach to the various problems and their solutions in the following chapters. This does not mean that I have been unaware of or negligent of the latest ideas, techniques, or principles in the teaching of English. Careful study of these chapters will reveal that long before certain practices were adopted to a large degree throughout the country, they were adumbrated or described in these chapters, some of which go back twenty years or more.

It is my considered opinion that no teacher can adequately evaluate the recommendations of the present and the projections for the future who does not know the philosophies and practices of the past. How much time, money, and needless effort could have been saved if teachers, supervisors, and administrators who too eagerly swallowed some of the specious solutions recommended for long-standing problems, had taken the trouble to become acquainted with practices that had been tried in the past and been discarded because they were found wanting.

After decades of countless suggestions for improving English instruction, ranging all the way from a plethora of electives to the utilization of expensive electronic gadgetry, teachers, parents, and members of boards of education are taking a second look at all these numerous innovations. They are going even further and asking for a "return to the basics," whatever that may mean. The author of this book has never left the basics, while at the same time he has been open-minded and responsive to worthwhile new instructional procedures for almost the past half-century. Hence you will find references in the Bibliography to books, pamphlets, and magazine articles of the 1930's, 1940's, 1950's, 1960's and 1970's because they were read and many of the ideas contained therein were applied to his own teaching and supervision of other teachers.

Perhaps in this respect *The English Teacher* is different from the scores of excellent methods books in the teaching of secondary English. Like Janus, I have by scholarly disposition been inclined to face the past to ascertain, to paraphrase Matthew Arnold, "the best that has been thought and practiced" in English teaching. At the same time, I have ever been on the alert for any principles and practices that pointed to more successful and more worthwhile results. As Toynbee and other historians through the ages have expressed so well, "He who knows only the present is bound to repeat the errors of the past."

If *The English Teacher* will enable you to avoid the pitfalls and egregious mistakes of your predecessors, and at the same time give you practical suggestions for meeting your many daily (and sometimes frustrating and seemingly insurmountable) problems, then my forty-five years of teaching and supervision will not have been in vain.

It would lengthen this foreword inordinately to express my acknowledgments to all who have helped make this book what it is. First and foremost, I must thank the thousands of students I have had in the past forty-five years who probably have taught me more about the teaching of English than I have taught them. The hundreds of teachers whom I have been privileged to supervise have taught me a great deal not only about methodology in secondary English but about patience, understanding and better human relations. It has been my good fortune to have had good supervisors both as chairmen and principals. My debts are great to my former chairmen, Abraham H. Lass, the late George J. Crane and Samuel Streicher. My Principal at Jamaica High School, Louis A. Schuker, the late Alfred A. Tausk of Boys High School and Wallace A. Manheimer of Long Island City High School have been towers of strength. One of the most creative individuals I have ever worked for is Dr. William H. Bristow, Director Emeritus of the Bureau of Curriculum Research of the New York City Board of Education. The privilege of serving in many local, state, and national professional organizations cannot adequately be evaluated. The thousands of dedicated English teachers whom I have met and spoken to in this way have enriched my understanding beyond price.

I wish to thank the various editors of the publications in which many of these chapters appeared for their permission to reprint them. Mr. Cornell Jaray, President, and Mrs. Alice Jaray, Vice-President of the Kennikat Press, have encouraged me in this venture and have served as editors far beyond the line of duty. This book is a much better one because of their advice and counsel, and my debt of gratitude is more than I can express.

My years of association with York College of the City University of New York have been especially rewarding, for which I am deeply grateful to Professor Elizabeth E. Seittelman, Head of the Department of Teacher Preparation, a supervisor of rare insight, humanity and understanding.

Finally, I wish to express my thanks to my patient and long-enduring wife, Estelle Joy Mersand, who has been the sounding board for many of my ideas, and who has been my most perceptive critic and wise counselor on countless occasions.

Joseph Mersand

York College of the City University of New York

THE ENGLISH TEACHER

PART ONE
INTRODUCTION

1

THE EMERGING CURRICULUM IN ENGLISH

A study of the English program in our country over the past sixty years would indicate that in one way or another it was always emerging. Thus in 1917, when J. Fleming Hosic and his colleagues from the National Council of Teachers of English and the National Education Association prepared that historic document, *The Reorganization of English in the Secondary Schools,*[1] many of our teachers felt at long last our bondage of domination by the colleges was broken and we in the secondary schools had emerged.

Later, in 1935, when W. Wilbur Hatfield and his committee produced *An Experience Curriculum in English,*[2] we emerged again, this time with a new philosophy, set of objectives and methodology. In 1946, Max J. Herzberg prepared a special issue for the *Bulletin* of the National Association of Secondary School Principals entitled, *The Emerging Curriculum in English.*[3] In 1952, under the direction of Dora V. Smith, the Commission on the English Curriculum, first organized in 1945, offered the first of five volumes, *The English Language Arts,*[4] and, in 1956, *The English Language Arts in the Secondary School.*[5] In 1959, the Commission on English of the College Entrance Examination Board was organized. In 1960, its first statement of objectives was widely disseminated and publicized; in the summers of 1961–1962 hundreds of secondary English teachers attended institutes organized by the Commission to study what many considered an emerging curriculum in English.

In that informative document by Arno Jewett, former specialist in Secondary Language Arts, U. S. Office of Education, *The English Language Arts in American High Schools,*[6] he studied some 285 courses of study in some 150 communities and concluded with some emerging trends as he observed them. James Moffatt's *A Child-Centered Language Arts Curriculum* published in 1968, is only one of many new studies in the 1960's and 1970's.[7] English in America in the past forty to fifty years has had no lack of emergings, as well as emergencies, no lack of trends, tendencies or directions. In fact, it would seem to some of us that no sooner had English emerged in one area and settled down than it began to emerge in quite a different

5

fashion in some other area. Some would even say: let us stop emerging for a while and get back to the fundamentals. This would be, in truth, a kind of emerging in reverse.

Nevertheless, the English instruction of the 1970's will be somewhat different in patterns and scope, in methodology and in content, from that of earlier decades. I should like to explore what I believe some of these emerging trends will be so that we may prepare ourselves to become more effective in our daily tasks.

1. *Greater importance will be assigned to English as the most important subject in the entire curriculum.* English to me is central, continuous, cumulative and all-pervasive.

There is no question that the public at large, members of boards of education, representatives in government and educated people generally are convinced that upon the literacy of our citizenry may depend the future of our nation. Although the extent of federal funds expended for English is minute in comparison with similar allocations in such areas as science, foreign languages and mathematics, these funds do increase yearly. In time we hope that we shall get the sums we need. The whole story of Project English is one of which we may all feel proud, although its results will not be known for several years.[8] The Fleischmann Report on the Cost and Quality of Education in New York State, published in 1972 again emphasizes the importance of reading and writing.

As for the view of enlightened citizens toward English, my favorite quotation still is that of W. W. Watson, former Chairman of the Physics Department of Yale University:

I feel that the most important subject in the entire course of study in the elementary and college preparatory years is the English language. What can be more important than to handle our own work-a-day language with facility, no matter what the life work, business or profession? I have some younger physics colleagues who obviously write with difficulty. They are promising scientists who love to work in the laboratory but they are laggards in writing papers that describe their results. But what good are research reports unless they are properly described in a well-written report?

Also, it is most important that a scientist or engineer be able to get on his feet and speak clearly about his work. Some practice in public speaking, debating, or dramatics should be a part of every student's course.

I am pleased to note that among Dr. James B. Conant's main recommendations in his various studies in secondary education is that all secondary school students should study English every year, and that half this work should be in composition.

2. *The second emerging trend is greater emphasis on written composition* by discovering better ways of teaching; by reducing the size of classes; by reducing the number of classes per English teacher; by more provision for individual conferences; and by the utilization of qualified lay readers. Exciting developments are taking place in written composition instruction at all levels. The brochure by Richard Braddock and his colleagues on *Research in Written Composition* demonstrates how little really has been known on a scientific basis, and, what is more important, what already has been discovered.[9]

The NEA Composition Project of 1963 undoubtedly revealed new concepts and valuable procedures. The February, 1964, issue of the *Bulletin* of the National Association of Secondary School Principals had a substantial article on this project by its director for the first year, Arno Jewett.[10]

Many of the Curriculum Centers funded by the Cooperative Research Branch of the U. S. Office of Education studied written composition in various sequences. From these centers much valuable data came.

3. *The third trend will be greater emphasis on individualization of instruction* for all students: the bright, the average, the culturally disadvantaged, the culturally different and the slow. We have given lip service to this trend for many years, but we have not quite known how to go about achieving our objectives. Consider the aspect of teaching the culturally different. This is one of America's most demanding educational problems; for years different communities have tried to find some solutions. I believe that a breakthrough has been made, which is well documented in the U. S. O. E. brochure *Developing Language Skills of the Culturally Different.*[11]

But the slow, the disadvantaged and the culturally different will not be the only students whose individual needs will be met during this decade. The average, the bright, the under-achiever, the late-bloomer, all merit the same careful study.

4. *The fourth trend will be greater interest in language growth and development and the modifications we must make in our teaching.* This means a greater understanding of historical linguistics, or the way in which our language developed, is constantly developing, and will develop in the future. This means also a reevaluation of our concepts of the place of grammar instruction in our schools, whether it be the formal grammar of my high school days, the functional grammar of my beginning days as a teacher, or the structural and the transformational grammar which is much talked about in many circles today.

I would not throw all grammar overboard or advocate wholly any single variety of grammar, but I do believe there is a need for more controlled experiments on a massive scale and over a considerable period of time to determine exactly what concepts of grammar we want to teach and how best to teach them. Even a few small experiments in teaching the new structural or transformational grammar may enable us to reevaluate our instruction for achieving our ends more effectively. Linguists are not agreed on many things, but they are all agreed on this: that there is a large body of verified knowledge about our language which has not even begun to affect the vast majority of our colleagues. Study takes time, and in the crowded schedule of the average secondary English teacher, with his 175-200 pupils a day, there is precious little time for study of the facts of our language, for newer discoveries in our literature, or in the methodology of both. The great popularity of workshops in linguistics and the various grammars is a desirable trend.

One of our most distinguished linguists, W. Nelson Francis, puts the matter thus:

My plea, then, is for English teachers who are specifically and professionally informed about the English language. Furthermore, I believe that this information is even more important for elementary and secondary school teachers than it is for college teachers. It is, after all, in the earlier school years that most of the direct teaching of language goes on. By the time a student gets to college, his language habits are formed for better or worse, and it is a major operation to change them. Yet the graduate schools seem to believe that linguistic training is necessary only for Ph. D. candidates. Little beyond rather simple courses in the history of English is offered to undergraduates. Indeed, many liberal arts colleges of high standing, some of whose graduates go directly into teaching, give no work at all in historical or structural linguistics. I believe that this is wrong and that nobody should be entrusted with the teaching of English in the secondary school until he has had some solid linguistic training. At present he may escape this in his undergraduate education, but he can make it up in summer courses. Before long, I would hope to see thorough, up-to-date courses in the English language offered everywhere to undergraduates planning to be teachers.

Linguistics is a broad field, too broad for the prospective teacher, whose primary concern must be with literature, to cover in any thoroughgoing way. It is all the more important that the content of his linguistic training be carefully chosen in the light of his future needs. Specifically I believe that he should have at least elementary acquaintance with four fields. He must know a good deal about grammar— not necessarily because he is to teach it directly, for he may not. But he must know how the English language works in order to help his students to a greater proficiency in its use. He must know something about regional dialects, social levels, and functional varieties of English and their relation to standard written English. Thirdly, he must know the outlines of the history of English and something about its older forms, so that he can see and perhaps reveal to his students the rich cultural heritage of the older literature and understand the growth and development of the English vocabulary. Fourthly, he must know something more about the English writing system than how to use it without error, so that he can understand the unique problems it presents and not simply classify all errors in its use as crimes against the state.[12]

5. *The fifth trend will be greater emphasis on preparation of teachers in English.* If English is the most important subject in the curriculum, it obviously cannot be taught by poorly prepared teachers. It has been said, and rightly so, that English is the easiest subject to teach poorly and the hardest subject to teach well. One of the disturbing revelations in the volume, *The National Interest and the Continuing Education of Teachers of English,* is the woeful inadequacy of preparation of many teachers of English in elementary and secondary schools.[13] We must provide in our pre-service training for a proper balance between subject matter and education within a matrix of the right teaching personality that is capable of growing on the job. It is heartening to note that in many states the qualifications for teaching English in secondary schools are being increased.

6. *The sixth trend will be greater attention to supervision of English teaching* and to the position of Supervisor of English for a state, a county or a city and to the Head of Department of an individual school.

For a long time to come, despite increased qualifications for new teachers, we shall be plagued either with a lack of English teachers or with inadequately trained ones. Who is to train them? Those cities, like New York City, which long have had licensed heads of departments who received higher salaries and allowances for supervision, have been more than satisfied with the outlay of funds for these valuable services in terms of improvement of instruction, teacher morale, and curriculum.

That the U. S. Office of Education considers the subject of instructional supervision of high priority was demonstrated on February 26, 28, and 29, 1964, when the first National Conference of English Supervisors was held at the Office of Education, to which distinguished supervisors of English from all parts of the country and from all levels of instruction were invited to discuss their problems and to share solutions. Out of these deliberations came a brochure which is of inestimable value in improving English instruction everywhere. In fact, all who were there wanted additional conferences sponsored either by the NCTE or the U. S. Office of Education, so profitable had they found this first one. And, in fact, many similar conferences have been held since 1964 all over the country.

7. *Curriculum Improvement.* I have written of the greater importance of our subject, about the importance of the individual student, and of the importance of the individual teacher and his supervisor. What can we expect about the curriculum of the 70's which will bring the student and the teacher together? It would be quite easy to say that the English curriculum of the 1970's will be an experience curriculum, or a correlated curriculum, or an individualized curriculum. But I believe it may be something else. Each of the Curriculum Centers funded by Project English, experimented over a period of about five years with new types of curricula. The results were made available to the Office of Education, which, in turn, made them available to all teachers and supervisors. I would venture to say that these curricula were based on more careful study than many promulgated in the past; that they had really been tried out with thousands of students; that they had been carefully evaluated; that they had been prepared by the best brains and teaching experience available in the respective Curriculum Centers.

Meanwhile, curriculum construction has been going on constantly all over the country, in individual schools, in large school systems and in many states.

New curriculum procedures are taking place, ranging all the way from those followed in the summer institutes of the Commission of English in 1961–1962 to the cooperative endeavor in individual schools. More and more school administrators and boards of education are realizing the value of released time to permit gifted teachers to meet for considerable periods of time to draw up curricula and to make plans for their implementation, evaluation and subsequent modification. The possibilities for individual growth as a result of work on curriculum in a leisurely atmosphere, among similarly devoted colleagues, are truly enormous. The more teachers we can involve in curriculum construction, the more deeply will they become involved when the curriculum is to be implemented and evaluated.

8. *New Instructional Materials.* What changes can we expect in instructional materials to be used to bring the curriculum, pupils and teachers into a working relationship for the realization of our objectives? I would venture to predict that there will be greater utilization of paperbacks in the literature programs, more building of personal libraries, thematic approaches to literature and reevaluation of the classics. More copies of the standard classics (*Silas Marner, A Tale of Two Cities, The Odyssey,* etc.) probably are sold today in paperbacks than were sold in the good old days when only standard classics were taught. Those critics who accuse us of having abandoned the classics do not know the sales figures. Each year about 400-million paperbacks are sold in America. Many college bookstore managers inform us that their greatest sales come from the paperbacks! Such firms as Avon, Bantam,

Fawcett, Dell, Pocket Book, Scholastic and New American Library are vying with each other for the greatest library of good literature for the schools. We would be unwise not to take advantage of their offerings. Perhaps the millions of secondary school students who are introduced to the quality paperbacks of today will become the enlightened readers of the future.

Closely allied to the use of paperbacks is greater utilization of all the mass media: television, radio, movies, newspapers, magazines and others. My point is that through the various mass media, wisely chosen, our students may have enriched experiences that were totally unknown in the days when we were in elementary and high school. I believe there will be more and more utilization of these media in the coming years.

9. *Instructional Hardware.* What will the technological advances be? Will the teaching machine replace the teacher? Hardly. Even the Latin language, which usually is considered a dead language and no longer subject to change, has had to accommodate itself to our own time; in the Latin language of our time, we read of a *typographica-machina* for typewriter and *via ferrea* for railroad. If the language of Cicero and Virgil is not afraid of machines, we as English teachers need not be. I well remember when my high school English teachers scoffed at the idea of a victrola, then at the moving picture projector, the tape recorder, etc. None of these eliminated a single teacher from his job. We now are being confronted with many new machines for teaching purposes. We simply do not know enough about how to use them, but we should learn more about them. Just as the typewriter enables us to write far more rapidly and, in many instances, more clearly than the old quill pen, so it is possible that some of the teaching machines may spare us from the more mechanical aspects of teaching and permit us to work more creatively. No machine will ever replace the capable teacher, but it might well enable him to do his proper job more effectively.

10. *The Place of Libraries.* The English program of the 1970's will make even greater use of libraries than ever before. Not only must the student in the seventies know there is such a thing as the Dewey Decimal System (usually ascribed to Admiral Dewey of *Maine* disaster fame; or to Thomas E. Dewey, former Governor of New York State), but also he must be aware of the countless resources of the well-equipped school library and be eager to use them. No longer can the *Encyclopedia Britannica* and the *Reader's Guide* be his only sources of reference for everything from the winner of last year's World Series to the Capital of Tanzania. Gradually the student must become aware of the countless treasures in his school and local library and the sources for more information about them. This means the status of librarian may have to be changed from that of a cataloguer to that of teacher-librarian or counselor. She will have to learn something about teaching library skills and then do everything possible to make the library a beehive of wholesome and worthwhile activity.

11. *English as a Second Language.* Finally, we must become aware of the new importance of English as a second language. In the March, 1961, issue of the *NEA Journal*[14] we were told that in the Soviet Union about three-fourths of all students in higher education study English; sixty percent of all foreign language majors are

in English. The figures must be even higher today. Throughout the world there are 700-million people who either are studying English or know it. Never in the history of the world was a single language known to so many people. To teach English in the high school today requires a new world view which will manifest itself in the use of materials, in methods, in attitudes. In truth, these old words are true today: *nihil humanum mihi alienum est.*

I believe that the 1970's will make great demands upon us all and upon our students as well. There is limited time for them to learn and limited time for us to teach them. We shall have to become acquainted with many new materials of instruction, with newer methods of utilizing them, with better ways to understand our students, and with devices for evaluating our instruction. The English teacher, armed with a grammar book, a literature anthology and a piece of chalk, may have been acceptable in my high school days, though he was rarely popular; in the demanding years ahead, he will be hopelessly out of date. If we are to cross the new frontiers of the mind, we must do so with all the weapons, all the ingenuity, skill and insight at our command.

Change, of course, is inevitable, and trends will continue to emerge. Our task is to prepare now to understand these trends, and, by adequate preparation and bold practices, to enable our students to meet the brave new world of tomorrow with understanding and courage, with humanity and wisdom, with faith in themselves and in the ideals of our nation. The old cliché that the pen is mightier than the sword has become a frightening truth, the sword is now so terrible. Man has the choice, it would appear, to utterly destroy the human race by the sword or to build a united and peaceful world by the simplest yet the most divine of all gifts: the human word. Was there ever a challenge to teachers more awesome, yet more inspiring?

2

THE AIMS OF ENGLISH INSTRUCTION

A definition of the aims of instruction in English has been the subject of discussion almost from the beginning of such instruction in America. These aims varied with the type of school in which English was taught, the nature of the student body, and the ulterior purpose of the student.

COLLEGES INFLUENCED INSTRUCTION

In the nineteenth century the comparatively small percentage of adolescents who went to secondary school almost invariably went on to college. Although the colleges did not actually prescribe specific books to be read or methods for teaching them, they did exercise a strong influence on English instruction through the college entrance examinations. The College Entrance Examination Board would announce several years in advance upon what texts examination questions would be based, and teachers whose students were trying to get into the best colleges would teach these "classics" in such a way that their students would answer the questions successfully.

Likewise, the composition program was affected by the nature of the essay questions asked on college entrance tests. If an English teacher in the high school of the 1890's were asked the aims of his instruction, he might have answered, "To enable my students to succeed in their English work in college."

A CHANGE IN PHILOSOPHY

Revolt against the real or fancied domination by the colleges was put into written form in 1917 by J. Fleming Hosic and his distinguished committee in their oft-quoted *Reorganization of English in Secondary Schools.*[1] Although the document is over sixty years old now, it is remarkably contemporary in its philosophy and can be read with profit as one of the basic statements in the history of the teaching of English.

The major aim of teaching English in the high school is no longer college preparation.

The college preparatory function of the high school is a minor one. Most of the graduates of the high school go, not into a higher institution, but into "life." Hence the course in English should be organized with reference to basic personal and social needs rather than with reference to college-entrance requirements. The school, moreover, will best prepare for either "life" or college by making its own life real and complete.[2]

Other statements of aims in greater or less detail have appeared in the decades since Hosic and his colleagues issued their historic pronouncement. Several of these will be listed, for only by studying the manner in which aims have changed to meet the times can the individual teacher formulate the aims which best meet the needs of his students.

AIMS OF ENGLISH TEACHING: 1942

The National Council of Teachers of English has been interested in aims of English teaching since its inception in 1912 and has issued several documents which are important for the historical understanding of the subject. A Basic Aims Committee issued a pamphlet in 1942 entitled *Basic Aims for English Instruction in American Schools*, listing the following aims:

1.   Language is a basic instrument in the maintenance of the democratic way of life.

2.   Increasingly free and effective interchange of ideas is vital to life in a democracy.

3.   Language study in the schools must be based on the language needs of living.

4.   Language ability expands with the individual's experience.

5.   English enriches personal living and deepens understanding of social relationships.

6.   English uses literature of both past and present to illumine the contemporary scene.

7.   Among the nations represented in literature, America should receive major emphasis.

8.   A study of the motion picture and radio is indispensable in the English program.

9.   The goals of instruction in English are, in the main, the same for all young people, but the heights to be attained in achieving any one of them and the materials used for the purpose will vary with individual need.

10.   The development of social understanding through literature requires reading materials within the comprehension, the social intelligence, and the emotional range of the pupils whose lives they are expected to influence.

11.   English pervades the life and work of the school.

12.   English enriches personality by providing experience of intrinsic worth for the individual.

13.   Teachers with specialized training are needed for effective instruction in the language arts.[3]

Each of these aims is developed in considerable detail in the pamphlet. In 1945 the National Council of Teachers of English established a Commission on the English Curriculum which has already completed and published all of its contemplated five volumes: *The English Language Arts, Language Arts for Today's Children, The English Language Arts in the Secondary School, The College Teaching of English,* and *The Education of Teachers of English.* In the course of gathering data for the various volumes, the Commission distributed "An Outline of the Desirable Outcomes and Experiences in the Language Arts Which Will be Illustrated in the Curriculum Study of the National Council of Teachers of English."[4]

AIMS OF ENGLISH TEACHING: 1952

To study the historical development of the aims of English, one needs to examine the ten aims listed below and compare them with the N. C. T. E. document published in 1942.

1.   Mental and emotional stability.

2.   Dynamic and worthwhile allegiances through heightened moral perception and a personal sense of values.

3.   Growing intellectual capacities and curiosity.

4.   Increasingly effective use of language for daily communication.

5.   Habitual and intelligent use of mass modes of communication.

6.   Growing personal interests and enjoyment.

7.   Effective habits of work.

8.   Social sensitivity and effective participation in the group life.

9.   Faith in and allegiance to the basic values of a democratic society.

10.   Vocational efficiency.

All of these aims are explained in detail in the Commission's first volume, *The English Language Arts.*[5]

CHANGES SINCE 1952

The 1950's and the early 1960's were years of many political, technological and social changes. By 1962 it became possible to broadcast television programs directly from the United States to Europe and vice versa. The African continent had almost entirely dropped its colonial status and added a score of nations to the United Nations. Mass methods of publication and distribution had made quality paperbacks ubiquitous, and their sales reached over one million copies a day.

The Conant Report on the *American High School,* with its recommendation for a composition a week and for 50-percent of the time to be devoted to written composition, has given greater emphasis to the whole subject of written composition. Also, the tremendous increase in the study of English as a second language has enlarged the entire scope of English instruction. The high school English instructor is influencing students who in a few years may be using their knowledges and skills in almost any country in the world in a host of capacities that were not dreamt of by the curriculum workers of the 1870's or the 1890's.

AIMS OF ENGLISH TEACHING: 1970's

What, then, should be the aims of English instruction in the American high schools of the 1970's? Practically every new course of study which appears today begins with a statement of basic aims. Investigation has revealed almost 2,000 such aims. An intensive study of many of these courses, and extensive correspondence and personal communication with many of the leaders of the profession, have resulted in the following ten basic aims and seven supplementary aims. They might well be considered for meeting the needs of the millions of our secondary youth of the 1970's.

Ten Basic Aims of English Instruction

1. To improve the communicative powers through listening, reading, speaking and writing, which are the four highways of human communication.
2. To bring to the individual the spiritual, intellectual and cultural heritage of the race through literature.
3. To enable the individual to live in all-time and all-space by means of literature (including the newspaper, magazine, radio, film and television) through vicarious experiences.
4. To provide the unique aesthetic experiences present in literature.
5. To guide the pupil into the safe channels of emotional release, leading to emotional poise, which are offered by speaking and writing.
6. To capture the rich satisfactions of creative activity in speaking and writing.
7. To endow some individuals with a means for leading others and for achieving social prestige for themselves by a superior command of the language arts.
8. To train in the ability to use, evaluate and enjoy newspapers, magazines, motion pictures, radio and television.
9. To develop a capacity for profitable use of leisure through education in the use of the mass media, in literature as well as speaking and writing.
10. To enable students to develop a degree of vocational efficiency through English.

Seven Subsidiary Aims

Other courses in the secondary school curriculum contribute to the realization of the following seven subsidiary aims, but the English teacher must also be aware of and strive to realize them.

11.　To lead pupils to the development of a worthy set of ethical values with the aid of literature and oral-written expression programs.

12.　To promote in students the devotion to worthy causes which can emerge from the best literary experiences.

13.　To promote in pupils those intergroup sympathies and that respect for the other man's right to his opinion which can and which should emerge from the best literary experiences.

14.　To train students to use the language arts as fundamental aids in correct thinking and in testing the thinking of others.

15.　To show the student how the language arts may assist him in solving his personal problems.

16.　To show the student how the language arts may assist him in becoming aware of social problems and may assist him in solving them.

17.　To train students to participate in classroom, group, family and community living by means of the language arts, especially listening and speaking.[6]

AIMS OF SECONDARY EDUCATION

The aims of English instruction have always been related closely to the aims of secondary education as a whole. As the latter have been enlarged to take into consideration a more heterogeneous type of student body, the former have been modified. Any teacher who is familar with the volume of the Education Policies Commission, *The Purposes of Education in American Democracy,* will recognize its four major aims:

1. The Objectives of Self-Realization;
2. The Objectives of Human Relationship;
3. The Objectives of Economic Efficiency;
4. The Objectives of Civil Responsibility.[7]

In the years since the appearance of these four aims, many courses of study in English have either referred to them or adapted them. Arno Jewett in his *English Language Arts in American High Schools*[8] makes an analysis of 285 courses of study from 44 states, the District of Columbia, the Canal Zone, and Hawaii, which appeared since Dora V. Smith's similar study in 1932.[9] It is interesting to study some of the ways in which the aims of English have been included among the larger aims of secondary education.[10]

ROLE OF THE ENGLISH TEACHER

There is, of course, a wide gap between the most complete statement of aims and its realization. Between these two, there are the experiences, instructional materials, methodology and the teacher's personality. Aims cannot be realized by their mere formulation, but they should be kept in mind if the teacher does not wish to waste his time and the time of his students. Arno Jewett has expressed this point well:

But aims are important. Before starting on a journey, a traveler usually knows his destination. If he knows where he wants to go, he can better select a direct and economical route. He can decide how he should travel. General objectives are like the ultimate goals of a man traveling on a long journey. The stopping places en route are the specific aims or immediate goals. The mode of travel and route are the activities in the English curriculum which enable the teacher and pupils to attain the objectives that are most significant. Unless the pupils and and teacher have clearly in mind where they are going and unless they believe strongly in the value of their goals and the means of attaining them, there is a good possibility that their classwork will be irrelevant, purposeless, and valueless.[11]

GENERAL AIMS AND SPECIFIC AIMS

Every lesson in English theoretically should contribute in some way to one or more aims of the total English program. It must also have a specific aim for that day or that unit. Much effort and time will be saved if the teacher knows exactly what he hopes to accomplish by the day's lesson and then devises the experiences and gathers the instructional materials which can best realize that specific aim.

Many beginning teachers make the error of starting the lesson without a clear formulation of the aim either in their own mind or in their students' minds.

It becomes a matter of the teacher's judgment as to how much time and effort is to be expended on the realization of any aim or series of aims. Somehow he has to be aware of all of them and may have to seize unexpected opportunities to realize some of them. An incident that happens in class may either be passed over or turned into a lesson in better human relationships. The death of a distinguished author, like Ezra Pound or William Faulkner, may either be passed over with a casual mention or it may serve as the occasion for a lesson on the significance of that author in the lives of the students.

Things happen so rapidly these days that the teacher cannot begin to catch up with the changes that are taking place. Yet the day's events can make excellent jumping-off points for teaching. The death of a movie glamour girl as the class is studying "Richard Cory"; the launching of the satellite *Telstar* as the class is doing a unit on one world; the television performance of a great play as the class is studying it—these are but a few of the examples of ways in which events in our daily lives can be utilized by the alert teacher to realize her daily and long-range aims.

PART TWO
INDIVIDUALIZATION OF INSTRUCTION

3

INDIVIDUALIZING INSTRUCTION IN ENGLISH
IN LARGE AND SMALL CLASSES

Those of us who are caught in the daily turmoil of instruction in overcrowded classrooms, often with unwilling or incapable students, may take some comfort in the thought that this is by no means a new problem. Twenty-five hundred years ago, some similar problem must have existed in Plato's time, for he says:

The elements of instruction. . .be presented to the mind in childhood, but not with any compulsion; for a freeman should be a freeman too in the acquisition of knowledge. . . . Knowledge which is acquired under compulsion has no hold on the mind. Therefore do not use compulsion, but let early education be rather a sort of amusement; this will better enable you to find out the natural bent of the child.

It is true that Plato was dealing at this point with early childhood education and not with secondary education; but his injunction against compulsion, and his counsels concerning discovering the natural bent of the child, are as valid today as they were in his day.[1]

Rousseau's educational principles contain three that are pertinent to this discussion:
1. That the natural interests, curiosity, and activities of children should be utilized in their education;
2. That the child should be taught rather than subject matter;
3. That a many-sided education is necessary to reveal child possibilities.[2]

In 1932 when R. O. Billett made his survey of *Provisions for Individual Differences, Marking, and Promotion* as part of the National Survey of Secondary Education, he stated:

. . .The facts and theories concerning individual differences, which have filled library shelves to overflowing during the past quarter of a century are still reposing on library shelves, or echoing through the lecture halls of schools of education, much more generally than they are incorporated in the practice of secondary schools. No fact has been established more firmly by this study than the fact that comparatively few schools are making thorough provisions for individual differences. . . .

21

In other words, only one principal in four or five using any one of these plans has any considerable measure of confidence in its success.[3]

The picture today is not as depressing. If Billett were making his survey in 1976, he would find that many more secondary schools are discovering and providing for the individual student.

I do not propose to summarize in this chapter the mountain of professional literature on individual differences that has accumulated in the past quarter-century, but rather to outline actual procedures which have been successful in my experience.

As a supervisor visiting hundreds of teachers and observing and writing reports on the lessons observed, I have been impressed by certain categories of teachers with respect to the problem of individualizing instructions, such as, the old-timer who is still "living by the book," although the book may have changed from *Ivanhoe* in the ninth year to *Johnny Tremain,* or from *Silas Marner* in the eleventh year to *The Good Earth.* This teacher recognizes individual differences to the extent that one individual knows the contents of the book, the others do not, and therefore they must fail and repeat the term. His attitude is the same for other areas of the Language Arts. In spelling one individual receives 100-percent when he spells correctly all the words in a list of twenty. All other individuals receive 0, whether they spell correctly nineteen, fifteen, ten or two.

He probably has never heard of the educational implications of television, radio, motion pictures or the magazines and newspapers. He has seen and condemned the comics and would prefer less reading of them among his pupils. This teacher not only has not discovered the individual in the large classroom, but also has not yet discovered the classroom.

In Category 2 is the teacher who genuinely wishes to know her pupils, but when she realizes she will have five sections of English, each about thirty-five in size, plus a home room of another thirty-five pupils and a study hall group of between fifty and one hundred, she throws up her hands in despair and rationalizes her failure to know her pupils by referring to the large number of students. "Since it is obviously impossible to know so many pupils," she says, "let us be sensible and do the best we can." True, she may make up assignments in which an extra project or two might be indicated, or extra credit may be given to the student who reads more than the usual four supplementary books a semester. Occasionally a gifted student may be recognized by permitting him to make a report to the class. On the other end of the scale, she recognizes the individuality of the troublesome child by sending him to the principal for a reprimand or by summoning his mother for a heart-to-heart talk.

Then there are various gradations of discovery of the individual until we get to the clearly defined Category 3 teacher who recognizes all the facts of individual differences and tries to do something sensible, practical and physically possible. There are probably more such teachers than we realize. My experiences in observing many teachers of this category will be the main contribution of this chapter.

RECOGNIZING THE INDIVIDUAL

Utilizing the Cumulative Records

Every student entering secondary school brings with him a cumulative record, containing among other valuable data his I. Q., the reading score, the grades in Language Arts in elementary school, the special weaknesses with respect to speech, special disabilities in reading, writing, etc. By the time he has been in high school several semesters, additional data about his work in the new type of program has accumulated which also can serve to familiarize his teachers with his capabilities, his natural endowments (to the extent that I. Q. and other objective tests can reveal them) and his work in Language Arts. Now, I will admit that for one teacher to examine 175 cumulative records and to jot down the pertinent data on a 3 x 5 or a 4 x 6 index card takes some time and may mean staying after school several afternoons. But to the teacher genuinely interested in getting background information about her students, such an investment of time is well worth while. Armed with the mass of information obtained from the Cumulative Records, the English teacher can make a little headway in recognizing the individuality of the 175 students with whom she will be spending the next six months or year. But this is only the beginning and is no substitute for what is to follow.

Uniform Lessons at Beginning of the Term

In many schools all English classes have Uniform Lessons at the beginning of the term, which are designed to acquaint teachers with their students in the hectic early days of a constantly changing class because of program difficulties, the arrival of new entrants and similar interruptions. I always have used such lessons to become acquainted with my new students. The most recent set of such lessons in my own Department consisted of the following:

Day	Activity
1	Registration of Pupils (usually a short period)
2	Oral English Work
3	Technical Errors
4	Organization of English Note-Books; First Diagnostic Test in Spelling
5.	First Composition written in class—Autobiographical
6	Instructions for Supplementary Reading
7	Appreciation of Mass Media
8	Vocabulary Study
9	Return and Correction of First Composition
10	First Lesson in Literature

Each teacher was given a ten-page brochure containing these ten lessons, carefully outlined with motivations, assignments for the next day and the many little suggestions for getting started on the right foot that all teachers welcome, especially the newly appointed ones. Thus in the first two weeks of the term each teacher can obtain some idea of the abilities of all her students in the areas of spelling, written composition, oral facility, interest in the mass media, vocabulary, and reading ability and interests.

Interest Questionnaire

Many teachers have long been using an Interest Questionnaire early in the term to get acquainted with their new students. As far back as 1934 Carol Hovious had included such a questionnaire in her manual, *Suggestions to Teachers of Reading.* There are many modifications of such a questionnaire.

Typical items in such a questionnaire might be:

1. My hobbies are. . . .
2. I am especially skilled in. . . .
3. I expect to earn my living by. . . .
4. My best school subjects are. . . .
5. I am weakest in. . . .
6. I consider myself a (slow-average-fast) reader.
7. I read about _____ books a month.
8. My eyes (always-sometimes-never) tire after reading.
9. I (wear-do not wear) glasses.
10. If I read a book for pleasure, I skip parts dealing with. . . .
11. I prefer (do not prefer) books with pictures and diagrams.
12. I have (do not have) difficulty understanding diagrams.
13. I wish our school library had more books on. . . .
14. In studying a book I (never-sometimes-always) use the index.
15. I (never-sometimes-always) go to my public library.
16. I (never-sometimes-always) use a dictionary.
17. I go the movies _____ a week.
18. My favorite type of movie is. . . .
19. The newspaper(s) we read at home is (are). . . .
20. My favorite features in this paper are. . . .
21. The magazine(s) regularly read in my home is (are). . . .
22. When I go to the library I look for _____ magazine.
23. On television I spend about _____ hours a week; on radio _____ a week.
24. On reading I spend about _____ hours a week.
25. I read the following books last term: _____

Card Index for Gathering Information

Those teachers who may not prefer such an elaborate questionnaire, may substitute a card index, usually 3 x 5 or 4 x 6. On these cards, information concerning I. Q., reading score, special interests, and favorite types of books can be entered. As students read supplementary books, they can make entries on individual index cards, which may be indexed with the vital data cards filled in by the teacher. An inexpensive cardboard, metal or wooden box can house all cards of all five sections of any teacher.

Daily Observation

The interest questionnaire and/or card index is but a first step in getting to know your pupils. It never can substitute for the day-by-day observation of the perceptive teacher. Traditionally, we always have kept records of daily recitations, homework assignments, daily and periodic or unit tests. Some teachers have not kept as accurate records as others, but there are plenty of record books on the market which assist the teacher in organizing the results of her daily observations so that she can formulate a sound judgment of the achievements of every student in her charge.

Numerical or letter ratings are not sufficiently meaningful for understanding the many aspects of a child's potentialities and capabilities. The perceptive teacher will make note of the following additional aspects:
1. Leadership and/or Followership
2. Social Relationships
3. Methods of Work
4. Sense of Responsibility
5. Willingness to Cooperate
6. Ethical Values

In this way, by means of the data from the Cumulative Record, by the Interest Questionnaire, the daily observation in class activities and by valid tests, it is possible to know one's pupils as individuals.

ADJUSTING THE CURRICULUM TO MEET INDIVIDUAL DIFFERENCES

If one compares the syllabus in English Language and Literature for Secondary Schools in New York State for 1916 and 1973 (only partially published as yet) he will notice both in size and content the changes that occurred in that period. The 1916 pamphlet was thirty pages; that of 1973 comes in several volumes. For example the volume on *Listening and Speaking K-12* is over 125 pages long. Interest in individualizing the curriculum developed during that time and has continued with ever-increasing momentum. Only a few significant changes can be mentioned in this chapter.
1. *Unit Instruction* providing for the pursuit of personal interests in addition to all-class activities.

The publications of the National Council of Teachers of English, most of the recently published courses of study in English, and most of the literature anthologies published for the past forty years have advocated the unit approach. The New York State Syllabus mentioned above gave actual examples of units in various aspects of the language arts as far back as 1935. *An Experience Curriculum* published by the Council in 1935 gives many other units, so that suggestions for unit teaching have been made for the last four decades. No teacher of secondary English today need say that she does not know what a unit is; why it is preferable to the "Next two chapters" approach of fifty years ago; or how to achieve greater individualization in the curriculum, by utilizing the unit approach. As usual, the curriculum makers are about forty years ahead of their times, for the unit approach is one of the best ways of providing for individual interests, needs and abilities.

In literature, particularly, it is possible to utilize the new courses of study and the new materials to individualize instruction. To give but a single illustration, I shall cite the course of study in Secondary English in New York City on which I worked as far back as 1957. While it has been superseded by more recent syllabi in 1970 and later, it is still useful as a means of providing for individual differences and should be examined by those teachers who are experimenting with the new, individual, approach for the first time.

To provide some unity in the diversity, each year of high school stressed a central theme:

9th - The Self-Reliant Individual
10th - The Individual as a Member of the Group
11th - The Individual and His American Heritage
12th - The Individual's Quest for Universal Values

Even the stress on the term *individual* in each of the theme centers is of significance for this discussion. For each theme center of the year there are suggested a number of subsidiary Centers of Study, varied in subject matter and differentiated in difficulty. Each Center of Study is intended as the basis for a teaching unit. Examples for the tenth year are:

Theme: The Individual as a Member of the Group

1. Learning to Live with the Family
2. Our School:
   a. It's Better to Work Together toward an Education
   b. Participating in the Extracurricular and Co-Curricular Programs
   c. Teams and Sports: Fair Play—The American Way
3. Making and Keeping Friends
4. As One Generation to Another
5. Appreciating the Backgrounds of Others
6. Finding One's Way into the World of Work
7. The Out-of-School Organizations for Teenagers
8. What Is Fun and What Isn't Funny
9. United We Stand, Divided We Fall: Many Groups of People Make America
10. Making the Most of Oneself
11. Around the World in New York City

For the eleventh year, the suggestions are:

Theme: The Individual and His American Heritage

1. Westward Ho!–The Pioneer Spirit
2. Great Americans and Their Legacy to Us
3. Let's See the Funny Side: American Humor
4. The Regions of America Contribute to Her Heritage
5. America in Song and Story
6. Guideposts to Liberty
7. The Union: Storehouse of Treasures from All Lands
8. Tell All the People: Mass Media
9. American Literature: Ideals in the American Heritage
10. New York City: Focal Point of American Culture
11. Secession vs. Union: A Drama of Human Relations, Many Became One

For the twelfth year, recommended units are:

Theme: The Individual's Quest for Universal Values

1. Heroes and Heroines of All Nations and Ages
2. The Search for Values in the Community of Work
3. Educational Values: To Go or Not to Go to College (Technical School, Trade School, Secretarial School)
4. Your Country Needs You: The Armed Forces and the Dignity of Man
5. The U. N.: An Experiment in the Living Together of All Peoples
6. World Understanding through Literature
7. Standards for Appreciation: Television, Motion Picture, Radio and Theatre
8. The Arts in Modern Living
9. The Literature of the Newspaper, Magazine, and Paperback
10. Land of the Free, Home of the Brave: the Development of Civil Liberties in America
11. Man's Struggle for World Peace
12. Truth vs. Falsehood: Stereotypes, Smears, Slogans, Insinuations and Fallacies

Although eighteen years have passed since this syllabus was promulgated, the themes are as valid in the 1970s as they were in the 1950s.

What a wealth of opportunity there is for the perceptive teacher to individualize her instruction in this approach! To assist the teacher in utilizing the new course of study, a resource unit for one of the themes each year was made available. Books suitable for that level, composition activities, speaking and listening activities are all suggested, as well as an introductory section on how to teach in this manner. It is constantly recommended that each English Department of the almost 100 New York City high schools, while following the four general themes, develop its own resource units suitable to the respective schools. Hence the multitude of Centers of Study for each Theme Center. In this way, the vast secondary school population of New York City was presented with the same general principles and approach to English, but with attention to individual needs.

2. *Instructional Materials.* What are the implications with respect to instructional materials in such a program of individualized instruction through units?

One obvious need is for classroom libraries. For example, the ninth year outline, *A Search for Adventure,* lists as suggested reading over 150 books in such categories as:

Adventures in Space; Air Flight Adventures; Adventures in Mountain Climbing; Adventures in Exploration; Adventure under Water; Adventure at Sea; Science and Science Fiction; Adventures with Wild Animals; Adventures in Growing Up; The Adventure of Helping Others.

In addition, a booklist was provided for each year with succinct annotations of hundreds of books suitable for the reading level of each year. Each teacher was thus enabled to familiarize herself with the wealth of adolescent literature that appeared in recent decades and to utilize it in her instruction.

3. *Audio-Visual Aids.* In this age of mass communication the printed book is but one way of reaching the individual student. There are many students for whom the various mass media will have an immediacy of appeal that the old-fashioned three-books-a-term approach never possessed. This does not by any means lead to discarding of textbooks or of the printed page generally. But the well organized English course cannot rely on the traditional *Silas Marner, Idylls of the King* and *Tale of Two Cities* approach to meet the needs of large segments of our population. Some of these segments may be stimulated by the mass media into reading. The film of *Moby Dick* stimulated the circulation of the book, as has been true of so many books made into films. In 1972 the film version of John Knowles' *A Separate Peace* was used successfully together with the paperback in thousands of classrooms throughout the country. A curriculum that is aware of individual differences must take cognizance of the audio-visual aspects of today's living. In New York City, for example, one teacher was relieved of all teaching duties to spend her time listening to hundreds of recordings, viewing scores of educational films and film strips for the express purpose of enriching each Center of Study's resource unit.

ADMINISTRATIVE CONSIDERATIONS THAT CONTRIBUTE TO INDIVIDUALIZATION OF INSTRUCTION

The administration of a secondary school must and does in many cases take cognizance of the needs of individuals. College preparatory, commercial, or general (non-college) courses are offered where enough students are present in the school.

For the English teacher such provision is made in some of the following ways:
1. Giving each teacher no more than two different preparations (e.g., English 3 and English 7).
2. Avoiding a program of five slow-learner classes even with only two preparations.
3. Providing two periods of instruction, followed by a period of preparation. Four teaching periods in a row will exhaust the hardiest and best-intentioned teacher. Even three consecutive periods of teaching at the end of the day can be tiring.
4. Making provisions for periods of conference with other teachers of the same grade, for attending district-wide curriculum meetings and state and national conferences.
5. Making provisions of time, place and facilities (motion-picture machines, film-strip projectors, record players and other audio-visual aids) so that teachers may become acquainted with the resources available for individualizing instruction.

ADJUSTING INSTRUCTION TO MEET INDIVIDUAL DIFFERENCES

The school system may have adopted the philosophy of individual differences. The Curriculum Bureau may have prepared the Course of Study that provides for meeting the needs of individual students. The perceptive teacher may have become acquainted with each of her 175 students a day. There is still left the great but by no means insurmountable task of teaching this large group each day. It is at this stage of the operation where the program most frequently collapses, and teachers fall back on either lip service to the program, or even further back to the old-fashioned assign-test method of fifty and more years ago, as the various texts on methods of teaching English of the time will testify.

Here follow some procedures that have proven successful in the classroom where the philosophy of individualization of instruction has been put into practice.

Differentiation of Assignments

Much has been written about differentiation of assignments for individualization and enrichment. A few obvious methods may be mentioned here:
1. Instead of assigning the same chapters to be read by the entire class, the class is divided into groups, each group being responsible for a certain segment of the work to be covered.
2. All students are given the same basic assignment with opportunities for special credit for additional work. An interesting example is supplied by the Aspinwall High School, Pittsburgh, Pa., for a class-wide assignment in Washington Irving's *Sketch Book*. (Fifteen points are required for a passing mark; 20 points for a mark of B; and 25 points for a mark of A).

Required of all:

	Number of Points
a. Reading of the following sketches	
1. Rip Van Winkle	1
2. Legend of Sleepy Hollow	1

3.	The Spectre Bridegroom	1
4.	The Author's Account of Himself	1
5.	The Voyage	1
6.	Rural Life in England	1
7.	The Country Church	1
8.	The Stage Coach	1
9.	Christmas Day	1
10.	Westminster Abbey	1
11.	Stratford-on-Avon	1
12.	Biography	1
	Subtotal	12

b. Earning passing mark on daily quizzes	1
c. Earning passing mark on test	1
d. Listing the best descriptive, narrative, and characterization passages	1
Total	15

Additional credit for a higher mark may be earned through the following special assignments:

a. Make an outline biography of the author	2
b. Write an essay on the character and personality of Washington Irving	2
c. Write an essay on the charm of travel in America	2
d. Write an essay on Christmas spirit in Pittsburgh	2
e. Write an essay on traveling by motor coach or airplane	2
f. Write an essay comparing rural life in England and America	2
g. Give an oral report on one of the parallel readings listed below	2
h. Write a theme on English dress and customs in Irving's time	2
i. Write a theme on American dress and customs in Knickerbocker's time	2
j. Make a colored drawing of Rip, of the schoolmaster, or of the bridegroom	1
k. Write a character sketch of Dame Van Winkle, Brom, Katrina, or Squire Bracebridge	2
l. Dramatize "Rip Van Winkle"	6

m. Any other project or problem approved by the teacher. Points to be determined.

Parallel readings. (Select one.)

a. Addison, *Spectator,* Paper No. 1
b. Franklin, *Autobiography,* "Voyage to England."
c. Dickens, *American Notes,* chapters 1 and 2. . .4

3. Providing for different activities based on the same literature selection. For example, the entire class may be assigned Act I of *Hamlet*. For written work Group I (the weakest) may be asked to write a summary of events. Group II may write an imaginary letter from Horatio to a fellow student in the University of Wittenberg describing the events that have recently occured at Elsinore. Group III may write a dialogue between Hamlet and Ophelia before the play opens. Group IV may write a dialogue between two courtiers describing King Claudius' opening session of his court after his assumption to the throne. Group V may write a dialogue between Claudius and Queen Gertrude as they discuss Hamlet's behavior at this first session of the court at Elsinore. Group VI will discuss the validity of Polonius's advice to Laertes. There are many other possibilities of differentiating this type of assignment.

In addition to the class-wide study of the play itself, the class may be given long-term committee projects on various phases of Elizabethan Life, such as Elizabethan Drama; Playhouses; Court Life; Costume and Daily Attire; Foods and Family Living; Military and Naval Practices; Housing.

Classroom Management

The old-fashioned classroom management of fifty years ago where the teacher sat at her desk with the textbook in one hand and her marking book in another while her docile charges waited expectantly for the question that would decree the 10 or 0 for the day should have died out with the flappers and the tin lizzie of the 1920's. Alas, there are too many such classes to be observed to this day. Happily, there are more and more classes where the exciting, exhilarating, creative atmosphere of learning and living is to be breathed. This does not mean the advocacy of "progressive" atmosphere which is more closely akin to chaos than to any progress. Nor does this imply the abdication of the teacher as guide, scholar and person of good taste. The classroom management that recognizes individual differences and makes some provision for them will employ one or more of the following methods:

1. *Committee and Group Projects.* As stated above in connection with the study of *Hamlet,* committees of students may be organized in the study of either a single classic like *A Tale of Two Cities, Idylls of the King,* or in the study of a unit like the *French Revolution in Literature, Victorianism in Life and Literature, The Generation Gap as Portrayed in Recent American Fiction, Youth's New Participation in Social Improvement as Portrayed in Recent Fiction and Drama, The Poetry of Soul, Rock Lyrics vs. Traditional Poetic Forms.*

It is not necessary to reiterate the direct and tangential values to be derived from such committee work. Values such as opportunities for leadership, for cooperative effort, for individual research, for self-expression in speaking and writing, for creative expression in painting, sculpture, music and industrial arts, are obvious. They can be derived without any loss of the generally accepted values in English skills and knowledge.

2. *Changes in Classroom Methodology.* Just as the assignment may be so given as to permit all of the class to do a portion of the work together, with provision for individualization in written and oral expression, so the classroom methodology

should be modified from the strict assign-test method to the numerous variations observable today. There should be fewer questions by the teacher to be followed by the "correct" answer directed by the student with one eye on the teacher and the other eye on the marking book. The "arrow of the recitation" should turn from student to student rather than from student to the all-important omniscient teacher. In such a classroom there is plenty of student inter-criticism. Students feel free to express themselves even if they may be proven wrong. The shy student is encouraged. The aggressive, the superficial, the supercilious, the snobbish are discovered and are met by disapproval or disagreement by fellow-students rather than by the teacher. Over and above the requirement that each student does his work and does not develop into a shirker or a mere glib talker, there are opportunities in such a classroom atmosphere for each student who has developed some talent or ability that bears on the work to express himself.

The gifted student-artist studying *Hamlet* can draw a series of costumes of the time. The craftsman can design a setting for a scene for the play or even build a model of the Globe, a standard project for the past fifty years. The scientist may bring in a microscope and a goldfish and demonstrate Harvey's discovery of the circulation of the blood, at about the time the play was written. The dancer can illustrate various Elizabethan steps and dances. Musicians can sing Elizabethan songs. How much more delightful is such a series of lessons—without detracting one iota from the comprehension and appreciation of *Hamlet* than the line-for-line, word-for-word dissection of the play that prevailed half a century ago!

Differentiated Book Reports

One instance has been given of individualized methodology with respect to the learning of a literary classic. Any aspect of the language arts can be so taught as to provide for individualization, enrichment and release of creative energy. Let us take the *bête noire* of many an English class, the hallowed four book reports per term. Since 1920 at least, when the writer entered high school, the four book reports besides the regular class texts have been standard operating procedure. Every teacher can testify to the boredom of hearing endless numbers of oral summaries of novels, biographies, plays, and non-fiction.

Reading and correcting these reports by the teacher rather than listening to them in class is little better because one of the values of supplementary reading is sacrificed: the interchange of students' opinions and the inspiring of fellow students to read books enjoyed by others. There need be no despair in this matter. Various modifications have been practiced for decades to provide a rich program of individual supplementary reading and opportunities to report on these books in class. Here are a few of the ways:

1. The usual summary for the slow or average student who wants the minimum passing grade;

2. Summary plus individual critical reaction, however immature it may be;

3. Genuine critique, imitating the pattern of reviews in the *Saturday Review/World*, the *New York Times Book Review*, the *New York Review of Books;*

4.   Summary plus (for extra credit) imaginary dialogue between characters in the book;
5.   Letters to friends describing the book;
6.   Contributions to class newspapers, school newspapers and local newspapers of the best reviews;
7.   A scrapbook of one's book reviews for the term or year, with decorative cover and decorations depending upon the artistic abilities of the student;
8.   Letters to the author describing one's reactions;
9.   Literary symposium in class in which various students analyze a single book;
10.   Imaginary conversations in the style of Walter Savage Landor's *Imaginary Conversations* or C. E. S. Wood's *Heavenly Discourse.*

Individual Conferences in and outside of Class

In all the four years of high school in the early 1920's a student might not have a single face-to-face or heart-to-heart conference with his teacher. To the latter he was a number; at best a name. Today, more and more teachers are scheduling time in their daily or weekly plans to confer with their students over their written work, their homework, their outside reading, their interest in the mass media, and their intellectual and aesthetic development generally. Such conferences are the essence of individualized instruction and may have far-reaching consequences for the student. Many a distorted or immature personality has been steered into the right path by an understanding teacher (frequently in English) who took the trouble to stay a while after school or give up one of her precious unassigned periods, to listen to his or her personal problem, whether in English or in other areas. There is eloquent testimony by creative writers, speakers, and lawyers who trace their first-forming interests in their fields to such conferences. One need only mention the public tributes that were paid by such outstanding American personalities as the writer Ernest Hemingway, and the statesman Ralph Bunche to their early English teachers. There are scores more by equally distinguished men and women.

Basic to the whole approach of discovering the individual in the large classroom is the belief on the part of the teacher in her own individuality, in her own creative powers, in her own unique contribution to her profession at large and to her students. Once she accepts that philosophy for herself, she will never view her class as a "sea of faces," as so many empty pitchers to be filled, as so many immature, noisy miscreants, bent on driving her mad. She will realize that each of her 175 charges may have the potentiality of becoming another Bernard Malamud, or a Dr. Arthur Compton, or a Martin Luther King, Jr., or an Edna St. Vincent Millay, or a Helen Hayes. The thought that she might become the igniting spark to another such as these or of many others of even greater potentialities must give one pause and make the daily heartaches and frustrations the petty things they well deserve to be.

4

THE ROLE OF THE DEPARTMENT HEAD IN PROVIDING FOR INDIVIDUALIZATION OF INSTRUCTION

There is nothing new in the concept of individualization of instruction. As far back as the fourteenth century a schoolmaster described his philosophy of education in a treatise now located in the Vatican in which he reminded his readers "that each boy has a different temperament and had to be treated accordingly," and he makes a further point: "Each boy learns his lessons at a different rate of speed, and it is the business of the schoolmaster to discover each boy's relative capacity for learning."[1] I am certain that educational literature of an even earlier period will have similar references. The problem is hardly a new one.

Nor are the solutions new. When Roy O. Billett wrote *Provisions for Individual Differences, Marking, and Promotion* in 1932 as part of the National Survey of Secondary Education, he could state quite truthfully:

...the facts and theories concerning individual differences, which have filled library shelves to overflowing during the past quarter of a century are still reposing on library shelves, or echoing through the lecture halls of schools of education, much more generally than they are incorporated in the practice of secondary schools.[2]

In the four decades since Billett made his statement, the volume of studies about discovering individual differences and making provisions for them has increased tremendously. The various books of the Report of the Commission on the English Curriculum of the National Council of Teachers of English, *The English Language Arts in Secondary Schools*[3] and especially Volume III, have had ample discussions of this topic. Of special interest to those of us in the field of English is Olive S. Niles and Margaret J. Early's excellent study of *Adjusting to Individual Differences in English,* with its many specific suggestions in the areas of reading skills, writing skills, uses of reading and listening.[4]

No teacher or supervisor of English can honestly say that nothing is available on how to meet the great problem of individual differences, if he will but take the trouble to read the vast and rapidly accumulating literature on this subject.

How one supervisor in a large metropolitan high school in New York City has endeavored to help his teachers meet the individual needs of their students is the subject of this chapter. Theory and practice are here interrelated, for only thus will the remainder have any value.

1. *The Supervisor's Philosophy.* Much depends upon the supervisor's own philosophy of education. If he conceives his function to be a dispenser of rubber bands and board erasers and theme paper, he may not have much time for individualizing instruction. Or, if he conceives his function to be that of an inspector who sees that classes, like Mussolini's and modern Swiss trains, begin on time, he too will be occupied most of the day with the trivia of instruction: proper ventilation of each classroom, removal of coats and chewing gum from the classroom, removal of papers and orange peels from the classroom and cleaning the blackboard before each lesson.

All these above-mentioned trivia of instruction must be put in their proper perspective so that the only excuse for the supervisor's existence can be given its due importance, which is the improvement of instruction. And, to me, improvement of instruction without individualization of instruction is meaningless. The supervisor must ask himself whenever he observes a teacher: "Is she aware of the differences of the students before her and is she doing something about these differences?" Of course, he must always be ready himself to show how these differences can be recognized and provided for.

2. *Providing for Differences by Programming.* Granted that he is aware of the importance of individualization, he must make some administrative provisions by programming at least in three large categories: the bright, the average and the slow. This sectioning may be extended in either direction. Thus the slow may need special sections in remedial written composition, remedial reading or remedial speech. The bright, at the other end of the spectrum, may need classes in creative writing, world literature (as compared to the standard 12th year English literature almost universally found). Thus, by sectioning classes, a first step is taken in the right direction. We need not amplify at this point the criteria to be used for selecting students for such classes because they are rather obvious; e.g., reading score, excellence in English in the preceding term, proven talent (in creative writing and dramatics, etc.), expressed interest (world literature). The literature for selecting slow learners is rich in discussing these criteria of selection.[5]

3. *Providing the Proper Teachers.* Unless the proper teachers are available or willing to be trained in the art and skills of meeting differences, the best educational philosophy and the most elaborate programming will not go very far. Where do these gifted teachers come from? I would urge every teacher to read Elizabeth Shepley Sergeant's "Charles Townsend Copeland"[6] and such books as Houston Peterson's *Great Teachers*[7] and Gilbert Highet's *The Art of Teaching.*[8] Many teachers, whatever their educational philosophy may be, have long recognized the paramount importance of the individual and have long made provisions for meeting individual needs. The perceptive supervisor, as he gets to know his department, learns to recognize those teachers who already are aware of this great challenge and are doing something about it; those who are dimly aware of it and would like to be told how to do something; and finally those who are not aware and must, by every supervisory technique, be made to realize that before them in their daily

classes are 150-200 separate individuals as distinct from one another as their respective fingerprints and vastly more interesting for these differences.

By recognizing the potentialities of his staff and assigning each teacher to the type of class to which she can make the greatest contribution for individual growth, the supervisor has taken the first step personnel-wise toward meeting the need. The rest is encouragement, training—in-service or otherwise—promotion of professional growth by all available techniques so thoroughly treated in the many text books on supervision that now appear almost annually.

4. *Providing the Proper Syllabus.* Sectioning classes and selecting the proper teachers must be followed by a course (or courses) of study that enables the teacher to make provisions for individual differences. An examination of the courses of study in English from many states and cities over the past twenty years reveals that hardly any one appears today without some chapter on meeting individual differences. The New York State *Syllabus in English for Secondary Schools, Grades 7-12,* as far back as 1935 made many provisions for individualization.[9] An examination of the annual volume published by the Association for Supervision and Curriculum Development about the new courses of study prepared each year will reveal a wealth of valuable material.[10] Throughout the country there is a great deal of curriculum building going on in English, and in almost every instance there is recognition of the need for providing for individualization of instruction. Any alert supervisor today must realize that as he and his staff work together to prepare a course of study in English that will meet the needs of today's American Youth, there must be no rigid list of spelling words, or set of grammatical rules and spelling devices that must be mastered, and that this hodge-podge cannot be dignified by the term, course of study. Rather there must be many possibilities for enrichment for the gifted, as well as modifications for the less gifted, each being challenged to do his best.There are many such multiple-track courses of study, but the one I know best is the one I was privileged to work with from its inception in 1952 to its publication in 1957.[11] To demonstrate how this may be carried out in the actual classroom situations, four large resource units have been prepared and distributed to all teachers of senior high English: *The Self-Reliant Individual* and *The Individual as a Member of the Group*[12] are for the ninth and tenth years. *The Individual and His American Heritage* and *The Individual and His Search for Values* were the units for eleventh and twelfth years. Many other school systems, both large and small, have individualized their courses of study in English. To name the courses of study from Philadelphia, Denver and Seattle is not to depreciate the many other examples that also are available.

5. *Providing the Proper Instructional Materials.* The best philosophy of education, plus dedicated teachers and a good course of study, must be implemented by instructional materials. The old days of the one grammar and one classic are (or should be) gone forever. The supervisor must obtain funds for many different texts, for series of remedial texts for the retarded readers and for enriched texts for the superior students. There are about fifteen different series of literature anthologies for senior high schools. It behooves the teacher to become acquainted with all or at least some of these series, their teachers' guidebooks and their student workbooks.

Only then can he choose which will be most suitable for his particular school situation.[13]

But grammar texts and literature anthologies are not enough in the modern English course. There must be many other instructional aids such as paperbacks, recordings, film strips, tapes.[14] The alert supervisor today must not only be a well-read man but also a "well-listened" man, well versed in many different kinds of audio-visual aids and the most effective ways of using them.[15]

6. *Practicing Methodology That Will Provide for Individualization.* Too many teachers still assign the next thirty pages of *Silas Marner* or *A Tale of Two Cities* and consider this an adequate assignment. A few go one step ahead toward individualization and ask for answers to three or four questions, with some extra credit for an additional answer or two. The supervisor must, through his various department publications, conferences and visits with teachers, stress ways of differentiating and individualizing assignments and methods of conducting the recitation.[16] Such topics as book reports, research papers, panel discussions, should be taken up with old and new teachers so that they get some idea of ways of varying the old question-and-answer technique of conducting the recitation of thirty years ago, and, alas, much too frequently today. Sometimes the supervisor himself should give a demonstration lesson or get one of his skilled teachers to give one. Intervisitation should be arranged, so that the neophytes may observe the newer techniques of the more experienced and gifted teachers.

Occasionally, good examples of superior individualized teaching techniques might be collected in booklet form and issued to the department. These collections not only boost staff morale by encouraging and giving due recognition to the outstanding teachers, but they can be used profitably by all.[17]

7. *Providing for Individualization through Tests.* Some kind of uniform testing program is carried on in large high schools throughout the country. Sometimes these tests are given in the middle of the term and in other cases at the end. Since these frequently are uniform for an entire grade, there is an apparent diminution of individualization. Yet certain provisions for individualization are still possible within the framework of the grade-wide uniform examinations. For example, the literature question can be unique to *each* class. All final examinations can be prepared for the particular class. Frequent quizzes or monthly examinations are further attempts to individualize examination procedure. Students in non-academic classes should get an entirely different examination from that given to those getting an academic diploma. Gifted students may be given a third type of paper.

8. *Bulletins for Individualizing Instruction.* Sometimes the best program may bog down or collapse entirely because the lines of communication are clogged. I have long made it my policy to state my own objectives clearly, give as many specific directions as are feasible and then trust to the intelligence and good will of my staff to carry on. Of course, there must be constant follow-up by the supervisor and encouragement and suggestions for improvement.

9. *Providing Facilities for Reproducing Instructional Materials Prepared by Teachers.* One of the most useful of all machines for helping to individualize instruction is the reproducing machine—whether it be the mimeograph, the Rexograph or

any other type. Teachers prepare an endless mass of materials for duplication daily: lists of words misspelled on examinations; lists of grammatical errors made on compositions; book lists for class units; reading passages for slow learners; class magazines; and last but not least a class novel to which every one of the thirty-nine students contributed. A student squad can quickly be trained to operate the machines. Student typists may prepare the stencils. I have found that this practice spreads like wildfire among the teachers as they tell one another about the success they have had with this or that exercise; this or that device, etc. One cannot expect the teacher to individualize instruction without individualizing materials, and individualized materials must be duplicated. The teacher has done her share when she prepared them. It is the chairman's responsibility to reproduce them.

10. *The Supervisor's Attitude toward His Staff.* The supervisor cannot expect his staff to individualize instruction if he himself does not individualize supervision. He must respect the integrity of each member of his staff, know her strong and weak points, praise her accomplishments and encourage her to do better all along the line. By this attitude of understanding, tact, and ever-present helpfulness, he can inspire his staff to their very best, to meet the fascinating challenge of individual differences and to do something about providing for them.

5

ENGLISH FOR THE BRIGHT STUDENT

Although teaching the gifted has received considerable attention in recent years, the problem is at least as old as Plato. Referring to these students he said: "We must watch them from their youth upwards and make them perform actions in which they are more likely to forget or be deceived, and he who remembers and is not deceived is to be selected, and he who fails in the trial is to be rejected. That will be the way."[1] In America programs for the gifted in English in high schools go back at least to the 1920's[2] in Cleveland, Rochester and New York City. Almost fifty years of research, experimentation and professional writing confront the teacher who is faced with his first class of gifted students and wants to know how to meet its needs. At least a dozen substantial volumes and many scores of pamphlets and periodicals are available for the inquiring mind.[3]

Reading the literature of the gifted in English will reveal that, like so many other problems in the teaching of English, this is not a new problem but is a problem we are pursuing more intensively and more scientifically today.

WHY IS THE PROBLEM CLAIMING OUR ATTENTION TODAY?

Although educators have long been claiming that our greatest resources are not our supplies of coal, oil and minerals but our children, the public at large has only begun to realize this fairly recently. The unrealized potential contributions of gifted students must give us pause in an age of tension and anxiety in which we need every possible intellectual and aesthetic contribution. The orbiting of Sputnik I jolted America into the realization that our instructional programs in science and mathematics needed "agonizing reappraisals" and reorganization. To this, the public who pays the bill gave its consent. The scientists themselves in recent years have been pleading for greater attention to English and particularly to the needs of scientists to be given rich programs in English. Typical is the following from a group of distinguished scientists:

We emphasize. . .that the future scientist or engineer needs adequate preparation in English, history, and languages. In fact, *minimum* secondary school requirements which a science major should bring to college should include four years of English.[4]

The race has always gone to the swift, and the future will present even more challenges than the troublesome present or the past. The future leaders, regardless of their professions or occupations, will have to read and digest more, will have to command their language more effectively, and will have to learn to listen with greater discrimination. The distinguished social scientist Peter F. Drucker in his study of the qualifications of the executive defined the demands upon the manager in these terms:

No matter whether the manager's job is engineering, accounting, or selling, his effectiveness depends upon his ability to listen and to read, on his ability to speak and to write. He needs skill in getting his thinking across to other people as well as skill in finding out what other people are after.

Of all the skills he needs, today's manager possesses least those of reading, writing, speaking and figuring.

. . .managers have to learn to know language, to understand what words are and what they mean. Perhaps most important, they have to acquire respect for language as man's most precious gift and heritage.[5]

If these are the demands upon managers, how much more important they are for our future teachers, writers, public speakers and the whole group of people who make their living primarily through the written and spoken word!

WHO ARE THE GIFTED IN ENGLISH?

The identification of gifted students in English has long been a topic of serious discussion in the field, for criteria vary and authorities are not agreed. Among the techniques discovered by a U. S. Office of Education project in 1954, twenty were listed and evaluated as to frequency. Since the beginning teacher of gifted students may not realize the diversity of techniques, they are listed below:
1. Teachers' marks
2. Group Intelligence tests
3. Teachers' estimates of school achievement
4. Standardized achievement tests
5. Information on physical health
6. Guidance counselors' appraisals of pupils' interests, aptitudes and abilities
7. Information on vocational plans
8. Information on reading interests and habits
9. Information on home environment
10. Anecdotal reports and records
11. Information on personality adjustment
12. Teachers' estimates of aptitudes
13. Information on physical maturity

14. Homeroom advisors' appraisal of pupils' interests, aptitudes and abilities
15. Information on social maturity
16. Information on hobbies
17. Teachers' estimates of intelligence
18. Standardized aptitude tests in specific fields
19. Individual intelligence tests
20. Parental appraisal of pupils' aptitudes and abilities

This list was compiled on the basis of information from 814 secondary schools, both junior and senior and is rated by frequency.[6]

Virginia A. Elliott sent questionnaires to 112 schools and administrators with high school programs for gifted students and has summarized her findings in Chapter II, "Identifying the Academically Talented in English" of *English for the Academically Talented Student in the Secondary School.*[7]

The characteristics that make up the gifted student are numerous, far more than a high I. Q. and outstanding achievement in English. Perhaps the most complete inventory of these traits in print was compiled by the Baltimore County Public Schools as an outcome of a Curriculum Workshop on Superior and Gifted Students. Because this list may reveal many new facets of identifying the gifted student in English it is printed in its entirety.

Characteristics of Pupils Who Are Superior in Language Arts

1. Intellectual traits
    a. Ability to comprehend abstract ideas
       Recognition of abstract terms in literature
       Effective use of abstract terms and concepts in speaking and writing
    b. Ability to generalize
       Attainment by induction of definitions and generalizations in areas of grammar, spelling, word attack and literary forms
    c. Ability to organize
       Organization of pertinent material preparatory to speaking or writing on a topic, issue or problem
    d. Capacity for intellectual curiosity
       Desire to do independent research in areas of interest
       Interest in language arts techniques
       Interests in different philosophies of life and psychological interpretations
    e. Capacity for extensive interests
       Development for wider range of reading interests
       Response to new language concepts and experiences
    f. Capacity for creative and imaginative thought
       Breadth and depth of vicarious experiences through literature
       Imaginative use of language in daily expression
    g. Ability to make comparisons, contrasts and analyses
       Understanding interrelationships among literary works and techniques
       Using comparisons, contrasts and extended analyses in oral and written expression

    h. Ability to grasp ideas quickly
       Interpretation and integration of that which is read and heard
    i. Ability to understand and use intricate and complex concepts and skills
       Involvement in long-term projects of all types
       Intensive analyses of literature
       Interest in intricacies and complexities of linguistic structures
    j. Ability to use a logical and orderly approach in critical thinking
       Extended investigations and arrival at sound conclusions in preparing for
speaking and writing

2. Personal characteristics and attitudes
    a. Impatience with routine assignments and drill related to accuracy in grammar,
mechanics and research
    b. Sense of humor
       Appreciation of types of humor in literature and speech
       Use of devices to achieve humor in writing and speaking
       An understanding that humor is a comment on life
    c. Power of self-criticism
       Intelligent criticism of their own oral and written work
       Objective analyses of themselves
    d. Desire to work independently in planning, selecting and developing language
activities of all sorts
    e. Ability for outstanding leadership
       Initiative in planning group work, discussions and class work
       Participation in extracurricular activities related to language arts
    f. Power of self-motivation
       Desire to do extended research
       Wide range of personal reading
       Selection of topics for study
       Interest in original creative work
    g. Ability to work well with adults and peer groups of own ability level
       Utilization of adults as resource people in language arts activities
    h. Capacity for aesthetic appreciation
       Recognition of relationship of literature to the other arts
       Development of an appreciation of our cultural heritage
    i. Tendency to question and challenge established conventions and ideas
       Desire to learn for themselves why a piece of literature is recognized as good
       Challenge of adult opinions about literature and grammatical structures
    j. Alterness and keenness in observation in writing and speaking; insight into
the problems and actions of people, both in literature and life
    k. Ability to memorize and retain material
    l. Ability to concentrate on one idea longer than the average age pupil
    m. Tendency to be individualistic
    n. Tendency to make premature generalizations; over-eagerness to reach a
generalization before getting all the facts

o. Impatience with group with slower children
p. Tendency to be overcritical
q. Tendency to procrastinate
r. Tendency to rationalize

3. Control of communication skills
   a. Use of more extensive and more difficult vocabulary
   b. Tendency to read intensively and extensively more difficult material
   c. Ability to become interested in language *per se*
   d. Experimentation with words
   e. Ability to understand and use metaphorical language
   f. Ability to communicate one's ideas with clarity
   g. Ability to write creatively and imaginatively

4. Areas of interest in language arts
   a. Word study and vocabulary development
   b. Structure of language
   c. Discussion
   d. Dramatizations
   e. Subtle forms of humor in literature
   f. Intensive analysis of literature
   g. Extensive reading for personal pleasure
   h. Experimentation with various written forms
   i. Opportunities to pursue interests in particular authors and themes of literature
   j. Enjoyment of aesthetic appeal of literature (rhythm, imaginative use of language, form)
   k. Creative aspects of English
   l. General semantics

Although not all gifted students will possess all of the characteristics above, many will show them in some degree. The alert teacher will have some definite frame of reference by which to recognize such students.

HOW TO PROVIDE FOR GIFTED STUDENTS IN ENGLISH

Basically provisions for gifted students are made in three ways:
1. Enrichment in regular classes;
2. Grouping in special classes;
3. Acceleration.
There are variations of these three basic patterns and advocates and opponents of each pattern.

Of the many ways in which gifted students in English may be given enriched programs while remaining in regular classes, the following are the main types:

1. Through broad units
2. Through supplementary activities
3. Through correlation with other subjects
4. Through reading
5. Through writing and speaking
6. Through extracurricular activities
7. Through use of community resources

Broad Units

Lack of interest and boredom sometimes result when the gifted student is given the same assignment as the rest of the class. He may have read the literary selection earlier, or he may read the entire novel or play in the time that it takes the rest of the class to read a few chapters or acts. Provision should be made for him to read and report on related materials or another novel or play. Sometimes the class may be pursuing a theme and several books related to the theme may be given to differing groups. The wealth of paperbacks makes such selection easy. A tenth-grade class reading *Silas Marner* or *A Tale of Two Cities* may have gifted students who are capable of reading, in addition to these novels, either other novels by Eliot and Dickens or other psychological and sociological novels. In all *genres* of literature, such enrichment is possible, whether they are poetry, essays, or biographies. Almost all anthologies of literature contain at the end of each unit copious bibliographies from which selections can be made. The Scholastic Book Services (50 West 44 Street, N. Y. C. 10036) has prepared several interesting units with rich bibliographies. Like-wise the Macmillan Heritage series in paperbacks offers promising opportunities. For bibliographies, the lists prepared by the National Council of Teachers of English, such as *Books For You* and *Your Reading* should be consulted.[8]

Supplementary Activities

Let us suppose that an eleventh-grade class is studying *Giants in the Earth*. The gifted student will probably finish it long before the rest of the class. He can supplement his reading in some of these ways:
1. Comparison with other novels about pioneer life, such as Willa Cather's *My Antonia* or *O Pioneers;* Bess Streeter Aldrich's *A Lantern in Her Hand,* or the works of Hamlin Garland
2. A study of original diaries of pioneers
3. Reading other novels of Rolvaag
4. Reading the reviews of *Giants in the Earth* to compare the critical opinions at the time the novel appeared
5. A compilation of articles on Rolvaag or his novel which are listed in *Reader's Guide* or other reference books.
6. An intensive study of Rolvaag's style, plot technique, or language

Correlation with Other Subjects

Many gifted students in English are also gifted in art, music, dancing or in crafts. These skills can be utilized to enrich the study of any classic or modern book. Stage settings for plays studied, dramatizations of scenes in novels or short stories: these are some of the correlated activities. In one class studying *Hamlet* a student gifted in art drew characters illustrating the various types of Elizabethans. This made an attractive display of the rear wall of the English classroom. Models of Elizabethan theatres have been made for decades.

Through Reading

The gifted student in English is most often a good and interested reader. He usually has begun to read early and has read much. Teachers of such students can build on these interests. Not only is there a good supply of books available in the English classroom (in many schools they are paperbacks), but also students are encouraged to learn about the sources of information about books. They frequently assume charge of classroom libraries, assist in the school library and supply information about current books for their classmates.

Through Writing and Speaking

Thousands of newspapers and magazines are produced in our secondary schools each year by students gifted in writing. A visit to the annual exhibit of The Columbia Scholastic Press Association will reveal the amazing talent that exists in our schools. Many students submit their contributions to one of the many magazines which sponsor such creative talent. Maureen Daly's "Sixteen," one of the most anthologized short stories, was originally submitted to *Scholastic* in one of its annual contests for student work.

In some schools teachers periodically collect the best materials from their classes and mimeograph or ditto them. Who can tell what future Ernest Hemingways or Arthur Millers or Willa Cathers may be found among such writers? In some instances departments other than English encourage publications in biology, chemistry, social studies and mathematics. Frequently the study of a classic may inspire the class to put out a newspaper like *The Raveloe Gazette* or *The Trojan Times,* or *The Elizabethan Courier,* with the gifted students assuming the editorial burdens.

A. J. Beeler, of the Curriculum Services Division of the Louisville Public Schools, spent the academic year 1955–56 studying the provision for individual differences in a dozen cities throughout the country. In his report in the Spring 1957 *Kentucky English Bulletin* he describes the many kinds of writing which gifted students like to engage in.[9]

Enrichment through Speaking

Gifted students not only frequently read and write well, but also their speaking ability is usually superior to the rest of the class. Their class recitations are more substantial in terms of content and language, and these students may show greater poise before a group. These students can be given differentiated assignments which will require them to address the class at length and also opportunities to address groups outside the English class. They are usually the announcers of student news on the P. A. system. They help to promote school drives and extracurricular activities.

Not only do bright students frequently have greater poise and larger vocabularies than their fellow students, but also their feeling for language is more highly developed. They should be given assignments which will stimulate them to think of the English language from its linguistic, semantic and historical aspects.[10]

Enrichment through Extracurricular Activities

Some of the activities most easily remembered of one's high school days are the extracurricular activities. Long after we have forgotten what took place in English 7, we recall with a glow of satisfaction our leadership in a club, our editorship of a school newspaper, our failure or success in a speech contest, our participation in a city-wide forum on current events. The activities may include the following:

1. Writing
   School newspapers
   Literary magazines
   Annuals
   Contests sponsored by *Scholastic, Atlantic Monthly* and other magazines
   Writing club that studies great writers and encourages student writing
   School publicity club
   Publication of anthology of best work in entire city
2. Speaking
   Drama Club to study plays as well as produce them in English classes, school
      assemblies, P. T. A.'s and fraternal and civic groups
   Speech contests
   Debate clubs
3. Mass Media
   TV Club, which watches TV with discrimination, prepares weekly list of
      recommended programs
   Motion Picture Club which does the same with motion pictures[11]
   Radio Club which may not only study radio programs, but also may partici-
      pate in local radio programs
   Recording Club. In one school in New York City the "audiophiles" listen
      to great recordings of poetry, drama and music. Discussions are held, evalu-
      ations are made, and recommendations forwarded to the English Depart-
      ment, to enlarge its recordings collection. Tangential values from such a

club are learning to write for varied catalogues, to evaluate new recordings on 4 x 6 cards, watching magazines like *Saturday Review/World, English Journal* and *Clearing House* for their evaluations of new recordings pertaining to the study of English.

The possibilities for a rich extracurricular program are numerous provided that teachers are willing to take the time to sponsor them and provide inspiration and guidance. Theirs will be the satisfaction of knowing that some of the most memorable experiences in secondary school English take place in such clubs.

HOW THE COMMUNITY'S RESOURCES CAN HELP

The world of the English classroom that is limited to the textbook is a truly limited one. Such a classroom can be enriched by community personnel and their own materials. Although not every community may possess a distinguished writer or actor, there are always editors, publishers, travelers and cultured people generally who would be happy to come and share their experiences with the class. The local editor, radio or television station operator or librarian may be invited to talk about his specialties. Parents frequently have had interesting experiences in their travels abroad or in their professions which may inspire, inform or entertain students.

On a more elaborate scale, sometimes theatrical companies or individual stars may come to perform. The Bureau of Audio-Visual Instruction of the New York City Public Schools has for several years invited theatrical companies to the schools with most favorable results. One teacher has been assigned specifically to coordinate such enrichment activities.[12] Frequently an enterprising English teacher or department head will invite a prominent author and thus give an unforgettable experience to many students.[13]

Far more rewarding in some ways are trips and excursions to the community resources. Thousands of students in Connecticut, New Jersey, and New York attend the Shakespeare plays in Stratford, Connecticut each year. It is not uncommon for a school to buy an entire performance for its students. Trips to local theatres, museums, motion picture theatres, radio and television studios have long been standard procedures. In some cities museums have special education departments which issue announcements of special exhibits of interest to certain classes or certain topics being covered. Thus students reading Greek myths or Homer may enrich their background with visits to the ancient art section of the local museum; when *Ivanhoe* or *Men of Iron* or a unit on chivalry is studied, a visit is arranged to the medieval art section.

The public libraries have long been cooperating with the public schools. Some of these activities have included:

1. *Book Lists for secondary students.*[14]
2. *Display of the latest books or for special occasions.* For example, the 100th anniversary of the outbreak of the Civil War was the subject for displays in libraries throughout the country. Many libraries feature displays which are unique. Thus, the Public Library of Greensboro, N. C., has a collection of O. Henry memorabilia

and books that may be unique in the country. Fortunate indeed are the bright students who can see the many priceless displays on the third floor of the New York Public Library where first editions, manuscripts, rare photographs and other memorabilia are on display. Items which a rare book collector would travel many miles to see are available in abundance. Likewise, such exhibits as those of the Folger Library in Washington and the Huntington Library in California are veritable treasure troves.

3. *Book Talks.* In many libraries throughout the country, librarians give talks either on the recent books of interest to gifted adolescents or on special topics. Sometimes the librarians may come to the English classes for these talks.[15]

4. *Story and/or Poetry Hours.* In many libraries, students are invited to readings of fiction, poetry or drama, to be followed by discussions. In Dallas, the children's librarian has gone one step further and invites gifted students to bring their creative writing once a week, to be discussed by fellow students. The librarian recommends other works which might be of interest.

Cooperation with the Mass Media

Radio and television programs have been arranged to provide opportunities for gifted students. Frequently secondary students will be invited to give talks on books or to discuss issues that are of interest to adolescents. Several tangential values can come from such experiences. There have been many television talk shows on which students have appeared.

Cooperation with Local Colleges

In communities where colleges and universities exist, opportunities to attend lectures may be provided.

Parents Can Be Helpful

Parents are, of course, the first source of enrichment of the gifted student by inheritance and the proper environment. When they travel, visit cultural landmarks, historical and literary sites, they can supply their students with precious experiences. Some school systems draw up recommendations for parents who would like to help their gifted children, by visits, trips and other extra-school experiences.[16]

Special Classes for Gifted Students

The second major method of meeting the needs for gifted students in English is to group them together. Authorities have argued the pros and cons of grouping by ability for decades, but those schools which are large enough to have one or more classes of gifted pupils per grade are quite satisfied with the results.[17] Assuming that the school or school system is committed to ability grouping, what has been done for the gifted student? In some instances the schools have developed separate courses of study for students from grades 9-12; in other instances they have added electives; in still others they have permitted teachers of gifted students to experiment without necessarily formulating a definite course of study. Each teacher or school system embarking upon a program of ability grouping can acquire the materials already available and thus avoid needless duplication of patterns which already have been found wanting. The New Trier Township High School in Winnetka, Illinois, has practiced ability grouping for over thirty years and has developed detailed courses of study for superior students.[18] The New York State Education Department has described fifty-six practices in various types of schools. Other school systems and individual authors have described their procedures. What we shall do here is to summarize the main procedures under the headings of Literature, Written Composition, Speaking, Language, and Listening.

Literature

To learn all the variations that have been introduced to provide for gifted students, the teacher would profit from the curricular materials which are available from such large cities as New York City, Cleveland, Birmingham, Los Angeles, Cincinnati, Indianapolis, Baltimore, Detroit, Washington, D. C., Portland, Seattle, to mention a few. Here are some of the approaches:

1. Thematic approach with both intensive study of some major works and collateral reading of several works. Thus in the Mt. Lebanon (Pa.) High School, when the whole class is studying *Moby Dick,* the outside reading may be based on such related ideas as the Problem of Evil, The Consequences of Sin, A Search for Faith, The Sea, Other Allegorical Works. For each topic several works are recommended.

2. More difficult works than would ordinarily be taught in average classes on the same level. Thus a gifted twelfth-year class might study *An American Tragedy* or *Crime and Punishment* or *Look Homeward, Angel* instead of *Ethan Frome* or a book of essays.

3. More emphasis on the ideas, the sense of values, and the style of a book studied by the class than would be done in the average class.

4. More intensive study of the manner in which several authors approach the same problem: or the several works of one author.[19]

5. Courses in World Literature in which several of the major works of several countries are read and analyzed.[20]

6. Intensive pursuit of the works of a single author. As A. J. Beeler writes, ". . .the reading of one of Jesse Stuart's short stories led into extensive study of his life and literary career. Included in the activities were a lengthy report on his life, a display of his nineteen books with some attention to requirements of various literary types, an attractive bulletin board, special reports on several short stories, an investigation of the Guggenheim fellowships. . ."[21]

7. Reading to study the techniques of fiction.[22]

8. Intensive study of a literary *genre.* A. J. Beeler states: "Biographical study is of never-ending interest and may be undertaken as a separate project or used as the need occurs. This provides an opportunity to study current biography as a literary

form, to have special reports on full-length biographies or selections from reference books, to make oral and written reports, and perhaps to stimulate extensive research."[23]

9. Comparisons between ancient and modern classics based on extensive reading. In the honors course in San Diego, California, oral and written reports are given on such topics as:

a. Compare the Circe episode in *The Odyssey* with Milton's *Comus*.

b. Use the *New Yorker* profile technique in describing a character in *The Canterbury Tales*.

c. Compare Addison and Steele with James Reston, Jim Bishop or another present-day columnist.

d. Compare Aeschylus' *Agamemnon* with O'Neill's *Mourning Becomes Electra*; Sophocles' *Oedipus Rex* with Shakespeare's *Othello* or Jean Cocteau's *Infernal Machine*.

e. Compare Swift's *Gulliver's Travels*, Part IV, with Orwell's *Animal Farm*.[24]

10. Study of contemporary literature.[25]

Writing for Gifted Students

Writing in Part II of the 57th Yearbook of the National Society for the Study of Education, Lou LaBrant outlines a program of writing for the gifted student which embodies many of the best practices.

1. In all high-school grades (ninth through twelfth) the student is able to relate a simple personal experience clearly. He selects events, rejects others, and follows a simple recognizable order—order of occurrence or order essential to understanding on the part of the reader. The experience chosen or its interpretation varies with maturity (a ninth-grader tells of a family event as of interest to classmates; a twelfth-grader uses the same event to point up a family relationship).

2. The high-school student writes formal pieces based on first-hand observations, reading, or laboratory experimentation. For example, at ninth grade a paper might report the visit to a factory, reading on local history, an experiment in nutrition. Reference should be made to sources, briefly but accurately reported. A gifted ninth-grader ought to give simple bibliographical credit and distinguish between quotation and paraphrase. By the end of the twelfth grade, the gifted student prepares carefully organized reports, synthesizes material found in reading, shows clear organization and approximates adult writing.

3. A considerable number of students find outlet for creative urges in writing stories, poems, and personal essays. Opportunity should be a constant in the English course as the gifted often have great need for self-expression through art forms.

4. The student also is able to state personal conviction in writing. A ninth-grade student may criticize school procedures, state his opinion concerning athletics, or explain vocation preferences. By the twelfth grade his papers may deal with social or political problems, religious doubts, or convictions, criticisms of ideas met in reading. At this level he distinguishes between data and unsupported judgment.[26]

To speak in specific terms in describing some outstanding programs, following are some procedures that have been successful:

1. Courses in creative writing[27]
2. Research papers showing intensive study of ideas, individual authors, trends in literature. Seniors in the honors classes of many high schools have to submit a paper of 1500-2000 words on one of the following topics:

Chekhov and the motionless play
The bizarre world of Franz Kafka
Sinclair Lewis as satirist
Steinbeck and American realism
Willa Cather: a Regionalist
The Importance of nature in Hemingway's Novels
The tragedies of Arthur Miller [28]

3. Original essays of all types. A. J. Beeler noticed after his year-long survey, "The writing of essays of all kinds stimulates the interest and creativity of good English students and may range from very informal autobiographical sketches to critical reviews."[29]
4. Special course in journalism. This is frequently the stepping stone for future members of the school newspaper, literary magazine and manual.[30]
5. The writing laboratory where gifted students may not only get individual help from their teachers, but may also serve to assist students who need help.[31]

Language Study for Gifted Learners

Where courses in semantics, linguistics or historical development of the English language are given in American secondary schools, they are generally offered to gifted students, either as units within a semester's course or as entire courses.

6

ENGLISH FOR THE SLOW LEARNER

For many years the problem of teaching the slow learner in English was solved by such simple means as dropping him from school at the age of fourteen. Thus, no slow learners went on to academic high schools. For those who were not interested in going to college, there were commercial or vocational courses which were among the earliest adaptations for nonacademic students. With the raising of the school-leaving age, more and more slow learners have come into our secondary schools. According to recent estimates, one of every five American high school students today is a slow learner.[1]

English teachers cannot ignore such a large segment of our high school population. Through the past four decades individual teachers, schools, and even school systems have experimented with new materials, methods and administrative procedures. Today there is considerable literature on teaching slow learners based on sound educational principles and successful classroom experiences.

CHARACTERISTICS OF SLOW LEARNERS

Specifically developed in the New York City high schools by Abraham H. Lass and Frank A. Smerling, the following outline of characteristics of slow learners and the methodological adaptations is still a useful starting point.

Student Traits	Methodology
1. Generally low I. Q. Lacking in verbal intelligence	1. a. Make appeal to the experience of the student. The curriculum must link very closely with the outside-of-school experiences of the student. Hence, there is necessity for discovering these interests before proceeding. b. Keep the pace of the recitation slower than with normal students. c. Use multiple activity within single units of work.

2. Reading ability almost always poor. Literary tastes undeveloped

2. a. Give training in reading skills of various kinds.
   b. Encourage copious reading of material within the range of student ability, or a bit beyond.
   c. Develop the reading skills in other subjects.

3. Lack of desire to excel scholastically or intellectually

3. a. Appeal mainly to the desire for immediate significant living. School to these students is a finishing process, not a fitting process.
   b. Stress experience values in literature. Place relatively little emphasis on literary forms or values. Make school work appeal concretely and positively through the validity of the school work chosen.
   c. Fact mastery is of little significance; stress attitudes and generalized habits.

4. Slow and incoherent thought processes. Impulsive in action, poor self-control. Guided by slogans, catchwords and common prejudices

4. a. In recitations and assignments, stress coherence, full transitions. Break up thought sequence into smaller steps than normal.
   b. The tendency in these groups to give concert answers presents a disciplinary problem. It shows attention and readiness to participate and grows out of the undisciplined character of the students. This tendency must be dealt with very early without crushing the undirected enthusiasm which produces it. The cue here is freedom within discipline. A device that works well in securing proper discipline with these students is the group construction of the class constitution which all students sign and to which they pledge obedience.
   c. These students love to hear the teacher talk. This trait may be used for the inculcation of correct attitudes and for substituting more rational values for the ones they now possess.
   d. Employ emotional impulses by providing desirable channels of self-expression.

5. Lacking in self-reliance and initiative. Highly imitative

5. a. Place less emphasis on individual project, more on group project.
   b. Utilize whatever initiative is present by getting the weaker students to imitate the stronger and brighter ones.
   c. The teacher must be more active and specific in his procedures than with normal or superior students. Give them a good part of the work, and enable them to perform the rest with some degree of success.

6. Slow in grasping abstraction; responsive to concrete and dramatic presentation

6. a. Individual case rather than abstract statement should be the point of departure in class discussion.

b. Use of dramatization of ethical dilemmas of interest.

c. Read poetry of marked rhythms—ballads, humorous poetry.

d. Fiction should be of stirring and romantic quality dealing with obvious conflicts on a physical plane and should involve vivid sensory and emotional appeal.

e. Enrich the vocabulary by the use and study of vivid words.

f. Teach through multiple sense appeal.

g. Judiciously employ radio, movie, television and tabloid techniques in the presentation of subject matter and the motivation of assignments.

h. Written work should be an essential part of classroom routine with these students. It serves to insure a greater proportion of student activity and gives greater concreteness to the recitation. Wherever possible, summaries and comments should be made in writing as well as orally.

7. Anti-school and anti-teacher attitudes

7. a. Don't stigmatize the student.

b. Don't lecture or scold.

c. Make school a joyous experience through the type of material presented and through teacher attitude toward the students.

d. Give the student a feeling of conquest in the subject. Make him feel that he is progressing significantly every day.

e. Be generous with praise and approval.

f. Link the work with the vocational and avocational interests of the student.

g. Expect industry of the student. Act as though you take it for granted.

h. Be sympathetic and cheerful.

i. Learn to ignore minor disciplinary infractions.

j. Give approval in writing. Mark often.

8. Orally inarticulate. Refusal to participate in recitations, the results of dammed energies and of inferiority complexes

8. a. Emphasize oral English in all phases of the English program.

b. Recognize all who wish to talk.

c. Make the students want to talk and give them the utmost encouragement. Have significant drill

	in corrective speech since these students have a great desire to cultivate social graces.
	d. Be patient. It takes time to break down this sort of self-consciousness.
9. Lacking in desirable work and study habits	9. a. Homework should be limited but fully motivated. The assignments should be well within the grasp of every student in the class.
	b. Make use of classroom routine to teach students orderliness and industry.
	c. Create a workmanlike attitude in the class by your own attitude toward the work at hand.
	d. Insist on thorough preparation.[2]

HELPFUL PUBLICATIONS

Another large school system which has devoted much time and effort to studying the nature of the slow learner and modifying the curriculum in English for that student is the Philadelphia Public School System. The publications that are extremely helpful are *An Inquiry into the Nature and Needs of Slow Learners at The Senior High School Level*;[3] *The Key to Reaching Slow Learners in the High School*;[4] and *A Guide to the Teaching of English—An Adapted Course, Grades 10-12 (Tentative)*, Curriculum Office, Philadelphia Public Schools, 1960.

An excellent survey of many successful practices observed during a year of visiting many schools is supplied by A. J. Beeler in the *Kentucky English Bulletin*, Fall, 1957-58 issue.[5]

More recent publications on how to teach the slow learner include: *Teaching English for Higher Horizons*, N. Y. C. Board of Education, 1965; *Resource Units in Language Arts for General Course Students in Senior High Schools*, N. Y. C. Board of Education Curriculum Bulletin, 1966-1967 Series No. 13; *Language Programs for the Disadvantaged*, a Report of the N. C. T. E. Task Force on Teaching English to the Disadvantaged, edited by Richard Corbin and Muriel Crosby for the National Council of Teachers of English, 1965.

These full-length textbooks have many useful suggestions: J. D. Brogden, *Developing Communication Skills in Non-Committed Learners* (West Nyack, N. Y.: Parker Publishing Co., 1970); Muriel S. Karlin and Regina Berger, *Successful Methods for Teaching the Slow Learner* (West Nyack, N. Y.: Parker Publishing Co., 1969); Robert D. Strom, Editor, *The Inner-City Classroom: Teacher Behaviors* (Columbus, Ohio: Charles E. Merrill Co., 1966); Arno Jewett, Joseph Mersand and Doris V. Gunderson, *Improving English Skills of Culturally Different Youth in Large Cities* (Washington, D. C.: U. S. Office of Education, Bulletin 1964, No. 5).

Publishers of textbooks who have realized that there is a large market for adapted or new materials for slow learners have prepared some useful brochures for teachers. Betty H. Yarborough's *Teaching English to Slow Learners* is extremely helpful.[6]

RECOGNIZING THE SLOW LEARNER

How the slow learner will be selected for special attention will vary, depending upon the size of the school, the philosophy of the school and the preparation of the teaching staff. Where schools are large enough, more special classes for slow learners are being formed.[7] Although there may sometimes be complaints from parents against ability grouping of slow learners as being undemocratic, the evidence seems to be that, given the right kind of teacher and materials, more can be done for such pupils in special classes than in heterogeneous classes.

The manner of selection will depend upon the guidance facilities in the particular school. In some schools one guidance counselor is given the job of helping slow learners. On the basis of I. Q., reading score and other data on the cumulative record card which accompanies the student to secondary school, the counselor programs these students into English classes marked "G" meaning *general*, as differentiated from *commercial* or *academic*, or "M" meaning *modified*. Other systems of designation may be used.

QUALIFICATIONS OF THE TEACHER

All teachers need patience and sympathetic understanding, but teachers of slow learners need these qualities in greater degree. As Featherstone expresses it so well in *Teaching the Slow Learner:*

Instead of tolerating him as a necessary nuisance—as a cross to be borne—the teacher must be able to accept him for what he is and believe that he has a right to the best and most conscientious guidance and instruction that can be devised.[8]

Patience and understanding alone will not make a successful teacher of slow learners. He must have a mastery of methodology, be willing to experiment, be willing to spend extra time on trips with the children to enrich their experiential backgrounds, to meet with their parents, to put in additional time on careful preparation, and to do a great deal of reading in "junior" literature suitable to this type of student. Because of the additional time required, in many school systems teachers of slow learners are excused from certain activities so that they may have more time for preparation and personal attention.

READING AND LITERATURE

Slow learners need extra instruction in reading because their skills have not been developed. When schools became interested in this group of students in the early 1930's, one of the first modifications in the curriculum was the introduction of reading-skills books and pamphlets. Teaching the reading skills is, of course, highly desirable, and many good materials are avialable. But a skills-building program without a rich leisure-reading program is inadequate. Many literature series now have a two-track program with reading skills closely allied to the various selections.

Teachers of slow learners have found that certain magazines, such as the various *Scholastic* magazines and the *Reader's Digest,* have been very helpful with slow students. Sometimes a teacher will prepare his own materials for improving reading. Comprehension and vocabulary questions based on a short passage or selection can be duplicated easily, and such material has the virtue of being prepared for the students by the one who best knows their reading problems.

Many attempts have been made to provide reading materials for slow learners. They range all the way from the second-track anthologies published by various publishers to the *Teen-Age Tales* of D. C. Heath and *Stories for Teen-agers* of Globe Book Company. Each series has its virtues. Each should be read by the teacher for the purpose of discovering which collection is best suited to his particular situation.[9]

More recently the following series especially designed for slow learners have appeared: Herbert Balish and Irene Patai, Editors, *The Way It Is,* a series of ten booklets containing a total of 45 stories (New York: Xerox Corp., 1967); Marjorie B. Smiley and Other Editors, *Gateway English* (New York: The Macmillan Co, 1966); Houghton Mifflin Action Series, containing such titles as *Encounters, Challenges, Forces, Crosscurrents,* all in paperback. (Boston: Houghton Mifflin, 1970); Benjamin M. Ashcom and other editors, *Stories of the Inner City* (New York: Globe Book Co., 1970); Charlotte K. Brooks, General Editor, Holt's Impact Series, containing such volumes as *I've Got a Name, At Your Own Risk, Cities, Larger than Life* (New York: Holt, Rinehart and Winston, 1968); Mary Frances Everhart, Consulting Editor, *The Voices of Man Literature Series* (Menlo Park, California: Addison-Wesley Publishing Co., 1969).

READING LITERATURE IN COMMON

Although slow learners may not speak well and may be poor readers, they will talk about literature which has interested them. Since their attention span is shorter than that of the academically minded, slow learners prefer short selections. Betty H. Yarborough expresses the opinion of many who have worked with these students:

When selections are assigned, they should be short and of high interest. The slow learner will not find it easy to "stay with" long, complicated passages. Since the slow learner usually confines his free-choice reading to newspapers and magazines, modern selections are more appropriate for him than classical ones. Of course, his tastes should be developed and his selection of reading material carefully supervised, but many of the traditional literary selections are inappropriate for the slow learner. Intricate, figurative writing escapes him. Subtle allusions or delicate shades of meaning are beyond his understanding. The beauties the English teacher sees in the magic enchantment of words will not be perceived by him. Indeed, he may build resistance to reading when confronted with what has little meaning for him.[10]

Some teachers, however, have found certain of the adapted classics satisfactory with slow learners. Since they are of varying quality, each teacher should decide for himself whether the adaptation or abridgement would be suitable for his group and at the same time not offend his own literary taste.

Slow learners like short plays and will participate in dramatization although their articulation and enunciation may leave much to be desired. Several good collections of short plays are available, several in paperback.[11] Among the longer plays, *Macbeth* has been quite successful, with much reading by the teacher. A recording of this play can be used to enrich and reinforce the classroom reading.

Many valuable suggestions for group enjoyment of literature with specific recommendations for teaching each type are found in the *Guide to the Teaching of English —An Adapted Course, Grades 10-12,* of the Philadelphia Public Schools.[12] Here are some practical suggestions concerning classroom procedure:

1. Motivation

    a. The teacher reads or tells the class the first part of the story, taking the plot to the point where the class is eager to know what happens next.

    b. The teacher leads the class discussion of the general problem or situation to be encountered in the story.

    c. The teacher points out the relationship between the pupils' own lives and the general theme of the story to be read.

    d. The teacher discusses with the class those elements of the book to be read which are likely to present difficulty—

        Unfamiliar background

        New concepts

        Vocabulary

2. Directed silent reading

    a. This may be done in or out of class, but there should be some silent reading periods in class so that the teacher can check on comprehension by direct observation.

    b. If the book presents considerable difficulty to the pupils, objective fact questions assigned before reading will help them.

3. Oral reading

    a. There should be much oral reading by the teacher.

    b. Pupils should be encouraged, but never required to read aloud passages which they find interesting.

    c. Poor readers who wish to read aloud (and many will) should be given the opportunity to practice for the teacher before reading to the class.

4. Group discussion

    a. Following directed silent reading, the class should have an opportunity to share their enjoyment of the story for these reasons:

        1. To compare notes on their opinions of characters and plot

        2. To clear up any difficulties they may have encountered

    b. The teacher should direct more difficult questions to less able readers.

5. Tests

Slow learners will wish to take "literature tests" like other pupils. The following types of questions are recommended:

a. Objective factual questions which follow the chronological sequence of the plot, answerable in one or two words

b. Sentence-completion questions

c. Vocabulary questions on some of the words discussed in class

d. Discussion questions calling for brief expressions of opinion about characters and central theme

THE PLACE OF AUDIO-VISUAL AIDS

Since slow learners have a relatively limited experiential background, anything that can be done to enrich their background will make the teacher's task easier. A trip to a Shakespearean production, whether to the Stratford Theatre in Stratford, Connecticut, or to the McCarter Theatre in Princeton, New Jersey, or to one of the many college theatres will do much to break down resistance to Shakespeare. There are also many film strips which are useful for English classes, as well as excerpts from films and 16 mm. versions of classics.[13]

The most complete annotated list of recordings suitable for all learners is Morris Schreiber's *An Annotated List of Recordings in the Language Arts,* with supplement edited by Robert Walk (Urbana, Ill.: National Council of Teachers of English, 1971).

The most recent handbook on the use of films is edited by G. Howard Poteat, *The Compleat Guide to Film Study* (Urbana, Ill.: N. C. T. E., 1972). The bibliography in this book lists many other valuable handbooks, as well as a complete collection of screen plays published in English.

A good source of audio-visual aids is *Educational Media Index,* fourteen volumes (New York: McGraw-Hill, 1964). Volume V deals with the English language (Grade 7 through College, Adult).

The newer equipment such as the overhead projector, permitting the teacher to face the class while demonstrating on the chalkboard, can be a useful aid to instruction. The chalkboard itself can be used effectively for outlining materials, for graphic illustrations and for defining difficult words found in the reading.

WRITTEN COMPOSITION

Slow learners do not like to write, and when they do write, their work needs much correction. The following suggestions have been successful in many classes:

1. Many short writing experiences are needed. The slow learner must learn how to write a note, a letter, a set of directions.

2. Begin with the simpler elements and proceed to the more difficult. The slow learner has to master the sentence, then group related sentences into a paragraph, and finally attempt a short composition.

3. If you make your letter-writing assignments realistic, you will get better letters from your students. Show your students that most newspapers and many magazines print letters from readers. Tell them about the sacks of mail that come to each

congressman every time an important issue arises. List real-life situations which will require letters later in life. (One teacher of slow learners had her students send letters across the sea. Then she arranged an exhibit in the library of copies of the original letters and the replies, with a map of England showing the areas from which the letters had come. The exhibit gave a certain dignity to letters, which the writers had not realized before.)

4. Slow learners need much help in organizing their written work. Instructions must be specific. Examples of topic sentences should be elicited and written on the chalkboard. Difficult words should be spelled. The more guidance that can be given before writing, the better chance there will be for acceptable written work.

5. Discussion of experiences which the class has had in common can lead to good written work. As the class discusses the experience, the teacher should list the points made, which later can be organized as an outline. Slow learners need much help in organizing their thoughts before putting them down on paper.

6. Much revision will be necessary. Teachers correct, but students revise and re-write. The proper form and the amenities of written composition should be emphasized.

7. Provide motivation for class newspapers and magazines. Even slow learners will take pride in their contributions to class newspapers and magazines. The teacher may have to correct many times, but, when the final products are mimeographed or duplicated, these students will experience a joy from their expression which they had not known before.[14]

8. There should be some written homework almost every day. To many slow learners, a reading assignment is not homework; they can do this in the cafeteria or on the bus. Some amount of writing done regularly in the English notebook, however, will help to habituate the writing act.

LIBRARY SKILLS

The library can play an important role in the slow-learner program. Unless the library stocks a sufficient number of suitable books, slow learners may lose interest even if they have been strongly motivated. In many schools, classroom libraries have been stocked with multitudes of "junior" novels, interesting biographies from such series as the Landmark Books and how-to-do-it books.

Slow learners have to be taught how to locate a book by using the card catalogue and by knowing how books are arranged in the library. Lessons may be conducted in the library or in the English classroom. Marie A. Toser's *Library Manual* has a wealth of suggestions for the classroom teacher who must teach library skills.[15]

Slow learners should be taught also how to get information from an encyclopedia, how to find an article in the *Readers' Guide to Periodical Literature,* and how to use other types of reference books needed in the term's work. The H. W. Wilson Company has prepared a handy little volume on *How to use the Readers's Guide to Periodical Literature and Other Indexes* which will be supplied in class sets, free of charge. Sample pages of several references books show exactly what these books look like, and there is much valuable information that can be used by the teacher to motivate her lessons.[16]

DICTIONARY STUDY

Since the dictionary is one of the indispensable tools for gaining an education, slow learners need instruction in how best to utilize this valuable reference book. Almost all grammar and composition texts contain chapters on the use of the dictionary. Sometimes, the dictionary makers prepare brochures which may be obtained in quantity, free of charge. Such is the pamphlet *An Outline for Dictionary Study*, for use with Webster's *New Collegiate Dictionary*.[17] Although slow-learning students cannot be expected to purchase a hard-cover high school dictionary, they may be able to afford one of the several paperbound copies. Dictionary-using is one of the most useful habits they can acquire. Anything the teacher can do to break down the dislike for words will be a victory in the battle for knowledge through reading.

KNOWING THE MAKE-UP OF BOOKS

Many slow learners can become quite interested in the make-up of a book if the information is presented properly. They like to know how a copyright is obtained, how permission to reprint selections in their literature anthology was acquired, and many other things about a book's evolution. Lessons can be prepared on how to use the table of contents, the index, the glossary, etc. The more interest we can engender in books as such, the greater the possibility that aversion toward them will break down and a liking will develop.

SPELLING

Since English is a language that is not spelled as it sounds, all students have difficulty with some words or with some combinations of letters. Some formal instruction in spelling therefore is required for all students. In addition, an individualized program is necessary for the words that each student requires. Each student, for example, should keep a list of difficult words which he needs to know.

Certain misspellings are predictable, and these words can be the basis for spelling lists to be learned by the whole class. Before any list is taught, a pretest should be given to determine how many words are already known by the class and what types of misspellings occur. The actual procedures to be used in teaching spelling words are well expressed by Yarborough:

1. Only a few words should be introduced in a given lesson.
2. Each word should be studied separately.
3. The meaning of each word should be clarified by using the word in both oral

and written sentences before teaching it as a spelling word.

4.   Each word to be learned should be pronounced by the class in unison and then by various class members.

5.   The letters in each word should be noted, each separately.

6.   Any known phonetic principles which are applicable should be applied (although it is not suggested that each phonetic element be studied).

7.   The word should be copied, then spelled aloud by the teacher so that each student can check his spelling, letter by letter.

8.   The student should then try to write the word from memory.

9.   After the words for the day have been studied, a brief test should be given to evaluate the extent to which the class has learned the words. Words missed by large numbers of students should be reviewed the following day, and each day's lesson should include a review (as a portion of the daily test) of several words from previous lessons.

10.   Weekly tests should be given.[18]

The dictionary can be a powerful tool for these students whose memory for configurations of words may not be strong enough. They should be taught how to look for words like *pneumonia, knowledge, gnaw;* for they may frequently look for such words under the letter *n*.

Above all, students must learn to employ the words they have learned, or the words will be forgotten. Hence, students should be given assignments which will require their use. As these words occur in reading, they should be pointed out for reinforcement.

PART THREE
READING, WRITING, AND
LITERATURE

7

READING FOR THE SUPERIOR STUDENT IN A COMPREHENSIVE HIGH SCHOOL

Guiding the reading of superior high school students is nothing new, brought on by the stress upon excellence after the launching of Sputnik. In fact, the author well remembers the excitement in his own high school days (1920-24) when students in the so-called X classes were given recently published anthologies instead of the battered old classics which were used by the Y and Z students (this is how our three-track system in English was labeled).

The excitement over the anthologies was due to three factors: the material was new; the selections were different from those used by the average students; we were expected to read these selections with greater maturity than was expected of other students. In essence, these are the three major factors in any reading program for superior students. Such students should be given a great variety of reading along with guidance in how to read different selections. Superior students should be required, with help, to read materials which would not be required of the average student and certainly not of the slow learner in English. Lastly, superior students should be expected to read many selections with real understanding.

GREAT VARIETY OF MATERIAL

In the high school years of which I have spoken (1920-24) the American drama was beginning to flower. O'Neill, Anderson, Howard, Rice, Behrman were beginning to have their plays produced. Very few contemporary plays could be found in school editions, however. It was with understandable excitement that the gifted students were asked to read some of the contemporary plays which were in print. This was the way in which I first became acquainted with the contemporary drama. Today, thanks to the omnipresent paperbacks, especially the ANTA Distinguished Plays, Dell, Anchor, and other series, scores of contemporary plays are available in inexpensive editions.

This principle of greater variety in reading extends both vertically and horizontally.

By vertically I mean that students will study the works of Plato and Sophocles as well as those of Anouilh and Chekhov. Similar examples can be given from fiction, poetry and biography. By horizontally I mean the geographical distribution of literature. No longer is the teacher of the gifted confined (as he usually was in the 1920's) to American and English literature. The world is our oyster, and students will read paperback editions of *Crime and Punishment, Kristin Lavransdatter, An American Tragedy* and *Of Human Bondage.*

Many lists of suitable works for superior students are available. The New York State Education Department, for example, has published three compilations:[1] *Fiction for High School Students of Superior Ability; More Books for High School Students of Superior Ability; Fiction for Superior Students, Grades 7, 8, 9.*

Every English teacher should possess the latest editions of *Books for You* and *Your Reading,* the senior high and the junior high reading lists published by Washington Square Press and New American Library respectively. Washington Square Press has published *The College and Adult Reading List,* prepared by a committee of the National Council of Teachers of English.[2] Finally, *Paperbound Books in Print*[3] should be available at all times either in the school library or in the teachers' professional collection. This last list is a veritable gold mine of books for all needs. Smaller collections of suitable paperbacks which have been compiled by Norman R. Lee[4] and a committee appointed by the Bureau of Independent Publishers and Distributors[5] should also be on the teacher's desk.

GUIDING THE READING

Obviously, it is not enough for the teacher of superior students to know where books may be found and to tell students what to read. Guidance assumes some kind of direction. This may take several forms. For example, a student may become interested in a certain author, in a certain idea as it is expressed in several authors, or in a theme of more universal application. The teacher, after making a preliminary survey of what is available in the school library (often with the cooperation of the school librarian) or what is available in paperbacks, will suggest a series of readings, with certain things to look for. A research paper is often associated with this kind of varied reading. Each student must work up his own bibliography on 3 x 5 cards to be submitted for approval or modification by the teacher. Periodic reports are then handed in by the student before the final paper is written. When the paper is submitted there must be a complete bibliography, showing considerable reading in both scope and depth. A variety of literary forms is insisted upon: novels, plays, essays and literary criticism. Frequently, personal conferences between teacher and student will give the best kind of guidance. Thus the student is exposed to a great variety of challenging materials which will enlarge his vision and understanding.

It is not enough to help the student to compile a long list of difficult books to read. Superior students need special guidance in reading. Here is a sample list of questions prepared by a gifted teacher[6] for her classes in world literature when they were studying *Antigone:*

1. What is the dramatic conflict that sets the play in motion?
2. Who are the persons involved?
3. Explain the three unities (of time, of place and of action). How are they maintained in this play? What is the emotional effect of this practice? Are the unities observed in English and American dramas?
4. Differentiate between the higher law and the lower law in the dispute. Which side do you support? Why?
5. What dramatic function is served by Ismene?
6. Antigone is considered by many the ideal Greek woman. What qualities of her character support this opinion? Is there any flaw that you can find in her? Discuss.
7. Is Creon a good or a bad man? Does he play the villain to Antigone's role of heroine? What motivates his behavior? Was he guilty of *hybris?* Explain. Has he led the "unexamined life"? Does he learn self-examination in the course of the play?
8. Is romantic love an important feature of this play? Compare Haemon's final act in the tomb of Antigone with Romeo's in the tomb of the Capulets.
9. What is Creon's attitude toward women? What was Socrates'? Does Ismene accept Creon's attitude? Does Antigone? Discuss.
10. What kind of father is Creon? Husband? Uncle? King? Man?
11. To what extent does fate control the events of the play? Does destiny absolve the characters of responsiblity for their action? What is the final moral of the play?
12. What functions are served by the chorus?
13. How much of the action takes place off stage? Why? Compare with modern practice.
14. Gather as many aphorisms from the text as you can find. For example: "No man loves the messenger of ill." "No thing in use by man for power of ill can equal money."

This kind of guidance in reading a Greek tragedy helps the student to read not for facts alone (something which we may have to settle for with the average student), but for principles and human motivation. The particular teacher who wrote these questions always prepared her assignments on ditto sheets at her own home and thus saved hours which her students might otherwise waste in writing the questions down from dictation or in copying them from the chalkboard.

Many contemporary literature anthologies for high schools contain questions on each selection or on an entire unit. The teacher of superior students does not ask her students to answer these questions wholesale, because many of them are too easy. But she goes through the questions (if she does not prefer to prepare her own) and selects the most challenging. Some texts on the teaching of literature in high school have reading plans which merit consideration. For example, Robert A. Bennett, Supervisor of English Language Arts of San Diego Schools has prepared a series of questions and activities in connection with the study of a unit on Drama in Dwight L. Burton's *Literature Study in High School.*[7] Loban, Ryan, and Squire's *Language and Literature in Secondary School*[8] has many such outlines with excellent guiding questions. The author has compiled *Index to Plays,* a handbook with page references to study guides as they appear in collections of plays and in anthologies, so that teachers may determine at a glance in which collection a favorite play is to be found along with suggestions for teaching it.[9]

The guidance demonstrated in the questions on *Antigone* is of the written variety, and the answers may be checked either orally or in a written test. Reading guidance, however, occurs in every oral recitation. The teacher can tell by the answer to a question whether a selection has been read on the elementary level (just for the facts) or on a higher level (for aesthetic appreciation). Guidance, thus, is a continuing process. As has already been mentioned, when time and place are available, personal conferences between pupil and teacher can reveal much. The success of the famous Professor Charles Townsend Copeland (Copey) of Harvard did not stem solely from his great scholarship in English or world literature; but more from his ability to guide his students in writing and reading through personal conferences.

SPECIAL TEXTS FOR CRITICAL READING

A number of texts have been used with superior students to develop their reading skills. These three have been quite successful: Richard D. Altick, *A Preface to Critical Reading;* Roy Lamson et al., *The Critical Reader;* Cleanth Brooks and Robert Penn Warren, *Understanding Poetry.*[10]

Many teachers make use of various reading improvement books in paperback form or make up their own selections from articles in newspapers and magazines.[11] As an example, a reading selection which was part of the Uniform Midterm Examination in Jamaica High School (New York City) for students in the first half of the twelfth year is reproduced below.

Such reading comprehension questions are given in each of the examinations which students at Jamaica High School must take throughout their high school career. Training is given in answering such questions, so that by the time they have to take their Regents Comprehensive Examination in English at the end of their high school careers, the superior students do quite well. In addition to providing reading questions for the uniform examinations which all students in the same grade must take, teachers prepare their own questions as the need arises. One teacher of slow students prepares an original reading comprehension question each week, and her students miss it when it is not given.[12]

Thus, by the three-fold approach described in this chapter, superior students are helped to develop the reading skills which they will need in college and in their life-work. The program has worked well for more than a decade, producing hundreds of scholarship winners in various fields in which the ability to read is important. Although Jamaica High School has more than four-thousand students and each teacher has from 150-175 students (except the guidance counselors, who may have about a hundred), we have been able to spend considerable time in developing this most important skill, as well as in fostering a love for literature, which is the ultimate aim of all teachers.

(Following is a Reading Comprehension Question prepared for superior students in the twelfth grade).

Read the Following Passage Carefully—Then Follow the Directions Which Appear Below It

A particular clue to their (the Greeks) uniqueness is a saying of Anaxagoras: "All things were in chaos when Mind arose and made order." More than any other ancient people, the Greeks put their trust in Mind, or reason. While elaborating one of the greatest mythologies, they achieved the greatest measure of freedom from myth. By rational inquiry they endeavored to explain miracle and *dispel* mystery, to rationalize the authority of both gods and the state. Their curiosity grew into a passion for understanding. Thinking for themselves instead of appealing to ancient authority, they began to think about thinking too; they established rules of reasoning, means to systematic thought. In time some even became conscious of their ignorance and of the possible wisdom of doubt. They realized the diverse possibilities and ultimate uncertainties that are the necessary condition of freedom of thought. For if man knows the absolute truth about God, the universe and his own condition, there is little room for inquiry, little reason for *countenancing* dissent.

Write the number 1-9 on your answer paper. Select the best completing statement; then, after each number, write the appropriate letter.

1. The title below that best expresses the ideas of this passage is: (a) Greek mythology, (b) Writings of Anaxagoras, (c) The Greek preoccupation with reason, (d) Degrees of freedom.

2. The passage states that the Greeks' most creative achievements followed from their reliance upon: (a) mind, (b) miracle, (c) myth, (d) authority.

3. Which of the following statements is *not* true?(a) Some Greek thinkers became convinced of the wisdom of doubt, (b) The Greeks valued freedom of thought, (c) The Greeks were enslaved by their belief in myths, (d) Absolute knowledge left no room for inquiry.

4. According to the paragraph, which one of the following ideas is considered an essential of the freedom to think?(a) acceptance of the state as ultimate authority, (b) reliance upon precedent, (c) recognition of many possibilities and of ultimate uncertainties, (d) prior acceptance of absolute truth.

5. From the following group, select the dominant technique used in the passage to clarify the Greek achievement: (a) exaggeration, (b) irony, (c) comparison, (d) contrast.

6. Which of the following statements best explains the meaning of the *last* sentence in the passage?(a) Freedom is the birthright of every human being, (b) There are requisite conditions without which freedom of thought cannot exist, (c) The right to investigate and disagree ultimately destroys freedom, (d) Because man's knowledge is considerable, there is no longer the urgent need for free inquiry.

7. As used in the last sentence, the word *countenancing* means: (a) rejecting, (b) grimacing, (c) permitting, (d) punishing.

8. The word *dispel* means: (a) alter, (b) remove, (c) add, (d) rebuff.

9. The most significant achievement of the Greeks mentioned in this paragraph is: (a) their art, (b) their mythology, (c) rules of reasoning, (d) their literature.

8

THE PAPERBACK IN THE HIGH SCHOOL

In one of the twenty-seven short biographical miniatures contained in John Dos Passos' *USA,* there is a sketch of J. P. Morgan, the great financier. One sentence has always fascinated me. "Every Christmas his librarian read him Dickens' *Christmas Carol* from the original manuscript."

You can easily imagine the powerfully built millionaire leaning back in his comfortable armchair, smoking one of his omnipresent Havana cigars and listening to Dickens' story of peace on earth and good will to all men from the only copy written in Dickens' own hand. Granted that he derived a certain amount of pleasure, yet I have always wondered whether Morgan could have derived more pleasure from this priceless manuscript than the poorest high school freshman reading the self-same story in a 95-cent paperback edition.

Whenever I tell this story to my students, whether in high school or in college, I tell them that theirs is the opportunity to derive the same kind of pleasure from a modest investment of only a few cents for which J. P. Morgan expended a small fortune. There are certain delights from literature which they can get which might very well have been unknown to Morgan, powerful and wealthy as he undoubtedly was.

And this is the pearl of great price, I go on to say, that we teachers of literature are holding out to them just for the asking. For as James Russell Lowell so aptly expressed it:

The benignities of literature defy fortune and outlive calamity. They are beyond the reach of thief or moth or rust. As they cannot be inherited, so they cannot be alienated.

Concerning the paperback in the high school, many terms have been used. Some call it a revolution; others call it an explosion; still others call it a boom. Without resorting to such high-pressure terms, I shall attempt in this chapter to confine myself to the known facts, and to make some predictions based on these facts.

1. What are the statistics about the use of paperbacks in the high schools?

2. What are the advantages of the use of the paperbacks in the high schools?
3. What are some interesting projects going on throughout the country with respect to the use of paperbacks?
4. What do some outstanding publishers of paperbacks say about the situation?
5. What does the future hold in store for us?

What are the statistics? To be quite frank, no one knows, and it would take a huge research project to determine the facts, which would be out-of-date almost as soon as the study was published. One would have to survey the use or non-use of paperbacks in the twenty-six thousand secondary schools in the United States. among a population of about 10-million students. Even the information thus obtained would be incomplete, for we would not know how many paperbacks were purchased out of school in drug stores, bookstores, grocery chains, by this segment of our population. We cannot make even an educated guess. We do know that over 400-million paperbacks are purchased each year, but we do not know how many of them are purchased by high school students, or how carefully they are read.

Yet some statistics are available, and they are certainly impressive. William D. Boutwell, former Vice President of Scholastic Book Services, wrote that during the 1960–1961 school year more than four million children in public and parochial schools purchased paperbacks regularly through more than one hundred thousand book clubs.[1] Since some of these clubs are in elementary schools, we cannot ascribe the annual purchase of four million copies to high school students alone.

John P. Ware, former Educational Director of Pocket Books, Inc., indicated that in 1960 his company alone sold 10-million paperbacks to schools or through schools. Here and there in the already growing magazine literature about paperbacks we learn of phenomenal purchases in individual schools. About all we can say is that paperbacks are being purchased and used by the tens of millions of copies by secondary students, but we do not know how many or even what types.

That paperback publishers are making vigorous efforts to appeal to this market is evident from these excerpts from personal letters written especially for this chapter.

Victor Weybright, former Chairman and Editor of the New American Library of World Literature, Inc. and now Senior Editorial Advisor of Weybright and Talley, Publishers, wrote:

In the past few years, NAL has greatly expanded the sale of its books for high school use, and we have dedicated our editorial program in the direction of greater service to young readers. Three quarters of the 120 Signet Classics which were published by the Spring of 1962 were widely used in high schools. In January we will launch the Signet Science Library. . . . It is our hope that the Signet Science Library will parallel the usefulness of the Signet Classics in high schools.[2]

And from the venerable House of Scribner, comes this comment from T. J. B. Walsh, former Editor, Trade Department:

All of us, from both "Trade" and "School" departments, keep up a steady search through our back list and our current list for titles suitable for use in the high schools to add to the Scribner Library. We are conscious of the problem at all times. . . .

We are much encouraged to pursue this course by the great number of letters which come in to us from high schools over the country setting forth their desires and needs in order to meet successfully the goals set in their various courses of study. Believe me, the curriculum experts, department chairmen, and teachers in our high schools are aware that many of their problems as to classroom material can be solved successfully, as well as inexpensively, by the paperback book.[3]

Space does not permit quotations from many other paperback publishers relevant to the importance which they attach to this ever-growing market.

The last sentence from Mr. Walsh's letter is a natural transition to my second point.

The Advantages of the Use of Paperbacks. Perhaps the most intensive survey of the use of paperbound books in the public schools and the parochial schools was made in 1959 by a Subcommittee of the National Council of Teachers of English Committee on Relations with Publishers of Paperbound Books, and published in 1960 by the National Council of Teachers of English. Every state was represented as well as the District of Columbia. The statistics of the use of these books you may read for yourselves but at this point I wish to list the advantages which were indicated: inexpensive; sold in many places; attractive; encourages student home library; more copies available; serve individual needs; easily replaced; students can own books; can make notes in their own books; inexpensive to replace in library; good way of acquiring more current material; broad range of material; good translations; enrichment of recreational reading; handy for supplementary text; many poor readers will read paperbacks; flexibility of programming; parents may also read books; increase volume for small school; students like them; teachers can easily have classroom library; channel students' allowances into wholesome areas; cut, adapt and present facts without unnecessary detail; easy storage; book club benefits; library can't furnish sufficient other copies; students can exchange books with each other; students buy more books; can have new books each year; prevent accumulation of books which are not reread.[4]

This list of advantages of the use of paperbacks in high school is so inclusive that it would be difficult to find additional reasons in all the literature on the subject that has appeared either in magazine or book form. Incidentally, for those who wish to know the disadvantages as voiced by administrators, teachers, and librarians, these also are listed in the same pamphlet.[5]

Some Interesting Paperback Projects. Interest in the use of paperbacks on the part of high school students has been aroused in many ways. At first it was the alert teacher, dissatisfied with battered old copies of textbooks which were assigned to him, who ventured to order a set of paperbacks with fresher, newer materials, who led the way. Gradually, more and more teachers saw the advantages which were listed earlier. Eventually, entire English departments and schools decided upon paperbacks for the realization of their objectives. Today there are thousands of English teachers throughout the country who are using them as primary or as supplementary instructional materials.

An interesting experiment in an entire school system was The Buffalo Plan of in-school paperback stores, which was begun early in 1960. This has been widely publicized, and its details are well known. In the years since this plan was inaugurated in 1960 in Buffalo, well over one thousand schools have established their own bookstores of paperbacks. As Alexander M. Butman, former Education Director of Bantam Books, Inc. writes:

No longer can one call the in-school paperback bookstore program "The Buffalo Plan." In two short years, the program has spread throughout the country, growing from the original four stores to well over a thousand; from Lynbrook (Long Island) to West Palm Beach (Florida), St. Louis, Chicago, New Mexico, Akron (Ohio), Washington, D. C., Rochester (New York), Baltimore (Maryland), Pittsburgh (Pa.), Detroit (Michigan), San Francisco (Cal.), to mention only a few. [This was written in 1962.] [6]

Book Fairs. Many schools have organized paperback book fairs at which they introduced hundreds of titles and permitted students to browse and purchase. Not only have thousands of copies been sold this way, but small profits have accrued to the student organizations as well. Cooperating in these projects have been the local or regional distributors of paperbacks. For many students this was a first opportunity to purchase books and start their own libraries.

Library Paperback Collections. Many high school libraries have established paperback sections. One of the most interesting articles in paperback literature, describing how such a library was started is "I Sing of the Paperback" by Sister M. Clarencia, librarian of The Incarnate Word High School, San Antonio, Texas. [7]

Since library funds are never as large as they should be, the inexpensiveness of the paperbacks has been a contributing factor to their use. For special assignments, where several copies are needed, they have proven to be one of the best means of enriching the curriculum.

Classroom Libraries. The advocacy of classroom libraries, especially in English classrooms, goes back at least forty or more years. Like so many other worthwhile educational practices, this, too, remained a good idea that could not be realized because of lack of funds. Today in thousands of classrooms collections of paperbacks are utilized to enrich and supplement the regular program. Various devices are employed to stock these libraries, but the end result is more good books at hand when they are needed.

One could discuss some interesting curriculum modifications which have been made possible in our high schools because of the availability of paperbacks, but space does not permit. References will be found in the footnotes. [8]

Views of Publishers on Paperbacks. Excerpts already have been read from three publishers of paperbacks. Many of their educational representatives have been among the most knowledgeable in the field. They have attended innumerable educational conventions where they have met thousands of teachers, supervisors and administrators. They discover what the needs are and try to bring ideas back to their editorial staffs.

Norman J. Elmes, Jr., late Manager of The Education Department of Dell Publishing Co., made an interesting observation on the effect of paperbacks upon the parents of high school students:

One of the most interesting sidelights in this paperback revolution is the tremendous effect that student reading has had on parents. The honest book consumption on the part of parents has spurted ahead noticeably. . . . Admittedly parents initially were concerned with the amount of obscenity direct or implied that could be scrounged from books their kids bring home—and they still are. But what fascinates me is the somewhat embarrassed interest parents are showing by nibbling at the classics "for their children's sake" and then swallowing them whole for their own sake. And since parents are a persuasive force in such American activities as the PTA, this accidental feeding on literature is bound to have a good effect—an effect that I hope will come full circle back to the student. . . .[9]

Freeman Lewis, late President of Washington Square Press and author of the sixteenth R. R. Bowker Memorial Lecture *Paperbound Books in America,* takes this interesting view of the matter:

It seems to me that the paperbound book is, at the moment, in a glorious, stimulating, ridiculous hodge-podge of a mess. With the passing of time, this infant gets to be more and more like its parents—the magazine business and the book publishing business. With this ancestry, it is not surprising that there should be such an enormous multiplicity, such a vast pattern of distribution, such a tremendous discrepancy between the quality of some and the lack of quality of others.
Despite the mess, it would seem clear that the paperback has now become respectable for school use, and that the very multiplicity of materials available will provide a real bonus to school teachers and administrators, if only they can chart their way through the maze.[10]

Finally, Alexander M. Butman, former Education Director of Bantam Books, Inc., sums up much of what has been said in this chapter:

The paperback revolution, which had been going on since 1956, finally became an educational reality in early 1959. At that time the finest of the world's writings were available in inexpensive paperback editions.
Today, through the efforts of the American Book Publishers Council, Committee on Paperbacks of the National Council of Teachers of English, and the realization on the part of the individual publishers of the needs of the educational market, this material's continuing availability is ensured. The major paperback publishers maintain large backlists which are permanently kept in stock. In this country over a hundred educational paperback titles are added to these lists each month. In December of 1961, there were over 13,500 paperbacks available, covering a scope of subjects that is staggering to the imagination.[11]

A LOOK INTO THE FUTURE

Many other aspects of paperbacks in high schools could be discussed, such as the excellent lists that have appeared like Bipad's *The Paperback Goes to School,* N. C. T. E.'s *Books for You* with starred notations for books in paperback form. Teachers now can easily find what is available in the area of their needs.

The following generalizations seem to me to be warranted:
1. There will be increasing use of paperbacks in all areas of high school programs both for in-class and supplementary reading.

2. More school systems will list paperbacks together with hard-cover books which administrators may order with school funds.

3. More high schools will establish paperback book stores along the lines of The Buffalo Plan.

4. The availability of many titles in paperback will permit more individualization and enrichment of instruction.

5. Paperback publishers and educators will work more closely together so that the most-needed titles will be made available.

6. More paperbacks either will be written or edited with the high school student in mind.

7. Because many retarded readers have shown more interest in the paperbacks than in the traditional textbooks, I believe that the paperback will play an increased role in developmental and remedial programs.

8. The interest developed through reading paperbacks will be transferred to other types of reading: the hard cover, the better type of magazine and the newspaper.

James W. Sanders, S. J. expresses this thought so well at the close of his article, "Soft Covered Culture," in the November 1959 *Catholic Educator:*[12]

The fact that high school students are reading, enjoying, and appreciating books, ...and asking for more of them, seems to prove beyond doubt that the average high schooler is capable of good reading if he can be brought into contact with it. The wealth of highest caliber literature at the lowest possible prices and in the most convenient and persuasive form made available by a paperback reading program can, perhaps, be the most successful means of establishing that contact, a contact destined to develop a solid appreciation of the finest in the world's culture.

9

HOW TO TEACH LIBRARY SKILLS

Over the entrance to the Main Reading Room of the New York Public Library on Fifth Avenue and Forty-Second Street is the following inscription:

A good book is the precious life-blood of a master-spirit,
embalmed and treasured up on purpose to a life beyond life.

How many of the thousands of readers who pass into the Main Reading Room every day stop to notice this inscription? How many would know how to locate the author by using the proper reference book? How many would be able to use the card catalogue properly in order to obtain a copy of the work in which that passage appears? Finally, how many would know how to look up proper reference books to obtain information about its author, the circumstances under which the work was written and its importance in the battle for freedom of expression today? All these skills should have been mastered by the graduates of senior high schools, as part of their equipment for college and professional life.

"Students should early learn," writes Blaisdell, "that the most valuable part of an education is not the information one accumulates, but the knowledge of how to find readily any desired information."[1]

AIMS OF LIBRARY INSTRUCTION

In planning a practical and effective library program in secondary schools, the following aims should be realized. Stated in terms of skills and knowledges they are:
1. Knowledge of the general arrangement of the library.
2. Use of the card catalogue.
3. Use of the encyclopedia and other reference books.
4. Use of the *Reader's Guide to Periodical Literature.*
5. Knowledge of the magazines and newspapers in the library.
6. Knowledge of the parts of a book.

7. Knowledge of the dictionary.

8. Skill in following a topic through various references and cross-references and in extracting only the pertinent information.

These skills and knowledges cannot be acquired in several easy lessons but must be exercised constantly during the secondary school years. In fact, new types of reference books are appearing constantly which we as adults have to learn how to use.

It will help to impress students with the importance of libraries today by mentioning how many business and professional organizations have extensive libraries in their specialities, and that these libraries are constantly being used by doctors, engineers, lawyers and writers as they search for important and necessary information. The acquisition of library skills, valuable for the entire life, cannot be measured in dollars and cents.

PRINCIPLES IN ORGANIZING A PROGRAM OF LIBRARY INSTRUCTION

More than half a century of library instruction in the secondary schools has provided several guiding principles which have proven most effective.

1. Library skills are learned best when they are needed for help with problems faced by the students. As DeBoer, Kaulfers and Miller indicate,

. . .When the skills are taught in isolation from situations in which they are needed, there is no guarantee of genuine carry-over, and what is worse, there is no assurance that students will develop the habit of consulting reliable sources in finding answers to questions in real life.[2]

2. Library skills are best acquired through the laboratory method, with the student going through each procedure, rather than just listening to a talk.

The introduction needs to be made largely through the laboratory method, giving him an opportunity both to see and handle the tools that he is expected later to use in connection with his class work.[3]

3. Instruction should be gradual, sequential and cumulative. The intricacies of the card catalogue cannot be mastered in one lesson. Several lessons, spaced over several terms, are more effective. The same principle holds true for all other library skills.

4. Once a library skill has been taught, students should put it to use in solving a problem and should be expected to use that skill on all future occasions where it is necessary.

If students in the course of reading contemporary essays have learned how to use *Who's Who in America* and *Twentieth Century Authors* to find out details about the lives of the essayists, they should be expected to use these reference works as often as the occasions demand.

5. Since the teacher knows best which classroom situations will require a knowledge of the library facilities, she should be equipped to give the greater part of instruction in library usage. Although the school librarian can best give instruction in certain

aspects of the library, she does not have the time nor energy to give all the lessons to all the students, particularly in a large school.

METHODS OF TEACHING LIBRARY SKILLS

Several factors enter into the methodology of teaching library skills: the knowledge which the students already have about the particular skill; the availability of first-hand materials; the curiosity aroused in the students; the proper timing; and the preparation of the teacher. Students who are new to the school need to know the arrangement of their school library, and this knowledge can best be acquired by a visit to the library and an explanation by the librarian. On the first visit for seventh graders in the junior high school or ninth graders in the senior high school, the librarian acts as the host and explains the arrangements of books (fiction, non-fiction, reference, magazines, etc.), the location of the card catalogue, the regulations for borrowing and returning books and rules of good library behavior. If there are any special features in the library, she as host is best qualified to describe them (periodic displays of new books, book jacket bulletin boards, cases for illustrated and valuable books). At the end of such a visit, students should be permitted to take books out and put into practice what they have just learned.

Lessons in other phases of library work will be given as needs arise. For example, if the class is reading certain selections and wishes to read other books by the same authors, the question will naturally arise: "How do we find out whether the books we want are in the library?" This leads into a lesson on the nature of the card catalogue. There are several procedures.

1. Enlarged forms of the various types of cards (author, title, subject card referring to a book, reference card) are used to demonstrate the various ways in which a book is listed.
2. Sets of cards are made available for each student so that he may see for himself the different types of cards.
3. Each student may be given a tray of cards to investigate as the teacher directs.
4. The chalkboard may be used to emphasize certain points.
5. Sometimes films and filmstrips are used to give this information.

The most important part of this lesson is the utilization of the knowledge acquired for actual problems. For this purpose, teachers have found worksheets helpful.

Following are some questions which might be prepared, duplicated and answered by each student.

Work Sheet on the Card Catalogue

1. Your literature anthology recommends Mark Twain's *Adventures of Tom Sawyer*. Without asking the librarian, find out whether our library has this book.
2. What other books by Mark Twain are in the library?

3. Your anthology recommends Rudyard Kipling's *Jungle Books*. What other books by this author does the library have?
4. List five other books about animals in our library.
5. Does the library have a book about rockets or satellites? Write the title and author.

As the library projects become more involved, the work sheets will become more difficult. Whereas in the seventh and eighth grades stress in instruction in the library may be upon locating books on the shelf by looking up authors and titles, in the ninth grade students should learn how to investigate a single subject. This is the time to emphasize cross references. Suppose a student is interested in rockets. He should know how to interpret a card with the following data:

> ROCKETS, see also
> MISSILES
> SATELLITES
> SOLID FUEL ENGINES.

Work sheets should be devised to test the student's ability to find books related to his topic by utilizing cross reference cards.

In grades eleven and twelve, four new uses of the card catalogue can be emphasized:
1. Material under Subject Headings.
2. Utilizing books with only a chapter desired by the student.
3. Utilizing cards for information about table of contents.
4. Getting information about the copyright date.

In this manner instruction about the card catalogue has been spread over the secondary school years, growing more challenging each year. Earlier instruction is reviewed and the whole effect is cumulative. The bright student might learn most of the information in the seventh grade. The slow and average student will learn a little bit more each year.

TEACHING THE USE OF ENCYCLOPEDIAS

Throughout the high school years, students make frequent use of encyclopedias, junior as well as adult varieties. Trips to the library should be arranged to show students where the various encyclopedias are kept, the lettering on the backs of each volume, the authorship of the various articles and the suggestions for further reading. Each student should be given the opportunity to study one or more volumes to find information he is seeking. Work sheets can be prepared relating to the specific encyclopedia being discussed. Suggestions for taking information down on separate cards, one for each topic, should be given, with caution for giving credit on anything to be quoted *verbatim*.

TEACHING THE USE OF THE "READER'S GUIDE TO PERIODICAL LITERATURE"

Although students may have been using the *Reader's Guide* earlier, the eleventh and twelfth years are appropriate for studying this valuable reference tool. They have learned in earlier years how to find books on topics which interested them and also authoritative articles in encyclopedias. Now they need to learn how to find more recent articles. Here again, there is no substitute for using current issues of the *Reader's Guide*. For a nominal sum the H. W. Wilson Company (950 University Avenue, N. Y. C, N. Y. 10452) will supply copies of their most recent monthly issue. If these are available, a visit to the library may be avoided. By using the actual current issue, students can be taught how to get information about an article when the author is known, when the title is known, or when the general subject is known (drama, poetry, missiles). They will learn the meaning of the various abbreviations, the volume number, the page number, the date and whether there are illustrations. The teacher, using the chalkboard, will work together with the class to explain the meaning of all the entries.

Several of the annual cumulative volumes should be on hand to show how the little monthly numbers are gathered together over a period of time.

The information is put to use immediately with individual assignments to find references to magazine articles which the students will obtain, read and report on to the class. The teacher must be certain that the magazines are actually kept in the library, individually or in bound volumes. Merely to copy magazine references without making use of them for actual research will make the lesson a purely verbal one.

INFORMATION ABOUT A SINGLE BOOK

It is surprising how many readers can use a book and be incurious about essential information in it. After students have used a textbook for many months, many of them have not bothered to learn the name of the author, when the book was published, the special appendices, etc. Direct instruction is indicated. Beginning with the seventh grade, students should learn the following information about their textbooks:

1. The Title Page
2. Table of Contents
3. Lists of Illustrations and Maps
4. Index

After these have been explained, the following work sheet may be distributed to be answered by consulting the book being studied.

Work Sheet on Contents of a Book

A good craftsman knows his tools. Books are among your most valuable tools. The more you know about your books, the better tools they will become. Answer the following questions by referring to your book:

1. Turning to the title page, give:
   a. The full name of the author
   b. What is his position?
   c. What is the complete title?
   d. Who is the publisher?
2. Turn over the page to find the following answers:
   a. What is the copyright date?
   b. Why is it important to know this (this is especially important for a book on science or social studies)?
3. Turn to the part of the book which shows how it is organized.
   a. What is the title of this section?
   b. What are the page numbers for this section?
   c. In what order are the items arranged (alphabetical, chronological, topics for study)?
4. What are pages for the index? If you wanted to find information about a single topic, which section of the book would you use to get information quickly?

In the last two years of secondary school when students will be working on research papers they will have to learn how to write their sources of information, from books, encyclopedias and magazines. Proper form for entering these sources must be learned. For books they will have to supply the full name of the author, the title, place of publication, year of publication and page references. For magazine articles, they will have to indicate the title of the magazine, the volume number, pages of the article and date.

TEACHING THE USE OF THE DICTIONARY

Beginning with the seventh grade, students should be given instruction in the use of an abridged dictionary, a copy of which each student should have. When schools do not own sets of dictionaries, paperbound copies may be purchased by students, which will serve well enough for instructional purposes. Among the uses of the dictionaries to be studied at this level are meaning, correct spelling and syllabication. If necessary, exercises should be given in alphabetization, using lists of proper names, or any other words supplied by the teacher.

In the ninth grade, students should become acquainted with the resources of the unabridged dictionary. Many secondary schools have one in each English classroom, thus avoiding a visit to the library. The publisher of Webster's *New International Dictionary* (G. & C. Merriam Co., Springfield, Mass., 01101) supplies free instructional materials about their dictionaries. Heretofore, students have gone to their dictionaries mainly for meaning, spelling and syllabication of words. They now should learn that in addition they can learn information about Proper Names, Persons, Characters in Books, Mythological References and Place Names in Geography and History. The following work sheet indicates how these new uses of the dictionary can be tested:

Work Sheet for the Use of the Unabridged Dictionary

Using an unabridged dictionary, find answers to the following questions. Unless you have found the answer in the main list of words, indicate the section in which you found the answers.

1. Who was Homer? Where did he live?
2. What is the meaning and pronunciation of *Iliad?*
3. What does the word *Atlas* mean?
4. After whom is it named?
5. What is Olympus?
6. What connection did Pluto have with the lower world?
7. Who was Charybdis?
8. Who was Circe?
9. Why is an *odyssey* so called?
10. Why is a strong man called a Hercules?

In the eleventh and twelfth years, students probably will have copies of dictionaries that will contain etymologies, synonyms and antonyms, and variations in meaning. As the needs arise in connection with class work, students will learn these additional uses of their dictionaries. Above all, they will develop the habit of using the dictionary constantly in connection with their school work.

LITERARY REFERENCE BOOKS

We as English teachers expect our students to develop a love for books and a desire to seek more information about them. Using the same principles of instruction in library skills enunciated earlier, we can develop an interest in literary reference books which will afford much pleasure both in high school and in college. Among the most useful are: Stanley Kunitz's *Twentieth Century Authors;* William Rose Benet's *Reader's Encyclopedia;* E. Cobham Brewer's *Dictionary of Phrase and Fable;* Paul Hervey's *Oxford Companion to English Literature;* James D. Hart's *Oxford Companion to American Literature;* Frank N. Magill and Dayton Kohler's *Cyclopedia of World Authors;* Max J. Herzberg's *The Readers' Encyclopedia of American Authors;* Oscar James Campbell's *The Readers' Encyclopedia of Shakespeare;* William J. Burke and Will D. Howe's *American Authors and Their Books.*

Among the items of information which can be found quickly in such volumes are: literary references, literary terms, brief summaries of important books, brief summaries of the lives of authors and their works. Too many students in high school who wish to get information in the field of literature will rush to the encyclopedia as the final source of information. Many items in the literary reference books are too recent for inclusion in an encyclopedia.

Since libraries, if they have these copies at all, will have but single copies, it may be best to assign each reference book to a committee of students who then will report to the class. Later there should be assignments for all students which will require them to use these books. The alert teacher will know best when to make these assignments to fit in with the unit being studied.

BOOKS OF QUOTATIONS

This chapter began with a quotation from John Milton's *Areopagitica,* and a question asked as to the source. In the eleventh and twelfth years, students should be given instruction in the use of books of quotations and the different arrangements to be found in Bartlett's *Familiar Quotations,* Mencken's, *A Dictionary of Quotations on Historical Principles, The Oxford Book of Quotations,* and Bergen Evans' *Dictionary of Quotations* and the various volumes compiled by Burton Stevenson. Here again, any explanation by the teacher should be followed by exercises performed by each student until he is able to use these valuable reference tools by himself.

10

CONTEMPORARY PLAYS FOR THE
ENGLISH CLASSROOM

The English teacher today who wishes to make use of contemporary plays in his instructional program has a field day compared to his colleague of forty years ago. All one has to do is to look at some exhibitors' books at any educational convention to see scores of plays in hard cover and paperback which can be used for such a program.

Forty years ago when I wished to break away from the requirements of teaching the plays usually assigned to my grades, I had two choices: *Representative Plays by Barrie*[1] and *Representative Plays by Galsworthy.*[2] Although *The Silver Box* was written in 1907 and *The Old Lady Shows Her Medals* in 1916, compared with *Twelfth Night* and *The School for Scandal,* these might be considered contemporary in 1931. Incidentally, if one makes a study of the teaching of the drama in American secondary schools from about 1885 to the present, one will be interested to learn that before 1917 hardly any dramatist other than Shakespeare or Sheridan was studied; educational history in drama-instruction was made in 1917 when Barrie's *The Admirable Crichton* was used in a school text for the first time.

Today the secondary school teacher has a wealth of plays of our own time from which to choose. Some are in anthologies such as Corbin and Balt's *Twelve American Plays* (1920–1960).[3] Others are in such books as Nagelberg's *Drama in Our Time*[4] and Sper's *Living Plays.*[5] A second source is the omnibus anthology which usually contains at least one full-length modern play. I made a study of sixteen such anthologies which were published fairly recently and found thirty-six such plays, ranging from Robert E. Sherwood's *Abe Lincoln in Illinois* to Moss Hart's and George S. Kaufman's *You Can't Take It With You.*

CONTEMPORARY PLAYS IN PAPERBACK

The large number of contemporary plays in paperback (and they now number in the hundreds, according to the latest issue of *Paperbound Books in Print*) are described in detail in three issues in *Today's Speech* for September, 1966; November, 1966; and February, 1967,[6] and in other publications. I have categorized them as: individual plays; several plays by one author; several plays by several authors.

Paperback Editions of Individual Plays

The latest edition of *Paperbound Books in Print* (November, 1976) lists several hundred volumes of individual plays by American authors, ranging from Edward Albee's *The American Dream* (Coward-McCann) to Jerome Weidman's book for the musical *Fiorello* (Popular Library). Some of our best known and most highly regarded contemporary American dramatists are represented by one or more volumes. Musicals as well as dramas are included. Some of the plays which are worth considering by the teacher of drama in secondary school or in college are the following:

Edward Albee: *Ballad of the Sad Cafe,* adapted from Carson McCullers' novel. (Co-published by Atheneum and Houghton-Mifflin); *Who's Afraid of Virginia Woolf?* (Atheneum and Washington Square Press). As everyone knows, Richard Burton and Elizabeth Taylor starred in the movie, which adheres very closely to the original script.

James Baldwin: *Blues for Mr. Charlie* (Dell).

Marc Connelly: *Green Pastures* (Holt, Rinehart and Winston). Connelly's tender play, originally presented in the late 1920's and later made into a successful movie, still has its appeal today.

Louis O. Coxe and Robert Chapman: *Billy Budd,* adapted from Herman Melville's novel. (Drama Books). The novel, although written in the late 1880's, was not discovered until the 1920's. Peter Ustinov starred in a memorable movie version. For classes studying a cross-media approach, the novel, the play and the excerpt from the film as prepared by the Teaching Film Custodians would be excellent examples.

William Gibson: *The Miracle Worker* (Bantam Pathfinder Edition). This, too, may be used in a cross-media analysis approach since a film has been made with the original Broadway stars.

Lorraine Hansbury: *A Raisin in the Sun* (New American Library), one of the most sensitive portraits of a Negro family and its problems in striving to better itself. The Broadway musical, *Raisin,* is based on the play.

Lillian Hellman: *Another Part of the Forest* (Compass Books); *The Children's Hour* (New American Library); *The Little Foxes* (Compass Books). Some of the most mordant satires of the 1930's were embodied in Lillian Hellman's plays. Today, forty years later, her ideas and her sharp characterizations of shady types in a declining Southern aristocracy are still meaningful. *The Children's Hour* has been made into a successful fim and had a successful Broadway revival many years after its original production.

William Inge: *Dark at the Top of the Stairs* (Bantam).

Jerome Lawrence and Robert E. Lee: *Inherit the Wind* (Bantam Pathfinder). This gripping dramatic version of the notorious Scopes evolution trial in the 1920's has also been translated into a film and television version. Students interested in the differences between journalism and drama will find the authors' preparatory note interesting.

Some Musicals in Paperback Form

Not many books of successful musical comedies were considered worthy of publication in hardback. With the coming of the paperback, some of the most literary of the musical comedies have been published, of which the following are representative samples:

Jerome Coopersmith: *Baker Street* (Doubleday).
Alan Jay Lerner: *My Fair Lady* (New American Library).
Joseph Stein: *Fiddler on the Roof* (Pocket Books).
Jerome Weidman: *Fiorello* (Popular Library).
Clifford Odets and William Gibson: *Golden Boy* (Bantam).

Individual Dramatists

Some of our greatest dramatists are well represented in several volumes. This section will deal with the individual plays by Arthur Miller, Eugene O'Neill and Tennessee Williams.

Since the late 1940's when Arthur Miller's *All My Sons* heralded a new and original talent in American drama, there have been numerous hard cover editions of his individual plays, a collected edition and numerous appearances in anthologies, for which the reader should consult John H. Ottemiller's *Index to Plays in Collections* (Metuchen, N. J.: Scarecrow Press, 5th Edition, 1969). Miller's plays may be studied now in the following paperbacks:

After the Fall (Bantam).
The Crucible (Bantam and Compass).
Death of a Salesman (Compass).
A View from the Bridge (Compass).

Eugene O'Neill has been the subject of critical study since his plays began appearing in the 1920's. The individual plays available in paperback are:

The Emperor Jones, edited by Max J. Herzberg (Appleton-Century-Crofts).
The Iceman Cometh (Vintage Books).
Long Day's Journey Into Night (Yale Paperbound).
More Stately Mansions, shortened from the author's partly revised script by Karl Ragnar Gierow and edited by Donald Gallup (Yale Paperbound).
A Touch of the Poet (Yale Paperbound).

Finally, there are the individual volumes of plays by Tennessee Williams:

Cat on a Hot Tin Roof (New American Library).
Fugitive Kind (New American Library).
The Night of the Iguana (New American Library).
Period of Adjustment (New American Library).
The Rose Tattoo (New American Library).
A Streetcar Named Desire (New American Library).
Suddenly Last Summer (New American Library).
Summer and Smoke (New American Library).
Sweet Bird of Youth (New American Library).

Several Plays by One Author

Maxwell Anderson: *Four Verse Plays* (Harcourt, Brace, Jovanovich). This collection comprises *Elizabeth the Queen, High Tor, Winterset* and *Mary of Scotland.* An even lower per play price edition is available in: *Three Plays* by Maxwell Anderson (Washington Square Press), which includes *Joan of Lorraine, Valley Forge* and *Journey to Jerusalem.* Few will dispute that the late Maxwell Anderson remains our greatest master of the verse play. No one—not even Christopher Fry—in modern times can approach his skill in dramaturgy and dialogue in verse. Recently a revival of *Mary of Scotland* took place at the New York City Center. Those who saw the original production almost thirty years ago can never forget Helen Menken and Helen Hayes in that play. Nor can I ever forget the opening night of *Winterset* in which Burgess Meredith, Margo and Richard Bennett starred. *Joan of Lorraine* was graced by the incomparable Ingrid Bergman in the title role. Who can forget the Lunts in *Elizabeth the Queen?* A true feast is in store for those who were not of the generation to see these plays when they were first produced. And for those who were so fortunate, the reading of the plays will revive rich memories of exciting theatre in rhythmic language never equalled in American drama before or since.

Edward Albee: From the theatre of the sublime to the theatre of the absurd in American drama is a step of less than a generation. Anderson and Albee are close in the alphabet and not far apart in time, but otherwise, what a gulf! *The American Dream* and *The Zoo Story* (New American Library); *The Sandbox* and *The Death of Bessie Smith* (New American Library); *The Zoo Story, The Death of Bessie Smith,* and *The Sandbox* (Coward-McCann).

These four short plays were Albee's first compositions before his first great hit, *Who's Afraid of Virginia Woolf?* In an interesting preface to the first volume he explains how *The Zoo Story* had its world premiere in Berlin after it had been turned down by several New York producers. Similarly interesting information about the other three plays in this series is included. Today, Albee is one of the most talked of American playwrights. One can see in these four early plays the budding of a talent which flowered in *Who's Afraid of Virginia Woolf?* and *Tiny Alice.* What William Saroyan was to the 1930's; Arthur Miller to the late 1940's; Tennessee Williams to the 1950's; Edward Albee was to the American Theatre of the 1960's.

Paddy Chayefsky: *Television Plays* (Simon and Schuster).

Horton Foote: *Three Plays* (Harcourt, Brace, Jovanovich). Contains *Roots in a Parched Ground, The Old Man* and *Tomorrow.*

The television drama is the infant of drama and has yet to develop readability. Yet of the dramatists of the past decade who have managed to rise above the level of most television drama these two are notable. Chayefsky went ahead from television successes to such plays as *The Tenth Man, The Middle of the Night* and *Gideon.* Horton Foote's plays have been produced on Broadway since his one-acter *Celebration* (1948), followed by *The Chase* (1952) and *The Traveling Lady.*

For the student of contemporary American drama these television plays have some historic interest apart from their own intrinsic values since they represent the work of two dramatists who "graduated" from video to the legitimate stage.

Jean Kerr: *Mary, Mary and other Plays* (Fawcett Publications).

In addition to her own play *Mary, Mary*, the book contains *Goldilocks* (1958) written with her critic-husband, Walter Kerr, and *The King of Hearts* (1954) written with Eleanor Brooke. Jean Kerr has been enormously successful with the public although the critics have not always written rave notices. In *Mary, Mary* she tells the tale of a divorced couple who finally remarry. *Goldilocks* is a satire on the early movies. *King of Hearts* is a close-up of a comic-strip artist at work and in love.

Eugene O'Neill: *Six Short Plays of Eugene O'Neill* (Vintage Books). Contains "The Dreamy Kid," "Before Breakfast," "Different," "Welded," "The Straw," and "Gold."

In the summer of 1966 at Provincetown, Massachusetts, the fiftieth anniversary of the first production of Eugene O'Neill's one-acters was celebrated. This collection will show how much the American drama owes to him and why he still remains the giant of American drama after half a century. "Before Breakfast" and "The Dreamy Kid" perhaps are the best of the collection, but all the others are worth reading. Long before many of our dramatists were grappling with vital human and social problems O'Neill had anticipated them in his one-act plays.

Three Plays (Vintage). Contains *Desire under the Elms, Strange Interlude,* and *Mourning Becomes Electra.*

Each of these plays is a landmark in American drama. What magnificent performances were given by Alice Brady and Alla Nazimova in *Mourning Becomes Electra* and Lynn Fontanne in *Strange Interlude!* O'Neill was always experimenting, and each of these plays represents a different type of experimentation.

Lost Plays of Eugene O'Neill (Citadel). Contains "Abortion," "The Movie Man," "The Sniper," "Servitude," and "A Wife for a Wife."

These short plays obviously are not the work of the master craftsman but they show how O'Neill was interested in topics which conventional dramatists of the time would not touch with a ten-foot pole.

Elmer Rice: *Three Plays* (Drama Books, Hill and Wang). Contains *Street Scene, The Adding Machine* and *Dream Girl. The Adding Machine* (1923) is perhaps the only exemplar of the drama of expressionism, which was so popular in the 1920's, that is still readable today. *Street Scene* (1929), one of the outstanding realistic plays of the 1920's, was made into a beautiful opera with music by Kurt Weill. The play is revived even today. *Dream Girl*, which starred Betty Field and was made into a successful film, was transformed into a TV drama not too long ago. Burns Mantle included it in his *Ten Best Plays* of 1934–1935. Rice's contributions to American drama go back to 1914 and his mark upon realistic drama has been made. The plays read very well, especially the first two in the collection.

Thornton Wilder: *The Long Christmas Dinner and Other Plays* (Harper). *Three Plays* (Bantam). Contains *The Matchmaker, The Skin of Our Teeth* and *Our Town.* This last has become a modern classic found in many anthologies and performed everywhere. *The Matchmaker* is a reworking of Wilder's earlier *The Merchant from Yonkers* and is the basis for the smash hit musical *Hello, Dolly.* The first collection consists of one-act plays of the 1930's and shows how early Wilder had mastered his craft.

Tennessee Williams: *27 Wagons Full of Cotton* (New Direction). Williams wrote some exciting one-acters before his *Glass Menagerie* established him as an outstanding playwright. These short plays are rich in variety of theme and expert in construction.

Several Plays by Several Authors

The Laurel Drama Series (Dell Publishing Company).

Famous American Plays of the 1920's, selected and introduced by Kenneth Macgowan. Contains: Eugene O'Neill, *The Moon of the Caribees;* Maxwell Anderson and Lawrence Stallings, *What Price Glory?;* Sidney Howard, *They Knew What They Wanted;* Dubose and Dorothy Heyward, *Porgy;* Elmer Rice, *Street Scene;* Philip Barry, *Holiday.* Macgowan knows this period well, having participated personally in the birth of modern American drama, and writes a perceptive twenty-page introduction which is very helpful.

Famous American Plays of the 1930's, selected and introduced by Harold Clurman. Contains: Clifford Odets, *Awake and Sing;* S. N. Behrman, *End of Summer;* Robert E. Sherwood, *Idiot's Delight;* John Steinbeck, *Of Mice and Men;* William Saroyan, *The Time of Your Life.* Harold Clurman, who was intimately associated with the Group Theatre as director and who has distinguished himself as a dramatic critic and historian of the theatre (See *The Fervent Years*), writes from personal experience of the theatre of the 1930's and hence makes his introduction meaningful.

Famous American Plays of the 1940's selected and introduced by Henry Hewes. Contains: Thornton Wilder, *The Skin of our Teeth;* Arthur Laurents, *Home of the Brave;* Arthur Miller, *All My Sons;* Maxwell Anderson, *Lost in the Stars;* Carson McCullers, *The Member of the Wedding.* Henry Hewes is one of our most gifted dramatic critics, having written for the *Saturday Review* as well as other periodicals.

Famous American Plays of the 1950's, selected and introduced by Lee Strasberg. Contains: Tennessee Williams, *Camino Real;* Lillian Hellman, *The Autumn Garden;* Robert Anderson, *Tea and Sympathy;* Edward Albee, *The Zoo Story;* Michael Gazzo, *A Hatful of Rain.* Lee Strasberg, a gifted director and teacher, has written a brilliant introduction, giving many insights based on his intimate personal involvement in the theatre of this decade.

The ANTA Series of Distinguished Plays (Washington Square Press). Whereas the Laurel Drama Series treats modern American plays by decades, a different approach is followed by this series. The six volumes edited by the writer all deal with themes illustrated by three plays about each theme. Each play has an individual introduction and a bibliography. The contents of these six volumes follow:

Three Comedies of American Family Life. Contains: John Van Druten, *I Remember Mama;* Howard Lindsay and Russel Crouse, *Life With Father;* Moss Hart and George S. Kaufman, *You Can't Take It With You.*

Three Plays of American Individualism. Contains: Clifford Odets, *Golden Boy;* Maxwell Anderson, *High Tor;* Emmet Lavery, *The Magnificent Yankee.*

Three Dramas of American Realism. Contains: Robert E. Sherwood, *Idiot's Delight;* Elmer L. Rice, *Street Scene;* William Saroyan, *The Time of Your Life.*

Three Plays about Marriage. Contains: George Kelly, *Craig's Wife;* Sidney Howard, *They Knew What They Wanted;* Philip Barry, *Holiday.*

Three Plays about Doctors. Contains: Henrik Ibsen, *An Enemy of the People;* Sidney Kingsley, *Men in White;* Sidney Howard, *Yellow Jack.*

Three Plays about Business in America. Contains: Elmer Rice, *The Adding Machine;* George S. Kaufman and Marc Connelly, *Beggar on Horseback;* Arthur Miller, *All My Sons.*

Additional volumes in the ANTA Series with the thematic approach are:

Three Plays about Crime and Criminals. Edited by George Freedley. Contains: Sidney Kingsley, *Detective Story;* Joseph Kesselring, *Arsenic and Old Lace;* Edward Chodorov, *Kind Lady.*

Three Distinguished Plays about Lincoln. Edited by Willard Swire. Contains: John Drinkwater, *Abraham Lincoln;* E. P. Conkle, *Prologue to Glory;* Mark Van Doren, *The Last Days of Lincoln.*

Representative Modern Plays: American. Edited by Robert Warnock (Scott, Foresman). After a sixteen-page introduction to Modern American Drama and a six-page section on Reading a Play, the book contains the following classics of the past forty-five years of modern American drama: George S. Kaufman and Marc Connelly's *Beggar on Horseback;* Sidney Howard's *The Late Christopher Bean;* S. N. Behrman's *Biography;* Eugene O'Neill's *Mourning Becomes Electra;* Maxwell Anderson's *Valley Forge;* Clifford Odets' *Waiting for Lefty;* Tennessee Williams' *The Glass Menagerie;* Arthur Miller's *Death of a Salesman.*

Each play is prefaced by a discussion of the author's work followed by an analysis of the play, and concluded with a bibliography. Additional bibliographical material at the end of the book includes readings in the History of Modern American Drama, Production and Criticism, and a complete list of all the plays by all the authors in the volume. Professor Warnock of Yale University has shown excellent judgment in the selection of these eight plays each of which he uses as a representative of its genre (e.g., Expressionistic Satire, Proletarian Drama, Naturalistic Tragedy). His perceptive critical introductions and bibliographies make this a valuable textbook for college and superior high school classes in modern American drama, as well as pleasurable reading for the drama-lover who likes to read plays.

Four Contemporary American Plays. Edited by Bennett Cerf (Vintage Books, a Division of Random House). The plays included are Paddy Chayefsky's *The Tenth Man;* Lorraine Hansberry's *A Raisin in the Sun;* Lillian Hellman's *Toys in the Attic;* and Saul Levitt's *The Andersonville Trial.* At the end of the book appear one-page Biographical Notes for each of the four authors included. For those who like to know when and where these plays were first performed and the members of the original casts, these data precede each play. Like all the publications in the Vintage Book series, the typography is pleasing to the eye and makes for a readable page. Each of these four plays deals with a subject quite different from all the others, and they ran the gamut of the post-Civil War, *The Andersonville Trial,* through the mystical Jewish play of *The Tenth Man,* to the striving for human dignity in *A Raisin in the Sun.* For those who did not see these plays on the stage, *Four Contemporary Plays* will make stimulating and interesting reading.

From the American Drama. Edited by Eric Bentley (Doubleday Anchor Book). The distinguished author of such critical works as *The Playwright as Thinker, In Search of Theatre* and *The Dramatic Event* has edited two valuable series for Doubleday Anchor Books. *The Modern Theatre* consists of six volumes of which the one in review is Volume IV. The second series is the *Classic Theatre in Four Volumes.* Both series should be in every drama-lover and drama teacher's library. *From the American Drama* contains five plays, including Clyde Fitch's *Captain Jinks of the Horse Marines* (1901); Langdon Mitchell's *The New York Idea* (1906); Thornton Wilder's *Pullman Car Hiawatha* (1931); William Saroyan's *The Man With the Heart in the Highlands* (1938); and Jo Swerling and Abe Burrows' *Guys and Dolls* (1950), published here for the first time.

In a brief Foreword, Mr. Bentley explains why he selected these five examples to illustrate the American Drama, and it makes interesting reading. At the end of the volume there are brief paragraphs about the opening dates and first publication in book form of each of these plays. The collection represents fifty years of American drama, from the comedy of Clyde Fitch in 1901 to the musical comedy of Swerling and Burrows. In one of those rare revivals that only the W. P. A. Theatre during the Great Depression could have produced it was this reviewer's privilege to see *Captain Jinks of the Horse Marines.* The female star was not the Ethel Barrymore who starred in the original cast, yet it was more interesting and amusing than the usual revival. The opening night of *The Man With the Heart in the Highlands* was sheer poetry recaptured time and time again in numerous readings. Like all the Anchor Books, this too is typographically a delight to the eye. For those who might like to obtain the other plays published in the Anchor series, they are all listed at the end of the book, as well as the Anchor Books on Drama.

New Theatre in America. Edited by Edward Parone (A Delta Book, Dell Publishing Company). Edward Parone, the editor of this interesting and provocative collection of seven contemporary American plays, has had wide experience as a poet, a writer of book reviews, production supervisor for the Phoenix Theatre, assistant producer of the film, *The Misfits,* stager of the West Coast productions of all the plays by Edward Albee, and director. Following a thirteen-page introduction written in the "hip" language of our time and not with the grace or charm of a Max Beerbohm or an A. B. Walkley are the seven plays: William Hanley's *Mrs. Dally Has a Lover* (about a middle-aged woman who tries to discover the world for a young man and uncovers her loss of him in it); Lawrence Osgood's *The Rook* (a sinister domestic quadrangle played out over a chess game in Washington Square); Harvey Perr's *Upstairs Sleeping* (a young man upstairs is wide awake to the talkative silences of the family below); Ben Maddow's *In a Cold Hotel* (an aging theatrical charlatan refuses to acknowledge the loss of youth and honor which his illegitimate son presents to him); Howard Sackler's *The Nine O'Clock Mail* (an American male wages his daily war against impotence); Lee Kacheim's *Match Play* (a spoiled young man takes on a girl, his father and the Army to get what he wants and doesn't need); LeRoi Jones' *Dutchman* (an encounter in the subway between a sensitive young Negro and a blonde not so sensitive). Four of these plays were presented in the 1960's in off-Broadway Theatres. The editor also directed *Dutchman.*

For those who would like to read some of the off-Broadway plays of recent years, this volume is an excellent introduction. If William Hanley's *Mrs. Dally Has a Lover* interests any reader, he may puruse his interest in Hanley with *Mrs. Dally Has a Lover and Other Plays* (The Dial Press).

Ever since the days of George Pierce Baker's English 47 in Harvard, in the teens of this century, plays by students in college drama workshops have been published. There were the several volumes of the English 47 Workshop, the Carolina Folk Plays, edited by Frederick Koch, and the Yale Workshop Series. It is good, therefore, to see this worthy tradition continued in *Three Plays from the Yale School of Drama* edited by John Gassner.

Beginning with an illuminating thirteen-page Introduction by Mr. Gassner on "The Meaning and Scope of Playwriting Study," there follow the three plays: Errol Hill's *Man Better Man* (a romantic folk comedy in verse); Joel Oliansky's *Here Comes Santa Claus* (a sardonic realistic drama); and Oliver Hailey's *Hey, You, Light Man* (an experimental play).

What makes this collection so different from the others by well-established playwrights discussed earlier in this chapter is that each playwright has written a short preface telling some of the things he learned from seeing his play produced. At the end of the book there is a postscript by John Gassner on "Invention and Creative Playwriting," biographical sketches of the three playwrights, and the casts for the premieres. The book is a Dutton Paperback Original.

For those who are curious about the methods of a master teacher like John Gassner and the ways in which some of America's potential playwrights are being developed, this book is a valuable addition to one's drama library.

The final two volumes contain some plays by American dramatists, and are included for the sake of complete coverage of the field.

Representative Modern Plays: Ibsen to Tennessee Williams. Edited by Robert Warnock (Scott, Foresman, Glenview, Illinois). Among the American plays included are Eugene O'Neill's *Desire Under the Elms;* S. N. Behrman's *Biography;* Tennessee Williams' *The Glass Menagerie.* For the pattern in which these plays are handled please refer to the discussion of Warnock's *Representative Modern Plays* .

Four Modern Plays. First Series. (Rinehart Editions, Holt, Rinehart and Winston). Two plays in this collection are American: Eugene O'Neill's *The Emperor Jones* and Arthur Miller's *Death of a Salesman.* No introductory or biographical matter is supplied.

AUDIO-VISUAL AIDS

To enrich the teaching of contemporary plays, the teacher has a wealth of recordings and some film strips. One should become acquainted with Helen Roache's *Spoken Records*[7] and Morris Schreiber's *Annotated List of Educational Recordings.*[8] For a listing of long plays in collections, consult Ottemiller's *Index to Play Collections*[9] and the author's *Index to Plays.*[10] Every secondary school and college should subscribe to *The Fireside Theatre* which brings each month one of the contemporary plays actually produced. Since not all of us are fortunate enough to live in New York City where new plays can be seen, one can at least read the best of them in the volumes of The Fireside Theatre Club.[11]

UTILIZING TELEVISION

Every teacher must surely be aware of the fine contemporary plays often commissioned for television and the excellent revivals of such contemporary classics as *Death of a Salesman* and *Pygmalion,* by the Hallmark Hall of Fame Theatre. Excellent Study Guides have been prepared to assist the teacher to make the most effective use of these plays. Some of the best drama lessons which I have observed have been based on such television performances. And I need not mention how valuable *The Forsyte Saga* seen on National Educational Television in the early 1970's can be.

SOME CONCLUSIONS

Finally, what has been the experience with our students in learning the contemporary drama in my own school? (Jamaica H. S.) Each teacher may have had similar successes. My teachers have used the following recent plays with considerable success:

Arthur Miller's *All My Sons, Death of a Salesman,* and *The Crucible*
Lorraine Hansberry's *A Raisin in The Sun*
Arthur Laurents' *West Side Story*
Shaw's *Pygmalion*
William Gibson's *The Miracle Worker*
Tennessee Williams' *A Streetcar Named Desire*
Thornton Wilder's *Our Town* and *The Skin of Our Teeth*
John Van Druten's *I Remember Mama*
Crouse and Lindsay's *Life With Father,* and
Kaufman and Hart's *You Can't Take It With You*

I have tried to survey briefly the history of the teaching of contemporary drama in our secondary schools, to list some of the sources of such plays, as well as some of the audio-visual aids to enrich instruction. The lover of contemporary plays who wishes to introduce them into his classroom is far better off today than his colleague of forty years ago who was given his first set of Barrie or Galsworthy and told to go ahead and teach. Whether he taught them well or not will never be known, but he certainly did a lot of running around trying to learn how.

11

HOW CAN WE HELP STUDENTS ENJOY LITERATURE?

The enjoyment of literature has long been one of the most important objectives of teachers of English. In one of the earliest of those heavily annotated classics, Scott's *Marmion,* edited by Robert Morss Lovett in 1896, we read: "...Although *Marmion* is often used as a book for study, yet few books are read by the average pupil with more pleasure."[1]

B. A. Hinsdale, in one of the earliest books on methods in English (*Teaching the Language-Arts,* Appleton, 1896), concludes his chapter on "Teaching English Literature" with: "Teach the children of the land how to read, teach them what to read, and give them a love for what is good in English literature."[2]

Since the publication of Hinsdale's book, there have been more than sixty volumes[3] on the teaching of English, most of them dealing in one way or another with some aspect of teaching literature. In the many decades of publication of the journals of The National Council of Teachers of English, *Elementary English, English Journal* and *College English,* there have appeared hundreds of articles on the teaching of literature. What, then, can be said about the topic which has not already been said so much better by such master teachers as Dora V. Smith, Lou La Brant, Louella Cook, Robert Pooley, James Miller, Dwight L. Burton and a host of others who have written on this subject?

Certainly there is no new magic formula which can be expounded that would solve all the problems encountered as we teach literature. The best to be hoped for is to express certain basic principles which have been found to be reasonably successful in the seventy-five years that teachers of English have been searching for ways to enable their students to enjoy literature.

Let us begin with objectives. I quote those operative in my own school system in 1922 when I was a student in high school, because they were probably as good as any that were in use at the time and because I can recall quite vividly the texts, the procedures, and my own reactions and personal growth under these objectives. The English syllabus for the high schools of New York City, adopted in 1922, states very clearly that:

The chief aim in the teaching of literature. . .is to get them to enjoy reading good literature and to desire to read more of it.

Other things to be accomplished by the reading of literature were: (1) To deepen and enrich their imaginative and emotional life. The teacher should help the pupils to see their own lives and experiences reflected in the literature they read. He should in his way lead them to understand others and to arrive at a better understanding of themselves; (2) to cultivate high ideals of life and conduct; (3) To give a knowledge of books and the power to read them with appreciation; (4) To improve their power of self-expression by stimulating thought and by supplying information and models of construction.

These are noble objectives which many of us would consider valid today. Certainly, the curriculum makers of 1922 were interested in fostering enjoyment through literature. Whether these objectives were realized in whole or in part by a large segment of the student body might make another interesting chapter. The matter of concern to us is how we English teachers in the high schools of the 1970's with their heterogeneous student populations, coming from diverse backgrounds, so different in capacities, needs and interests, can perform this all-important task. A few misconceptions must be cleared up before a positive program can be established.

We can no longer assume that students entering our high schools have the ability to read on their level. W. S. Gray years ago stated: "Scores made on reading tests show that from twenty-five to forty per cent of the pupils who enter high school are reading below the ninth grade level."[4]

A necessary corollary is that teachers of English in high schools must stop bemoaning the situation mentioned above and blaming the teachers in the lower schools for failing to do their jobs. Rather, they have the responsibility of maintaining the skills already acquired, providing remediation for skills undeveloped or underdeveloped and guiding their students toward the mastery of the new reading skills necessary for high school work.

The day of the "one-shot" classic is about over. We cannot expect a feverish search for the beauties of thought and expression of either George Eliot or Charles Dickens and any degree of growth, intellectual, emotional, or aesthetic, from such a search.

As far back as 1896, B. A. Hinsdale cautioned against excessive preoccupation with a few literary compositions.[5] Hence, those of us who warn against studying a classic to shreds are following in a tradition that is at least eighty years old. We hardly are pedagogical radicals or innovators.

We cannot afford blithely to ignore the fact that individual differences with respect to reading are here to stay. For any teacher to ignore differences in reading abilities, in interests, in rate of growth and in possibilities of growth, is to be teaching truly in the pedagogical dark ages. Individual differences constitute at once the major problem and major challenge in education today. Not that they did not exist in the "good old days" of the 1890's or the early 1900's. Teachers, because of the highly selective nature of the secondary population, could afford to ignore these differences with fewer dangers than today. Even if we wished to ignore the individual differences in our classrooms today, the Four Horsemen, Retardation, Repetition, Boredom and Poor Discipline, would rear their ugly heads to remind us that they were present.

We cannot assume that growth will come automatically by exposure to literature, even to enthusiastic, over-bubbling exposure on the part of the teacher. A favorite cliché of poetry teaching when I began my career in the 1930's was "Poetry is caught—not taught." We want to be certain that our students are catching the right things about poetry and all other imaginative literature, not an aversion that will never be eradicated.

How many times have we been confronted by our successful returning graduates whom we thought we had taught to enjoy literature? Too often, even the most friendly will admit that they do not recall the classics over which we waxed so enthusiastic. And some who recall the classics, even with some degree of pleasure, will confess that they never read another book by the same author.

We cannot afford to cry defeat because of the onslaught of the mass media. Literature and enjoyment of literature have survived every holocaust since the burning of the Library of Alexandria and will still be here long after the last TV antenna becomes only an object of historical interest. Rather than bemoan the impact of the mass media on our times in general and on our students' reading in particular, let us learn how to utilize them for our own advantage. All of the mass media, TV, radio, movies, magazines and newspapers, have long had educational departments whose purpose is to demonstrate how these media can contribute to valid educational objectives. As far back as the February 8, 1958, issue of the *Saturday Review of Literature,* Lester Walker in his article "Boom in Good Books" stated: "Part of the interest in good reading has been stimulated by an unexpected source: the movies."[6] Correspondence with Mr. Walker, *Publishers' Weekly,* the American Library Association and the Public Library of Washington, D. C., confirmed the statement of Mr. Walker and elicited additional information about the stimulation of worthwhile reading through television.

In the publication, *Teachers Guides to Television,* in which the outstanding television programs of the fall and the spring seasons are listed and annotated, there is always a section on related reading for both students and teachers.

We cannot stimulate enjoyment in others unless we enjoy literature tremendously ourselves, know a great deal not only about the great classics but also about the ever-increasing wealth of suitable adolescent literature, and learn how to apply that knowledge and enthusiasm in our classes.

We cannot do this in one lesson, one term, or even one high school course. Our own love for literature took a long time to develop. Let us not expect miracles overnight.

STIMULATING ENJOYMENT OF LITERATURE

Accepting that a large proportion of students entering high school are deficient in reading, each teacher of English (and other content subjects as well) must familiarize himself with the various ways of evaluating reading growth, the many reading skills subsumed under the term *reading,* the techniques of providing remediation within the classroom, and the teaching of the new and advanced skills that are now required. This implies in-service training for the multitudes of high school teachers who have never taken a course in the teaching of reading or who have never even read a book on this subject. The field is now so rich that no high school English teacher honestly can maintain that he doesn't know where to get the information. The pages of such professional journals as *The Reading Teacher, The English Journal, The Clearing House* and many others have a host of articles for those teachers who are genuinely interested. Let us stop complaining about the shortcomings of our colleagues in the lower echelons of the educational system and do something ourselves about improving the situation.

I list only a few of the reading improvement books that have appeared in the past few years: Robert Karlin, *Teaching Reading in High School,* Second Edition (Bobbs-Merril, 1972); Albert J. Harris and Edward R. Sipay, *Effective Teaching of Reading,* Second Edition. (David McKay Company, 1971); Albert J. Harris, *How to Increase Reading Ability,* Fifth Edition. (David McKay Company, 1970); Emerald Dechant, *Diagnosis and Remediation of Reading Disability,* (Parker, 1968).

In addition there are at least twenty-five books designed for college students who wish to improve their reading.[7]

THE PASSING OF THE STANDARD CLASSICS

We must stop hoping that assigning a portion of a hallowed classic to every member of the class will result in comprehension, appreciation, enjoyment or any noticeable growth. The teacher of literature in high school today must abandon his reliance on teaching a dozen or so major classics in English literature as a *modus operandi.* As Dora V. Smith has cogently stated it:

...there is little place in high school teaching today for the old approach to the novel by having every pupil read the same book at a set pace of thirty-five pages a day. Some should finish such a novel in three days. Others lack the capacity to read beyond the second chapter.[8]

This implies that the teacher must know a great many books on various reading levels and must know the interests and abilities of each of his student. Whereas one student might not be ready to appreciate *Silas Marner,* he may find much to interest him in such books as: Golding's *Lord of the Flies;* Heller's *Catch 22;* Knowles' *A Separate Peace;* Camus' *The Stranger,* and a host of others.

In New York City, to implement the 1957 course of study in senior high schools, a reading list of hundreds of books pertaining to the dominant theme "The Self-Reliant Individual" was issued to each ninth-grade teacher.[9] Similar reading lists and suggestions for integrated activities in the language arts were issued to teachers in the tenth, eleventh, and twelfth grades to illustrate the following annual themes: Tenth grade—The Individual as a Member of the Group; Eleventh grade—The Individual and the American Heritage; Twelfth grade—The Individual's Quest for Universal Values.

Instead of building a literature course in senior high school on two classics a term, the teacher has a wealth of books both from the classics and contemporary authors to meet every taste, every stage of development and every interest.

The publishers of literature anthologies have given us fine examples of profusely illustrated, attractively printed and intelligently edited compendia of suitable materials for personal and social growth. Some of the following four-volume series certainly deserve careful study by our English teachers interested in fostering personal development:

Harcourt Brace's *Adventures Series,* Classic Edition
Scott, Foresman's *America Reads*
Henry Holt's *Our Reading Heritage*
Houghton Mifflin's *Reading for Enjoyment*
Lippincott's *Reading for Life*
Ginn's *Good Reading*
Macmillan's *Literary Heritage Series*
American Book's *The Mastery of Reading*
Laidlaw's *Cultural Growth through Reading*
Prentice-Hall's *Life in Literature*
McGraw-Hill's *Themes and Writers*

These texts not only will open new worlds for our students, but also for many teachers. The thematic or unit approach followed in these anthologies (and such reading lists as supplied by the New York City schools) will probably go much further toward our objectives of enjoyment than the careful analysis of a dozen standard classics and nothing more.

MEETING INDIVIDUAL DIFFERENCES IN READING

Part of this misconception of teaching only a few classics can be corrected if the teacher begins to realize that *Silas Marner* may be pleasure for some, but poison for others; that *Idylls of the King* will thrill some and chill others; that Burke's *Speech on Conciliation* may conciliate a few, but alienate the many; that *Much Ado about Nothing* may, alas, be taken quite literally by many in his class. He has taken the first step on the long, hard road of recognizing individual differences within even the most homogeneously grouped class. Space does not permit the summary of the studies made by the Commission on the English Curriculum of the National Council of Teachers of English on the provision for meeting individual differences in the teaching of literature. Reference must suffice at this time to Chapter 11, "The Challenge of Individual Differences," in *The English Language Arts.*[10]

The perceptive teacher who knows his students will understand which books out of the teeming multitudes on hand will contribute to Johnny's growth in understanding himself, to Mary's growth in sensitivity to poetry, to Henry's growth in understanding the ways of other people, to Loretta's growth in understanding her American heritage. To all these and to other aspects of growth, books can contribute. The teacher should know them and know when best to bring the book and pupil together for maximum effect. The reading of an alert English teacher in high school never ceases.[11]

Does this mean that we must lower our standards as we attempt to provide for individual differences? That we must accept a comic book version of *Macbeth* instead of the real thing? The answer is decidedly in the negative. Providing for individual differences does not mean descending to the lowest common denominator. Like the reverse of Gresham's law in economics, good literature will eventually drive out trash. A perceptive and well-read teacher armed with a multitude of books of interest to teenagers is more than a match for the purveyors of trash.

Many teachers and administrators have accepted the need for individual conferences in teaching written composition. We are more and more coming to realize that the individual conference in enjoying literature is just as important. Lou La Brant in her *We Teach English* writes cogently about this important way to understand our children and to guide them to enjoyment of literature.[12]

THE FALLACY OF GROWTH BY EXPOSURE

If personal growth could be achieved by exposure alone, then our most cultured young men would be attendants in library stacks or salesmen in bookstores. Exposure to good literature, however, is not enough. More has probably been written on the methodology of teaching literature than any other subject in the high school curriculum. There are at least sixty textbooks on the teaching of English and almost every one has a substantial section devoted to literature. No teacher can honestly contend that he doesn't know where to get information about teaching literature. Many of the publishers of literature anthologies mentioned earlier also provide substantial teaching guides for each of the volumes.

Many teachers with the best intentions in the world fail to establish contact between the book taught and the student striving to grow up. Such an evanescent form as poetry has been particularly difficult to get across. Commenting upon the contrasting ways of teaching Amy Lowell's "Lilacs," Dora V. Smith indicates:

The old way of teaching was to begin with characteristics of Amy Lowell's poetry and stories of how she smoked a cigar or with definitions of free verse, examples of which were then sought in books. The new way is to help students realize how effectively poetry reveals what he himself has seen and felt and to discover something of the technic the poet has used. Then each pupil can read more poems by himself, under the teacher's guidance, finding what best meets his own need.[13]

There is no royal road to knowledge. There are many roads, probably as many as the young people before us. Too many of us think that the road which we took, and which led us to delight in literature, is the one along which we must lead our youngsters. We must be on the alert to read new (and old) books which we can utilize in our reading-literature program. We also must be experimenting with, reflecting over, and evaluating the results of new methods of guiding our students to the understanding, appreciation and response to a work of literature. Once that right contact has been made, the pupil is never quite the same. Flaubert spoke of *le mot juste* in describing his search for the perfect word to express his ideas. The teacher of literature should also search for *la méthode juste* (if I may coin the phrase) to achieve the results outlined above. This is the reverse of the old-fashioned question-phrasing and daily mark-giving which is so unhappily associated with the literature experiences many of us had several decades ago.

ENLISTING THE MASS MEDIA

Prophets of doom have been lamenting the effect of the mass media upon reading and reading habits of our population. At each stage, alert teachers of English have tried to utilize these media to strengthen their educational programs rather than attack them as Don Quixote's windmills were attacked. From Edgar Dale's *How to Read to a Newspaper,* to the N. C. T. E. volume *Radio and English Teaching,* the N. C. T. E. volume *Using Periodicals* and the current guides to TV shows, we have many valuable procedures for utilizing the mass media. Rather than detracting from reading time, many students have demonstrated that requests for books frequently rise when there has been a movie or TV version of a classic. The complete sellout of Stendhal's *Red and Black* after Fred Zulli's initial lecture on *Sunrise Semester* is well known.

When such TV productions as *A Tale of Two Cities, Hamlet, Jane Eyre, Romeo and Juliet, Richard III, David Copperfield, Vanity Fair, Père Goriot, The Forsyte Saga,* and other classics are produced live on TV or revived on film, the alert teacher can surely capitalize on them in presenting the literature program. Thus by means of comparisons and contrasts between the mass media version and the literary work being discussed the teacher can open ever newer avenues toward enjoyment. No mass medium will ever take the place of reading, but it should be utilized profitably toward achieving the goal for which we are all striving. The novelty of a new medium wears off quickly. The love of literature which we instill lasts a lifetime.

The public library in Washington, D. C. informs us that:

The production of *The Lark* aroused interest not only in the play but also in other books about Joan of Arc—as did the earlier stage production. Many viewers were prompted to read Shaw's *Man and Superman* and Shakespeare's *Romeo and Juliet* after seeing the plays. TV programs led readers to ask for Fitzgerald's *Great Gatsby* and other titles, Sherwood's *There Shall Be No Night,* and Lindsay's *Great Sebastians.*[1]

THE CONTAGION OF PERSONAL ENJOYMENT

The testimony is so overwhelming that it is almost axiomatic that enjoyment in literature is contagious from teacher to student. How many teachers are still using books, not because they are themselves strongly moved by them, but because they happen to have a set (or somebody else's set) of lesson plans? Or because they can obtain three sets of these books for their three sections? When there are almost one hundred thousand paperbacks in print and when the price is so low that few students will object to purchasing their own copies, need any teacher use a battered, torn and dirty set of *Tale of Two Cities* just because she has been teaching it for years and has a set of questions for each chapter?

No teacher should teach a work of literature who is not herself fired with enthusiasm for it, is widely read in as many periods of literature as she has time for, and is acquainted with the scholarship in the fields. Such a book as Lewis Leary's *Contemporary Literary Scholarship* should be read by each one of us! And how can we afford to neglect some of the 1,500 books published each year for children and adolescents?[15]

ENJOYMENT OF LITERATURE IS A SLOW PROCESS

Unless we were all precocious, we developed our love for literature and our burning desire to communicate it over a period of years. If we followed the traditional pattern, we did not enjoy *The Brothers Karamazov* or *War and Peace* before *Frank Merriwell* or the *Bobbsey Twins*. More likely, we went through a period of reading what we now know to be little better than trash, until we began to see the light, the light that shone from the beacons of the great lighthouse-keepers of mankind, those authors who showed us the way out of the darkness of our own minds or limited environment into the clear light of self-knowledge and world-knowledge and all the satisfactions pertaining thereto. We probably are stirring more of our students than we presently realize. Time works many miracles on seeds properly planted. Let us at least be certain that we are not wasting our seeds, or planting them at the wrong time, or failing to nourish them properly.

As an indication of how gifted students themselves regard their development of enjoyment of literature, I have appended thirty-seven statements from students in a twelfth-grade class. All had received ninety percent or above in English and had an I. Q. of 130 or above. Their comments on such subjects as the influence of their parents, friends and relatives, teachers, book reports, class discussions, television and movies are revealing of the role that each of these factors play in developing the ability to enjoy literature.

Gifted Students on Enjoyment of Reading

The Influence of Reading. "Nevertheless, I might dare to say that through reading one grows far beyond his mortal years and one actually does become a little bit wiser in the ways of man. For every chapter, every page, every paragraph, and every line of a book bring to their reader a little bit of the truth that is in the world."

The Influence of Parents. "My parents, being teachers, introduced me to books at an early age by reading to me such children's books as *Winnie the Pooh*. As I got older and began to learn to read, they read with me, helping me with the words I did not know."

"My parents are both avid readers, and they belong to numerous book clubs. Within the walls of my house I have always been able to find interesting reading material and the encouragement to peruse through it."

"My parents provided me with a store of volumes from which to choose, and encouraged me to keep a small library of my own."

"My mother is an avid reader and so we occasionally discuss special books of interest. I am surrounded day and night by books, books and more books which pleases me no end."

The Influence of Friends of Parents. "My parents' friends have influenced my habits as well. They have always looked upon reading as a social necessity, since books and ideas are a main topic of conversation."

The Influence of Parents and Teachers. "Firstly, I believe that a person does not develop a love for reading. It is developed for him by his parents and teachers. If the parents help and greatly encourage the first awkward attempts of the student to choose and read a book, I believe that a gradual liking will develop."

Conversation of Parents. "Their mention of good reading also has influenced me. It was the frequent mention of Thomas Wolfe that influenced me to make a term project of him and his works. When time permits I hope to read all of his works."

The Influence of Parents' Oral Reading. "My parents read to me nursery rhymes, bedtime stories and fairy tales among others. They would show me pictures and all this, because I was interested."

Discussion by Parents. "Now it is not uncommon for my whole family to read the same book and then sit down for an hour or two and discuss and analyze it."

Reading of Parents. "My parents are avid readers of current periodicals, and consequently such magazines as *Scientific American, Atlantic, U. S. News and World Report,* and *Harpers* are part of the decor of my home."

The Influence of Parents by Gifts. "At home my parents have greatly influenced my reading by their choice of books which they have presented to me—Dickens and Dostoevski to name two."

Books in the Home. "Reading has always been a part of our family life, so much so that there are bookcases in almost every room, and they're still not enough."

The Influence of Friends and Relatives. "My friends and relatives also play an important role in my appreciation of literature. We recommend books to each other and, by so doing, I have broadened my scope by learning to enjoy reading many types of books in many fields. By discussing various books with my friends, I get their reactions and interpretations and in turn give them mine. This leads to a greater understanding of the book and therefore to a much deeper appreciation of what is read."

"My friends and relatives also played a role in my own development as a reader. In a relationship where one person admires another, it is only natural for the worshipper to emulate his ideal. If the second person happens to proffer an atmosphere of cultural dominance (reading, music, etc.) then we may expect his companion to absorb this."

A Wholesome Diet. "In conclusion, I enjoy reading because I was fed a wholesome diet of good books when I was young, and had the good fortune of having inspiring English teachers in school."

Introduction to the World of Books. "I also feel that an introduction at an early age to the world of books is quite advantageous. However, at this age (8-9) books must be chosen very carefully so that they will be of adequate interest to the adventuresome youngster."

Early Inspiration by Teacher. "When I was in the third grade the teacher I had was a very intelligent woman. In the course of a lesson she would mention several facts about a book or a story she wanted us to read. However, she very rarely assigned the stories for home reading. The clues or facts she mentioned often interested the class so much that the next day the first topic of discussion more often than not was the story the teacher supposedly never assigned for homework."

The Influence of Teacher. "I think it might also be very helpful, as it was in my case, for the teacher to make extra books available to the more avid students for use in their spare time."

The Influence of Teachers. "My teachers also influenced my reading to some extent. Although lower grade teachers did little to steer me to extra reading for they were more interested in teaching students to read, my fourth- and fifth-grade teachers set aside a few library periods where we were given a choice of books to read."

The Influence of a Teacher. "Only recently has my interest in reading returned and I think this is due to my English teacher of last year. He stressed literature a great deal and made the required class reading interesting."

The Effect of the Teacher's Oral Reading. "I do remember one teacher in elementary school who had a unique way of getting the class to read more. She would take time out of the class periods every once in a while, sit down and start to read aloud from some book. Whenever the story reached an interesting point she would stop and put the book away. The same book would never be taken out again. This caused many of us to get the book from the library and finish reading it outselves. We read just for enjoyment and not for marks."

Lessons in Literature. "Although I like to read I don't like the literature lessons the school gives. I don't like the phrases 'teaching literature' or 'teaching pupils to like to read.' In my opinion a desire to read or an appreciation of literature cannot be taught; it can only be communicated from teacher to student. I don't think you can interest students in reading just by assigning them books to read and analyses to do. I always have hated to do written work such as analyzing books chapter by chapter, comparing characters, or explaining why I liked or disliked a book. I think the only proper way to appreciate a book is through discussion."

The Effect of Required Book Reports. "Whenever I was expected to read a book it was assigned as a book report. This developed hostilities against reading. I don't want to sound like a psychiatrist but I feel their idea of assigning books for reports at an early age is something that discourages reading. Each time a child would normally pick up a book and start reading he thinks that it is too much like work he had to do in school and puts the book down again."

The Danger of Book Reports. "In this connection I have one complaint. This is against book reports. True, a student should supplement his formal schooling with some extra reading but to make him write a report on the book, reading becomes a drudgery, all enjoyment is lost and the student gets very little out of what he has read. If instead, more books were read at home and then were discussed and analyzed in class the student would not lose interest and would benefit from the ideas of his classmates."

The Effect of Required Book Reports in Junior High. "During the next phase of my education, junior high school, my literary instruction consisted of a series of required monthly book reports. I recall reading the first fifteen chapters of *David Copperfield* as a class unit, and handing to my teacher a folder, prettily decorated, containing a summary of each separate chapter. We never discussed our opinions of the book and were not encouraged to finish the book on our own."

New Classics for Old. "The teacher should not compel the reading of outdated novels, which no longer have the significance they had at the time of their original publication, such as *David Copperfield, House of Seven Gables* and *Silas Marner.* The Board of Education should require novels of such contemporary authors as Dreiser, Hemingway, Steinbeck. Then high school literature would be more beneficial and more enjoyable."

Dislike of The House of Seven Gables. "Another of these extremely uninteresting novels was Hawthorne's *House of Seven Gables.* During the period of time when this novel was written it might have been interesting, but one century later it does not belong on the required book list of a high school student."

Dislike of Silas Marner. "In high school I first encountered books which I did not enjoy. The first of these was *Silas Marner* by George Eliot. I have never found a more deterring novel for any student who is attempting to find a love for reading. In my opinion the only thing the reading of *Silas Marner* accomplished was to discourage me from indulging in any of the other works by Eliot.

Class Discussions. "In Jamaica High School much of my desire to read was augmented by discussions of various books and authors. Criticisms by my classmates and teachers, as well, have introduced me to many books which I have enjoyed immensely, and I maintain that this is the best method of getting high school students interested in literature."

Required Reading a Block to Reading. "I enjoyed reading until I entered junior high school. Required book reports and the reading of certain books just didn't agree with me. I'm not sure that I know why, but I just seemed to rebel against the idea of having to read a book for school. My reading slacked off until I read only what I was required to read."

Liking vs. Disliking Books. "I developed a liking for reading because I never developed a dislike for reading. This may sound paradoxical. The only explanation I can give for this fact is that I never was assigned dull books to read in school. When Homer and Dickens were assigned, my teacher presented these works in such an enjoyable fashion that even they were a pleasure to read."

Forcing the Child to Read. "The child must not be forced to read, for if he is, he may develop an aversion for reading from which he may never recover."

Influence of Library. "With the aid of library techniques taught in the seventh grade, the lock to the numerous volumes in public libraries was opened to us. In these buildings I never found it difficult to get lost among the written pearls of wisdom."

The Effect of Movies on Reading. "Movies have been instrumental in my selection of 'popular' novels. After viewing an interesting film I am often impelled to read the novel upon which the movie is based."

Television vs. Reading. "Another reason I would say for my developing the habit of reading is because television is not encouraged in my home. I am permitted to watch a few choice programs that have been approved and often selected by my parents."

Suggestions for the Limited Reader. "Find out something that interests the student—romance, baseball, fate—and then dig up a book on the subject that is written in a manner pleasing to the tastes of the student."

12

SELECTION OF ADULT BOOKS FOR SCHOOL-AGE READERS

The discussion of this topic is particularly appropriate at this time in our cultural and educational history for several reasons. First, there is an ever-increasing proportion of school-age students compared with the population of our country as a whole. Teenagers, for example, now form an important segment of American consumers for which American businessmen are showing an increasing awareness. Second, books are more available today than ever before in our history, thanks to the omnipresence of paperbacks—good, bad and indifferent—and to the construction of more public and school libraries. Finally, thanks to the interest of the federal government in improving education at all levels, more funds now are available to librarians for purchasing books and other instructional materials.

To formulate any worthwhile criteria for selecting adult books of interest to school-age students requires a knowledge of these three pertinent factors. Those who are responsible for making such selections, whether teachers, librarians or parents, obviously must know something about interests, ideals and aspirations of adolescents (here considered as the secondary school students, grades 7 to 12). Knowing the nature of the adolescent, however, is not enough. The selector of adult books must have a rich acquaintance with the best books of the past and the present. He also must have that rare and undefinable quality of "good taste" so as to know what to recommend. The third requisite in the obvious availability of adequate funds.

The development of the procedure for recommending adult books for adolescents has progressed through several stages. At first, such recommendations were made by adults, ostensibly interested in good reading and eager to inspire young people with the same enthusiasm. Booklists have been compiled by experienced teachers, librarians and bibliophiles for the past seventy-five years and undoubtedly longer. In fact, when the so-called Standard Classics of the 1880's began to dominate secondary school English programs through the first two decades of the twentieth century, there were usually two lists of books recommended, one for intensive class study and the other for individual reading. Publishers then came out with their lists of classics to meet the demands of the College Entrance Examination Board[1]. These recommendations for individual reading were, for the most part, literature of the nineteenth century or earlier. Hardly a contemporary book was included.

Lists later were prepared by curriculum committees of state and local school systems. In large-city school systems, almost every high school felt it necessary to prepare a list of what came to be universally known as "supplementary reading." I still have retained the *Brooklyn Boys' High School Handbook,* which was purchased in 1920 when I entered, with its substantial list of recommended books, term by term. Many libraries prepared their own lists, and these served as guides to teachers and parents. There has never been a dearth of recommended lists of books for young people. In fact, one or more doctoral dissertations in library science could profitably be written about these recommended lists, their preparation, promulgation and influence. To my knowledge, this kind of study has not been made, and it should be useful to those who are interested in knowing how to build lasting reading interests in students.

WHAT EARLY LISTS LACKED

The only trouble with the early lists was that, from the evidence offered by the students themselves, the books did not appeal to young readers. For every adolescent who developed a life-long interest in books as a result of reading the books on these lists, there must have been a thousand who continued to read trash or nothing at all. Something must have gone wrong, somewhere along the road, between the selectors and the adolescents. What many of the early list-makers failed to take into account was the young reader for whom they were making these recommendations. The intentions were good, but the results were disappointing.

HAVE CURRENT PRINCIPLES OF SELECTION BEEN IMPROVED?

Today, helpful guidelines are available for those who would select suitable adult books. The Bill of Rights of the American Library Association certainly contains valuable suggestions and lists the following responsibilities of a school library:
1. To provide materials that will enrich and support the curriculum, taking into consideration the varied interests, abilities and maturity levels of the students served.
2. To provide materials that will stimulate growth in factual knowledge, aesthetic values and ethical standards.
3. To provide a background of information that will enable students to make intelligent judgments in their daily lives.
4. To provide materials on opposing sides of controversial issues so that young citizens may develop, unaer guidance, the practice of critical reading and thinking.
5. To provide materials representative of the many religious, ethnic and cultural groups and their contributions to our heritage.

6. To place principle above personal opinion and reason above prejudice in the selection of materials of the highest quality in order to assure a comprehensive collection appropriate of the users of the Library.

While these principles no doubt are unobjectionable, they are far too general to assist the busy librarian who has a great deal of money to spend but too little time to read the thousands of adult books that are suitable for the student readers in her library. Of course, there are easy ways out by consulting such compilations as *Doors to More Mature Reading,*[2] or *Books for You,*[3] or the *Senior Book List,*[4] and *Junior Book List,*[5] that used to be published annually by the National Association of Independent Schools through *Books for the Teen Age*[6] published annually by the Young Adult Division of the New York Public Library. All these and many others can assist the well-intentioned but harassed librarian or teacher or parent in the quest for the best adult books for young readers.

However, some librarians and teachers may ask, when making selections based upon their own reading and judgment, "What criteria do I follow?"

Here, too, there is help in sight. The first is a series of suggestions on selecting adult novels, taken from Hanna and McAllister's *Books, Young People, and Reading Guidance:*[7]

Sometimes young people find adult novels unsatisfying because the content proves dull and uninteresting. The theme may be too mature, the construction too involved, the style too contemplative, or philosophical, or too weighted with description. Often small print and narrow margins make the format unappealing. . . . Many novels are too long, for the adolescent is usually in a hurry and wants books he can finish quickly. After all, there are a great many other things to do besides read and all of them are important and very pressing.

There is, furthermore, the ever-present problem of the suitability of adult fiction for school-age readers. In this respect, too, Hanna and McAllister offer helpful guidance:

Of the novels that are considered interesting and readable by the adolescent, many are considered unsuitable by his elders. Too often "unsuitable" has not been properly understood either by the adolescent or the adult and so has been interpreted as censorship. Good book selection for young people accepts the fact that adolescents are not adults and therefore do not hold the same perspective or place the same importance on ideas in novels as do adults. For this reason certain incidents in otherwise fine adult novels are often not as harmful to them as many adults think. On the other hand, young people tend to place emphasis where adult readers would not, and too often they miss the real point of what the author is saying and see only the apparent result. The reading of some adult novels, therefore, should be postponed, just as many other experiences of adult life are postponed, until there is enough maturity for full understanding. Book selection does not deny any novel to young people, but rather makes available to them a wide variety of more suitable novels, better and more appealing because they reflect the needs and interests of young people on their own level of understanding. Not denial of a book but the provision of something better is a basic principle of book selection.

WHAT DO THE BOOK SELECTORS USE AS CRITERIA?

To determine criteria used in selection, sources such as *Books, Young People and Reading Guidance* and numerous articles in the various library journals were consulted. In addition, it seemed profitable to find out what librarians and teachers who have served on book selection committees have used as their criteria. Hence, a letter was sent to all the members of the Committee on Senior Booklist, the Committee on Junior Booklist, to the committee that prepared *3,000 Books for Secondary School Libraries,*[8] and *Doors to More Mature Reading*, and to Richard S. Alm, former editor of *Books for You*. Their answers, appearing in print for the first time here, represent the latest thinking on this subject and hence merit attention. Those who responded to this limited survey, many of whom answered in considerable detail, deserve profound thanks and appreciation.

Pauline Anderson, Librarian of the Andrew Mellon Library of The Choate School, Wallingford, Connecticut, and a member of the N. A. I. S. Committee that compiled *3,000 Books for Secondary School Libraries* mentions the following as basic principles, in addition to the American Library Association's Bill of Rights already mentioned:

1. No books in the "gray areas" of acceptable taste to be included.
2. Materials of literary value to be chosen.
3. The authors of the selected books to be the best authorities in their fields available at the time.
4. Materials hinging on the sensational side to be avoided.
5. In case of translations, the most accurate ones to be selected.
6. No book to be included which would not contribute to the academic, moral or personal growth of the individual student.

Mrs. Locke K. Brown of the Springside School, Chestnut Hill, Philadelphia, reveals the criteria employed by the Committee on Senior Booklist of the N. A. I. S.:

Generally, the criteria for evaluating these books include excellence of writing and some relationship to the student's actual, vicarious or potential experience. Thus, for example, Molly Mahood's *Joyce Cary's Africa* was rejected by the committee, because, although it was itself excellent and a real contribution to the understanding of Cary, it was too specialized to be of general interest at the high school level. Without departing from these guidelines, indeed consistent with them, we may list a book which appears on the surface to be racy, and for which we have occasionally been criticized. The point in this instance should be made that the committee does not reject a book merely because it is racy. If sordidness or violence plays an integral part in an artistically viable and significant book, then the committee has no objection to it. On that basis, for example, the committee included Jesse Hill Ford's *Liberation of Lord Byron Jones*. For failing to meet these standards, the committee rejected a very bad novel, *The Beasts*, by Leslie Garrett, because it was vicious with no objective other than being so.
In all of this, of course, it must be remembered that the student body of a demanding school has a great deal of freedom in what it reads, both in its leisure and in its curriculum. It can be relied on to exercise a full degree of discrimination and critical

judgment. Because of this, it can read certain books with profit that would be devastating to less able students. This is a particularly important aspect of what I mean when I say that we choose books in some relationship to student experience. Because the experience, as far as training and judgment are concerned, is relatively wide, so can the selection be broad.

Although Mrs. H. L. Richardson of the Committee on Senior Booklist did not suggest any criteria, she commented with insight on the reading of adolescents in this way:

I think the one thing important to adolescents in their reading is reality. They are anxious to know how the world really is and how other people solve their problems. This explains, I think, the popularity of *The Diary of a Young Girl* (by Anne Frank) and *Death Be Not Proud* with young people. They certainly do not want to read that strange breed of book, the teenage novel—a book of dating problems written about teenagers for teenagers by adults who are still children.
Because they are looking for answers, books of controversy and books expressing views not generally held by their parents and teachers are interesting to adolescents. I have the feeling that although the adolescent has had more thoughtful attention from adults in this generation than in previous ones, he has also had less understanding and comprehension.

Elinor Walker, Coordinator of Work with Young People and one of the compilers of *Doors to More Mature Reading,* has some revealing comments on the criteria which she uses for the Carnegie Library of Pittsburgh:

It always amuses me to hear young teachers who indiscriminately recommend Faulkner and his ilk to teenage readers say that librarians are trying to protect young readers from the facts of life. I wonder if they think that teenagers live in a vacuum. Actually, the seamy side of life is thrown at them from every direction. Some magazines, many newspapers, radio, and most TV, theatre, and movies are concerned with little else.
My theory and practice have always been to buy only books which have some positive value. Any negative qualities have to be *far* outweighed by the positive. We buy some books which we know are mediocre as far as writing goes, but this is justified by contents which have something worthwhile to say to the young person. No matter how beautifully a book may be written, we do not buy it if it has nothing to say to teenage readers. Some books are too nostalgic or too far outside the young people's experience to be appreciated by them. I think it is important that books give young people some assurance that there is good in the world, and that it often triumphs over evil. I maintain that realism includes the good as well as the bad, although many people do not agree with me.
You will note in the Preface to *Doors* we said that we chose books "that bring challenges to young people, that widen their horizons, and that deepen their appreciation of language, of truth, of beauty, of life itself."
We often refuse to buy some of the titles recommended by A. L. A. as being appropriate for teenage readers. We do not buy a new title on a subject just because it is a new title. If it does not add anything to what we already have, we think it is not worth buying. We have teenage readers who review books for us and discuss them at reviewing meetings, and we find they are more choosy than we are. We do have to keep the slower, poorer reader in mind.
I am sure that I have not said anything new or startling. We used these same criteria in selecting books for *Doors*. For that publication we had the advantage of having

tested everything with our readers, and we knew what their reactions were to the titles we chose. That is one reason we have teenagers help review new books here in Pittsburgh.

Donald W. Allyn, another member of the committee that compiled *Doors to More Mature Reading,* made the following statement of principles that guided the members of this committee as well as those who compiled its companion volume, *Book Bait:*[9]

In the preface to *Book Bait,* the companion volume to *Doors to More Mature Reading,* is the statement that the books included not only "give lasting pleasure, but they also contribute to the growth and understanding of the young people who read them. They help in building a sound philosophy of life, and they offer some of the knowledge, tolerance, and courage which will enable young people to face their problems with a determination to solve them." I like to think that there is no such thing as a "young adult book." There are thousands of books, some of which young people like to read and which contribute something to their particular stage of development. Identifying these books is a matter of listening and watching to find out which titles are duds and which are demanded year after year. When we put together *Doors,* we were combining our collective opinions about books which we knew appealed to some young people and which could be introduced to other teen-agers with a good chance of success. When a new book is published, the librarian reviewing it may sense that it will or will not appeal to young adults, but its true test comes when the students pick it up.

WHAT ARE THE READING INTERESTS OF YOUNG PEOPLE?

Throughout, mention has been made of the reading interests of the school-age reader; the remainder of this chapter will be devoted to this topic. Perhaps the most extensive investigations of this subject are those made by George W. Norvell over a period of twenty-five years. In 1950, he published his *Reading Interests of Young People,*[10] in which more than fifty thousand students and 625 teachers participated from all types of communities of New York State. In all, 1,700 selections widely used in secondary schools were listed in the order of choice by boys and girls of grades 7 to 12. In 1958, Norvell published *What Boys and Girls Like to Read,*[11] in which he studied the opinions of 24,000 students in grades three to six. The statistics are probably the most impressive of any similar study.

Whereas Norvell's studies are valuable for their statistical significance, there have been complementary studies of the adolescent's reading tastes that should be helpful in the search for criteria. Space will permit mention of only a few of them. In the January, 1965, issue of *Top of the News,*[12] Helen Wilmott of the Young Adult Services Division Board of the American Library Association describes the results of a questionnaire addressed to senior high school students who were leaders in sports, in honor societies or other groups within the school. The question asked was phrased as follows:

Because we feel the above to be true (the quotation from Aldous Huxley used to end this article) we thought it would be fun and interesting to have you tell us what book or books have influenced you. We are asking your opinion because, though still in your teens, you have already shown traits of leadership and have the respect and good will of your fellow students.

Over three thousand questionnaires were returned from 138 areas. Of these, seven hundred came from non-leaders of the schools. Although three thousand replies may not represent the viewpoints of millions of teenagers, nevertheless they do represent the groups surveyed. As Miss Wilmott analyzed the findings, she found that young adults are primarily concerned with three areas:

1. The individual—his growth, personality and philosophy. This may be brought out through character development in fiction; religiously and ethically, as in the Bible and Gibran's *The Prophet;* through ideas set forth by the "great minds" of all time or through career-based fiction and nonfiction. Basically, this is the teenager's search to find himself. . . .

2. He has concern for social problems and social responsiblity, whether it be the great national concern of Civil Rights or the problem of the mentally retarded, the alcoholic or the juvenile delinquent.

3. He is concerned for the world he lives in on both the national and the international levels, and he often shows a deep interest in and appreciation for his American heritage. He often mentioned that what he has read has given him a determination to do something about a situation—if only to better inform himself.

Those of us who have been teaching for the past few years and have read the literature dealing with adolescents' reading interests may find nothing particularly new about the three above-mentioned points. They have been found in the literature of at least the past three decades. What is of interest is that conclusions of the 1930's were found to be valid in the 1960's. Thus, despite all the apparent changes in behavior, dress, social activities and attitudes of today's adolescents, basically their reading interests have not changed, and probably will not change much in the next three decades. This fact ought to be of some comfort to the teacher or librarian who has to make long-range purchases.

Among the recent publications covering a range of literature for school-age readers is G. Robert Carlsen's *Books and the Teen-Age Reader.*[13] Professor Carlsen is one of the most knowledgeable experts in this field, and his book is a useful guide to teachers, librarians and parents. He has provided a handbook that answers the question raised in this chapter, as well as many other related questions. His chapters 6, "The Popular Adult Book," and 9, "The Place of the Classics," contain a wealth of practical suggestions with many specific titles at the end of each chapter. It is the kind of book that can be read and reread and will continue to enrich the reader and provide deeper insights into this fascinating area. In addition, Professor Carlsen's address given at the American Library Conference in St. Louis, July 2, 1964, is reprinted in the January 1965 issue of *Top of the News.* The article, which is written with his usual clarity and perceptiveness, is entitled, "For Everything There Is A Season."[14] It is valuable because it describes both the reading habits and the reading content of adolescents. Rarely has so much good sense based on sound scholarship been expressed in so few pages. In a certain degree, his book is an amplification of this discussion. The four areas of content are quite familiar to those who have had much to do with developing the reading interests of adolescents. The topics are:

1. *The Search.* Young adults choose books in which individuals are looking for a direction for their lives. . . .
2. *Problems of the Social Order.* Just as young people are involved with their own personal problems, so they are concerned with the problems of their society.
3. *The Bizarre, the Off Beat, The Unusual in Human Experience.* Apparently, in looking for direction, the young adult is curious about the fringes of human life. . . .
4. *The Transition.* Perhaps the single theme most sought by the young adult is the book that details the movement of a character from adolescence into early adult life.

These four areas of content happen to be the most popular, but there are many more. Luckily, there now is a much greater understanding of both literature for adolescents and their tastes in literature than was true in the past.

HOW TO KNOW THE BEST

The words "taste in literature" raise the question as to how teachers or librarians can be sure of showing the best taste. Here a field of inquiry is opened that goes back to Aristotle's *Poetics* and has by no means ended with the New Criticism. More than a quarter of a century ago when the author was asked to discuss the subject "What Makes Great Drama Great?" his criteria eventually became a chapter in *The Play's the Thing.*[15] Although these were originally intended for selecting plays, they are just as applicable to other literary *genres:*
1. Universality of appeal, in time as well as space.
2. Creation of living characters in convincing situations.
3. The play must stir, move, enrich or transform you.
4. The language of a great play is superior to one that is inferior.
5. Great plays, in common with great literature of all varieties, will teach you about life, how people think, act, and should strengthen your hand in facing your life problems.
These five simple criteria have helped many a teacher and librarian and hopefully may continue to do so.

CONCLUSION

This chapter has attempted to present some of the major problems involved in selecting adult books for school-age students by demonstrating some of the principles that have been used for the past seventy-five years. Some of these principles have never succeeded in accomplishing their purpose. The more successful practices have been revealed by actual practitioners in the field of book selection. With a better knowledge of the adolescent's interests and a richer acquaintance with literature of both past and present, perhaps individuals can succeed in achieving the goal so well expressed by Aldous Huxley: "Every man who knows how to read has it in his power to magnify himself, to multiply the ways in which he exists, to make his life full, significant and interesting."[16]

13

WHAT HAS HAPPENED TO WRITTEN COMPOSITION IN THE PAST FIFTY YEARS?

Judging from the stories in the newspapers, not much has happened in written composition by way of improvement. The United Press carried a dispatch on October 24, 1960 with the headline, "Students Stumble on English." "Specifically," reads the story, "they have trouble with English, the language they are supposed to use in communicating their ideas. To put it another way, Johnny can't read, write or talk properly."[1]

Almost seventy years ago in Percival Chubb's pioneer volume in methodology, we learn that

In the complaints drawn up by the colleges against the high schools, it is the inability to write passably correct English that is most severely complained of.[2]

Fifteen years later in Sterling Andrus Leonard's *English Composition as a Social Problem*, we hear the same complaint.

In spite of years of training, our students fail to become easy, clear and forceful writers. We are told that the Americans who can speak and write with effective fluency have learned the art outside of classrooms.[3]

A study which the writer conducted in 1960 on attitudes toward English teaching indicated that the largest area needing improvement was written composition. Of the seventy-nine college presidents (or their representatives) who replied, twenty-four criticized the written composition of the students who had entered in the past five to ten years (this was in 1960). Of a total of seventy-six recommendations made to improve the teaching of English, the largest number, thirty-nine, was made for written composition.[4]

The writer's files of newspaper clippings are bulging with similar complaints about the writing skills of students at all levels of our educational system, but most teachers are aware of this attitude. Our purpose is not to recite the charges against our instruction and results in written composition, but rather to trace patterns with respect to aims, content, methodology and evaluation during the past half-century.

114

We shall discover that, as our critics were denouncing our meager results, our forward-looking teachers long before had enunciated the principles which today are so widely proclaimed.

For example, as far back as 1902 Chubb was asking for small classes and personal conferences with students about their written work. "...This must mean a liberal amount of individual work with our students; and this means small classes and frequent personal conferences between pupil and teacher."[5]

This plea for small classes was repeated in that clarion cry for reorganization of English by J. F. Hosic and his courageous colleagues:

The conditions surrounding the work of English teaching are susceptible to vast improvement. The large number of pupils now commonly assigned to an English teacher makes thorough teaching all but impossible, both because of the consequent lack of attention to the individual pupil and the physical exhaustion of the teacher. No teacher, though a Hercules and a pedagogical genius both in one, can be expected to do justice to 200 pupils in English.[6]

Those of us who look at each new pile of compositions with a mixture of frustration and dread may find some consolation in the knowledge that it was ever thus. Even in the halcyon good old days (whenever those days were) teachers had their burdens, intellectual, professional and ocular, even as you or I. Charles W. Eliot has told us why Harvard introduced the entrance examination in written composition in 1873:

As to the motives which determined Harvard requirements during the "70's" and "80's," they are chiefly the hope of improving the teaching of English in the secondary schools, and in the belief that college instruction in English language and literature could be much advanced if the elements thereof had been mastered before the boys came to college.[7]

That writing was an effort which was difficult and distasteful in 1873 and even later is obvious from the reports which we have from students and teachers alike. What modifications have been made in method which have made it less distasteful in our time? Let me list a few changes which have come in our century, and which are incorporated in the newest texts.

1. In composition it is peculiarly important to enlist the interest and pleasure of the pupil.[8] To illustrate what not to do in this respect, I shall read a composition by one of my students. It is one of a set which was turned in when I told the class that I had been invited to address a group of English teachers on this topic. No motivation was required other than my candid statement that it was possible some of their views about good and bad teachers of composition whom they had had might influence English instruction elsewhere. The papers turned in were so frank and so interesting that we planned a classroom publication which we hoped to distribute not only to the teachers in my own department but also to our colleagues in other schools.

Roger wrote about an English teacher who obviously had not heard of enlisting the interest and pleasure of the pupil. Here is his paper:

I once had a perfectly frightful experience in junior high school which has made me terribly shy of teachers, especially English teachers. It was just an example of the kind of thing that often happened to me in my stirring days at school, but the Midnight Oil Affair (which is the term by which my mother always grumpily refers to the frightful incident) was rather more spectacular than most of my scholastic troubles.

The whole brain-taxing mess had its roots in the disreputable fact that mine was the noisiest class in the entire school and consequently brought back atrocious marks on the section sheet every day. [The section sheet, in the happy event that you never went to junior high school, is a card on which each subject teacher marks a class's behavior in the course of a day.]

Our beloved homeroom teacher (name on request to right parties) was very upset by the whole thing. She was a mean old lady who wore high collars and a pocket watch. Anyway she had a very novel approach to the problem of correcting her class's conduct. At the end of the week she would assign an interesting little composition for every bad mark on the section sheet.

Don't get the idea that these compositions were little nothings on the importance of good manners in school. Not at all. They were thousand-word theses on such thought provoking topics as "What Fools These Mortals Be" and "Why I am a Conservative-Radical-Reactionary."

I was quite dismayed by the whole thing. I mean, why was I a conservative anyway? And what was a conservative in the first place?

Obviously these were not questions for my twelve-year-old brain, and looking back on the nights I sat up thinking about these things I sometimes wonder that I survived my youth at all.

I always hoped that somebody would suddenly pile a lot of work on this teacher whom I considered to be an unfeeling monster and looking back on it all I guess that's exactly what happened. The next year she became Chairman of the English Department.

2.   The first essential of real success in composition work is to make proficiency in it seem worthwhile to our students.[9]

3.   Classroom activities in composition should be founded upon and should grow out of the experiences of the pupils.[10]

4.   We must not make the mistake of assuming that training in composition is purely an individual matter. Most self-expression is for the purpose of social communication.[11]

5.   Formal grammar has limited value in the improvement of written composition. I might say that the argument about how much grammar, when to teach it, and how to teach it is still going on. But there is no argument about the uselessness of learning many grammatical terms which will never help the student to read, speak or write better.

6.   Defective motivation has been one of the greatest causes of poor instruction in composition.[12] We have learned a great deal about motivation in the past half century, and the variations of motivation in a single class.

7.   Whatever adds to the pupil's store of fact and ideas, enhances his power to think and augments his linguistic resources will minister to the art of expressing himself in written words.[13] Especially in the elementary school, and certainly in the high school, we now know that enriching the experiences of our students by trips and visits will stimulate greater expressiveness. The textbooks of the early

1900's emphasized almost exclusively the close dependence of written composition upon literature study. Thus one might appreciate an occasional tidbit about Sir Roger de Coverley or Brian de Bois Guilbert, but a steady diet of these two gentlemen as sources for writing became surfeiting and at times indigestible.

8. All of the teachers of a school should share equally this task of supervising the English writing.[14] For almost seventy years it has been recommended that teachers in other subject areas have a certain responsibility to require that their students meet certain minimum standards of organization, clarity and mechanics. As more of our colleagues in the other disciplines realize their responsibility in improving their students' written work, our efforts will be more successful. The Professional Growth pamphlets of the Arthur C. Croft Publications on "Writing—Everybody's Job" showed how this cooperation is going on in many parts of the country.[15]

9. A good textbook in composition and rhetoric may be used for reference and for occasional exercises but for little else.[16] As one studies the multitudinous textbooks which have been written for high schools during this century, he is impressed by several significant changes.

The earliest books were almost all written by college teachers. George R. Carpenter of Columbia University, an author of Carpenter, Baker and Scott's *Teaching of English* (1903) wrote a series of books beginning in 1891 with *Exercises in Rhetoric and English Composition*. Fred Newton Scott, another co-author of that methods text, with J. V. Denny wrote another series beginning with *Composition—Rhetoric* (Boston: Allyn & Bacon, 1897). Ashley H. Thorndike, then of Northwestern University, wrote *The Elements of Rhetoric and Composition* (New York: The Century Co., 1905). Franklin T. Baker, the third author of the well-known methods book, had his own *English Composition,* written with Herbert B. Abbott Smith (New York: Henry Holt, 1908). Even as late as 1913 we had Thomas H. Briggs of Teachers College and Isabel McKinney of Eastern Illinois State Normal School write *A First Book of Composition for High Schools* (Boston: Ginn, 1913).

It was unusual indeed for a high school English teacher in the early decades of this century to write a composition textbook. One of the first was Charles Maurice Stebbins' *A Progressive Course in English for Secondary Schools,* which appeared in 1905 (New York: Sibley & Company).

Another change in the composition texts is shown in their nomenclature. Thus, to show the new emphasis on the dynamics of English, J. C. Tressler began his *English in Action* series which is now in its eighth edition.[17] And to show the pleasure that might be had, another publisher has issued *Enjoying English.*[18] The emphasis on action is seen also in the *Building Better English* series.[19] To show the personal aspect, another publisher has the *Your Language* series.[20] The modernity of another series is found in the *Guide to Modern English* series.[21]

A third change in the composition textbooks is their more interesting and attractive formats. Perhaps the best statement is from W. Wilbur Hatfield in his "A Quick Look Back":

Place any high school English text of 1911 beside the handsomely bound, attractively printed, beautifully and pertinently illustrated successor of 1960! And the present model is as much superior in content as in appearance.[22]

10.   Composition correction has changed from a pursuit in red ink by a bleary-eyed teacher-detective to a constructive evaluation which is shared by the student-writer and the class. Almost sixty years ago, Alfred M. Hitchcock, a prodigious author of composition textbooks, wrote his now classic essay, "A Composition on Red Ink" for *The English Leaflet* of the New England Association of Teachers of English. It is still meaningful today, and its twelve-point program for theme correction should be standard operating procedure.[23]

Many other teachers' manuals, methods books and magazine articles have gone into ways and means of lightening the burdens of correction of themes, and it is needless to repeat them here. The point I am trying to make is that for sixty years teachers apparently have been quite effective in improving their students' writing without going blind or having a nervous breakdown in the process.

11.   About fifty years ago, the extra-class outlets for students' writings began to be emphasized. Today there is hardly a high school of any considerable size which doesn't have a student newspaper, a literary magazine or an annual. Many teachers know the volumes *Creative Youth* and *Creative Power* which were so popular in the 1920's and which gave encouragement to so many teachers who were of the opinion that youth could be made to enjoy writing, even verse.[24]

12.   It is a mistake, too, for the teacher to allow himself to be thought of as an unscientific and unlearned person who merely knows how to say things. He is instead an expert in adolescence.[25] It is obvious that the revelations of character in writing and the sympathetic understanding by the teacher of composition may be among the most powerful influences in the entire elementary and secondary program. We probably can all testify to the influence of a wise teacher of English upon our own lives.

13.   Finally, we come to the recognition of the individual, which is such a frequent rallying cry among our professional colleagues everywhere. Today we still are struggling to find ways to individualize instruction in composition. Such publications as *Adjusting to Individual Differences in English* by Olive S. Niles and Margaret J. Early show us how much can be accomplished even in large classes.[26] If we had to designate the decade 1960–1970 by any title, we probably would call it the decade of the recognition of the individual.

Time does not permit discussion of many other fascinating aspects of the changes in written composition of the last half-century, such topics as:

Best methods of motivation.

The effect of research upon composition instruction.

Frequency of writing and its effect upon improvement.

Grammar and usage in composition instruction and their relation to excellence.

The place of semantics and structural linguistics.

The influence of the home as a factor in learning to write.

I should like to include another of the brief compositions which were written by my students. I asked them to discuss either "How I Developed an Interest in Writing" or "Why I Learned to Dislike Writing." One student wrote:

A teacher enamoured by the written word; a teacher and a student; one overwhelmed by the music of poetry, was the inspiration of many of the written words of my own.

Indeed, what can be more effective than love, love for what you know and the desire to share it with your students? What can be more inspirational in the field of communication than the desire and the need to communicate? For myself, I can say that I have always written my best, and the most, when I had a teacher who cared. That is a teacher who cared about what I had to say, a teacher receptive to my thoughts and my desires. To me this is the most important quality of any English teacher, or of any other subject for that matter.

For writing is not mere technique, it is a means of expression, of communication. And one is most inspired to express oneself, to communicate, when one is encouraged to think and is assured of a recipient. This is the function of an English teacher. It is not merely to teach grammar—this can be learned from any textbook—but to impress upon the student the importance of self-expression and communication and the satisfaction which can be realized only after this first step is allowed, if not encouraged.

The methods of accomplishing this are myriad, I am sure. There are probably as many methods as there are teachers. However the important thing it seems to me is not the method, for this I expect comes naturally, when one has the patience to hear the awkward expressions of a student become words profound and meaningful.

PART FOUR
TEACHING THE ART
OF LISTENING

14

WHY TEACH LISTENING?

The subject of listening is not new in the history of the cultural development of mankind. Long before man tried to communicate his thoughts in written form, whether in ideograph or alphabet, he communicated them orally. The cultural traditions were handed down from speaking father to listening son. Even today, peoples of the Orient rely more on the retention of large bodies of important knowledge by repetition and memorization of the spoken word than do the western peoples. From the listeners of blind Homer to the millions of our contemporaries who may be watching a United Nations broadcast on television, there has been a tradition of communication through reading and listening.

Listening has been so familiar to us as a daily experience that we have taken for granted that it has been developed in our students. It is only within recent years that we have begun to realize that, just as students now come into the secondary school unable to read, so they are unable to grasp meanings, concepts, appreciations through listening.

We have always lived in a world where listening occupied most of our waking time. Rankin pointed out as far back as 1926 that we spend about forty-five percent of each day in listening, thirty percent in speaking, sixteen percent in reading, and nine percent in writing. Yet the amount of instruction in effective listening has been rather incidental, haphazard, or nonexistent until comparatively recently. Most teachers have assumed that their students would learn to listen as naturally as they learned to speak. Just as we have gradually become resigned to the realization that from twenty-five to thirty-five percent of our secondary school students are retarded in reading and need a program of remedial and developmental reading, so we are beginning to realize that a considerable percentage of our students have not learned to listen for comprehension and that an even larger percentage cannot listen discriminatively or appreciatively.

It was thought in the early days of printing that a populace that could read the printed page would therefore develop into a more civilized and cultured group. The sad spectacle of the most literate nation in Europe falling sway to the deceptive spoken words of Hitler smashed once and for all the notion that a well-read people was necessarily a discriminating or thoughtful one. The era of dictatorship and totalitarianism has indicated to the world that our future civilization may be saved or destroyed by those who listen. The totalitarian governments have long known what we are only now reluctantly admitting: namely, that the great masses of the people are more easily swayed by what they hear than by what they read. It was that realization which prompted the formation of the National Psychological Strategy Board during World War II, to spend millions to tell our side of the story of our domestic and foreign policies to the peoples of the world.

We then, as English teachers, must teach listening because the spoken word is becoming more and more the powerful medium of communication.

Our students must be trained to listen for the purpose of comprehension. Who among us has not had the almost daily experience of discovering that although we have tried to be interesting, exciting and dramatic, our students have absorbed only a fraction of what we have presented? We petulantly call it "not paying attention." It is actually nonlistening.

It is rather disconcerting, too, that even those of us who meant to be attentive in our listening have discovered how little we retain of what we have heard. How wise and clever we should all be if we could remember even a fraction of the college lectures we heard on literature, history, science, philosophy and education! The saddest fact in the history of culture is the certainty of forgetting. And it is precisely because we are destined to forget so much of what we have heard that we must learn to remember more of the important things.

Psychologists have long told us how quickly we forget what we have learned. We as teachers must train our students to learn through listening in such a manner that they will retain most vividly and most fully.

Making our students walking encyclopedias of information acquired through the senses, however, has long been discarded as an important goal of education. The author well remembers how the head of the chemistry department of his university admitted one day that he did not know the answer to a student's question. Some of us were surprised to hear him state that he was not expected to remember every fact in chemistry. What was important, he declared, was that he could go to the exact reference work and get the answer in a few minutes. He had learned to discriminate as far as his memory was concerned between the essential and the less important. In teaching the art of listening, we must impress upon our students the necessity for critical evaluation of what we hear. This is a second major reason for teaching listening. First comes comprehension, but more important is critical evaluation. We have long said the same in the teaching of reading: "Do not believe everything that is in print just because it is written down." Verily the truth shall set ye free, but the truth is not necessarily set in type. Francis Bacon tells us that we should read not to contradict but to weigh and consider. Similarly we must devise ways of teaching our youngsters to weigh and consider what they hear. That this is a more difficult undertaking than the similar deliberation of the printed word is obvious. We may always return to the printed page to ponder every word and phrase, to grasp every nuance of meaning. The spoken word cannot be subjected to such an analysis. Yet it will be the spoken word which will move our generation toward good or evil. "As the world grows more ominously voluble by the hour," states Professor Wendell Johnson of the University of Iowa, "the words we hurl at each other are no more confusing and maddening, or clarifying and calming, than our habits of listening permit them to be. Until they reach our ears they are mere sound waves, gentle breezes, harmless as a baby's breath. It is through the alchemy of listening that they become transformed into the paralyzing and convulsant toxins of distrust and hate—or the beneficent potions of good will and intelligence.[1]

The necessity for teaching listening for comprehension and for evaluation is obvious to all of us. Students at all levels of education need instruction in listening as part of the regular curriculum. As the study of listening gets the attention from educators that it deserves, we undoubtedly shall build up a structure of information which can be utilized by all of us. Remedial and developmental listening will be taught just as are the equivalent phases in reading. Writing in 1949, Professor James I. Brown of the University of Minnesota decried the fact that there were over 26,000 worthy articles on reading in the professional journals and only about a score on listening. Today there are over one thousand professional articles on various phases of listening and more are appearing constantly.

A few areas deserve our special attention. They are listening for enjoyment, for the improvement of oral expression, and for literary appreciation. Listening for enjoyment brings up the whole matter of radio listening, which occupied the attention of researchers in this field thirty years ago. When it was discovered that our students were spending an average of two hours a day listening to their radios (a greater amount of time on leisure listening than on leisure reading), alert teachers began to realize they would be remiss in their duties if they did not take advantage of this medium of communication. The National Council of Teachers of English in 1941 published that excellent volume *Radio and English Teaching* edited by the late Max J. Herzberg.

Closely allied to the utilization of radio in the teaching of listening for enjoyment is the use of recordings and transcriptions. The tape recorder, the record-player, the cassette and other devices used to preserve sound have untouched educational possibilities, and the gifted teacher will learn ways to utilizing them. Even the commercial theater has given a prominent part to the tape recorder. The radio, television and the comics have shifted the emphasis in communication away from the printed word in type. Rather than deplore that we are living in a nonreading generation, we must seize our opportunities to instruct in these new mass media. They never will replace the written word and, in fact, can be utilized to direct students toward the printed page for additional information, for new pleasures, for a more varied treatment.

It may be appropriate at this time to mention that most interesting series of experiments which was conducted in the Phoenix, Arizona, schools and which has been published in *Projects for Listening*. Experiments are described in the attempt to answer the following questions:

1. How can we evaluate experiences in appreciative listening?
2. What do students gain from listening to a discussion of group reading?

3. What can students learn by listening to each other?
4. What do we learn by listening to people?
5. What do students listen to and remember?
6. What kinds of listening experiences do students have?

The answers that are given justify many times over all the time and effort invested in these experiments and lead one to wish that teachers all over the country would attempt similar experimentation.

The need of teaching listening for the improvement of oral expression is clear to all of us. It is obvious that the child learns his mother-tongue by listening. When he comes to school, his speech is such as would be learned in the immediate environment. In school he enlarges his vocabulary of comprehension and speaking; he adopts new speech patterns based on the correct speech of his teachers. In communities where English is not necessarily the language spoken at home, this function of the English teacher is most important. Speech teachers have been aware for several years that their subject no longer is confined to the various ways of making different types of speeches but is as much concerned with listening to the speeches as with content and delivery.

Listening for literary appreciation has long been a cardinal tenet of our objectives in English. English teachers agree that for drama and poetry, at least, enjoyment should come from hearing good readers or actors.

Instruction in the appreciation of the drama is at least one hundred years old in the United States. There is still room for instruction in how to listen to a play. In Alan Downer's book *The British Drama,* we are told that the Elizabethan audiences had "an incomparable ear for verse, an intellectual delight in word play." What was to the illiterate groundlings a daily experience—namely, the appreciation of blank verse—became a topic for esoteric discussion in the 70's. Is it too much to hope that we may expect to say of the playgoers of any large metropolis of our country what Downer says of the Elizabethan Londoners: "A large percentage of Londoners had become habitual playgoers experienced in following through a complex plot and appreciative of poetic speech"?[2]

Still another aspect of listening concerns the various types of students we are receiving in our secondary schools today. Experimental psychologists say that some of us are more sensitive to the auditory stimuli, some to the visual. We know that there are some students who will not learn readily from the printed page. They may learn more from listening to a teacher who knows their needs and interests and abilities. Interesting experiments are being conducted in various parts of the country on ways to teach students with low I. Q.'s. Such listening experiences as interviewing, the psychodrama and the sociodrama have led to hopeful results. In New York City, by the use of FM broadcasts from the Board of Education's own station, interests have been aroused in such students who ordinarily would be maladjusted, who would wait only for their dropout age, and who would be problems to their teachers and to themselves.

Ambrose Bierce defined a bore as a person who talks when you want him to listen. In this hurried generation of ours, when he who reads frequently must run to have time to listen, the gentle art of listening to others is rapidly losing out.

The art of living with dignity has always been identified with the art of gracious listening. The age of the great conversationalists was the age of the great listeners as well as the great talkers. Listening for gracious living is, therefore, another aspect of this subject. It has been said of the late Ethel Barrymore that she could inspire her fellow-actors to great heights because she made them all feel she was really listening to what they said. Our students need to be taught the art of listening to others so that the minds and the hearts of two people will be bridged.

Finally, what can the teacher of English do to help students in listening? Rather than give a detailed list of suggestions and devices, it seems that the following three courses of action are desirable:

1. Each teacher of English and of every subject, for that matter, must value the tremendous importance of the spoken word in the lives of the children of today and must resolve to make proper provision to prepare them to listen accurately, completely, discriminatively and appreciatively. Having made that resolution, it is incumbent upon him to familiarize himself with some of the outstanding statements of the philosophy and objectives of the teaching of listening such as those by Harold Anderson, Wilbur W. Hatfield, James I. Brown, John Caffrey, Mildred M. Finch, Paul T. Rankin and H. W. Wells.

2. Many articles already have appeared in the professional journals which describe actual procedures, and it behooves us to acquaint ourselves with this literature. Following are the names of some of the pioneer methodologists in the field: Althea Beery, Evelyn F. Carlson, Leonore Dakin, Earl J. Dias, Sam Duker, Bernice Freeman, J. N. Hook, Muriel G. Jacobs, Ruth Ann Korey, Jessie Mercer, Nathan Miller, George Murphy, Ralph G. Nichols, Elizabeth Goudy Noel, Francis J. O'Reilly, and Miriam E. Wilt. Their procedures are by no means definitive or ideal, buy they indicate some of the methods which have been successful on the elementary, high school and college levels. Practically every series of English textbooks that I know of has devoted substantial sections to units in listening. They merit each teacher's examination and study.

3. There is need for constant experimentation and evaluation on the part of each teacher. You would be amazed at what you could accomplish with a little thought and ingenuity. Having once adopted the general philosophy of the teaching of creative listening, you will discover that ideas, devices and procedures will occur to you as they have in other areas of English, which will make the teaching of this skill a true adventure for yourselves and for your students.

The Good Gray Poet tells us: "I hear America singing." Are we preparing our students to listen to that voice?

15

DEVELOPING COMPETENCE IN LISTENING
IN SECONDARY SCHOOLS

The student of speech and drama cannot help being amazed at the fact that 15,000 spectators of the theatre of Dionysius in Athens could hear the greatest of all tragedies in open daylight, without any artificial means of voice magnification. How much more amazing is the number of listeners today to a radio or TV speaker who may be heard in almost all parts of the world! That one should be heard by 100-million or even 500-million people simultaneously seems beyond credibility, but radio and TV communication have made it possible. The first landing on the moon was witnessed by hundreds of millions of people all over the world.

Listening today is the dominant means of sensory comprehension. It has been so for most of mankind's past, with the exception of those few hundred years when the printed word became an important medium for the transmission of facts and ideas. Today, the radio, motion pictures and television are capturing the attention of our secondary school and college populations as the printed word never could. It is commonplace now that our students listen much more than they read as a means of acquiring information, ideas and attitudes. In this hurried and confused age when he who reads must run, listening has come into its own again as the primary means of acquiring facts and opinions.

As English teachers, we cannot afford to forget that in approximately ninety-five percent of the homes of this country radios and/or TV sets are operating on an average of five hours a day. We dare not estimate the number of homes in which good reading is carried on five hours a day. Nor can we ignore the 80-million television sets in American homes in 1975. It is a common experience for us to discover in our classes the paucity of knowledge about cultural matters in our students. Some of us long ago gave up trying to develop aesthetic concepts and would settle for the understanding of simple printed matter. Yet, it cannot be denied that our students have absorbed an impressive amount of their information and ideas from non-written sources. Listening, not reading, has given them information or misinformation about themselves, their communities and the world at large. For every fact which a student can trace to a book, there are many more that can be traced to the spoken word.

The history of educational method is largely the history of listening, whether it be in the nursery school or in the graduate seminar in linguistics. In the secondary school, students spend most of their day listening either to their teachers or to their classmates. The proportion of school time devoted to non-listening activities is relatively small. When the adolescent leaves school for home he engages in additional listening activities: directions from his parents or older members of the family, conversation with friends and neighbors, programs on radio and television. Rankin discovered in the 1920's we spend about forty-five percent of our waking time each day in listening; later studies by Bird set the figure at sixty-three percent.

In view of the important part which listening plays in the daily lives of our students, it is disappointing that so few scientific studies have been made of the most effective ways of teaching the development of listening ability. In this regard, it is significant that one of the articles in the first issue of the *Journal of Communication* (May, 1951) was entitled, "Needed Research in Listening Communication." Rather than list the many areas in which research in listening is desirable, we can indicate some definitely established facts about listening which the secondary school teacher should know. Regarding listening in general, the following facts are worth remembering:

1. Reading and listening seem to be of approximately equal efficiency as media of learning.
2. Reading and listening are closely related skills.
3. Variations in the rate of assimilation do not significantly alter the comparative efficiency of the two processes.
4. Almost all students are afflicted with a number of very bad listening habits.
5. Effective listeners possess and practice certain specific skills.[1]

The last two generalizations are most challenging to the teacher of English or Speech. To these, a sixth might be added: training in listening skills brings about decided improvement.[2] Several of the students of listening have stated cogent reasons for instruction in this neglected area. Perhaps the best summary is by James I. Brown, one of the pioneers in listening research:

1. Listening is the most frequently used of the language arts.
2. Critical listening is more difficult than critical reading.
3. The most important affairs of this country are carried on around the conference table.
4. We cannot excuse ourselves by saying that people automatically and without effort learn how to listen effectively.
5. We cannot claim that in every respect except listening there are individual differences which must be taken into consideration in planning and conducting educational experiences.[3]

Lou LaBrant sums it up briefly in her statement: "Teaching young people to be listeners may be of more importance than teaching them to read or to write."[4]

J. C. Tressler as far back as 1950 stated: "Radio, motion pictures, television and telephones have made our generation the most talked to people in history."[5] Yet this does not mean that our students are making the most of their listening activities. Being exposed to auditory stimuli is not listening. It may be partial listening or even non-listening. The obvious distinction between hearing and listening is that in the latter case some significance is attached to the aural stimuli. J. N. Hook defines the kind of listening we teachers hope for as "the conscious, purposeful registration of sounds upon the mind, and it leads to further mental activity."[6] A more descriptive definition given from the speech teacher's point of view is that of Baird and Knower:

Profitable listening requires more of the listener than his presence. He must recognize the ideas presented, evaluate the ideas presented, discover relationships among them, and select from what he hears those ideas he finds worth remembering. If a listener makes his listening a thoughtful process, he controls his own thinking; if he does not listen critically, he is little more than a sponge, and often not a very good one.[7]

Just as reading is an all-inclusive term that encompasses many kinds of activities of extracting meaning from the printed page, so listening has been divided into the following types. Writing as a teacher of speech for secondary schools, Karl F. Robinson lists these purposes of listening:

1. Listening in order to recognize and discriminate (speech sounds, especially, but also words, inflection, etc.).
2. Listening for information, facts, ideas, principles, with recall as a goal.
3. Listening for pleasure, entertainment or enjoyment.
4. Listening in order to make an intellectual judgment, to criticize, to evaluate ideas.
5. Listening to appreciate (to make an aesthetic judgment).[8]

Other classifications of the types and/or outcomes of listening have been made by Harlen M. Adams,[9] W. W. Hatfield[10] and J. N. Hook.[11]

It is obvious that different degrees of mental alertness are required for the realization of the different purposes of listening.[12]

HOW TO TEACH THE ACHIEVEMENT OF THE VARIOUS PURPOSES OF LISTENING

Creative teachers are convinced that secondary students will learn anything better if they are convinced of its importance for themselves. This is why so many of the pioneers in listening instruction have stressed discussion by students of the importance of good listening and its positive elements. Students frequently will bring forth conclusions that might do credit to their more experienced teachers. Among those who have reported such discussions are Jessie Mercer,[13] Lou LaBrant,[14] Harlen M. Adams,[15] J. N. Hook[16] and Lucile Lohnas.[17]

Textbooks on technical English and speech have included many activities along this line, including those by J. C. Tressler,[18] Sterling, Olsen and Huseby,[19] Gray and Hach,[20] Weaver and Borchers[21] and Hedde and Brigance.[22] It might be profitable for any teacher in secondary school to compare the conclusions of her students on what constitutes good listening with those arrived at by Miss Lohnas' class:

1. Have desks clear; sit in comfortable position with eyes on speaker.
2. Show by expressive faces that you are "with" the speaker.
3. Be patient if he has difficulty.

4. Be able to offer intelligent criticisms.
5. If the final bell rings, do not interrupt the speaker.
6. "Listen unto others as you would have them listen to you."

Miss Mercer's class concluded that good listening is characterized by quietness, appreciation, discrimination and reflection.

A natural transition from characteristics of good listening in general to the different purposes or outcomes now can be made. Students probably will formulate most if not all of the major purposes. The natural question arising would concern how to develop each of the listening skills required for achieving the purpose indicated.

Let us assume that a unit is to be developed on listening for information, facts, ideas and principles, with recall as a goal. This is a listening skill which students will need throughout their years of secondary school, their college career and their lives. Instruction either has been generalized or specific in this area. For example, Hedde and Brigance list seven basic principles of good listening, which include:
1. Get ready to listen.
2. Start listening with the first sentence.
3. Get the central idea.
4. Get the chief supporting idea.
5. Separate the important from the unimportant.
6. Make mental summaries.
7. Analyze what you hear.[23]

Similarly, J. C. Tressler gives these five general rules for improving listening:
1. Stay awake.
2. Look as if you were listening.
3. Force yourself to pay close attention.
4. Be interested. The time will pass faster.
5. Follow the questions your classmates ask and your teacher's explanations.[24]

Sterling, Olsen and Huseby likewise have a generalized list of rules.[25]

So much for student discussion and some general rules. One principle of teaching listening which is characteristic of all good teaching is establishing a purpose for the particular activity. W. W. Hatfield in a most stimulating article on "Parallels in Teaching Students to Listen and to Read" stated this principle clearly: "Purposeful listening, like purposeful reading, is more successful than that which is without purpose."[26] J. N. Hook refers to this precept in his suggestions to the teacher on listening.[27]

Various exercises have been suggested for listening to remember facts. Sterling, Olsen and Huseby,[28] J. C. Tressler,[29] Bernice Freeman[30] and J. N. Hook,[31] describe such activities. It has been discovered that students will recall more facts if they are told beforehand that they will be tested on the contents of the passage read aloud. The listening experience may be a newspaper article, a radio broadcast, a student dramatization, a tape recording or a conversation.

Sooner or later the subject of taking notes will arise, and instruction will have to be given. Weaver and Borchers, in their chapter on "Creative Listening" in their book *Speech*, give these rules for taking notes:
1. Have pencil or pen and notebook ready when the speaker begins.
2. Do not try to make a full word-by-word record of any considerable part of the

speech. Listen and note words, phrases and figures which will help in recalling the most important statements.

3. Be especially alert for points which the speaker emphasizes in his presentation. If he is a good speaker, he will indicate the relative importance of the various parts of his speech by the way in which he delivers them.

4. When the speaker has finished discussion of one point, watch carefully for what he says concerning his next point; often he will state this in a topic sentence.

5. It is usually more helpful to put down a striking phrase than it is to write out a complete sentence.[32]

Additional excellent suggestions on how to take notes are given by Sterling, Olsen, and Huseby[33] in their sections on "Listening to Take Notes" and "Listening by Interviewing"; by Gray and Hach in their "Rules for Taking Notes"[34] and by Smith and Littlefield in their *Best Methods of Study*.[35]

Although using the test as a means of motivating better listening is not the most modern kind of motivation, it will work with many pupils. Life is full of examples of chance remarks that became significant out of all proportion to their original meaning. The great lawyer, psychiatrist, general or statesman may recall what others would consider a minor statement and read into it some great significance. Trivia are not always trivia to the mighty mind. Students should be made to realize that there are many things said in class that were not based on the day's assignment and were not even spoken by the teacher, but which should have been remembered. Irvin C. Poley in his article "Teaching Obliquely and Testing Directly" evaluated what was being learned, and he stimulated in the pupils careful listening and thoughtful note-taking by announcing that every fortnight or so there would be a new-type, teacher-made test on miscellaneous matters, many of which came up incidentally.[36] The old story about Flaubert's instructions to Maupassant to remember what he had seen in the shop windows as they strolled along the streets of Paris might be applied here in regard to listening with greater alertness to the things spoken in and out of class.

There always will be the student who will ask why it is necessary to spend so much time in learning how to listen better, since he will never go to college and wants to become a garage mechanic. This creates a natural opportunity for motivating the need for listening to follow instructions. If all the time and money lost in the course of a single day because of failure to follow instructions given orally were calculated, it would add up to an impressive total. In school, the student who fails to follow instructions given the first time may be given a second chance. In business and in later life, he may not be so fortunate.

Several successful procedures have been described in articles and in the textbooks which are designed to teach *listening for the purpose of following instructions,* including those by J. N. Hook[37] and J. C. Tressler.[38] For example, following are the latter's six suggestions on "Listening to Instructions, Directions, and Explanations":

1. Listen to each detail carefully.
2. In your mind, picture each step.
3. If convenient, jot down notes on important points.
4. If given the chance, ask questions about doubtful points.

5. If possible, say out loud the directions, explanations or instructions.

6. In the case of instructions, repeat the directions as you carry them out. The quickest and surest way to learn a new job is to repeat your instructions as you practice.[39]

Vocational listening has been known to mankind throughout history and pre-history. It will not require much convincing on the part of the teacher to make clear the importance of this skill to those students who are going to work immediately after they graduate from secondary school.

The bane of the teacher of oral or written composition is the lack of organiza-tion in the speaking and writing of our secondary school population. We try to teach Beginning, Middle and End and all the standard ways of organizing our thoughts. Teachers of rhetoric give models of written composition for the purpose of studying their organization. In listening to a speech, students should be made aware of the organization and the effects achieved by good organization. Great speeches don't "just happen." They are prepared carefully, after much blood, sweat and tears. Students can be trained to watch for organization. One device recommended by J. N. Hook is:

. . .to review the possible methods of organization and to discuss ways of identifying the chief supporting points. A few comments on the use of transitions is *apropos* here. Then the students listen to the next assembly speaker, or to presentations by their classmates, and make analyses. Students who have been taught to listen for the organization of a talk tend to comprehend it rather well; they also tend to be highly critical of rambling discourse.[40]

J. C. Tressler in each of his volumes gives concrete suggestions on how to listen for organization.[41] He has made them specific under the titles: "How to Listen to a Speech," "Listening to a Talk," and "Hints on Listening to Understand."

Such practice in listening for organization has the two-fold benefit of improving the student's ability to summarize what he has heard and impressing him with the need for organization in his own speaking and writing. Listening for organization also was part of a project undertaken by Ollie Stratton of the Brackenridge High School, San Antonio[42] and Doris De Lap of Phoenix Union High School, Phoenix, Arizona.[43]

Every high school student who has studied *A Tale of Two Cities* is impressed with Sidney Carton's labors as Stryver's jackal, in extracting important facets of a legal case for the purpose of presentation in court. Extracting the main ideas of a speech is one of the more advanced phases of listening for comprehension. It is much more difficult than the mere recall of several items of a newspaper story. Such training is of great value for the college preparatory student who will have to read a great deal in law, medicine, engineering or literature. This skill will be necessary to him when he listens to college lectures on these subjects. Specific procedures for developing this skill have been described in articles by Earl J. Dias,[44] Harlen M. Adams[45] and W. H. Ewing.[46]

Typical of this type of exercise is the one described by Dias and summarized by Hook. Three increasingly difficult passages are read and students are required to extract the main ideas.[47] Sterling, Olsen and Huseby have an exercise called "Listening Leads" which is also designed to teach the selection of main ideas.[48]

LISTENING IN ORDER TO MAKE INTELLECTUAL JUDGMENTS, TO CRITICIZE, TO EVALUATE IDEAS

Important as is listening for comprehension, of far greater importance is listening for evaluation. Never before has mankind been exposed so mercilessly to millions of words. Each of us must make decisions on matters for which we have not the time nor energy to find adequate written reference materials. Running through the literature on the methodology of teaching listening is a warning that unless critical listening is developed, our civilization may be destroyed. Excellent statements have been made by Edgar Dale,[49] Wendell Johnson,[50] S. I. Hayakawa[51] and Lou LaBrant.[52]

Essential to democracy is making intelligent choices. Apologists of various persuasions flood the ether with their raucous or mellifluent utterances. The harassed listener or televiewer frequently has not the background for making a wise decision on a matter of great moment. The tragic case of Hitler's Germany is the classic example of the power of the spoken word to sway even a well-read nation into the paths of brutality. Critical evaluation of what is heard has long been the practice in Speech and in English classes, and numerous texts contain check-lists and other student-aids to be used when listening. In the upper terms of high school, when argumentation and propaganda are taught, the various fallacies in reasoning may be included in the listening unit.

Listening to the radio, however, offers a difficult problem in teaching critical listening. No one will deny that listening to the radio is quite different from listening to live speakers in the classroom, under the teacher's guidance. As Lou LaBrant states:

If we believe that listening to the radio requires different skills from listening to someone in the room with us, we will include radio programs in our assignments and bring into our schoolrooms recordings of such programs for study.[53]

The field of utilization of the radio in the teaching of English has been amply covered in such National Council of Teachers of English publications as *Skill in Listening*,[54] and *Radio and English Teaching*.[55] Alice P. Sterner, one of the co-authors of the first volume, has issued her own *A Course of Study in Radio and Television Appreciation*,[56] containing twenty-one units on radio. A Syllabus in Communication Arts is used in some high schools.[57]

However, merely listening to radio, either voluntarily or as an assignment, is not learning to listen critically. In addition to Alice P. Sterner's *Course of Study*, which contains a wealth of suggestions for evaluating radio programs, other authors have suggested definite procedures. Lou LaBrant describes a unit which began with a questionnaire that discovered the radio interests of the students. They then helped in preparing, summarizing and analyzing the data. In the resulting discussion, new programs were recommended, comments were exchanged, and values established.[58] In a tenth-grade class, the students compared a radio play with the printed form:

Deletions were noted. Devices for conveying line and color were discussed. A similar play and a movie were next compared. Students began to think of radio as having special techniques. Several reported that the radio play lacked color; but other experienced color in their personal visualizations. Some disliked, other enjoyed, the brevity of the radio drama. Most of them preferred listening to the radio play to the reading of drama.[59]

The ability to discriminate between a good and a bad radio program or between a radio version and the printed version of a play is of minor consideration, compared with the problem of discrimination between the true and the false. Wendell Johnson presents the dilemma vividly in his article, "Do You Know How to Listen?"

We are engulfed by a sea of sound. Only the deaf are privileged to know the peace of utter stillness. Sound is so much with us that we perform the wonder listening almost as unconsciously as the beasties afield. We listen for the most part as artlessly as we breathe. But, while under practically all circumstances Nature and the *medulla oblongata* will attend to our breathing for us, we can entrust our listening to our reflexes only at the risk of losing our birthrights.
As speakers, men have become schooled in the arts of persuasion, and without the counter-art of listening a man can be persuaded—even by his own words—to eat foods that ruin his liver, to abstain from killing flies, to vote away his right to vote, and to murder his fellows in the name of righteousness. The art of listening holds for us the desperate hope of withstanding the spreading ravages of commercial, nationalistic and ideological persuasion. Unless the gentle watchword "Listen!" becomes an arresting command, we may not halt in time the stampede of humanity in its pursuit of the enchanting tooting of the Pied Piper of Doom.[60]

To be a discriminating reader is difficult enough for the secondary school student. The discriminating listener has greater challenges. Some of them Lou LaBrant has described:

The skillful speaker who is attempting to influence opinion—and most speakers are doing just that—moves so rapidly that the listener is likely to be influenced in ways which he does not recognize. The hearer cannot interrupt, question or argue. He hears the uninterrupted speaker, who follows his own line or argument to his own chosen end. It takes great skill to compare the points made and to get at the basis of contradiction.[61]

Students who have heard a program on controversial issues frequently will have different interpretations of what the speakers said. Many of them will come away with the same viewpoints they had before they listened. In such instances, the use of recordings of radio programs or scripts, if they are available, will be helpful.

LISTENING FOR APPRECIATION

The transition from listening for critical evaluation of the thought to the manner in which the effects have been achieved is a natural one. Listening for appreciation of the beauties of poetry and drama has long been a part of the English and Speech program. There is no end to the books on reading poetry, reading drama and oral interpretation of prose and verse. The modern tools of the teacher have extended her resources. The earliest teachers of drama appreciation were essentially elocutionists, excerpt-readers attempting to convey by the power of their own voices the vocal beauties of a Julia Marlowe, a Margaret Anglin or a John Barrymore. The gifted teacher could hold her students spellbound by the beauties of her voice. Today, thanks to the magic of recorded poetry, prose and drama, the great stage successes of the past and the present may be brought into the classroom. From the Shakespeare Recording Society recordings of Shakespeare to *The Death of a Salesman, The Cocktail Party, Abe Lincoln in Illinois, The Consul, Peter Pan,* and scores of other plays come rich opportunities to develop skill in listening for appreciation. Poetry recordings produced by the National Council of Teachers of English and many others have extended the ability of the teacher of literature to instill in her children love of the "best words in the best order."

As Henry W. Wells of Columbia University has stated, "Hundreds of literary records are for sale, thousands are in a much more limited way available."[62] Many valuable teaching suggestions may be found in Adams' *Speak, Look, Listen,*[63] Sterner, Saunders and Kaplan's *Skill in Listening,*[64] *Recordings for Classroom and Discussion Groups,*[65] and in the various catalogues of commercial recording companies.[66] The best of all lists is Morris Schreiber's *An Annotated List of Recordings in the Language Arts* (N. C. T. E., 1971).

The tape recorder, which has been characterized as the greatest advance in the field of audio-visual instruction since the advent of the sound-film, is an excellent tool for teaching listening. At least four publications are at present available, indicating the many uses of this instrument. *The Nineteenth Yearbook of the Institute for Education by Radio* lists twenty-three examples of school use under the headings:

Implementation of Classroom Instruction
Making Educational Program Recordings for Class-Group Listening
Recording in Connection with Dramatics and Radio Workshop Activities
Recording Services to School.[67]

Edward G. Bernard, former Director of Audio-Visual Instruction of the New York City Public Schools, has written an excellent brochure on the tape-recorder. Vincent McGarrett, former Principal of the Francis Lewis High School of New York City, has prepared a brief brochure on *The Tape Recorder in the Classroom;* Harry Levine, Coordinator of Audio-Visual Instruction of P. S. 188 in Brooklyn, New York, has issued *Tape Recording for Schools;* the Minnesota Mining and Manufacturing Company has issued the booklet, *Tape Recording in the Classroom.* Libraries of tape recordings have been collected by the Minnesota Department of Education and Cornell University of New York, Kent State University, to mention a few.

More recently, cassettes have entered both the educational and entertainment field. Schwann's monthly *Record and Tape Guide* lists all available records and tapes, and is obtainable at most record shops all over the country.

The conscientious teacher may find satisfaction in the availability of the above-mentioned mechanical devices to assist him in his task of teaching listening. Yet the voice of the teacher will never be replaced by them, no more than the teachers themselves can be replaced by the instruments. No machine will ever be an adequate substitute for the artist-teacher, an educational truism that needs reaffirmation with the advent of each new mechanical device. Long before the invention of the phonograph or tape recorder, the reading aloud of good literature made lovers of man's most beautiful way of self-expression. The living voice of the teacher can still be the most potent influence in developing a love for the beauties of language. Whether it be the listeners of blind Homer in ancient Greece, the royal court of a German princeling in the days of the minnesingers, or a wardful of hospitalized G. I.'s in World War II listening to the late Charles Laughton read from the Bible or from Charles Dickens, people have always loved to listen to a story well told. The memoirs and diaries of our American ancestors repeatedly refer to family gatherings where the father or grandfather of the house read from Holy Scripture or Shakespeare or the classics of the day. No tape recorder or cassette player was needed to convey the never-dying beauties of the mother-tongue. Teachers must not and undoubtedly will not lose sight of the place of good oral reading on their part for the inspiration of their students. In all this mad confusion of our mechanized world, there is still an important place for oral reading by teachers, by well-trained students and by verse choirs. Many suggestions are to be found in the recent texts on methodology in English and Speech.

It would be unfortunate if, in the emphasis on critical listening and informative listening, we lost sight of the social value of courteous listening. The ages of enlightenment were also ages of gracious listening. Plato's *Symposium* implies good listening as well as good talking. The Enlightenment of the Eighteenth Century was also the era of the great conversationalists. Good conversation must have as its counterpart courteous listening. Students always should keep in mind that the good listener is frequently the socially acceptable and frequently the honored and respectable. It is rather a disturbing commentary on our time that the paid psychiatrist has become the symbol of the patient listener in our neurotic era. It would be an interesting piece of social research to study the experiences that many neurotic and psychotic cases may have had with listeners. Would there be a smaller incidence of nervous disorders if there were better listeners, if there were more time for listening to others?

LISTENING FOR ORAL IMPROVEMENT

In the hurry of our tense civilization, few have time to listen. The rapid tempo of the time has affected the speech patterns of our secondary school population. Indistinct speech, over-rapid speech, mangled speech long have been the daily linguistic stimuli of our confraternity. We have struggled valiantly with the final *ng*, the unvoiced *th*, and the many slings and arrows of outraged speech, only to feel so frequently, "What's the use?" Yet we realize that instruction in listening will contribute to improvement in speaking. The expression "mother-tongue" implies listening as the first means by which we learned to speak. If our models have been good, and we have listened well, we came to school equipped properly and ready to improve and enlarge our speaking faculties. The pronunciation of new words, their proper use in oral discourse and the automatic use of correct grammatical forms in the normal rhythm of the language were the outcomes of early classroom listening experiences. The poor speech that is noticeable in so many secondary schools today is due to many factors: foreign or underprivileged home environment, lack of desire for self-improvement, hesitancy about standing out of the crowd by closer attention to one's speech, listening laziness, or just plain lack of interest.

Teachers of speech have emphasized the importance of good listening in building better speech habits, and almost all recent textbooks contain appropriate exercises. Speech correction is greatly concerned with listening to correct sounds and their correct formation. The blackboard and the textbook alone never made a good speaker.

The English and the speech teacher today have the advantage of instruments that strengthen their effectiveness. When the lisper or careless speaker can hear himself on the tape recorder, he may be convinced of his defect and make an effort to improve it. Some of the uses of the tape recorder in this area are:

1. Helping students overcome poor speech habits, such as faulty pronunciation, poor choice of words, grammatical errors, speaking too fast or too slowly, "bunching" words and poor inflection or accent.

2. Helping students correct actual speech defects, such as nasal resonance, slurring of syllables, giving incorrect vowel values, breathiness, lisping, giving too much force to sibilants and stammering.

3. Training students to express ideas clearly, concisely, logically, and forcefully.

Mention already has been made of the use of recordings for teaching appreciative listening. Additional suggestions on methodology are given by Norman Woelfel and I. Keith Tyler in their *Radio and the School,* and summarized by Edgar Dale in his *Audio-Visual Methods in Teaching.*[68] More recently, recordings have been recommended as effective means for securing oral improvement. DeBoer, Kaulfers and Miller suggest them as an extension of the area of language experience:

If the pupils' language environment has been so underprivileged or restricted, however, that they cannot distinguish between normative and nonnormative language, it is possible that they will see little need for supplementing speech habits that are perfectly intelligible and acceptable to almost everyone whom they meet outside of school. In such cases, enrichment of language experiences with opportunities to hear standard English, and with life situations in which such English is clearly the most appropriate, becomes essential both in developing insight into what constitutes standard English and in building a desire to use it one's self. Recordings by competent actors of stories, short plays, or abridged novels from the pens of well-known modern authors provide excellent means for interesting young people in the effective use of oral English in modern life. Among such recordings are Ronald Colman's interpretation of *Lost Horizons* and *Tales from the Olympian Gods,* and Herbert Marshall's moving rendition of *The Snow Goose.*[69]

Other suggestions can be found in Robinson[70] and Sterling, Olsen and Huseby.[71] If students listen to good English long enough they eventually will develop acceptable patterns of their own. Harold A. Anderson, in one of the most stimulating of the articles on listening, speaks of the "listening climate" in the classroom.[72] Can every teacher of English be certain that the speech heard in her classroom contributes to the best patterns of our time? Is she always aware of the countless directed and incidental stimuli which she can utilize?

LISTENING FOR ENJOYMENT

It may seem to many students that no training is necessary in listening for entertainment. They will either affirm they do not need further stimulation to have a good time while listening, or say they know what they like and nobody can tell them what to like. *Chacun à son goût* or its English equivalent will frequently be met with. Yet some profitable discussion usually can take place on what constitutes humor and wit, or the varieties of humor to be found in television programs, the specific *fortes* of the prominent comedians, the enjoyment of laughter. For the brighter student, such a unit might be tied in with such celebrated studies of humor as those of Henri Bergson, Sigmund Freud, George Meredith and Max Eastman's *The Enjoyment of Laughter*. Ollie Stratton gives the following suggestion in her stimulating article, "Techniques for Literate Listening":

The assignment was: "Next Tuesday let's listen to a humorous program." Then followed a discussion of such programs and a vote to choose the one that the class as a whole would enjoy that evening. "Be able to give examples of different kinds of humor: exaggeration or understatement; peculiarities of language; play on words— parody and pun; unexpected endings; satire, irony, sarcasm; ridiculous situations; other forms that are noticed.[73]

The English or speech teacher can borrow from the teacher of music, who has long been providing enjoyable listening experiences for her students. It is common knowledge that some background information about a musical composition enhances enjoyment. In listening to stories, poems, plays or speeches, students should become aware that their enjoyment is increased in proportion to the background they bring to the experience and the concentration with which they listen. There are levels of enjoyment, the highest of which are reached by the trained and the cultured. Nor must the enjoyment be confined only to humor. Sounds, words and apt phrases can give pleasure to the initiated. Passages can be read of inspired and routine descriptions of the same scene or experience, so that pupils may be shown the pleasure which can come from the arrangement and rhythm of words. A passage from Browne's *Hydriotaphia,* Ruskin's *Modern Painters* or Pater's description of La Gioconda may be read for sheer pleasure of sound, aside from the beauty of meaning.

Extension of the pleasurable sensations from listening should be the goal of this type of instruction. The yokel who could recognize but two tunes, "Pop Goes the Weasel" and the one that wasn't, needed some enlargement of his faculties for enjoyment. It is revealing how many things students will miss in any inventory of sounds they enjoy hearing. It is not so much a question of whether heard melodies are sweet and those unheard are sweeter; we must aim to equip our students with the ability to hear melodies where before they heard mere sounds, experience enjoyment where before they were bored, enjoy every living moment where before they merely existed. Such is the essence of listening for enjoyment.

16

TEACHING THE USE OF TELEVISION

WHY TEACH THE UTILIZATION OF TELEVISION?

When the Columbia Broadcasting Company presented Joseph Papp's production of Shakespeare's *Much Ado About Nothing* in the spring of 1973, more people saw the production than all the people who had seen it since it was first presented at the Globe Theatre in 1598. Similar records were set by other productions of Shakespeare such as Maurice Evans' *Macbeth,* Laurence Olivier's *Richard III* and many other classics. No one can estimate how many tens of millions have seen John Galsworthy's *The Forsyte Saga* which first appeared on the British Broadcasting Station in the 1960's. Since our students spend several hours every day before their television sets whether we assign programs or not, it would be in the interest of more meaningful viewing if English teachers made the best possible use of this omnipresent medium.

As Theodore W. Hipple so aptly expresses it,

Few homes, even those in the nation's pockets of intense poverty, are without television. The two-television set family is as common as the two-car garage or the two-bath home. Numerous evening meals are eaten in the company of the network newscaster. Sunday's professional football games provide topics of conversation among millions of Monday morning quarterbacks, including an increasing number of women who have joined their husbands and sons among the ranks of television's superspectators. Series performers become instant heroes to the viewing public. The nation's business all but halts as the populace sits glued in fascination before the gripping spectacle of an astronaut's television moonwalk. Television has shaped Presidential elections, changed family sleeping habits, altered pre-school education, indeed, transformed American society.[1]

Although television as a means of communication is the newest of the arts, it has already stimulated many significant studies which English teachers can hardly omit if they wish to accomplish their main objectives. For example, Neil Postman's *Television and the Teaching of English* since 1961 has shown countless teachers successful ways in which to utilize this most powerful medium of communication known to man.[2] An excellent bibliography of about 100 books and articles in this volume will enrich the background of any teacher.[3] For those who are interested in television as an art form, there is *TV As Art,* a series of essays by distinguished scholars and critics commissioned in 1966 by the National Council of Teachers of English edited by Patrick D. Hazard.[4] A more recent book of readings about all media including television is Thomas R. Giblin's *Popular Media and the Teacher of English.*[5]

OBSTACLES TO CLASSROOM INSTRUCTION IN TELEVISION

One of the most frequent excuses given by English teachers for not making greater use of television is that they are often not aware of the good programs that are being presented. There are many sources of information often printed months in advance. Perhaps the best of these is *Teachers Guides to Television,* published by Edward Stanley and edited by Gloria Kirshner. It appears twice a year, in the fall and in the spring. In each issue there are listings of what the editor and publisher consider to be the programs of most educational value and study guides to many of them. Each study guide consists of the following elements: aim; suggested activities before viewing; suggested activities after viewing; for further explanation.

Bibliographies are provided in each issue by the Children's Services Division of the American Library Association.[6] These study guides are among the best in the entire field of appreciation in the mass media. Although teachers could not be expected to utilize all the recommendations, there are enough of them to be adaptable to any grade in secondary school and any type of class—slow, average or bright.

The Television Information Office is an agency funded by the National Association of Broadcasters for disseminating information about significant television programs and the appreciation of television. Its monthly listings of outstanding programs is distributed to many thousands of English teachers and other interested parties.[7] In addition to publishing its monthly television highlights, the T. I. O. also publishes occasional studies of the medium, and maintains perhaps the best equipped library on television to be found anywhere. Its services are always available to teachers and researchers. Those who cannot come to the office in New York City may write for information.

Other sources of programs that are available are:

1. *TV Guide,* which not only lists the programs one week in advance but has several interesting articles about these programs or their stars in each issue. For those teachers and students who are interested in movies that will appear that week, each issue of *TV Guide* lists them all. It is the best source of information about current TV programs available today, and its enormous circulation, running into the millions each week, testifies to its usefulness.[8]

2. *Media and Methods,* perhaps the best all-round periodical for teachers who are interested in the utilization of all the mass media, begins each issue with an annotated Telelog one or two months in advance of the presentations.[9]

3. *Scholastic Teacher* also publishes lists of programs in each issue and frequent

excellent study guides to programs especially suitable for students.[10]

4. *Education USA,* published by the National School Public Relations Association, also lists TV programs of educational interest.[11]

5. The daily newspapers, of course, are a good local source of information.

6. *Cue* magazine has a weekly listing of all sources of entertainment in the New York Metropolitan area covering New York City, Long Island, New Jersey and Connecticut.

7. Most Sunday newspapers publish the television programs for the forthcoming week and thus enable the English teacher to look ahead for suitable programs for her students.

SOME EFFECTIVE STRATEGIES AND TECHNIQUES

Becoming acquainted with suitable programs is just the first step. Such knowledge, while better than no knowledge at all, can contribute very little to developing more appreciative and sophisticated TV viewers. What the interested teacher needs now is a series of strategies and techniques that have been proven successful during the past two decades since television became a popular entertainment and educational medium.

Every textbook on the teaching of English for the past twenty years has a substantial list of activities for developing classroom appreciation of television. For example, J. N. Hook in his *The Teaching of High School English,* published in 1972, lists the following sixteen activities suitable for radio as well as television:

1. Analyzing Amount of Time Spent.
2. Discussing "Getting Your Time's Worth."
3. Preparing a Class List of Worthwhile Programs.
4. Letter Writing to Sponsors and Networks.
5. Discussing Changing Tastes.
6. Reading and Writing Reviews.
7. Summarizing Plots.
8. Estimating Probability and Truth to Life.
9. Applying Literary Tests.
10. Reading Books on Which Broadcasts Are Based.
11. Showing Kinescope or Film Versions of Good Programs.
12. Writing Original Radio and Television Plays.
13. Teaching the Power and Responsibilities of the Mass Media.
14. Analyzing Speeches.
15. Reporting Events as if Students Were Newscasters.
16. Developing a Class List of Standards.[12]

Neil Postman's *Television and the Teaching of English,* the most extensive book on the teaching of this medium, gives detailed examples of how to handle the following:[13]

1. A Special Class Assignment.
2. A Brief Unit Isolated from the Regular Curriculum. e.g., a unit on a play by Ibsen.[14]

3. A Brief Unit within the Regular Curriculum.[15] Examples are a study of the TV version of Ernest Hemingway's short story, "The Killers," or Edwin Cranberry's "A Trip to Czardis."

4. An Extensive Unit, dealing with a study of television programs as an expression of American life.[16]

Theodore W. Hipple in his *Teaching English in Secondary Schools* (1973) lists additional successful experiences in English classes under the headings, The Study of Television and Television as an Adjunct to Other Aspects of English.[17]

Hardly any curriculum in English appears today without a substantial section on Television Study. Based on an examination of many recent curricula and my own teachers' practices, the following suggestions should stimulate each teacher and supervisor of English to adapt whatever items are most suitable to each situation.[18]

While the topics are arranged in outline form on a semester basis, any teacher can feel free to select whatever topics belong to an earlier grade for a later one and vice versa. Enough provision has been made for individualization of instruction to satisfy all needs of the contemporary classroom situation.

Ninth Year-First Half

Topic: What does the public get for its money?

1. How does the public pay for television programs?
   a. Sponsored programs
   b. Sponsored vs. sustaining programs
   c. Public service programs
   d. Educational programs such as the Corporation for Public Broadcasting
2. Vocabulary of TV terms: *Sponsor, sustaining, commercial, public service, educational cable television, network, local station, "huckster," advertising agency cable television*
3. The pros and cons of advertising on television
4. Comparison of American Television with that of the British Broadcasting System

Ninth Year-Second Half

Topic: Study of the types of daytime programs.

1. What is a soap opera?
   a. Who listens and why?
   b. What values does it have for the listener?
   c. If you don't like it what do you recommend in its place?
2. Sustaining programs
   a. Definition
   b. Why are most sustaining programs on the air during the daytime hours and the late evening hours only?
   c. Which type of station (local or network) can offer better day-time programs?

d. What suggestions would you make for improving daytime and sustaining programs?

Tenth Year-First Half

Topic: Discussion of public issues on television.

1. Free Speech on television.
   a. What guarantees are there for free speech on the air?
   b. Who guarantees it? How?
   c. How are election campaigns handled on the air from the viewpoint of fair play?
   d. Have you ever heard a program on the air that you considered one-sided?
   e. How does the viewer secure fair play on such programs?
   f. Describe several programs of public discussion that you are familiar with; for example, *Meet the Press, Face the Nation, Newsmakers.*
2. How are television programs influenced for good or evil?
   a. Political pressures
   b. Network pressures
   c. Advertising agency pressures
   d. Private censorship agencies
   e. Government regulation of television. How does it operate?
   f. The influence of the Federal Communication Commission
   g. How does our system compare with that in England, France, U. S. S. R., China, from the point of view of regulation?

Tenth Year-Second Half

Topic: Guides for judging television programs.

1. Evaluative Criteria. Although tastes may differ, intelligent persons choose and judge television programs on the basis of certain standards. Here are a few:
   a. Is the advertising excessive, misleading, in poor taste?
   b. Does the TV program express false ideas of life and/or false values?
   c. Is the program free from propaganda or faulty reasoning?
   d. Are the actors outstanding, mediocre, downright poor?
   e. Does the program assume that you have at least an average intelligence; or is it condescending or prejudiced?
   f. Is there good craftsmanship evident in plotting, characterization, choice of language, music, décor?
   g. Is there a worthwhile purpose noticeable behind the program and is it intelligently and appropriately accomplished?
2. Contributions from other art forms
   a. What evaluative criteria for judging literature can be applied to television?
   b. What criteria from the fine arts?

c. What criteria from music?

d. What help can come from the professional TV critics?

Eleventh Year-First Half

Topic: Judging newscasters and commentators.

1. Newscasters
   a. Is the reporting of the news accurate and impartial?
   b. Is comment on the news authoritative—based on personal experience or on a thorough knowledge of history, government, economics?
   c. Is there a plan evident—a grouping of items or a planned alternation of types of news?
   d. Is the newscaster's voice intentionally emotional and sensational?
   e. Does the newscaster spend too much time on trivialities in the news?
   f. When he or she gives an opinion, does the newscaster make it clear that it is a comment, not straight news?
   g. Does the newscaster transform unwieldy, hard-to-remember statistics into arresting familiar terms?
   h. What kind of voice does the newscaster have. How suitable is it for this type of work?
2. Commentators
   a. Does the newscaster also serve as the commentator or are there two different personalities? For example, Dan Rather on CBS as the newscaster; and Walter Cronkite as the commentator.
   b. Does the management of the station occasionally express an opinion through a special editorial commentator?
   c. How well qualified is the commentator to express an opinion that may well affect millions of viewers?
   d. What do you think should be the qualifications of a good TV commentator?
3. Comparing two newscasters. Take notes on the topics included by two newscasters during one morning, afternoon or evening.
   a. Compare the number of items of local, national, and international news.
   b. Did either newscaster omit anything of importance covered by the other?
   c. Did they report straight items or include "human interest" items? Was there a difference in the amount of detail given?
   d. If you were writing a letter to each newscaster what suggestions would you make?
   e. The same comparison techniques can be used for two commentators or editorial personalities.

Eleventh Year-Second Half

1. Judging the television play
   a. Does the action begin immediately and move rapidly toward the climax?

b. Is the plot probable, avoiding reliance on coincidence and far-fetched events?

c. Are the characters clearly differentiated?

d. Are the characters individuals or stereotypes?

e. Is each character consistent throughout the play with the personality presented at first?

f. Is the music appropriate?

g. Are the costumes and décor appropriate?

h. Does the play convey a significant idea?

i. How has the director contributed to the excellence of the play?

2. The effect of television programs on behavior and morals. Have the class discuss either as a whole or in committee some or all of these topics:

a. Does television contribute to crime by its various crime programs?

b. Do horror stories have an adverse effect upon the easily impressed person?

c. How does the speech of television actors affect the listeners of secondary school age?

d. Does television watching have a deleterious effect upon students' study habits? Can one watch a reasonable amount of television daily and still do one's required homework?

e. Does watching television destroy the habit of reading? Has any student ever read a book because of its TV adaptation? Which did he prefer? Why?

f. Would television be improved by a tax on TV viewers as in the case with the BBC in England?

g. What advantages are there to cable television?

h. Have you ever watched an "Emmy" award presentation? What effect did it have upon you?

i. Write to the U. S. Government Printing Office, Washington, D. C. for a report of the hearings on the effect of violence on television upon the listeners. Study it and report to the class on the significant findings. There will be a nominal charge for this and similar publications.

Twelfth Year-First Half

1. How to Improve Television Programs. Discuss the following ways to improve programs.

a. Use of ratings such as the Nielsen ratings

b. Use of opinion polls such as the Gallup and Harris polls

c. Writing to authors, sponsors, networks about good or bad programs

d. Having a Board of Consultants for each network

e. Having an Ombudsman for the television industry to hear complaints

f. Boycotting objectionable programs

g. Allowing representative citizens to sit in on previews of forthcoming programs

h. Improving television criticism

i. Making kinescopes available for schools for study purposes

Twelfth Year-Second Half

1. Intensive study of some outstanding current programs.
   a. Using the criteria elaborated in the first seven terms, evaluate some of the outstanding programs in such areas as drama, news, documentaries, spectaculars, serials, etc.
   b. Students may form in committees each concentrating on one *genre* for intensive study and then reporting to the class.
   c. Papers might be written on various aspects chosen by students.
   d. Resource persons might be invited to discuss topics of their special competencies.
   e. Visits might be arranged to the local TV station to watch a live interview, news broadcast, or play being performed.
   f. For gifted students there should be opportunities to write their own TV plays and have them produced in their English classes or on the stage before the entire school. Other students might write documentaries, interviews, etc.
   g. Students might be asked to keep scrap books of television criticisms over a semester to notice the trends in plays, documentaries, news programs. A prize might be awarded for the best one.

Television is here to stay and it is our responsibility to either prepare our students to become more sophisticated viewers or let them develop their own tastes. Long experience of many devoted teachers has proven that time spent in developing better viewing habits in school paid rich dividends in future years. If the better programs on television today are much more numerous than they were five or ten years ago, then we may be certain that instruction in television viewing by forward-looking teachers has played an important role. The future of television is in the hands of many people: its writers, producers, actors, directors, and all those who participate in this astonishing industry; but it also depends upon the growing awareness of excellence on the part of future adult watchers. English teachers cannot afford to take their challenge lightly.

PART FIVE
LIGHTENING THE BURDEN OF
THE ENGLISH TEACHER

17

HOW TO PLAN A LESSON

It is almost axiomatic today that government agencies, big business, colleges and other public institutions have officers in charge of planning and development. Planning for effective action is a by-word in almost all walks of life. Planning for more effective classroom teaching has been urged from the first time an educator prepared to write a textbook on methods of teaching English. Today most methods books in English have a section or chapter on planning the lesson.

As early as 1902, Percival Chubb in his pioneer work, *The Teaching of English,* wrote:

We have more than once laid stress upon the initial importance of planning one's work. Good, clear, large planning is indispensable.[1]

Writing the following year, Carpenter, Baker and Scott in their *Teaching of English in the Elementary and the Secondary School* likewise emphasized the value of planning:

Some plan, however, the teacher must have: a few large points, carefully thought out and associated firmly in his mind with a considerable number of details.[2]

Through the past seventy years similar expressions of the importance of planning one's lesson can be found in such authorities as Dorothy Dakin,[3] Craig,[4] Stratton,[5] Hook,[6] Loban, Ryan and Squire,[7] Fowler[8] and many others.

THE NEED FOR PLANNING LESSONS

The field of English is so vast and the time so limited even under the best of teaching conditions that the teacher must plan carefully if he is to achieve even his minimum objectives. Perhaps the greatest enemy of effective teaching is the inevitable bell which signals the end of the English period. Sometimes the best plans do not succeed, but no plans at all surely will lead to wasted efforts on the parts of both teachers and students and to frustration and failure to master the skills, appreciations, knowledges and attitudes which comprise the field of English.

The inspired teacher frequently will explain his lack of planning by claiming he will be hampered and restricted. Chubb answered that fallacy when he stated:

Plans are essential even for the most inspired, just because they are inspired. Their inspiration must be under control; and it must be assisted and get its chance by being unhampered by any anxiety as to the purpose it is serving. Inspiration runs to waste if it is not wisely employed.[9]

ELEMENTS OF GOOD LESSON PLANNING

In planning a single lesson or a series of related lessons, there are indispensable elements to be considered:
1. The objectives, remote as well as immediate.
2. The nature of the class.
3. The content.
4. The materials at hand with which to achieve the objectives.
5. The most effective teaching procedures.
6. The learning activities of the students.
Modifications will result depending on the nature of these factors. For example, the teaching procedures in a drill lesson will differ from those of the appreciation lesson. Slow-learning students will be asked to perform certain activities in mastering English skills which are unnecessary for gifted students. The teacher's activities will vary with the materials at hand. A lesson on *A Tale of Two Cities* utilizing a film will differ from a recitation on several chapters assigned the night before. A lesson using a recording of *Macbeth* or *Hamlet* will differ from one based on several questions assigned to be answered for homework.

Objectives also determine the procedures of the lesson. It is obvious, therefore, that effective lesson planning combines strategy, tactics, logistics and, in many cases, good common sense. Good intentions and a love for children help, but they do not necessarily lead to effective teaching.

Good lesson planning is hard work. But the well-planned lesson, time-consuming as it necessarily is, leads to ease and confidence in the classroom, and the teacher has the great satisfaction of contributing to an educational experience for her students which is a truly creative act. It is an old common-sense principle that you get out of your teaching just about what you put into it.

Planning the Objectives

A distinguished principal of a large metropolitan high school, on entering his term of office, decided to visit each class briefly to become acquainted with the staff, the students and the curriculum. As he entered each class, he gave a slip of paper to the student sitting beside him, containing the following questions: (1) Name of teacher? (2) Name of class? (3) What's going on?

In a certain class, a student answered the first two questions adequately, but answered the third with: "Search me." The principal, in announcing the topic for his first faculty conference, simply listed "Search Me." What ensued, because of the curiosity aroused by such an unusual first conference topic, was an excellent discussion of the need for clear objectives in the minds of both teacher and students. If the objectives are clear the teacher will not plan too much in a single period or in a series of lessons. Likewise no lesson will be over in half the period because the objective was so picayune. One candidate for a license as a teacher of English in a large metropolitan high school planned so poorly for his trial lesson in poetry that he finished long before the period ended. After many random questions which were getting nowhere and only serving to make the students more restless, he pulled a newspaper clipping out of his pocket, containing a bit of doggerel in very poor taste, and read it to the class. The verses had nothing to do with his objectives. He left the classroom a failure in the examination, another victim of bad planning of objectives and their realizations.

Long-Range and Immediate Objectives

Objectives in English have occupied the minds of the leaders of our profession since English became a subject in the secondary schools. Many statements of objectives have appeared, not one of the scores of methods books being without its statement of objectives. Elsewhere in this book, there is extensive discussion of the ultimate objectives of English. They always should be borne in mind by the perceptive teacher. *The English Language Arts in Secondary Schools* recognizes these three major goals: (1) cultivation of wholesome personal living; (2) development of social sensitivity and effective participation in group life; (3) linguistic competence necessary for vocational efficiency.

Certainly we can try to plan our lessons so that we shall not prevent or thwart the realization of these goals. If, for example, we want our students to develop social sensitivity, we shall plan by our words, our deeds and our instructional procedures to develop this highly desirable goal, rather than deprecate it or cause our students to develop negative attitudes.

Likewise, if we are constantly aware of the importance of effective communication for almost any profession or occupation today, we shall seize every opportunity to point out the value of this or that particular skill for vocational competence; this or that body of knowledge for success in one's chosen walk of life; this or that appreciation that contributes to making a finer person, hence one more respected and trusted, hence one more likely to be considered for vocational advancement.

One of the desirable goals of English teaching—and, in fact, of education generally—is good mental health. The alert English teacher does not have to teach specifically for good mental health (although this has been advocated persuasively by some) but is always aware of good mental health practices. He will not make a shy child shrink further into his shell by his tone of voice, by his way of handling an answer to his question, by any one of a dozen unsound mental health practices.[10]

Another long-range objective of English teaching is good speech. In some cases we and our colleagues in speech departments try to teach directly for acquisition of such good speech habits as clear articulation, proper intonation, pleasant pitch. Awareness of the need for good speech habits is omnipresent in the alert teacher's mind. Every lesson is, or should be, a lesson in good speech. No careless or indistinct speech should be tolerated by the English teacher in any type of lesson. It would be easier if our colleagues in other departments likewise would insist upon acceptable speech practices. This is another long-range goal to keep in mind all the time, without specifically writing in our daily lesson plan that the first five minutes will be a drill on *ng*.

Good social habits are a *desideratum* in the English class, and these too need not be planned specifically for each lesson. Every period can contribute to their development by the way students handle the answers of their fellow students, by the way they stand and speak to the class, rather than slouching in their seats and mumbling, by the words they choose in differing with others.

Other long-range habits and attitudes will quickly come to mind as the teacher becomes aware that his students are developing every day intellectually, aesthetically and emotionally, and that it is his responsibility at all times to contribute to their formation.

Planning for Immediate Objectives

Every daily lesson, in addition to contributing to long-range objectives, should have one or more specific objectives. These may range from enabling students to use quotation marks properly to appreciating Browning's "My Last Duchess"; from helping them acquire knowledge of the proper form of a business letter to appreciating the degeneration of the character of Macbeth; from learning how to use commas in a series to perceiving the significance of the terminal twist in a typical O. Henry short story.

These specific objectives may be prescribed by the school-wide, city or state syllabus in English. They may be left to the teacher who has studied his students' needs and now plans to meet them. The first question the teacher must ask is: "What do I want my students to get out of this period of time spent with me?" In answer to that question he formulates his objectives in terms of student growth. Care must be exercised to limit the objective to one that is realizable in the time available. A student doesn't learn to appreciate poetry in one lesson on Monday in the third week of the term in the junior year of high school. He may, however, sense the nature of the simplicity of Robert Frost's language in "Mending Wall"; he may appreciate the value of rhythm in Browning's "How They Brought the Good News from Ghent to Aix"; he may perceive the nature of dialect in the scenes in the Rainbow Inn in *Silas Marner*. These are a few illustrations of specific objectives which teachers may set in the domain of literary appreciation.

In the area of written composition, the student does not learn to write a composition in one lesson Friday (composition day!). He perhaps may learn that each paragraph should have a topic sentence, especially in exposition. The student may learn how to develop a topic sentence by instances and examples. He may learn to detect lack of unity in a series of poorly constructed student paragraphs and thus avoid this error in his own. Although he may not learn how to write a story like Galsworthy's "Quality" or Conrad's "The Secret Sharer" in the composition lesson, he may learn to use more vivid words than he has previously employed. He probably will not write another essay like Huxley's "On a Piece of Chalk" or Chesterton's "On Running after One's Hat," but he may learn the elements of the Harvard Outline as a means of organizing his thoughts; even the Harvard Outline is not mastered in one easy lesson.

A bookstore, selling several sets of classics designed for the busy reader who wants "culture," displayed several such sets in the window. In the center was a sign in large letters:

You Can Have These on Easy Terms.

One cannot master any branch of English "on easy terms." Chubb stated at the beginning of the century one of the cardinal principles of method:

To teach one thing at a time, but always in relation to one's plan as a whole; as an out-growth of what has gone before, and as pointing to what is to succeed.[11]

The need for specifically stating immediate aims so that provisions may be made for their realization cannot be overemphasized. Too often, however, aims are stated in terms of the teacher. They rather should be stated in terms of pupil growth. As every experienced teacher will testify, there is a vast gap between a teacher's aims and his students' mastery. One of the reasons for this gap is the failure of the teacher to put himself in the place of the student. We as English teachers cannot help thinking that our subject is the most important thing in the day's work. The high school student may study four or five other subjects, equally or more important in his eyes. Hence, we must put ourselves in place of these teenagers before us, with their tensions, their fluctuations of interests, their shifts in loyalties, their hopes and fears. How can we best build them into thinking, sensitive, humanized, responsible citizens? We cannot do this with pious hopes, with vague objectives, with derogation, sarcasm or reprimand. The first step is to formulate what we want them to learn, and then we begin the battle.

The Nature of the Class

Once the specific objectives have been realized, the nature of the class (already determined by diagnostic testing, by examination of cumulative records and by daily observation) will determine the procedures. The best objectives are those designed to meet the needs of a specific class and the individuals in that class. Hence the futility of using the same set of lesson plans term after term or even for two sections of the same grade. Some objectives, however, are prescribed in courses of study, having been arrived at after generations of teaching. For example, many students in secondary school will still make errors in sentence structure, in the use of the semi-colon, in dangling participles. These are some of the skills which are planned for in courses of study. Other skills and appreciations are anticipated because new challenges will face the students and they must be equipped to meet them. The student whose literary diet has been prose fiction and narrative poetry must learn new reading skills as he prepares to enjoy essays or plays for the first time.[12]

Certain things, therefore, will have to be taught to almost every class at a certain level in secondary schools. Yet no two classes are ever alike. Some can learn a skill or concept more quickly. Others, sometimes labelled "G" or general classes, are slow-learning in nature. A third group might be entirely of bright students, and they will require different treatment. Some classes will have many leaders who can carry the class discussion along. Others have to be pushed or dragged. Some classes have students with a friendly spirit toward one another. Others may have to be kept within bounds. In some classes, students have traveled widely, or are talented musically or artistically, and they can contribute much to the class's pace. Some classes are composed entirely of underprivileged students, and they create a learning problem. Some classes, composed of well-fed, well-housed and well-bred students, present their own problems of snobbishness, of clannishness or old-fashioned spoilage. These are a few of the factors which determine the planning of the lessons from the point of view of the class as a whole.

Providing for Individual Differences

Difficult as it is to provide for meeting the needs of the individual class, the teacher in his planning must make some provision for individual differences. The reader is referred to Chapter 3 for some of the ways in which provisions have been made for meeting the needs of individuals.[13]

Basically such differences are met in daily planning by differentiation in assignments to groups within the class or to individuals; by differentiating in questioning and treatment of answers; by provisions for variations in class procedures; by variations in textbooks, in outside reading and testing.

The Content of the Lesson

A teacher teaches something to a class. The something is the content of the lesson and must be planned carefully. This content may range from a series of short poems, a chapter in a novel or a scene from a Shakespearean play, to a series of drill exercises to eradicate misplaced modifiers. Sometimes this content may be a skill, some segment of knowledge or an appreciation. Attitudes usually are derived from the lesson and are not easily planned for because they are so intangible and individual

The content should be specific, manageable in the time allotted, and capable of being evaluated to some extent. Appreciations and attitudes are not easily evaluated, but they should be in the mind of the teacher as she plans her lesson.

In planning the content of any particular lesson, one can take the easy way out and say "pages 56 to 80 of *Silas Marner*" or "Act I of *Macbeth*," but that is not as effective as specifying the special quality of the particular content. The opening scene of *An Enemy of the People* as an example of Ibsen's method of exposition of the past is much more meaningful as content than "the first ten pages." Galsworthy's "Quality" as a study of varying values in daily work is much more meaningful than pages 50 to 55 in Zilch's *Modern Short Stories*.

Too many teachers conceive of their content as so many pages in a literature or grammar textbook. The page numbers soon are forgotten, but the significant ideas or concepts exemplified may be remembered.

Frequently the vividness of the content of a lesson will depend on the way the assignment of the day before was worded. If students have been given interesting and challenging assignments, the probability is that when the lesson takes place there will be more than mere regurgitation. There will be evaluation, revision of half-baked views, introduction of new views and at times some original thought.

Questions which a teacher should ask about the content of a lesson are:
1. Is it appropriate to this class?
2. Is it related to preceding content and does it lead to new content?
3. Has there been adequate preparation by the students for mastery?
4. Can it be covered in the time allotted?
5. Is it significant?

The Most Effective Teaching Procedures

Writing in 1930, Virginia J. Craig put her finger on a grave weakness in today's English teaching:

The fact is that many English teachers go into their classrooms knowing neither the questions that they are to ask nor the ideas and views that they wish to develop. They believe that they have planned their work because they have read the material. They somehow trust that the classroom exigencies will guide them. The result is that they are as helpless as mariners adrift without chart or compass.[14]

There are many ways to teach English. Some are more effective than others in achieving certain objectives. Some lessons consist of questions by the teacher and answers by the class. An unvaried diet of this procedure can lead to educational scurvy. Certain lessons demand more active participation by students than others. A lesson on how to write an outline without some practice by the students in outlining becomes pure verbalism. Talking about the elements of a good speech without providing many opportunities for students to speak does not make for improvement in speech.

Among the weakest procedures are those involving lessons utilizing audio-visual aids. Playing a recording without adequate preparation, suitable questions and challenging follow-up activities may fill a period but is not effective teaching. Showing a film strip or film for which the class is not prepared can be a deadly educational experience.

The art of questioning as an element in the teaching-learning process has been the subject of extensive chapters in methods textbooks. The careful teacher does not trust to the inspiration of the moment to ask the right question. These are thought out prior to the lesson and written in the lesson plan. The master teacher knows how to direct them to arouse the maximum amount of thought, how to distribute them throughout the class. Not to plan this way is to invite inconsequential questions, to repeat questions, and to engage in a kind of verbal duel more akin to cross-examination than effective teaching.

In planning procedures, the teacher should always be aware that he is teaching all four aspects of the Language Arts simultaneously. As J. N. Hook expresses it:

Therefore in the teaching of communication it is usually wise to combine the four types of activities. Instead of teaching the semicolon today, "Miniver Cheevy" tomorrow, the complex sentence Wednesday, a short story Thursday and "public speaking" Friday, it is better to plan one's work in units that will incorporate, to some extent, all four aspects of communication.[15]

Such a fourfold approach cannot be left to chance. Previewing the day's work will indicate the opportunities that will arise.

The Learning Activities of the Students

It is an educational truism going back thousands of years that we learn best when we are actively engaged in learning. The day of students as educational pitchers to be filled with educational wisdom is, or should be, over. Too often the pitchers turned out to be sieves. The more actively our students participate in the lesson, the greater the probability that they will remember and apply the content, master and apply the skill, react more sensitively to literature. To talk about sonnets to students is hardly the best way for them to develop the ability to read and appreciate them. To talk about the *ie-ei* rule in spelling is not the same as having students practice writing words containing these letters, correcting exercises and actually trying to incorporate such words into their writing.

Some of the classroom activities in which students can engage, and which should be included in lesson planning are:

1. Dramatization of scenes from plays, dialogues from short stories or novels and original work.
2. Panel discussions for reports on books, plays, films and television programs.
3. Delivering reports on research.
4. Working together in committees.
5. Writing compositions or exercises on the chalkboard, to be evaluated by fellow students.
6. Spelling bees and other types of quiz games.
7. Mock interviews.
8. Drills to establish habits.
9. Reading aloud from works studied.
10. Teaching the rest of the class with or without visual demonstrations.

Some of these activities are suitable for one type of lesson; others are more suitable for other types. The teacher must weigh and consider how best to utilize the responses of the class to achieve the objectives listed.

THE WRITTEN LESSON PLAN

Most authorities in the teaching of English would agree with Dorothy Dakin's statement:

For your daily lesson plan I believe these are the points to keep in mind. . .I should write a plan for each class period.[16]

Just as we think through a problem when we write it down, even in a sketchy fashion, so do we prepare ourselves for better teaching when we write the lesson out. Detailed listing of each point may be advisable for beginning teachers. Gradually, with experience, the teacher may be able to rely less on the written plan. Although there are many forms of a written lesson plan, they all usually embody the following items:

Class_____   Date_____

Topic_____

Objectives: Long Range_____

                                      Immediate_____

Method

1. The Approach.
2. Pivotal Questions.
3. Materials for Illustration.
4. Student Activities.
5. Summary or Conclusion.

Content

As an illustration of detailed lesson planning, an example is given in its entirety. It was used by the late Dr. Samuel Streicher, formerly Principal of Seward Park High School, New York City, and a member of the Board of Examiners of the Board of Education of the City of New York. Used for a ninth grade slow class, it deals with the use of the apostrophe to indicate possession. Although it is not suggested that every lesson plan be written out in such great detail, it is reproduced here because it embodies many of the principles enunciated in this chapter.

Typical Lesson Plan
Developmental Type

Class E126X (slow) Use of the Apostrophe to Indicate Possession

Aims of the unit (3 lessons):

1. To secure variety of expression (sweaters that belong to Sam: Sam's sweaters)
2. To review the formation of plurals of nouns, regular and irregular
3. To indicate possession by use of the apostrophe with common and proper nouns, singular and plural
4. To refrain from misuse of the apostrophe (the hat is your's; Giants' games' on home grounds')

Specific objectives of this lesson (third in series):

1. To review use of apostrophe with singular and plural of possessors and singular and plural of things possessed
2. To indicate possession with irregular plurals, pronouns, collective nouns, proper nouns ending in s, and interrogative pronouns (whose)
3. To give mixed drill on all combinations.

Time	Procedure	Subject Matter (including optimum anticipated answers)
3 min.	Motivation: It seems that we'll have to re-open the "Lost and Found Department." In your composition just returned, many pupils mention things belonging to people but they don't make clear to whom these things belong.	
	1. In telling what certain boys found on returning to camp after looking for firewood, one pupil wrote: The boy's lunches were missing (at board).	
	a. Why did he fail to make his idea clear?	The lunches belong to all the boys but only one boy is mentioned.
	b. Correct the sentence.	boys' lunches
	2. Other class members tackled problems we have not yet studied: blankets of James; uniforms of the squad; yours (apostrophe?); policemen's clubs; etc.	
6 min.	Review:	
	1. Use the apostrophe to make clear to whom each thing belongs (at boards and writing at seats).	
	a. camping kit belonging to Jerry	Jerry's kit
	b. blankets for a Scout Why no apostrophe in blankets? Give rule learned yesterday.	Scout's blankets Apostrophe only with possessor, not thing possessed.

c. hiking shoes of Harry — Harry's hiking shoes

d. entertainment by the boys — boys' entertainment
   Why apostrophe after s? — To show that more than one boy took part

e. song of the Cubs — Cubs' song

f. camp of the Boy Scouts — Boy Scouts' camp
   What wrong impression would be given by Boy Scout's camp? — It would belong to one only Scout.

g. names of the officers — officers' names
   Why no apostrophe in names? — Plural is indicated. (Use word if class doesn't).
   Why apostrophe after s? — Rule repeated.

h. tricks by the boys — boys' tricks

i. clothes of the campers — campers' clothes

j. The lunches of the campers were missing. — campers' lunches

2. Partial Summary: When is the apostrophe placed after the s? — When the possessor is plural, place the apostrophe after the word.

15 min. Presentation (of the new) and Comparison:

1. Give the plural of the following:

man	woman	men, etc.
policeman	child	
fireman	baby	
lady	key	

2. (at board)
lady-bag	lady's bag
ladies-club	ladies' club
babies-nurses	babies' nurses

   a. How do these cases differ from the earlier ones? — First form the plural by changing y to i, before adding es.

   b. Why is the apostrophe after the s? — Apostrophe comes after the last letter of the plural.

3. (at board)
   hats of the men-men's hats
   clubs-policemen-policemen's clubs
   ball-firemen-firemen's ball
   women-shoes-women's shoes
   children-games-children's games

a. How do these cases differ from those we have just discussed?	Plural formed without s.
b. Why the apostrophe before the s?	Apostrophe comes after the last letter of the plural.

4. (at board)
mascot of the team-team's mascot
tents of the troop-troop's tents
uniforms of the squad-squad's uniforms

a. Why the apostrophe before the s?	Only one possessor is given.
b. Why no apostrophe after tents and uniforms?	Apostrophe only for possessor, not thing possessed.

5. (at board)
The ball is yours.
The gloves are theirs.
The badges are ours.
The bird hurt its wing.
Whose picture is this?

a. Why no apostrophe?	The words (pronouns) themselves indicate the possessor and don't need an apostrophe.

6. (at board)
clothes of Charles-Charles' clothes
blankets of James-James' blankets
stories of Dickens-Dickens' stories

a. Why the apostrophe after the s?	Apostrophe after last letter of the name.

3 min.	Generalization: There are really a few rules that govern all these combinations. Let's state them and give a model phrase to remember with each rule.	Apostrophe only with the possessor, not with the thing possessed: Sam's skates. When possessor is plural ending in s, add an apostrophe after s: ladies' hats. When possessor is plural not ending in s, add apostrophe and then s: firemen's ball. When possessor is singular ending in s, add only an apostrophe: Charles' clothes.

6 min.   Drill (mixed):

Note: Some teachers prefer to give drill on each type presented in the presentation directly after each is taken up and before the generalization is called for.

1. Sentences listed at board, or mimeographed sheet, or in composition text.
2. Rationalization reduced to minimum.

5 min.   Application:

Composition papers examined for all instances of use of the apostrophe and corrections made.

Assignment (for the sake of convenience, it is usually given at the beginning of the period):

To be dictated and wording corrected: from this evening's newspaper, copy ten expressions containing apostrophes. It may be taken from the women's page or ads.

18

HOW TO TEACH BY THE UNIT METHOD

As early as 1932 Dora V. Smith, in her survey of English instruction in the United States, pointed out the advantages of the unit method of teaching:

The prevalence of the unit method of instruction throughout the country has been exceedingly beneficial in helping both teacher and pupil to see a literary selection as a whole and to consider it in relation to others of similar theme or type. It had led to broader discussion, to less emphasis upon meticulous detail, and to the seeking of wider relationships both in literature and with other forms of expression. It is responsible also for the coming in of more laboratory procedures, where actual reading and use of books in the classroom supplement more discussion of materials read outside.[1]

A textbook on methods now would not be without a detailed discussion of the unit method, and hardly a literature anthology for secondary schools appears without unit arrangements of its selections.

WHAT IS A UNIT?

Various definitions of a unit have appeared in the educational literature of the past four decades. To Dorothy Dakin in *How to Teach High School English,* it is a "block of work." To plan one's teaching in units or blocks, allotting a definite period of time to cover the work in each unit, is always desirable.[2]

J. N. Hook in his *The Teaching of High School English* defines the unit as "an organized study, lasting from one to six or eight weeks, and centered upon a given theme to which everything in the unit is in some way related."[3]

The English Language Arts in Secondary School, Volume III in the N. C. T. E. Curriculum Series, devotes an extensive section to Chapter 4, "Building Instructional Units." Unit as defined in this volume is "varied activities in the language arts . . . developed around a central theme or purpose, clear and significant to the student."[4]

Loban, Ryan and Squire in *Teaching Language and Literature* state that "a unit of work organizes instruction for several weeks around a core of ideas and pertinent activities and includes instruction in all language skills."[5]

THE VARIOUS TYPES OF UNITS

If the word unit is mentioned to a group of teachers of varying experience and pedagogical persuasions, the chances are that varying concepts will arise. To one teacher a unit might mean a concentrated attack on grammar; she might be speaking of her work as a unit on grammar. To a second teacher the same word *unit* would mean spending several weeks of intensive study on a group of poems, and she would describe herself as doing a unit on poetry (American, Elizabethan, Romantic). A third teacher who likes to spend a month or more on *Silas Marner, A Tale of Two Cities* or *Macbeth* would be quite correct in describing her work as a unit on that particular classic. In fact, units have so far grown in variety that they have been classified into eight distinct varieties, and more will probably develop. Arranged more or less in the order of complexity, they are:

1. The unit that emphasizes a skill:
   Examples: "Group Discussion and Debate,"[6]
   "Business Letters."[7]
2. The unit that concentrates on a single text:
   Example: *Macbeth.*[8]
3. The unit that concentrates on a type of literature:
   Examples: "Unit on Drama,"[9]
   "Unit on Short Story,"[10]
   "Unit on Biography,"[11]
   "Poems of the Sea,"[12]
   "Travel Unit."[13]
4. The unit based on the works of a single author or a group of authors:
   Examples: "The Novels of Thomas Hardy,"
   "The Elizabethan Sonneteers,"
   "The Plays of Eugene O'Neill."
5. The thematic unit:
   Examples: "The Search for Adventure,"[14]
   "Tall Tales and Tunes,"[15]
   "Youth and War."[16]
6. The unit around a single topic:
   Examples: "Revelation of Character and of Human Relationships as shown in Monologue, Dialogue, or the Dramatic Lyric,"[17]
   "Sports and Sportsmanship,"
   "Heroes, Past and Present."
7. The unit that concentrates on the problems of students:
   Examples: "Getting Along with Others,"
   "Getting Ready for My Life's Work."[18]

8. The unit that culminates in a specific project:

   Examples: "Producing *Romeo and Juliet* as a Contemporary Play,"

   "Producing a Class Newspaper,"

   "Producing Models Illustrating Stage Design through the Ages."

Practically any series of literature anthologies on the market can supply numerous examples of units. Likewise many composition textbooks are arranged in unit form.

STEPS IN DEVELOPING A UNIT

It might seem startling in a discussion of so modern a topic as the unit method to quote Aristotle by saying that unit activities concern the beginning (or initiating activities), middle (developing activities) and end (culminating activities). The good unit obviously must begin somewhere, continue over a period of time, and culminate in some worthwhile activities. Some authorities subdivide these three major phases into six: points of approach; orientation; research; enabling materials; culmination; evaluation.[19]

All of the points have been so well developed in the following resource units that it would be useful for teachers to consult them:

Power over Language, in *Teaching Language and Literature* by Walter Loban, Margaret Ryan and James R. Squire (New York: Harcourt Brace Jovanovich, 1961) pp. 162-179 (for junior high);

Science Fiction: Radar of Man's Curiosity, ibid. pp. 257-272;

Macbeth; ibid., pp. 405-413 (senior high);

Fortitude, the Backbone of Courage; ibid., pp. 414-422 (junior high);

Meeting a Crisis, ibid., pp. 589-598 (senior high);

The Consequences of Character, ibid., pp. 631-646 (senior high);

An Approach to a Novel: Cry, the Beloved Country, in *Teaching Language, Composition and Literature* by Mary Elizabeth Fowler (New York: McGraw-Hill, 1965) pp. 252-259;

Teaching the Play: Death of a Salesman, ibid., pp. 299-307;

Teaching Biography: World Heroes and Leaders, ibid., pp. 326-331;

A Tale of Two Cities, in Resource Units in Language Arts for Senior High Schools, Curriculum Bulletin, 1962–63 Series, No. 3f, Board of Education of the City of New York, pp. 1-26;

Giants in the Earth, ibid., pp. 27-42.

In addition, several textbooks on teaching English in secondary schools have fairly well-developed units. The pages of *The English Journal* and other magazines of local or state-wide associations of English teachers contain other examples of units of various types.

OUTLINE OF THE UNIT PROCESS

Points of Approach

Here the teacher and students become highly interested in a topic on which they will spend considerable time. The approach will vary with the type of unit. If the unit is to be concerned with intensive study of a great classic, the approach could utilize all the time-honored devices for arousing an interest in the work.

If the unit is to be typological, the teacher may begin by reading several poems, a portion of a story, an essay or play. Or she may play a recording of any of these types. The better television programs may offer opportunities for arousing interest. Events in the daily newspapers may offer good opportunities.

Sometimes an approach may be made through discussing personal problems of the students: how does one succeed despite hardships? How can one become popular without losing integrity? How do we prepare for a world which is ever-changing? How can we overcome shyness before others?

A unit on a certain skill may be stimulated by studying the results of a diagnostic test, by asking what skills are necessary at a certain point in one's development.

In short, the alert teacher has a rich arsenal of devices for arousing class-wide interest in a topic that will be worth pursuing for a period of time.

Orientation

Once the motivation (remember that this word is related to *motor* and movement) has taken place, the class must move along toward common goals, not just aimlessly fan out in separate directions.

In the orientation phase, the teacher and class (if possible) select certain problems for investigation, the experiences they wish to share, the skills that must be mastered and the knowledges that should be acquired. Sometimes the teacher does most of the delimiting, since she knows best what she hopes to accomplish through the unit. Sometimes, especially with gifted students, the class can make significant contributions. The procedures are discussed and decided upon. So that all may contribute, committee assignments are tentatively set up. Since one of the advantages of the unit method is the more active participation of every member of the class, the committee procedure is desirable.

Research

Although the word research has been given strange connotations in recent years, in the context of the unit method it means finding material that will contribute to the goals envisioned. This information mostly will come from books (in the school library, public library and home). Magazines, reference books and other printed sources of information will be utilized. One of the outcomes of this method is development of independent search for knowledge; students are encouraged to write for materials from numerous agencies, public as well as private, for information. They likewise are encouraged to visit museums and other educational institutions in their quest for knowledge. Authorities may be interviewed or written to. In short, the students will be doing what the educated adult is doing all the time when he seeks answers to his problems.

Through the committee method, students learn how to divide their tasks and help one another. A work schedule is drawn up with a time limit for reporting and sharing. Various procedures can be utilized for sharing: individual reports, group reports, interviews, mimeographed reports. As sharing takes place, students learn to evaluate what they have done and how to improve. They also decide what form their culminating activity will take.

Maintenance and Development of Enabling Skills

Many teachers who have debated use of the unit method have asked what provisions are made for the skills. Don't students become so excited about high adventure that they use sentence fragments and forget the use of the apostrophe? Are they not so concerned with the quest for permanent values that they get lost on the way in the bogs of slipshod thinking and faulty organization? The advocates of the unit method (particularly the thematic and problem-centered) claim that adequate provision can be made for mastering new skills and maintaining old skills. Characteristic of the resource units listed above is their detailed listing of many skills to be learned in reading, writing, speaking and listening. Sometimes the teacher can anticipate what her students will need to know, and she can teach directly for mastery. For example, if students are to write for materials, they must know the correct form of a letter of request. If a diagnostic test reveals weaknesses, then time must be taken for direct teaching of that skill. If students are going to interview the local editor or the District Attorney or a local author, they should know or must learn something about the correct procedure in interviewing. Many other necessary skills can be anticipated. Others will be taught as deficiencies occur. There is nothing in the doctrine of the unit method which forbids the teacher from interrupting the unit for necessary drill in spelling, grammar or other basic skills.

Culmination

The culminating activities will vary with the unit. Units on types of literature frequently have ended with individual compilations of either the works of established authors or the fledgling efforts of the students. A class studying the eighteenth-century essayists ended the unit with a collection of original essays, all modeled on Addison and Steele but dealing with current topics.

A class studying a problem frequently collects all the papers written by the students, binds them and presents them to the school or public library. Sometimes a tape recording is made of the final presentations. Other types of culminating activities are: original scripts, exhibits, posters, models (the Globe Theatre is popular), annotated bibliographies, assembly programs and P. T. A. programs. One high school dramatics class toured several European countries with Wilder's *Our Town,* after marked local success.[20]

Evaluation

Some aspects of growth can be measured by standardized and teacher-made tests. Anecdotal records, pupils' self-evaluation and observation by the teacher can help in measuring outcomes in habits, appreciations and attitudes.[21]

WHAT ARE THE VALUES IN UNIT TEACHING?

The teacher who has enough to do in "covering the syllabus" naturally asks the question above. Apparently more work is involved in planning, in conferring, in evaluating and in personal reading. The following answer is supplied by *The English Language Arts in Secondary Schools,* which devotes an entire chapter to "Building Instructional Units":

Unit teaching, therefore, provides a natural situation for well-motivated learning. It places the skills of communication where they belong—in purposeful activity in a social setting. It demands orderly planning and assumption of responsibility for carrying out the plans. It furnishes opportunity for extensive group work and for individualized procedures to meet the needs, the interests and the capacities of all members of the class. It stimulates curiosity and creativity, giving those with unusual powers of self-direction a chance to forge ahead on their own. Yet it keeps the entire class working together on a common problem. It permits the use of all types of literature—new and old, prose and poetry, easy and mature—and the development of skill in reading each of them. It recognizes the place of the library in the learning activities of the classroom and teaches economical use of the facilities available. It takes advantage of the natural relationships between speaking and listening and writing and reading in the normal pursuit of well-integrated problems. It gives opportunity for enjoyment of literary selections by the class as a whole and at the same time develops personal standards of literary appreciation and personal habits of reading to suit individual interests. It gives opportunity for careful evaluation of progress by the students themselves and for the planning of next steps in learning.[22]

19

HOW TO TEST AND EVALUATE

"Appraisal of outcomes is an essential feedback of teaching. The evaluation process enables those involved to get their bearings, to know in which direction they are going." Thus state the writers of the pamphlet, *Testing, Testing, Testing.*[1] Teachers are evaluating and being evaluated constantly. In the same fashion, entire English departments, entire schools and entire school systems occasionally are evaluated.

The beginning teacher—and the experienced teacher as well—must realize that good teaching cannot exist without effective evaluation and that effective evaluation leads to better teaching.

First let us examine what a comprehensive evaluation program does. In an excellent chapter in *The English Language Arts,* the following purposes are listed:

1. Identifies the need of the learner.
2. Provides important information for use in guidance.
3. Stimulates self-direction.
4. Aids in planning and replanning the language arts curriculum.
5. Provides a record of growth and development for learners, instructors and parents.[2]

As will be seen, such aims cannot be achieved by dashing off a twenty-item True-False test in a few moments between class sessions. The intricacies involved in evaluating the outcomes of instruction in English can be seen as the teacher studies such a classic volume as Dora V. Smith's *Evaluating Instruction in Secondary School English* in which she reported her findings in New York State.[3] Many of the principles and methods employed in this survey have significance today and will continue to be meaningful for a long time.

For the teacher who is specifically interested in making the classroom test, there are several helpful volumes and pamphlets. One of the most helpful brief treatments is *Improving the Classroom Test* prepared by Sherman N. Tinkelman formerly of the State Education Department of New York (Albany, N. Y., 1967). *Testing and Evaluation,* a reprint of articles from the April, 1958, issue of the *N. E. A. Journal* is another valuable practical aid.

The question frequently is asked: what is testing and how does it differ from evaluation? A simple distinction is given by Helen Heffernan in her article, "Evaluation—More Than Testing":

Testing is limited to the quantitative aspects of evaluation. Evaluation includes, in addition, the qualitative aspect. Good instruments of evaluation should help us to determine more than what the child is doing in his school work; they should help us to discover what the school program is doing to the child.[4]

To make a test is easy as compared to establishing a complete evaluation program.

WHAT ARE THE CRITERIA OF A GOOD EVALUATION PROGRAM?

De Boer, Kaulfers and Miller in their *Teaching Secondary English* list the following:
1. Does the evaluation program include measurement of the extent to which the offerings in English are compatible with the needs and abilities of the students?
2. Does the evaluation program include adequate means for individual diagnosis of pupils' needs and difficulties?
3. Does the evaluation program provide for a cumulative record that can be passed on from teacher to teacher as the student progresses through school?
4. Does the evaluation program include tests of special abilities, such as spelling, vocabulary or usage, as diagnostic instruments to assist in locating possible causes of difficulties in using language for purposes of communication?
5. Does the evaluation program include appraisal of outcomes in the way of reading interests, speech habits (including usage outside of the English class) insights into human relations through literature, and other traits or qualifications cited as objectives of the course of study?
6. Does the program include pupil participation in self-evaluation?
7. Does the evaluation program de-emphasize grades as ends in themselves?
8. Is the evaluation program appropriately differentiated to accommodate terminal as well as college preparatory students?[5]

Many school systems have incorporated into their courses of study evaluative criteria and evaluative devices which show how theory has been put into practice. These are the four principles that guide the Seattle English teachers: evaluation is in terms of goals set and understood by students and teachers; evaluation is in terms of all the goals set; evaluation must be at all times consciously in the minds of both teacher and students; evaluation, if it is to be effective, must be so handled that it is a stimulus to further study and achievement.[6]

To show how these principles may be realized, *Guideposts to the English Language Arts* recommends the following measuring devices:
1. Diagnostic tests at the beginning of a term or of a unit.
2. A file of the themes of each student.
3. Periodic examination of the students' notebooks, to discover study habits, accumulation of vocabulary lists, exercises on language skills which have given the student

trouble in his oral and written work, and notes taken from reading and discussion.

4. Teacher-made and student-made tests in writing skills, grammar, speaking skills.

5. Sets of criteria for reading and for oral and written work.

6. Standardized tests.[7]

PREPARING A CLASSROOM TEST

Soon after the beginning or experienced teacher starts the new term, she will be thinking of tests. In order to know where the class as a whole and each student individually stands as far as skill and knowledge are concerned, she will plan a diagnostic test or series of them. Summer vacation is the time for forgetting much that has been learned in the preceding year. Students may be coming from lower schools in the same district or they may have transferred from other areas. Mobility is a constant factor in education today.[8]

What can be learned by these diagnostic tests? Reading skills, spelling skills and grammatical knowledge can be diagnosed by objective short-answer tests. Skill in written composition can be estimated to some extent by the first composition of the term. Other aspects of the English program such as appreciation of literature and attitudes toward language are more difficult to perceive in a diagnostic test.

Later in the term the teacher will be interested in ascertaining the achievement of her students, and here again tests will be used. The end of the term is frequently occasion for either a composite test (the Final Examination) or a series of shorter tests. The information obtained through these tests can be very valuable if the tests are properly constructed. They may indicate growth in language power. They may lead the teacher to change her methods. They may lead to individual counseling of students when indicated. A test should not be a means of getting a grade for purposes of promotion or retention.[9]

Because the classroom test is still the most frequently used measurement of evaluation, we must understand what it is and what it can best do. As Sherman N. Tinkelman stated in his helpful brochure *Improving the Classroom Test:*

Before a single test question is written, therefore, the teacher should have clearly in mind what purpose the test is to serve, what skills and content areas are to be measured and what their relative weights should be. To ignore these factors at the outset in preparing a test is to court the danger that the test, if it constitutes a poor sample of questions, may provide a misleading picture of pupil progress.[10]

TYPES OF TESTS

Basically tests today are of two types: the essay and the objective (short answer). Much controversy has taken place as to the relative merits of each type. For many years the essay type was popular in secondary schools. Then came the great interest in measurement and in testing in the 1930's. Objective-type tests were prepared and marketed, and whole libraries were written defending or attacking these short-answer tests. In the 1960's there was renewed interest in the essay test, particularly as a gauge of accomplishment in written English. The controversy will continue because of several factors, among them the time consumed in marking essay questions and the subjective element always present in the marking.

Strengths and Weaknesses of the Various Types of Tests

Of the values of the essay question, Tinkelman says:

The fundamental contribution of the essay question is that it requires the pupil to develop an answer from his own background and fund of experiences without benefit of suggested possibilities or alternatives, and to express that answer in his own words.

By requiring pupils to present evidence, to evaluate, to analyze and to solve problems or approach problems in a new way, essay questions can serve to measure some higher level abilities and can thus contribute to knowledge about the pupil.[11]

Examples of essay questions which were actually used in the Comprehensive English Examination in New York State follow:

The very nature of man makes it impossible for him to live "by bread alone"; he must live by faith—faith in an ideal or principle, faith in his country, faith in mankind. From the poems and essays you have read, choose any *four* selections. In *each* case show by definite references that the author expresses one of the kinds of faith mentioned. Give titles and authors.

"History records changes. Literature makes them real for us." Using two novels, or a novel and a short story, explain how each of the two selections has made some phase of history more real to you. Refer directly to the incidents and portrayals in the stories to support your discussion. Give titles and authors.

From books that we read we get many pictures of family life, some of which reveal sympathy, understanding and cooperation among the members, while others reveal discord and lack of harmony. From one novel and one play you have read, select a family group (parents with children; children with one another; family with servants, guests or relatives) and discuss what leads to cooperation or prevents cooperation. Give titles and authors.

The major difficulty with the essay question is that the rating is subjective. In spite of numerous attempts to make rating of test essays more objective, "considerable variation of assigned marks has been found, not only between one teacher and another, but in ratings by the same teacher from day to day."[12] Among the interesting experiments in trying to determine more objective criteria is the study in the Spring, 1958, issue of the *Newsletter* of the Michigan Council of Teachers of English, "Evaluating a Theme."[13]

Another helpful booklet, distributed by the State Education Department of the State of New York, is "Suggestions on the Rating of Regents Examination Papers in English," with a special section on the rating of literature essay questions of the type described above.[14] Many local and state courses of study have indicated ways of correcting compositions. The Guide for Evaluating Written Work and Criteria for Evaluating a Theme from *Guideposts to the English Language Arts* of Seattle Public Schools merit serious attention.[15]

Objective-type tests

Objective tests are usually of two types. In the first, the student supplies the answer; in the second, the student selects the answer from several supplied. Examples of the first type are: *Eminent Victorians* was written by _____; Iago is a character in _____; Wessex is the setting for the novels by _____.

The advantages of such questions are: the answers are definite and specific; they can be rated quickly and accurately; wide sampling is possible, since a large number of questions can be answered in a unit of testing time.

The disadvantages are: the teacher tends to concentrate on details; the teacher must be certain that there is only one correct answer to each question. Whereas the average student may give the answer the teacher expected, the bright student, who has read widely, may think of several answers; it is difficult to measure the higher processes of thought and reasoning.

How to Write Good Completion Items

Write your test item so that only one correct answer is possible. For example, in these items several answers are possible: Shakespeare wrote _____. Coleridge was born in _____ . (This might be answered by the year, century, city, country.)

It is better to place the blank space at the end of the statement, rather than at the beginning.

Avoid extraneous clues to the correct answer. If the class has been studying forms of poetry and has learned about the sonnet, ode, triolet, you give an extraneous clue in this question: A long, serious poem is called *an* _____ . (Obviously the student would not write "an sonnet" or "an triolet.")

The Selection Type of Question

There are three forms: true-false, multiple choice and matching.

True-False. In this question, the students write T or F or True or False, depending upon the answer. For example: Ernest Hemingway won the Nobel Prize. (T or F); Shakespeare was born in the 17th century. (T or F); *The Scarlet Letter* was written in the early 19th century. (T or F).

Advantages are that these are fairly easy to write; that a large sampling can be covered in any given test period; that scoring is objective and quick.

Disadvantages are that it is limited almost entirely to testing facts or specific information; that many of the larger outcomes of English instruction, such as generalizations, explanations, evaluations, cannot be tested by true-false questions; that there is encouragement to guess at the correct answer; that it is difficult to write questions that can be marked true or false without qualifications. Even a sample question like "Shakespeare wrote *Hamlet*" may draw a negative answer from the bright student who has read something about the Baconian Theory or who remembers that on the title page of his edition is *The Tragedy of Hamlet*.

How to Write Good True-False Items. Make statements that are absolutely true or false without qualifications or exceptions. Avoid statements that contain elements that are partly true or partly false. Avoid trick questions (students resent them!). Avoid long involved statements with qualifying clauses.

Multiple-Choice Questions. These questions are very popular with the various College Boards, civil service, and Army Intelligence tests because the answers can be indicated on a separate sheet which can be scored electronically and quickly.

The advantages are: the correct answer is limited to the choices given, thus eliminating any possibility of students' concern over universal application; the guessing factor is less than in the true-false questions; reasoning ability, fundamental understandings, as well as facts and principles, may be tested; many items can be tested in a period of class time; the scoring is objective and rapid.

The disadvantages are: it is applicable when there are a number of related possible answers (Where the choices are obviously unrelated, the student can guess the answers easily); it is time-consuming to prepare four or five choices for a single question.[16]

Matching Items. A series of items is listed in one column to be matched with those in another column. It is advisable to have more possibilities than correct answers in the second column so that students who know some of the answers will not guess at the others by elimination.[17]

WHAT ARE THE CRITERIA OF A GOOD TEST?

Validity. A well-constructed test should measure students' progress toward realization of the objectives of the course or unit.

Reliability. A well-constructed test should distinguish those who have mastered the subject from those who have not. It should consist of items carefully selected from the whole range of factual materials or principles taught. Poor administration of tests decreases reliability.

Clarity. A test should be clear as to directions, construction of test items, assignment of credit, and should be free from ambiguity or error.

Objectivity. In evaluating an answer to a question several teachers marking the same paper should arrive at approximately the same mark.

Administrability. In a good test the exercises are arranged as to difficulty, convenience in scoring, and with provision for a reasonable allotment of time.

Originality. The test should challenge thought, stimulate imagination, arouse interest, provide for variety, and generally serve as a teaching as well as a testing device.[18]

For additional information on the entire scope of evaluation, the reader should consult the following excellent resumes:

Chapter 18, "Methods of Evaluation," in *The English Language Arts.*[19]

Various sections under Evaluation in *The English Language Arts in Secondary Schools.*[20]

The March, 1962, issue of *The Reading Teacher,* which deals with Evaluations of Reading Instruction.[21]

Encyclopedia of Educational Research, 3rd Ed., article under "Evaluation" pp. 464-466, where additional references are given.[22]

The May, 1960, issue of *English Journal* in which Louella B. Cook, Chairman of the Committee on Evaluation of the National Council of Teachers of English, presents some of the basic problems in evaluating growth in English.[23]

PART SIX
THE ENGLISH TEACHER AND
CURRICULUM IMPROVEMENT

20

HOW TO PLAN A CURRICULUM

February 20, 1962, Astronaut John Glenn orbited three times around the earth, the first American to accomplish that feat. Before this could be successful, over $400-million had been spent in planning, personnel and equipment. Objectives had been set years before the event, astronauts had been given special training for many months, and thousands of technicians working in various phases of this project cooperated for the successful outcome.

English teachers might learn a profitable lesson from this feat. To be successful in our field, we too must formulate our objectives in terms of the needs, interests and abilities of our students. We too need experiences and materials to achieve these objectives. And all of this must be accomplished in an orderly, rather than a hit-or-miss manner. How can we plan a curriculum for youth in the 1970's that will achieve our chosen objectives most successfully?

In curriculum planning for the secondary schools, these elements must be kept in mind: personnel involved in preparing the curriculum; procedures in preparing the curriculum; formulation of objectives; scope and sequence; materials used to realize objectives; relationship of the English program to the total school program; reaction of teachers to the curriculum in tentative form; publication in more permanent form; use in the classroom (implementation); revision on the basis of classroom experience.

PERSONNEL

The problem is simplest in the school with only one English teacher. He is obviously the person who will prepare the departmental curriculum in English. Where there are a few English teachers in the typically small secondary school, all of them should cooperate in the project.

As the school becomes larger, or as the curriculum is designed for a school system, an area or an entire state, the matter of selection enters. Ideally, everyone who was going to use the new curriculum would have some share in preparing it. The chances are that it then would be better utilized. The problems of numbers in such a large school system as New York City become almost insuperable. It is unrealistic to expect three thousand or two thousand or even five hundred English teachers to sit down over a period of time and construct a new curriculum. There is neither the time nor the money to release such a large number of teachers. Many would not be interested and would have nothing to contribute; the whole project would quickly bog down. To be realistic, therefore, we must be selective.

Let us assume that we have a secondary school of about fifteen hundred students with ten English teachers. This number is small enough for everyone to contribute and yet large enough to have a variety of viewpoints, an array of talents and abilities, and a workable number for achieving a consensus. When a large school system is preparing a new curriculum, a steering committee of about twenty-five has been a workable combination.[1] In a state-wide curriculum study a similar number has been found workable.

Some member of the steering committee should be placed in charge. In a department where there is a department head, he would be the chairman. In cities with language arts coordinators, that coordinator would assume charge. Where there exists a state-wide coordinator or supervisor of English, the State supervisor would be in charge.

Good representation of various educational levels and various points of view is important. In the steering committee of a large city school system, there should be several heads of English departments from both the academic and vocational high schools. Junior high school and elementary teachers should join for proper articulation with the lower divisions. One or two college teachers of English and/or education will secure better articulation with the colleges. Other members should be English teachers in the senior academic and vocational high schools, one or more representatives from the community, students, and representatives from bureaus of audio-visual instruction, libraries, evaluation and guidance. On a state-wide basis similar representation should be arranged.[2]

PROCEDURES

How does curriculum improvement in English arise? *The English Language Arts in the Secondary School* states it in this manner:

A teacher not fully content with results he is achieving begins to study the problem afresh. He reads recent literature on instruction and curriculum planning in English. He attends conferences, enrolls in workshops, consults other teachers, examines new courses of study, or by himself thinks realistically and creatively about the objectives and goals that must guide his work with boys and girls. He investigates the kinds of experiences and activities he may use to these ends; he studies materials, instructional procedures, the nature of unit organization, and other means for improving the program he follows. A vitalized teaching of English in the classroom emerges. His colleagues hear about it and begin to study their own problems.[3]

Such is the origin of curriculum change when a single English teacher is involved.

Numerous illustrations can be found of the way in which such large groups have worked together as: the village curriculum committee;[4] the city school system;[5] study councils and regional association;[6] workshops sponsored by state English associations;[7] state-wide approach.[8]

A complete explanation of the evolution of the city-wide course of study for the senior high schools in New York City may be used to suggest similar large-scale revisions.[9]

Time and effort are required to prepare courses of study. Where a large committee is operating, it has been the practice to release at least one person full time to prepare the agenda for meetings, to carry on correspondence for materials, to prepare materials, to organize the minutes of the meetings and to carry out the many other tasks involved. At times other members of the committee might be released. For example, the librarian or librarians might spend a few days preparing bibliographies for resource units; another member might take a day or more to list audio-visual aids; a third might prepare a bibliography of related articles from professional journals.

How often should such a committee meet and for what period of time? Generally, one meeting every two weeks would be sufficient to make all the necessary preparations. A year of meetings before even a tentative document can be circulated is not too long a time. In some instances teachers and supervisors have been remunerated for working on a curriculum during the summer months or during several vacation periods. De Boer, Kaulfers and Miller have stated the case forcefully for releasing teachers to work on curriculum:

The preparation of resource units requires extensive library work, much reading and careful study of the needs of boys and girls in high school classes. Teachers who are called upon to meet class after class, attend to the routines of the home room, supervise extra-class activities, and make periodic reports to parents and administrators, cannot be expected to devote a great deal of time to the preparation of original resource units. Smaller teaching loads, and systematic provision for free time in which cooperative planning and research may be conducted, will be needed in order that basic improvements may be made in the English curriculum.[10]

Periodic meetings may be attended by members of the staff, students and representatives of the community, who are not on the steering committee, as resource persons. For example, an expert in guidance and/or mental health may be asked to comment on the new evolving curriculum from the guidance and/or mental health point of view. Occasionally a vocational or academic high school principal may be invited to comment from the point of view of the administrator. An evaluation expert, or a careers expert are examples of other specialists whose views should be welcomed.

The reasons to bring such a group together are numerous. General dissatisfactions with the results of English instruction have long been expressed. They run the gamut from the famous *Reorganization of English in Secondary Schools* of 1917[11] to the various pronouncements of James B. Conant in the 1950's and the 1960's.[12] There never has been a dearth of critics of our products.[13]

Sometimes the criticisms come from graduates of high schools who discover that they were not adequately prepared when they came to college or entered a vocation.

Local employers may be critical of the poor spelling and sentence structure of recent graduates. Pollsters of reading habits have criticized the amount and kind of reading done by our graduates. Our colleagues in other subject areas often have found fault with the students' speech and written work in their subject classes. All these criticisms have been the stimuli for curriculum change.

THE OUTCOMES OF ENGLISH INSTRUCTION

After the initial agreement that "something must be done" to answer these (and many more) criticisms, any curriculum committee must agree on the desired outcomes of the English program for the particular school, school system, area or state. Hundreds of such outcomes have been listed, and some of them will inevitably arise in the discussion. The chapter on "The Aims of English" reviews some of these statements. It is, of course, better than nothing to adopt a list of objectives such as the National Council of Teachers of English or the National Education Association has prepared. Far better, however, is a list that is based on the needs of the local situation and a list expressed in the language of the workers on the curriculum. Many a list of objectives or outcomes has been printed in a course of study, to be honored by lip-service only. When the local committee has thought this matter through and expressed outcomes in its own language, and when the teachers involved have both understood them and agreed to strive for them, the possibility for realizing them in actual practice is much greater. This does not mean that each new curriculum committee must start with a *tabula rasa* and refuse to look at any other courses of study. By all means, let there be publication of many lists of outcomes for serious study; let there be rearrangement, omissions, and, finally, a new organization to fit the needs of the community. It is obvious that the objectives of English instruction for students living near an Ivy League college, most of whom plan to go to that college, cannot be the same as those of a small agricultural community, most of whose high school graduates will go to work on the farms or into early marriage, although some objectives will be the same for all high school graduates.

Somehow, after all of the lists of outcomes and objectives have been studied and restudied, they come down to three large basics: personal, social and vocational. It would be the exceptional curriculum which did not make provisions for these three areas of living. The English curriculum, then becomes a matter of providing experiences which realize these goals.

CRUCIAL ISSUES

Every curriculum committee, once it has leaped over the hurdle of defining its objectives, has had to face crucial issues. It was always thus. It will plague the curriculum committees of the 1970's, the 1980's and those to come. In the 1950's, when the Commission on the English Curriculum of the National Council of Teachers of English labored, these were the crucial issues, and they are still crucial:

1. What should be the relative emphasis upon the various phases of the Language Arts and how can they be interrelated?
2. Shall there be planned or incidental programs in the Language Arts? What should the schools do about grade placement, minimum essentials and promotion practices?
3. What is the relationship of the Language Arts to the total curriculum, to the library, and to the life of the school?
4. How can the needs of individual pupils be met most effectively?
5. What shall be taught in grammar and linguistics?
6. What should be the program in speech and writing?
7. How can the program in the Language Arts recognize the importance of listening in life today?
8. What should be the place of the mass media of communication in the Language Arts program today?
9. What should be the nature of the program in reading and literature?
10. How should results of the program in the Language Arts be evaluated?[14]

The ways in which these crucial issues were resolved by the Commission on the English Curriculum are described in detail in *The English Language Arts,* comprising most of the contents of this volume. Many answers, therefore, will be found by local committees to their own crucial issues in this volume, although not all answers can fit any local situation. This is one of the reasons for releasing one or more persons full time to gather the materials relating to these and other issues. In the case of the New York City course of study, the coordinator prepared scores of mimeographed sheets extracted from many sources bearing on some of these critical issues. Thus when the members of the steering committee met fortnightly, they were supplied with materials that would have taken each of them many days to compile.

MAKING INITIAL AGREEMENTS

Fairly soon in the course of the discussion of an English curriculum committee, a series of initial agreements will be reached. They may range from such simple agreements that there will be four years of senior high English to something much more controversial. In any cooperative process it is wise to get some agreements down on paper (there will always be plenty of disagreements). A list of thirty initial agreements of the Production Committee which prepared the volume *The English Language Arts in the Secondary School* will give some idea of what other curriculum committees agree on. These run the gamut from: "The program in the Language Arts must be broad enough to give students freedom and opportunity to develop their potentialities, to pursue their own ends, and to learn the processes of effective participation in group life,"[15] to "Reading is a means of emotional, aesthetic, and intellectual growth."[16]

The agreements arrived at will give a sense of accomplishment and purpose to the curriculum committee. They need not be those of the Production Committee of the Commission on the English Curriculum, but they should be some basic statements of belief on which the curriculum can be built. Here, too, a study of other courses of study will be of value, but only as stimuli for the thinking of the local committee.

DETERMINING SCOPE AND SEQUENCE

For any English curriculum to have value, it must tell its users what is to be taught and in what sequence. Teachers, even the most creative, want to know what experiences to provide for their students, and in what order. In this regard there are two schools of thought. The majority of teachers would like a course of study which is pre-planned, but which they can adapt to the needs, interests and abilities of their individual classes. A much smaller group would prefer that "classes should be free to select their problems and activities in accordance with their current interests and with current happenings."[17] The dangers of the latter method are several. Students' interests, though strong, may be unimportant. One can't spend four years discussing the ethics of going steady in junior high school or early marriage, both interesting topics, especially for adolescent girls. Too much reliance on students' interest may result in inordinate wastes of precious time, repetitions and omissions. Students may come out of such a four-year course as experts in dating but unable to read, write or spell. This is not to imply that there should be no pupil-teacher planning whatever. When used properly it is a desirable procedure.

The vast majority of courses of study in print are pre-planned, with adequate provision for differentiation and adaptation.[18] How wide the scope of each course of study will be depends on the philosophies of the school and the committee and the demands of the community. There are six major factors to consider in preparing the scope and sequence (i.e., an orderly progression of learning activities): the student population; the community; faculty resources; school facilities; consultant services; time and funds.[19]

The Student Population

Obviously the course of study, since it is made for students, must consider the students in the following aspects: interests; capacities; scholastic achievements; instructional needs; occupational outlook.

The information can be obtained from the following sources:
1. Cumulative records.
2. Work-study experiences.
3. Scholastic and aptitude tests.
4. Interest inventories.
5. Interviews.
6. Exploratory situations in which linguistic competence is observable.
7. Follow-up studies of previous graduates in employment or in college.

Only when a curriculum committee knows its students can a course of study be prepared for their needs today. All this takes time, and provision must be made for teachers to study the cumulative records, the answers to the questionnaires and the replies from graduates in college and at work. One caution must be given. Teachers should not form their final opinion about a student or a class on the basis of data on records alone. Only first-hand experiences after a period of time can enable the teacher to gain the necessary insight. Yet data, when used judiciously, can be of valuable corroborative help in forming the true picture.

It must become clear, by considering these factors, that students are not only people, but also prime factors in any scope and sequence. Communities vary in their hopes and ambitions, in their social and economic values, in their opportunities for their children. It would be unrealistic to prepare a curriculum that is designed to send students to Harvard, Yale and Vassar when most of the students using it know they will be going into business or a factory after graduation. The sad fact about American secondary education today is that over forty percent of our students never graduate. A college preparatory course is not the answer to all needs.[20]

In many schools, students' autobiographical essays at the beginning of the term supply valuable information about ideas, ideals, hopes and aspirations. Guidance interviews also can be helpful, as well as interviews in the English classroom about reading and written composition.

The Community

The scope of an English course of study must take into consideration the community in which the students live. It would be helpful to know:
1. Where do the students live?
2. What do the students see on their way to and from school?
3. What cultural and recreational opportunities exist in the community?
4. What kind of youth organizations are available? (Gangs or Boy Scouts?)
5. What members of the community are equipped and willing to serve as resource persons?
6. What job opportunities are available?
7. What are the entrance requirements to local institutions of higher learning?

Any experienced teacher of English knows how difficult it is to make American students realize vividly the opening chapters of Hardy's *Return of the Native* or Eliot's *Silas Marner*. Nothing in their immediate environment "connects" with these descriptions of British scenery, and imaginations cannot be stirred. Hence the curriculum committee must be aware of the community in which the students live, for English is mastered by vital experiences, both in and out of the classroom.

Faculty Resources

A curriculum committee can prepare a wonderful course of study that really is designed to meet the present and future needs of the students, and yet it can come to complete frustration and failure. The staff using the course of study also must be considered. These are some aspects which determine the quality of a staff with respect to implementing a new course of study:
1. Aptitude as teachers.

2. Interests.

3. Formal and informal education.

4. Availability of teachers in other subject areas as resource persons.

5. Availability of in-service facilities to train teachers in implementing the new course of study.

In those school systems like New York City, Chicago, Philadelphia, Baltimore with well established in-service programs, it is possible to train new or experienced teachers in aspects of English which they may not have covered in college work. For example, if the curriculum committee abandons the skills-centered course of study for a theme-centered one and organizes one or several in-service courses to show teachers how to teach by the new approach, there is a greater possibility for the success of the new course of study.

Likewise, if the curriculum committee, after surveying the training of the teachers who are going to use the new course of study, realizes that many of them have been attending professional conferences and workshops to become acquainted with the latest thinking about their subject, then the committee will be confident about innovations in the new course of study. The reverse holds true. A "traditional" staff will not accept a course of study radically different from what they have been using for many years. In this case, the curriculum committee would do well to make haste slowly and introduce changes gradually.

The availability of qualified teachers in other subject fields will make possible certain types of correlation and integration, which might better not be attempted when such teachers are not present. It is one thing to talk about a school-wide reading improvement and writing improvement program when teachers in other subjects are qualified and eager to participate. It is a sure path to frustration and failure when the teachers are interested only in their own subjects and have no time to do what the English teachers should be doing. Therefore, a realistic curriculum committee hopeful of a modicum of success must give attention to the teachers who will utilize the course of study. Where the teacher turnover is large because teaching wives move along with their non-teaching husbands in other professions or for other reasons, the course of study has to be such as to be meaningful to the many new, young teachers who will appear each September.

School Facilities

The presence of certain facilities in a school will influence the contents of a course of study. Where classrooms are built with shelves for libraries, contain filing cabinets, audio-visual equipment, movable furniture and the like, it makes some sense to incorporate a program of wide supplementary reading. The practice of maintaining folders of the students' written work, student committee work, and students' oral reports is desirable when the English classrooms are equipped to permit such a program. On the other hand, such a program becomes a pious hope where few such facilities exist. Hence the curriculum committee must be acquainted with the school environment in which the new course of study will be tried out. It is not surprising that some of the newer experiments in English on the secondary level have originated in fairly new buildings in which each English room has electrical outlets for audio-visual equipment, movable furniture to permit whole-class or small-group work, plenty of storage space for classroom libraries and recordings. This does not mean, however, that significant curriculum change cannot go on in any type of room. But the right environment does make our work a little easier.

Consultant Services

Many curriculum projects have been speeded up and enriched by the presence of consultants of rich experience in this field. The scope of a new course of study may be influenced by their presence. Even if their views are not always accepted, these consultants can suggest ways of operation which will save time and effort. They have worked with many groups and know how to get things started, how to get the "ball moving," how to arrive at a consensus, and how to summarize points of view. They also can inform curriculum committees about new developments or developments that have been abandoned and thus spare the committee the embarrassment of producing a course of study which has been found unworkable time and time again.

Consultant services need not always be in the form of a consultant in the flesh. The many valuable publications like those of the National Council of Teachers of English, the Association for Supervision and Curriculum Development, the National Education Association all are consultative in character. Such a publication as *The English Language Arts* is the result of the collaboration of some four hundred teachers and supervisors. An equal number or more contributed to the companion volumes, *The English Language Arts in the Secondary School, The College Teaching of English,* and *The Preparation of Teachers of English.* These and many more are excellent sources of information and guidelines for any curriculum committee. The E. R. I. C. bibliographies and articles available from N. C. T. E. Headquarters are also very helpful.

Many consultant services are available before a curriculum project is begun or during the project. For example, the National Council of Teachers of English has organized for the past few years a series of workshops to which teachers and supervisors come from all over the country for three days prior to the opening of the convention. Problems of vital concern are discussed by vitally interested parties. When these participants return to their own schools they certainly can contribute in a consultative capacity to their curriculum committees.

In recent years the N. C. T. E. has co-sponsored a number of summer workshops concerned with improving instruction in various phases of English. Highly qualified workshop leaders bring their vast experience and wisdom to these workshops, from which the participating teachers have derived so much. Similar workshops have been arranged by state education departments and by state English councils. From all these sources, consultants may be produced for any curriculum project.

Time, Place and Funds

As has already been indicated by De Boer, Kaulfers and Miller, curriculum improve-

ment takes time and money. The volume *The English Language Arts* makes some practical suggestions on this point. Things to be explored are:
1. Time for committees to work other than in the weary after-school hours of a teaching day.[21] Some school boards provide time before school opens in the fall for all teachers to work a few days. In some instances the curriculum committee may prefer to work during the summer, Christmas or Easter vacation, with compensation.
2. Budgetary provisions also should be made to purchase curricular materials from other school systems, for payment of consultants and for attendance by the curriculum committee at conferences and workshops. If many questionnaires are to be prepared and mailed, provisions should be made for time and funds.

HOW TO PROVIDE FOR SEQUENTIAL LEARNING

So far in our discussion of curriculum improvement in English we have dealt with content and its scope. Now it is time to consider how to provide for sequential learning. From our studies of child growth and development, we now know what secondary students are prepared to learn at different stages. To avoid a wrong sequence or to avoid unnecessary duplication, a proper sequence in learning English skills, ideas, attitudes and appreciations is most important. Many materials are available to assist the curriculum committee.

Chart of Sequential Skills

Many school systems (New York City, Chicago, Indianapolis, Minneapolis, Oakland) have worked out charts of sequential skills. These can be obtained from the Curriculum Bureau or Curriculum Coordinator of these and many other cities. Although they may not be applicable to every local situation, they have been prepared after much care and study and may spare a curriculum committee considerable time in avoiding needless repetition.

Publishers' Charts of Skills

Many publishers of language arts series (Macmillan, D. C. Heath, Harcourt Brace Jovanovich, L. W. Singer, Scott Foresman) have prepared large charts showing how the various skills are provided for in their series of composition texts. They are always glad to oblige with copies in quantity. Each member of the curriculum committee might be asked to study and report on these skills charts until the best possible sequence is decided upon to fit the local situation.

Care must be exercised, however, not to make these charts of sequential skills into minima of every student in the class. Each teacher must find out where each student in the class is with respect to any particular skill and must then help him maintain that skill and go on to mastering others.

Study of Problems of Articulation

The question of articulation will be discussed in Chapter 22. Here it should be noted that effective articulation will assist in achieving a better sequence of learning. It is not enough to hand all English teachers from grade seven through twelve a course of study with a recommended sequence and expect it to be carried out. Teachers of one level of the school system can profit from visits to colleagues at other levels. Sometimes meetings are held to discover the obstacles to orderly development of the program and then adjustments can be made. College teachers meet with high school teachers to discuss problems of common concern. In this manner a sequence on paper can be helped to become a sequence in reality.

Themes vs. Skills

Inevitably the topic of how to organize the sequence will arise. Should it be by skills alone? Should it be by problems of genuine concern to adolescents? Should it be by theme centers? There are strong advocates of each of these points of view. The committee must examine many of the newer courses of study, find the reasons for preferring one approach to another, and makes its own decision, knowing the local situation best. An examination of Arno Jewett's *English Language Arts in American High Schools* will reveal the many different courses available and their characteristics. The unit and thematic approach are found in many of them. Yet there are many new courses of study without this approach. It is fatal to force any one approach, however effective in one locality, upon another that is unprepared by philosophy or training or community understanding.

Selection of Instructional Materials to Fit the Curriculum

"At the heart of the sequential program in the language arts," says *The English Language Arts in the Secondary School,* is the selection of instructional materials to meet the wide range of differences among the students at any grade level.[22] Today there is such a wealth of instructional materials available that the curriculum committee will be bewildered as it attempts to select what is best suited to the local situation. Even if the problem is to be solved quickly by selecting a literary anthology and a grammar-composition test for each year, there still is the matter of deciding which anthology out of almost two dozen competitors is to be chosen. To base the sequence on the anthology, whether it be literature or grammar-composition, is the easy way out but is not necessarily the best for the local situation. Anthologies were made to assist teachers, not to enslave them.[23]

In addition to many excellent anthologies, there are literally thousands of books written for adults and for adolescents which may be well suited to accomplish the sequence of learnings. How is the curriculum committee to determine what to include?[24] To enable teachers to keep up with the newest materials, workshops and in-service courses have been organized by many school systems in which these books are discussed. Many schools of education are offering courses in children's literature and adolescent literature.

Adjustment of Grouping and Promotion Policies to Curriculum Goals

We know that no two students develop in quite the same way whether it be in English or in any other subject. Hence any sequence of learning must be governed by these considerations:

1. The curriculum committee should come to some agreement on this important principle: the rate and progress of individual students and the ultimate level of their accomplishments differ according to their innate potentialities and to the stimulation of their surroundings.[25]

2. Appreciation of the fact that growth in language power is gradual. It can be continuous; it should be cumulative.

3. The faculty should agree on what kinds of growth are essential for promotion and when to hold the student back in the same grade.

4. To achieve maximum results with any sequence, it may be necessary to group students by sections or within the class.

Since this entire aspect of grouping has been discussed in detail in Chapter 4 it will not be repeated here.

The Use of Cumulative Records

"To the extent that the teacher adds to the records significant data concerning the rate and pattern of the student's learning, the next teacher will be able to maintain an unbroken sequence of the student's development."[26]

MATERIALS TO BE USED IN REALIZING THE OBJECTIVES

Some aspects of this subject of materials have already been discussed under the heading of Sequence, but materials include more than anthologies of literature and grammar-composition texts. Films, film-strips, video tapes, recordings, cassettes, pictures, magazines and newspapers are part of instructional materials. All of these are designed to provide experiences which will stimulate maximum growth toward the realization of objectives. The curriculum committee can make recommendations. The local administrator must make provisions for having them when they are needed. The individual teacher must make the decisions as to when and how to use them. To show a film of *A Tale of Two Cities* to all tenth-year students because it happens to be in the building at a certain time, even if many students are not working with this text, is pretty much a waste of time. To play a recording of *Macbeth* in the twelfth year because it happens to be around, without adequate preparation on the part of students or the teacher, is another waste of time. Careful planning is the answer here as in so many other instances of the English program.

RELATING THE ENGLISH PROGRAM TO THE TOTAL SCHOOL PROGRAM

For more than three quarters of a century writers of methods books in English have been saying that every teacher in the school should have some responsibility for the English spoken and written by his students. "Every teacher is an English teacher" has long been a slogan. This is not the same as saying that no special qualifications of training, temperament and sensitivity are needed to teach English. What is meant is that every teacher in the secondary school should insist on certain standards in oral and written English; that every subject teacher should teach the reading skills pertinent to his subject; that he should give help in understanding the special vocabulary difficulties of his subject.

More and more subject teachers are becoming aware of these responsibilities.[27] Such a publication as *All Teachers Can Teach Reading* by the New Jersey Teachers Association indicated various ways in which all subject teachers can teach reading skills in their subjects.[28]

This cooperation may be shown in other ways. Subject teachers refuse to accept papers that are not written in ink, in proper form, and with a modicum of good English. In correcting examinations, subject teachers fail a paper that is written in sub-standard English even though the facts may be correct. Wide reading is encouraged in all areas by all subject teachers. They may assist English teachers in compiling book lists in their areas. These are only a few of the ways in which cooperation has been secured.

Interdepartmental committees have been formed in some schools for discussing such problems as reading improvement, standards of written English in all papers, standards of oral English. Faculty conferences have been held in which English teachers or supervisors have explained their philosophy, the content and the procedures in the English classes. From such deeper understanding has come closer cooperation. Other aspects of interdepartmental cooperation are discussed more fully in the chapter on "Correlation and Integration."

REACTING TO THE NEW COURSE OF STUDY

After the curriculum committee has prepared a first draft of the course of study, there should be an opportunity to react to it by a number of teachers and supervisors. People who have worked intensively on a project over a period of time tend to become so preoccupied with it that they miss many little facets. Hence it is wise to submit the rough draft in mimeograph or rexograph form to selected teachers and supervisors for their reactions. In a large school system like New York City or Philadelphia, all chairmen of English of the vocational and academic high schools might be sent copies. These chairmen at their department conferences might discuss the drafts with all their teachers. The comments would then be forwarded to the steering committee. In smaller school systems this might be carried out directly with the teachers in the individual schools. The greater the number of reactions by qualified people, the more likelihood there will be that the final form will be free of obvious errors and ready for adoption. Sometimes these rough drafts are sent to distinguished members of the profession in other cities, who can give a more objective view. Representatives of the junior high schools, elementary schools and the colleges also might be sent copies.

When all the comments have been gathered, the curriculum committee has the task of accepting or rejecting them, and revising the course of study prior to publication. If time permits, certain schools or certain teachers might be asked to try the course of study for a term or year in its tentative form. The reactions from such teachers are particularly useful because the workability of a course of study can be tested only in the front lines, the classroom. Many valuable suggestions have been received in this manner, many egregious errors have been avoided, and better statements have usually resulted.

PUBLICATIONS

The publication of a new course of study must be considered carefully. Its format and size may make or break the document. A comparison between the courses of study published in the 1920's and the 1970's will show that many improvements have taken place in the appearance of printed courses of study. The type is more readable, the pages are of convenient size, and many printer's devices to enhance the page have been utilized. Since several years will elapse before a new course of study will be issued, the binding should be durable. Some courses of study, like those of Seattle, for example, have a spiral type of binding which permits the pages to be opened at any place and lie flat. Caution must be taken not to make the document so thick and heavy that it is cumbersome. An attractive cover helps.

Every English teacher in the school or school system should obviously receive a copy. A sufficient number of copies should be printed to provide for the new teachers who will be coming in from time to time.

IMPLEMENTATION

For a new course of study to win the approval of the majority of teachers of a community, there must be sufficient time to study it and try it out in the classroom. In the first year of operation only the ninth-grade teachers might be required to use it. The following year the tenth-grade teachers come in. In the next two years the two upper grades implement it. This is better than requiring all the teachers to change over in one fell swoop. Confusion and frustration will result and the school system may lose all the advantages of the old course of study and gain none of the new. If implementation takes place over a four-year period or even longer, the course of study and the results can be evaluated more effectively.

REVISION

Curriculum improvement is an ongoing process, and there is no such thing as a final course of study. Rapid increase in knowledge about child growth and development, about the nature of language learning and linguistics, have compelled teachers to modify their methods of teaching. New books by the hundreds appear each year. New problems arise, which can be used for themes or units. The unit that seemed so exciting five years ago will seem dull now. Hence the need for careful evaluation for the purpose of revision. As the *English Language Arts in the Secondary School* so aptly expresses it:

No classroom teacher or organized curriculum group can afford to call its work finished when a new course of study is produced. The fact that many courses of study recently appearing as printed documents have the title "A Progress Report" is indicative of the realization that curriculum work must be continuous. The most important result that could emerge from a curriculum study—local, area, state, regional or national—would be an awakened interest among all teachers in study of the needs of boys and girls, the impact of the changing times, the richness of materials available to improve teaching, and the almost limitless and tremendously important possibilities that challenge a teacher of the language arts continually to study and improve the curriculum.[29]

21

ARTICULATING OUR EFFORTS IN THE
TEACHING OF ENGLISH

The problem of the articulation in English between the elementary and the secondary school, and between the secondary school and college, has been discussed for almost three-quarters of a century. As a problem, it is closely connected with overall articulation among the three major levels of American education.[1] Just as there were many difficulties in making a smooth transition from one school system to another because each level had arisen independently, so there were difficulties in maintaining continuity, avoiding useless repetition, and achieving adequate preparation in English as the student moved from grade school to secondary school and then on to college.

The National Council of Teachers of English in May, 1912, appointed a committee specifically to study the matter of articulation of the English program between the elementary and secondary schools.[2] After receiving three hundred replies from all parts of the United States, this committee, through its chairman Ernest C. Noyes, issued a report at the November, 1913, meeting of the Council. Some of the recommendations made sixty years ago have significance for us today and merit listing below:

1.   That the large and complex terminology of English be clearly defined by those whose position enables them to speak with authority so that the work to be done in any particular part of the school course can be accurately stated and clearly understood.

*2.   That the ground to be covered in each phase of English in each type of school be carefully defined.

3.   That in both schools the courses of study be simplified and revised so as to include much less formal grammar but much more thorough drill in applied grammar, so as to include a wider range of reading matter and more oral composition, and so as to appeal more to the sympathies and interests of pupils. That in the high school course a separation be made between what may be called "practical English," which every pupil should study, and so-called "cultural English."

*4.   That full, definite syllabi, rich in specific details, be prepared and printed for the guidance of teachers, and that representative teachers of various grades be consulted in the preparation of such syllabi.

*5.   That the organization of the two schools be planned and the courses administered in such a way as to contribute to good articulation by the employment of such and as many of the schemes following as may be feasible in any particular locality:

a. The assignment of the most efficient teachers in the high school to the charge of first-year classes.

b. The more general use of departmental teaching in the elementary school, or the plan of one teacher in several subjects in the first year of the high school, or both.

c. The promotion of acquaintance and mutual cooperation between teachers in the two classes of schools by means of joint conferences, exchange of visits, notification by the high-school teachers of the prevailing faults in the English of entering pupils, and similar means.

d. The assignment of successful elementary-school teachers to the first-year work of the high school and vice versa, for a year at least.

e. The complete reorganization of the two schools on the plan, giving six years to each.

*f. The close correlation and continuous supervision of the two courses by a supervisor of English or other competent authority.[3]

The recommendations that have been starred seem particularly contemporary, in spite of the time lapse since they were first promulgated. It is interesting in this brief history of attempts to achieve articulation between elementary and secondary schools to see what one school system attempted more than fifty years ago, because much can be learned from that experience today. Charles Swain Thomas, who was head of the English Department in the Newton (Mass.) High School, describes in his *The Teaching of English in the Secondary School* the experiences in articulation in that city.[4]

Among the procedures used were:

1. Assignment of only the most expert members of the English staff to teach the first-year high school English.[5]

2. Temporary assignment of outstanding grade-school teachers to teach first-year high school English.[6]

3. Visits of high school teachers to observe what is going on in English instruction in grade schools.[7]

4. Group conferences between representatives from the upper grammar grades and from the high schools. These conferences discussed profitably many of the aspects of proper articulation. In the 1917 edition, Thomas lists twenty two topics, most of which still are high on the list of problems in articulation. In the 1927 edition of his methods text, Thomas lists fifty six topics.[8]

5. Plans to print the results of such conferences. During the three years of such collaboration at Newton, three reports were published—one on spelling, one on sentence structure, and one on letter-writing.[9]

6. For those who may be planning joint conferences specifically to achieve a clearer understanding of aims and standards, Thomas has printed the notice which was sent

to all the grammar schools in the city which might well be adapted for conferences in articulation in our own day.[10]

7. The six year organization of the grammar school followed by the six year secondary school is suggested.[11]

8. The appointment of an English supervisor either for the entire English program or for the upper grammar grades and high school.[12]

Thus Thomas anticipated many of the articulation procedures in practice today.

WHY DO WE NEED ARTICULATION?

Lack of articulation results in certain deficiencies in the continuous educational development of the student, which may be removed by the means already described and others to be mentioned later. Alvin C. Eurich and John J. Scanlan, in their article on Articulation in the *Encyclopedia of Educational Research,* list four kinds of waste resulting from faulty articulation. Although they are discussing articulation between high school and college, these wastes are evident at both the lower and upper levels of our educational system:

1. Repeating work already done.

2. Dropping a subject before it has really done much good.

3. Concern with less important aspects of a subject at the expense of the more important.[13]

4. Gaps in the student's secondary education which have to be filled when he reaches college.[14]

The practising teacher in today's secondary school can testify to other deficiencies. For example, students in the ninth year or tenth year (if they have been to a junior high school) have not been prepared for the more rigorous demands of the senior high school. They need help in how to do an assignment in English; in how to utilize the school and public library; in how to take notes on what they read, listen to, or watch on television. Frequently one hears the lament, "We never had this in junior high school or elementary school." The senior high school teacher never can be sure if: the students never "had it"; they were exposed to it (whether it be a fact, an idea or a procedure) and never mastered it; they were exposed to it, but under different terminology. Whatever the situation may be, the teacher becomes discouraged, frustrated and tempted to censure his colleagues in elementary school, and starts the whole chain-reaction of recriminations which has been the great obstacle to better articulation.

As to the positive benefits of articulation, one of the best statements is from Frederic W. Heimberger, formerly vice-president of Ohio State University, made at a conference of high school and college teachers of English:

First of all, while there may be varying phases of development and maturation, there are no separate and isolated segments in the process of education. In its best sense it should be directed toward a lifetime of learning. Try as we may, we can never begin from scratch once learning has started. What is learned today must be related to what was learned yesterday—and, furthermore, to what should be learned tomorrow.

At each new level we must take full account of what has happened before. And, of great importance, we must cast an eye to the future unless we are so foolish as to think that the learning process ends with our particular efforts to teach within a particular segment of time.[15]

Dora V. Smith, in her study of the teaching of English in New York State in 1941, expressed the importance of articulation thus:

In the pursuit of all these purposes it (i.e., a modern English program) aims so to articulate the program between the upper and lower levels of the school system that gradual and continuous growth on the part of the individual is assured.[16]

EFFECTIVE METHODS FOR ACHIEVING ARTICULATION

The remainder of this chapter will deal with the most effective methods now being employed to achieve articulation. Some of them go back to the recommendations of the 1913 report to the N. C. T. E. already alluded to. Others are more recent, and must still be tested by time and experience.

Inter-level conferences. Designed for discussion of mutual problems, this was tried sixty years ago in Newton, Mass., and has already been described.

When the Commission on the English Curriculum was set up by the National Council of Teachers of English in 1947, the subject of articulation was studied seriously. Since the members of the Commission represented all levels, from elementary through the graduate school, their view on the importance of mutual understanding merits most careful consideration:

It is obvious that neither the college nor the high school can solve the problem of articulation alone. Each one from the point of view of its own philosophy and its experience with young people has a contribution to make to the solution. If the view of the Commission on the English Curriculum is accepted—that a curriculum must grow, like the student himself, from the ground up—the problem of the college is to understand the elements which have gone into the background of the high school student, and the particular stage of development he has attained. On the other hand, the colleges have had years of experience with students who represent for the most part the upper half of the high school population, and have, in general, given serious thought to the problem. High schools have equally serious problems to cope with in the interests of all the students of secondary school age. *Articulation can never be a one-way process.* It demands adjustments on the part of both high school and college and constant conferences between their representatives. The question of preparation for college is not alone, what do the colleges what, but what is the next step in the education of able young people if they are to reach their fullest potentialities and contribute to the welfare of their communities, their country, and the world?[17]

To determine how some of the conferences advocated by the *English Language Arts* have operated, the following are some typical recent examples worthy of examination.

All teachers who are interested in articulation between high school and college should read the following reports on successful conferences designed to facilitate articulation:

Joint Statement on Freshman English in College and High School Preparation prepared by the Departments of English of Ball State Teachers College, Indiana State Teachers College, Indiana University, and Purdue University [18]

Freshman English at Ohio State University, a report of a Principal-Freshman Conference held on March 1, 1957[19]

Teaching Composition and Literature, a report of a conference held at Goucher College, January 18, 1958[20]

A College Seminar to Develop and Evaluate an Improved High School English Program, held at Ball State Teachers College, Muncie, Indiana, 1958-1959[21]

Although this series of conferences was called primarily for improving instruction in English, rather than for improving articulation, the methods would be useful for any articulatory conference.

STANDARDS IN FRESHMAN RHETORIC AT THE UNIVERSITY OF ILLINOIS[22]

Although this is not a report of a conference between high school and college English teachers, one of the purposes was to improve high school teaching of English so that graduates from the high schools might be better prepared for English at the University of Illinois.[23]

During such conferences, many false notions can be dispelled, many fresh points of view may be generated, many understandings may be fostered which will lead to mutual respect for their respective efforts.

In that epoch-making document, itself the culmination of a series of conferences among English teachers of all levels, *The Basic Issues in The Teaching of English,* Issue No. 33 deals with closer communication and cooperation.

If the English program is to become ideally sequential and cumulative, there must be much closer communication and cooperation among the teachers at the various levels. Some states and some national organizations have made efforts toward better articulation in recent years, but much remains to be done.[24]

Intervisitation and Orientation

One step beyond the conference approach is that of intervisitation. This plan has been in operation in Baltimore for several years. As described in *The English Language Arts in the Secondary School:*

For orientation purposes, elementary pupils are given an opportunity to visit the secondary school, and, when feasible, senior high school students visit the college which they are planning to enter. The junior or senior high school teacher confers with the former teachers of his students. Visits to classes are arranged. Teachers from "feeding" schools confer with the teachers in the junior or the senior high school, as the case may be, and observe classes to which their students go. Teachers from the higher level visit classes in the lower school. At times, too, a teacher follows up a particular child as he moves on to the next school because of some special problem he has. Through these conferences and observations a study is made of curriculum materials, techniques and procedures at all levels.[25]

The Carnegie Institute of Technology and the Pittsburgh Public Schools have long been experimenting with interchange of teachers for the purpose of discovering ways of improving the program of instruction for superior students.[26]

Intervisitation within a single school can take place more easily and will help achieve better articulation from grade to grade. No elaborate preparation is necessary for such intervisitation, except that the administration should cooperate by providing free periods for conferences among the teachers involved, to compare notes on what they have observed and to plan for future action.

The Supervisor as a Means for Better Articulation

Both the N. C. T. E. 1913 committee[27] and Charles Swain Thomas in 1917[28] recommended that an overall English supervisor be appointed who, among other duties, would work for the achievement of better articulation. No one, at this date, needs to argue about the paramount importance of the head of department of English or the supervisor of English in the local school system or state. His contributions to curriculum construction, to improvement of instruction and to better articulation are indisputable. Since the supervisor sees the program as a continuous one from K through 12, he is at a vantage point. As Charles Swain Thomas expressed the matter in 1917:

... the influence of a strong guiding hand is one of the most helpful factors in effecting closer articulation between the grammar school and the high school—and even if this were his only accomplishment, his services would be extremely valuable.[29]

Likewise in that other significant document, *The National Interest and The Teaching of English,* a strong plea is made for increased supervisory services:

To provide the needed leadership in program development and in-service education, specialists in the teaching of English are needed on the staff of every state department of education. Such supervisors should be persons especially prepared by education and experience to promote sound articulation of programs in English from the Kindergarten through the high school, as well as articulation between the high school and the college.[30]

Curriculum Construction

One of the recommendations of the N. C. T. E. committee on articulation in 1913 was that "full, definite syllabi, rich in specific details, be prepared and printed for the guidance of teachers, and that representative teachers of various grades be consulted in the preparation of such syllabi." Today such school-wide and city-wide procedures are almost standard practices. An examination of *Guideposts to the English Language Arts* of the Seattle Public Schools (1962) will indicate not only the many representatives of all levels who have participated, but also the process, which sometimes may be almost as important as the product.[31] Committees of teachers who may wish to consult additional recently published courses of study should make use of the annual list of *Curriculum Materials* published by the Association for Supervision and Curriculum Development.[32]

The advantages of this method of preparing an English curriculum are many:

1. Representatives of the different levels get to know and understand one another, their objectives, their methods and their concepts of standards of evaluation and achievement.

2. Much time can be saved since questions at issue can be solved by personal conferences.

3. The accumulated experience and wisdom of the group can be utilized, rather than that of one or even a few persons who used to be charged with the task of preparing a curriculum.

4. Limitations caused by problems of budget, space or the nature of the pupils for whom the curriculum is intended, can best be expressed by the teachers themselves, for they are in the front lines every day.

5. Frequently the matter of "minimum essentials" for each level can best be settled in such conferences because the experienced teachers know what their slow, average, and bright students can accomplish.[33]

6. Teachers who will use the courses of study so prepared will have greater faith in them because they have been prepared by their colleagues rather than by one who "doesn't know what goes on in the classroom."

High School and College Articulation with Special Reference to Superior Students

In the decade of the 1950's and 1960's special attention was given to articulation between high school and college because of the great interest in the superior student. Because so many of them were bored by courses which they found too easy in high school, or by courses which they studied in college similar to their high school courses, efforts were made to eliminate the waste and duplication. Of these efforts, two main plans have evolved.

Early Admission. In the early admission plan, students are admitted to college before they graduate from high school, thus saving a year or more from their educational program. In the volume *They Went to College Early,* published by the Fund for the Advancement of Education (1957) the experiences of one thousand three hundred and fifty high school students of superior ability are described. Between 1951 and 1955 they entered twelve participating colleges and universities. Although they were about two years younger than the average college freshman, they did remarkably well both scholastically and extra-curricularly.[34]

Advanced Placement. Advanced placement began as an experiment in 1952 by the School and College Study of Admission with Advanced Standing. By 1955, when the study was concluded, it had accomplished four things:

1. It had developed through committees of school and college teachers college-level courses in eleven subjects which were given to a small group of public and private secondary schools.

2. Students who took these courses were tested carefully and thoroughly.

3. An agreement was made among fifteen colleges to give credit and advanced placement to those students who did satisfactory work in the courses and the examinations.

4. A conference was arranged for high school and college teachers who were interested in improving articulation.[35]

In 1955 the College Entrance Examination Board decided to continue the work on a national basis. Now students in high schools throughout the country may participate.

The examinations are now open to any able student wherever he may be and whether he achieved his knowledge through his own efforts, through tutorial assistance, or by taking special courses.[36]

The College Entrance Examination Board has issued various publications describing the program.[37] Some state departments of education as well as local school systems have issued their own booklists, suggested activities and sequence of studies.[38]

The Use of Cumulative Records. In many large school systems, cumulative records accompany the student from lower schools to the secondary schools. Individual marks in English are given in each grade. Thus the tenth-grade English teacher can ascertain what every member of the class has achieved in English. The I. Q., the reading score, and individual strengths and weaknesses are included. By studying these records, the senior high English teacher can form some idea of the nature of the class, what special emphases need to be given, and provide for individual differences. These records are continued throughout the high school career of the student. Since each English teacher's name is indicated as well as her mark for the student, it is easy for several teachers to get together (providing that administrative allowances have been made for such conferences) and discuss individual students' problems.

The Individual Approach to Articulation

In the final analysis, the best kind of articulation must be made on an individual basis; only the paucity of time and the pressure of other non-teaching assignments militate against the individual approach to articulation. After labeling articulation in English as one of the seven important curriculum problems in the program in New York State, Dora V. Smith continues with:

The answer to the problem (i.e., of articulation) would seem to lie less in the meticulous listing of graded items for mastery at each level of instruction than in the consideration of a basic philosophy of education, a study of the actual needs of all boys and girls within the school system, and an analysis of the major powers, attitudes and skills with which it is desirable that they should be equipped, apart from the specific content by means of which these ends are to be achieved.[39]

The individual's approach to articulation is cogently expressed in *The English Language Arts:*

Thoughtful consideration of the ways in which skills and concepts actually develop in the language arts, as in other fields, makes it clear that there is no uniformity in the amounts of development in different pupils during any given period of time. Instead of all pupils having reached the expected levels at the end of the elementary school or of the high school, they are actually scattered at various points far up and down the scale in each different aspect of development. The only realistic way in which any useful articulation can be effected is to begin the work of each new year or division of the school by determining just where the student is in each area of language development and then to help him move ahead from that point. To try to help him to begin new development at some more advanced point "where he is supposed to be" would usually be a waste of the teacher's time and effort, as well as an unwarranted attack upon the student's integrity.

The articulation of one grade to another, or of higher-level to lower-level schools, can never be accomplished effectively in any aspect of language development except pupil by pupil.[40]

Three quarters of a century of explorations in means of articulation have not solved the problem, but at least some successful techniques have evolved. There is less complaining about the work in the lower echelons and more of the spirit of mutual respect and understanding. If, as Dora V. Smith said, articulation is not a one-way street, we have discovered some ways of meeting one another in the attempt to contribute to the maximum growth in English of all our students.

22

CORRELATION AND INTEGRATION IN ENGLISH

Correlation, fusion and integration in the English program have a long history, going back to Herbart's doctrines. With slight modification, they also appear in new approaches labelled core, broad fields and unified learning. Definitions, therefore, are in order before we can describe procedures and evaluate them for the English program of the 1970's. *An Experience Curriculum in English* (1936) makes the following distinctions:

Correlation may be so slight as casual attention to related materials in other subjects, for example, noting while reading the spirited, polished, superficial verse of the Cavalier Poets the ideals and social graces of the cavalier as studied in history. Correlation becomes a bit more intense when it is planned in advance to make the materials of one subject interpret the problems or topics of another.[1]

Fusion designates the combination of two subjects, usually under the same instructor or instructors; supposedly the partners are equal, but usually one dominates and uses the other. One of the most common fusions is the blending of literature and history, which has the more definite outline usually dominating. Fusion may extend to the combination of a whole group of subjects, for example, literature, music, dancing, architecture, plastic arts and graphic arts. Such courses are organized by common principles, common themes, or other common elements of the subjects included.[2]

Integration is the unification of all study and other experience. It comes about, for the most part, not through conscious combining of different subjects or activities but through initiation of vital activities which reach out into vital fields and absorb subject content as the roots of a tree absorb food from the soil—without regard to fences on the surface.[3]

ADVANTAGES AND DISADVANTAGES OF CORRELATION

Alert teachers for generations have correlated their teaching of English with other subjects. The extent and the validity of the correlations they made depended on their cultural background and their good judgment. It is almost impossible to teach *Silas Marner* without some reference to England's Industrial Revolution, just as it is almost impossible to teach *A Tale of Two Cities* without referring to the historical facts of the French Revolution. Likewise, enlightened teaching of *The Scarlet Letter* would require some explanation of Puritan ideas and conventions, just as the teaching of *My Ántonia* and *Giants in the Earth* would require explanations of America's Westward Movement. English teachers have for decades helped their students to comprehend the literature they studied by explaining the historical backgrounds of which the literary work was the artist's interpretation.[4]

As to the reasons for correlation, Hatfield has expressed them well:

It should be self-evident that the more numerous the connections which are established between subjects the better, and also that the greater the number of subjects connected the more correlation will contribute to a perception of the general pattern and significance of life. Probably all *sound* correlations, discoveries of *live* connections, are worth all they cost.[5]

English, or any phase of English, cannot be so compartmentalized as to avoid references to other subject areas. How can vocabulary growth be stimulated without references to Latin and Greek prefixes, roots, and suffixes (correlation with classical languages)? How can the history of English be developed without references to the contributions of words, phrases, and cognates from modern foreign languages? A word like "cosmonaut" or "astronaut," both coined in the early 1960's, naturally leads to correlations with space science. A mention of the etymology of "antibiotics" naturally leads to a study of modern chemical destruction of germs. The opportunities are too numerous and too obvious to require further repetition. English teachers have used the subject matters of other areas in the secondary curriculum to exemplify concepts which they were explaining, to enrich the backgrounds of their students so that the literature being studied might be seen in its contemporary as well as its universal setting, and to strengthen the strands of learning.

One step removed from such casual references to other subject areas is a more organized attempt to find enriching materials for students so that they may read historical, biographical and autobiographical materials (letters, diaries, memoirs) at the same time they study the literary works for their emotional, aesthetic and ethical values. Several collections of such correlative materials have been gathered. The English Life in English Literature Series is a case in point.[6] Six volumes have been published, each containing contemporary historical materials which furnish a background for understanding the literary period being studied. Each has been compiled by an outstanding scholar. The series consists of the following:

England from Chaucer to Caxton, by H. S. Bennett
England from Caxton to Spenser, by J. M. Berdan
England in Shakespeare's Day, by G. B. Harrison
England from Bunyan to Defoe, by J. Isaacs
England in Johnson's Day, by M. Dorothy George
England from Wordsworth to Dickens, by R. W. King

Various book lists have been compiled which can be used to enrich the English course of study, among them *Books for You* and *Your Reading* of the National Council of Teachers of English; Edwin R. Carr's *Guide to Reading for Social Studies Teachers,*[7] and the publications of the American Council on Education, *Literature for Human Understanding* and *Reading Ladders for Human Relations.*[8]

Magazines frequently contain materials which can serve for correlation, such as the various *Scholastic* magazines, *The Saturday Review/World* and *Reader's Digest.*

A third step in meaningful correlation takes place when the English teacher ascertains what his students in social studies are studying and tries to make the reading in literature parallel the period studied in social studies. Thus, if in eleventh-year social studies the history of America is studied and if a survey course in American literature is pursued in the English class, attempts have been made to reinforce both subjects by teaching them at approximately the same time. The difficulties in this closer type of correlation have long been pointed out. One obvious disadvantage was pointed out as early as 1902 by Chubb; namely, that inferior literature might be used merely because it can be correlated with social studies.[9] Another is that the chronological approach may not always be the best approach in certain schools or with certain classes. A third difficulty is the inflexibility which may result. Students may wish to linger over certain literary works because they are appealing, but which must be laid aside because a new topic in social studies is to be taken up next. Finally, there is the matter of going to the point of diminishing return: to the point of monotony with too frequent emphasis on correlation.

THE GROWTH OF THE CORRELATION MOVEMENT

In the 1930's many schools were experimenting with various types of combined courses. Ruth Mary Weeks and a committee of The National Council of Teachers of English prepared *A Correlated Curriculum* in 1936, which included numerous examples of experiments. Although many of these experiments are no longer existent, the volume is an excellent survey of the state of correlated studies in the 1930's.

In the course of breaking down barriers between subject matters, some teachers went the whole way and no longer called their subject English-Social Studies, but by more striking names describing the overall theme and concept. Theoretically, such courses were not integrated. Perhaps a list of the titles of such courses will give an idea of the scope of these integrated courses. Interested readers can obtain complete details about each of these in the footnotes. It must be cautioned that many of these courses no longer exist, either because their teacher retired or because the school decided to return to more traditional methodology. Yet they deserve to be studied as part of the alert English teacher's quest throughout the twentieth century for more effective teaching.

1. *Western Youth Meets Eastern Culture,* by Frances G. Sweeney, Emily F. Barry and Alice Schoelkopf. This was taught in the Horace Mann-Lincoln School at Teachers College, Columbia University, and combined junior high school English, history, geography and art.[10]

2. *Builders Together* was an integrated unit conducted by E. Louise Noyes of the

Santa Barbara High School and is described in great detail in *Conducting Experiences in English.*[11]

3. *An Analysis of an American's Rights.* This was carried on in the high school at Chico, California. As Mirrielees described it in her *Teaching Composition and Literature,* the course consists of six units, each unit motivated by one of the six rights of American citizens set forth in the preamble of the Constitution: (A) to form a more perfect union; (B) to establish justice; (C) to insure domestic tranquility; (D) to provide for the common defense; (E) to promote the general welfare; (F) to secure the blessings of liberty.[12]

4. *Why Do We Act This Way?* An integrated twelfth-grade course. This was taught by Grace D. Broening at the Forest Park High School in Baltimore and is summarized in *The English Language Arts in the Secondary School.* Its goal was "to understand why people are acting the way they are in the twentieth-century by discovering relevent patterns of thought and action in the seventeenth, eighteenth and nineteenth centuries."[13]

5. *Social Living,* a two-year course for freshmen and sophomores in which English, social studies, art and music are integrated. "The course opens with discussion of the pupils' own problems—economic, social, moral. It then broadens to the community problems and to the problems confronting the pupils' parents. Finally, a study is made of national and international problems."[14]

THE INTRODUCTION OF CORE

In addition to the terms *correlation, fusion,* and *integration,* the 1930's saw the introduction of the terms *core* and *unified studies.* The latter two terms refer to programs in which "a series of social problems were attacked in the classes, the resulting curriculum being substituted for the previous courses in English, history, and, in some cases, science and fine arts."[15] The core program has by this time developed an extensive literature, much of which is summarized in Roland C. Faunce and Nelson L. Bossing's *Developing the Core Curriculum.*[16] Added elements in the core program, in addition to breaking down the subject-matter barriers, are considerable pupil-teacher planning, considerable use of cooperative student effort, use of outside resources and atypical methods of evaluation.

In all of these combined programs students spend considerable time together under a single teacher or a team of teachers. Thus, teachers get to know their students better and can provide for individual differences to a greater extent than in the traditional class. Since a pre-planned course of study usually is not followed, students can attack their problems more leisurely and under less pressure for covering ground. Advocates of core programs for the non-academically minded contend that under this program students develop more interest in their work, do not get discouraged so easily, and develop desirable attitudes to school and society.[17]

ADVANTAGES OF COMBINED COURSES

Teachers of English, new or inexperienced, might well ask themselves what the advantages and disadvantages are of such combined courses. They find teaching English difficult enough without having to add new bodies of subject-matter and new methodology to their training. From the many expressions of opinion from English teachers who have engaged in one or more of the types of combined programs, the following advantages are stated more frequently:

Mastering the Skills

1. The longer period of time permits more time for developing, practising and applying a skill.
2. Since the subject-matter of two or more disciplines (i.e., English, social studies, science) are included in the longer period of time, good reading, speaking, writing and listening habits can be stressed. In a program that separates the subjects, it is conceivable that such good habits might be stressed only by the English teacher.
3. Skills can be taught as the needs arise. In the traditional program, the pupils may feel the need to learn something just as the bell rings for class dismissal, and that need may never be met.
4. Where individual and social problems are the starting point of student inquiry, the human values in literature may be more meaningful. An assignment which asks students to "take the next 30 pages of *A Tale of Two Cities*" has seldom been known to develop a passionate interest in this or any other piece of literature.
5. More time is made available for providing for individual differences. The teacher meets one class of students instead of two and meets them for a double period or sometimes longer (e.g., a home room, a study hall or both). Not only has he more time to study the needs of fewer students, but the longer period permits him to organize the class into a series of activities with time available for personal attention.
6. The combined class by its very length of time permits procedures that contribute to development of higher thought processes. For example, the committee work may stimulate thinking, evaluating and creativity. The question-and-answer method which dominates most traditionally conducted classes may not work as effectively.

Developing Proper Behavior and Social Concepts

English is not learned as something to deposit in one's memory in order to possess it. English is for understanding one's self, for communicating with others, for contributing to one's community vocationally and avocationally. Hence attitudes and social concepts assume great importance in our world and will be even more important in the world of tomorrow. Advocates of one or another of these combined courses claim that pupils grow in behavior and social concepts to a greater extent than in the traditional English class. These are the ways:

Cooperativeness. In the double period there is time for cooperative activities. The success of an individual report, a panel report, an original dramatization depends on the cooperation of the entire committee. While it is true that in the traditional English class one may observe an occasional panel discussion or a group report, there simply is not time in the 45-minute or hour period to do as much of this type of work as the teacher would like. This cooperativeness manifests itself in many ways: in accepting assignments from a student chairman even though these may be onerous, distasteful and not of one's choice; in learning person-to-person relationships which are so important to the process of growing up and in later life; in taking pride in contributing to a group project.

Work habits. Longer periods of time under the guidance of a superior teacher (and only a superior teacher can handle such a combined class) can contribute to developing better habits of work: ability to plan individual and group tasks; complete a job once it is started; organize material; use many resources; feel pride in neat and almost perfect work. The double period permits more student and teacher evaluation, and honest evaluation leads to self-improvement.

Ability to work with and respect others. In a pluralistic society the contributions of many are welcome. The student of today may in a few years occupy an important business or government post in any of a hundred countries both new and old, with different languages, traditions, heritages. The world of learning to work together in the combined class may be a microcosm of what the student will do tomorrow.

Self-discipline vs. imposed discipline. Once a project gets underway and student interest is aroused, the problem of discipline may be reduced. Particularly in the case of non-academic students who may become behavior problems, this double period has resulted in greater interest and hence better self-discipline. Some advocates have proof that the holding power of this program is greater for the non-academics.[18]

Advantages for the Teacher

1. He can get to know his students better and provide for individual differences.
2. He is free to experiment because he is not restricted by the need to cover ground in either English or social studies.
3. He is constantly growing in the process of teaching. A canned set of questions in the back of a classic does not satisfy him. Evidences of pupil growth and change are there every day, and new techniques must be found to stimulate growth and direct it into useful channels.
4. The wide variety of classroom activities which can be carried on in a combined double period class are lacking in the traditional class.

SOME DISADVANTAGES OF THE COMBINED CLASSES

Almost from the very beginning of the introduction of the various kinds of correlation in the English programs, certain cautions were expressed. These cautions which were found in Carpenter, Baker and Scott in their book of 1903 are still expressed today. Experiment in English is desirable and will, in fact, always be carried on, but one must be careful not to lose sight of the important values in English as a separate subject. Among the disadvantages of the combined programs are:

One subject may be neglected if the teacher of the combined class is trained in one of the disciplines and only has a smattering of the other. Technically such a teacher should know English and social studies equally well and should have a good background in adolescent psychology, guidance, evaluative procedures and the use of many resources. There are not too many teachers of such background available. The teachers who have described their correlated work in the professional literature have all been outstanding teachers. It is conceivable that they would have been successful regardless of the method they tried.

Such a teacher must be extremely well read not only in the best of English, American and world literature but also should have read a good portion of that adolescent literature which some authorities have designated, "junior novels."[19] Particularly in teaching the slow learner, such knowledge is all-important if the teacher is to take each student from his present level and lead him to higher levels of comprehension and appreciation. Such novels, biographies for younger readers and similar works now number in the thousands. Teachers who would really like to do justice in such a program should accept the fact that there will be much reading to do.

Although it is a comforting thought for the English teacher to hear an administrator say that "every teacher is a teacher of English," he knows that it takes many years of hard work for the English teacher to become a good English teacher, let alone the industrial arts teacher or the sewing teacher. The greatest criticism of the non-English teacher is that he is not trained to teach literature as appreciation. Consequently, students may be able to read factual prose well in preparing a class report but be deficient in the appreciation of literature as an art and as a source of inspiration and pleasure for a lifetime.

A combined course requires many resources of materials and plant, the absence of which may condemn the program to failure. For example, such a class cannot succeed with a set of literature anthologies, a set of history books and a few drill books. Classroom libraries, multitudes of magazines or articles clipped from magazines carefully filed and easily available, are necessary. Such classrooms often have audio-visual equipment in the room. Movable chairs and desks permit group activities. Libraries must be richly stocked and easily accessible.

Preparation for such a class is arduous. No teacher should go into such a program who is not prepared to spend hours a day in preparation.

CORRELATION AND THE THEMATIC APPROACH

Many of the aspects of correlation, fusion and integration described in this chapter are incorporated into regular English classes using the unit approach. (See Chapter 18.) The teacher of a particular unit may be handling a theme or a problem which requires content from many subject areas. A study of Elizabethan drama, even in the regular English class, can make use of Elizabethan music, would include some understanding of Elizabethan daily life, costume, international politics and other knowledges which other disciplines can contribute. All of these facts are discovered by students, presented to the class by various means, and help the students to get a more complete view of life than from a close analytical study of the text.

Likewise, student problems do not necessarily have to arise in the combined class. Many a brilliant unit has begun in the English classroom under the guidance of a teacher who knows the unit approach. Cooperative behavior, although it cannot be exercised in a single period as long as in a double period, nevertheless can be emphasized in all classes. In short, the contemporary English teacher who uses good methods of teaching may be the heir of such crucial volumes in the history of American education as *An Experience Curriculum in English* and *A Correlated Curriculum* without necessarily following the patterns described in these volumes in the mid 1930's.

English instruction in America has grown because of many contributions of outstanding teachers who have experimented with better ways to develop in their students the skills, knowledges, attitudes and appreciations that make up the subject called English.

PART SEVEN
THE HIGH SCHOOL ENGLISH
CHAIRMAN: PERSISTENT
PROBLEMS

23

CREATIVE SUPERVISION IN THE SECONDARY SCHOOL

In 1921 Charles A. Wagner in his *Common Sense in Supervision* states: About all the knowledge obtainable on this topic is a series of individual opinions, mostly the opinions of teachers who give expression to their dissatisfaction with supervision as they have experienced it. No statistical study appears to have been made at any time.[1]

We have come a long way since 1921. Some thirty to forty major studies of instructional supervision have been published in book form. Between 1935-1945, *Educational Index* listed 278 articles. This did not include curriculum planning or in-service training. The topic of supervision in general, and creative supervision in particular, is one therefore that has come into its own in the past five decades and well merits our deep consideration.

It is always helpful in discussing supervision to define one's terms. By creative supervision, I mean the encouragement, stimulation and guidance of each teacher in a department to his maximum capacity so that he may in turn contribute to the maximum development of every pupil in his class. To think of creative supervision without considering the effect upon the pupils is to think of means without awareness of the ultimate end, which is instructional improvement.

If one accepts this definition of creative supervision, he then will agree that there is no one best means of supervision, no one royal road to teacher improvement. What may work successfully with one type of teacher would be destructive and stultifying to another. John A. Bartky in his *Supervision as Human Relations* lists seven types of supervision: autocratic; inspectional; representative; cooperative-democratic; invitational; scientific; creative.[2] I am sure that there are several other types that are modifications or combinations of these and that newer concepts will develop in the future.

The modern concept of education for all American youth is predicated on the philosophy that the teacher takes the pupil where he finds him and, by whatever means at his command, develops him to his maximum capacity. The supervisor does pretty much the same thing with the teachers under his direction. It is pointless to try to make a Horace Mann or an Elizabeth Peabody of every teacher, and many of us will settle for written daily lesson plans, knowing that for some teachers that is a professional victory. Common sense and a modicum of knowledge of human nature and human relations will make one realize there are limits beyond which one cannot go as a supervisor.

Based on my three decades of experience as a supervisor of English teachers, I have devised some guiding principles of my own philosophy of creative supervision. These are so simple and obvious that one often wonders at the ponderous tomes on instructional supervision that pour forth from the educational presses.

Supervision works best in an environment of mutual respect and understanding.

Teacher growth through instructional supervision is a slow process. This means that the supervisor's level of frustration must be high. I personally did not expect even a small change in my entire department before eighteen months passed.

The supervisor himself must be a master-critic, quick to perceive the strengths and weaknesses of every lesson; a master teacher, ready with worthwhile suggestions to improve the lesson; and a master diplomat, capable of pointing out to the teacher how he best may improve himself without offending him.

Communication lines must be clear between teacher and supervisor. This means face-to-face conferences, small group conferences, department-wide conferences and various types of supervisory bulletins.[3]

Supervision is both an art and something of a science. Some supervisors may become skilled technicians, but never artists, for the art of supervision is not quickly learned, whereas the preparation of a rating sheet is a comparatively simple process.

Methods without materials are as undernourishing as sandwiches composed exclusively of bread. The supervisor must make available textbooks in sufficient quantity, reference books for both teachers and students, audio-visual aids, duplicating facilities, so that his suggestions for improvement may be more than mere words on paper.

Encouragement is the best fuel to light the flame. This does not mean a phony slap on the back or a comforting arm around the shoulder, but rather a genuine desire to see something good and praise the teacher for it. I found my day as a supervisor incomplete if I could not write one or two notes of encouragement. If one looks for good things, one will find them. Some supervisors follow the practice of writing notes of commendation at the end of the school year, and the practice is a good one. But on-the-spot encouragement for anything outstanding goes far toward improving teacher morale and inspiring the teacher to seek ever-higher levels of improvement.

Fairness, firmness and fidelity to the staff are important. The staff must know that the supervisor has no favorites, that all members are important players on the team. Even the weakest teacher is better than an inexperienced substitute (usually out of license) or no teacher at all because no one will come in inclement weather.

Although some teachers may call the supervisor unreasonable, he must be firm when he is definitely in the right. I was proud to be considered inflexible because I insisted that every teacher in my department should be well prepared daily in writing, should see that his or her room was attractively decorated, should prevent the floor from being littered, and should stand on his or her feet as much as possible when teaching. I was called inflexible for insisting on these minima; I welcomed the appellation.

Closely allied to fairness and firmness is fidelity to your staff. Our subject, particularly, has long been under unwarranted attacks from unqualified or biased critics. I never permited these attacks to go unchallenged, whether they came in my own school or in the public press. When the staff realizes that the supervisor has faith in them and is confident of their ability to grow, and that he is always ready to give them support when it is needed, he will go a long way toward achieving that mutual respect which is the most nourishing environment for maximum stimulation of teacher growth.

The supervisor must strive to develop leadership in others by providing opportunities for growth. Even the weakest teacher may excel in some aspect of teaching.

The supervisor must develop the art of good listening, and must make time for listening, to his teachers' gripes and satisfactions, joys and sorrows, successes and frustrations.

Sometimes supervision must be interpreted in its literal sense: "oversight." Sometimes it may seem wiser to be blind in one eye and deaf in one ear. It may be wiser to lose the minor supervisory skirmish in order to win the major instructional battle.

Finally, there is the principle so wisely expressed by the Chinese poet and philosopher, Lao-tzu:

> A leader is best
> When people barely
> Know that he exists,
> Not so good when people obey and acclaim him,
> Worst when they despise him.
> Fail to honor people, they fail to honor you;
> But of a good leader Who talks little
> When his work is done, his aim fulfilled,
> They will say "We did this ourselves."[4]

Rome wasn't built in a day, and a happy and efficient department takes years to develop. Yet the English staff and the supervisor must grow or retrograde in these times of many changes. Teachers, like plants, will grow and flourish. Given the proper environment, the right kind of intellectual nourishment and the proper dosage, the English staff is bound to grow into an efficient team that makes the work as a supervisor the daily rewarding experience for which we as supervisors have dedicated ourselves.

24

THE PRINCIPAL AND HIS INFLUENCE ON
THE ENGLISH PROGRAM

Let us begin with our first problem: how to convince our students and our colleagues in other disciplines that English is our most important subject and that every teacher, to some extent, is a teacher of English. Whenever this question arises, we like to quote from Professor W. W. Watson, former chairman of the Physics Department of Yale University, a member of the Manhattan Project group which worked on the atom bomb:

I feel that the most important subject in the entire course of study in the elementary and college preparatory years is the English language. What can be more important than to handle our work-a-day language with facility, no matter what the life work, business or profession? I have some younger physics scientists who work in the laboratory but they are laggards in writing papers that describe their results. But what good are research reports unless they are properly described in a well-written report?

Also, it is most important that a scientist or engineer be able to get on his feet and speak clearly about his work. Some practice in public speaking, debating or dramatics should be a part of every student's course.

I am pleased to note that one of President's Conant's main recommendations is that all school students should study English every year, and that half this work should be in composition.[1]

For those skeptical students who are interested in business, we like to quote from Emil Hubka, Jr., a former executive of Motorola:

I have often stated to former colleagues of mine that after nine years in industry, I would like very much to be able to return to the classroom and tell the students just how desperately they will need the ability offered them by their English courses. . . . Allow me to assure you and your colleagues in the Council that you can, in truth, tell your students that no other part of their training in school will be so vital to them in their careers as their work in English.[2]

216

THE PRINCIPAL AND THE IMPORTANCE OF ENGLISH

Where does the obligation of the principal lie? As the chief administrative officer of his school, he can set policy. He can direct his teachers in all disciplines to require reasonable standards of English in all written work, all oral work in every class. He can encourage wide reading for enrichment by providing adequate library facilities in all areas.

Why should English teachers alone require supplementary reading of their students when there is such a wealth of books in science, mathematics, social studies and other fields? By encouraging reading throughout the school, the principal can be a potent force for development of life-long habits in one of life's greatest pleasures.

Let us give a single example to show how departments other than English can fortify our program. For many years in Jamaica N. Y. C. High School, we gave mid-term examinations in all of our major subjects. Our English paper always began with a reading-comprehension question. A few terms ago the Social Studies examination also began with a reading question. When this occurred, our principal made it a point to praise the chairman of the Social Studies department for introducing this particular question and strongly recommended that all major departments include such a question. More recently, other departments have introduced reading-comprehension questions.

The principal can dignify the position of English in various other ways: by providing adequate sums for textbooks and supplies. We have never had enough. Funds from N. D. E. A. have helped a little; by providing the chairman with clerical assistance, so that he can be relieved to perform his supervisory function; by rewarding students' excellence in English just as excellence in sports, music and art are rewarded. This can be done in assembly programs or at commencement; by seizing every opportunity to emphasize that in his school English is all-pervasive and all-important.

THE PRINCIPAL AND WRITTEN COMPOSITION

Of all the phases of English which have come in for criticism in recent years, written composition leads the list. We need not repeat here all the criticisms or the many valuable suggestions which have been made. Putting the matter very simply, English teachers have had too many papers to mark and too little time to mark them. In addition, too many have come into the profession without adequate preparation in proper methodology of teaching written composition.

What Can the Principal Do?

Most experts on the teaching of English advocate a class size of twenty-five and four classes of English to a teacher. This has been advocated by the Dusel, Conant, the Foley Reports, and the National Council of Teachers of English. We realize that just as soon as a principal reduces an English teacher's load to one hundred students in four classes, other teachers will find good reasons for reducing their load. Well, one must make decisions, and the improvement of written English is a truly important decision for a principal to make.

The principal can contribute by relieving the English teacher from non-teaching duties so that he can have time to confer with his students. One of the practices of the beloved Charles Townsend Copland (Copey) of Harvard was his personal conferences with his students. Likewise the great George Lyman Kittredge of Harvard was at his best in small seminars with his graduate students. We need not belabor the point. If more English teachers had time to meet with their students to discuss their written work and a quiet place for such consultations, we believe that much improvement would result.

The principal can dignify excellence in written composition by encouraging students to contribute to their school newspapers and magazines, to such magazines as *The Student Writer,* and to the *Scholastic Magazines* annual competition. An outstanding article, poem or story might be read at assembly, a P. T. A. meeting, a Rotary Club or similar meeting.

Finally, he himself should have some idea of the difficulty in teaching written composition and should himself have a fairly good prose style.

THE PRINCIPAL AND LANGUAGE STUDY

The principal, like his English teachers, must have a clear perception of what language is and how it has grown and developed.

This means a greater understanding of historical linguistics, or the way in which our language developed, is constantly developing, and will develop in the future.

This also means a re-evaluation of our concepts of the place of grammar instruction in our schools, whether it be the formal grammar of our high school days, the functional grammar of our beginning days as a teacher, or the structural and transformational grammars which are much talked about in educational circles today.

We would not throw all grammar overboard or advocate wholly any single variety of grammar, but we do believe there is a need for more controlled experiments on a massive scale and over a considerable period of time to determine exactly what concepts of grammar we want to teach and how to teach them. Even a few small experiments in teaching the new structural and transformational grammars may enable us to re-evaluate our instruction for achieving our ends more effectively. Linguists are not agreed on many things, but they are agreed on this: there is a large body of verified knowledge about our language which has not even begun to affect the vast majority of our colleagues. Study takes time. In the crowded schedule of the average secondary English teacher, there is precious little time for study of the facts of our language, newer discoveries in our literature, or in methodology of both. The great popularity of summer workshops in linguistics is a desirable trend.

What is the role of the principal in the area of language study? In the first place he should be aware of some of the new concepts. He should encourage experimentation among those English teachers who have taken courses in structural linguistics, transformational grammar and other aspects of language study, and who wish to experiment with newer approaches. He should make attendance possible for members of his staff who wish to attend such linguistic workshops. Or he might make it possible for some teachers to visit school systems where the entire junior and senior high school English program has become linguistically oriented. Finally, he can provide funds for the purchase of some of the best books in the area of language study for his teachers' library. Student textbooks now are available on the junior and senior high levels. An excellent bibliography[3] was published by the School of Education of the University of Oregon and might serve as a guide.

By becoming acquainted himself with new concepts about language, encouraging experimentation and enabling his teachers to procure in-service training in this area, the principal may go a long way toward improving the program of language study in his school.

THE PRINCIPAL AND STAFFING THE ENGLISH DEPARTMENT

English is the easiest subject to teach poorly and the most difficult subject to teach well. Hence the principal must be especially careful in selecting his English Department. It would never occur to him to fill in an extra science class with an inexperienced teacher from the home economics department or the industrial arts department. Yet it is a practice to give classes in English to any teacher who happens to need a period to complete his program.

The philosophy has been that anybody can teach English. We would like to change that to anybody can nonteach English. If a scientific study could be made of the damage that has been done to our English program by this nonteaching of English by non-experts, we are sure we should all be chagrined at the results. Yet this obnoxious practice continues all over the land. Read *The National Interest and the Teaching of English*[4] and you will be depressed by the number of unqualified persons who are in our English classrooms.

This problem is easily solved by insisting that only qualified English teachers teach English. In the event, however, that a school is too small to be permitted a choice of teachers, it behooves the principal or his English chairman to give poorly qualified teachers all the help they need, through observations, conferences, bulletins and other supervisory devices generally utilized for improving instruction. In too many instances an inexperienced teacher is thrust into an English classroom with a battered old grammar text and an antiquated anthology and told to sink or swim. Most often he drowns and takes his unfortunate class with him. It is time to call a halt to this short-changing, by a rigorous adherence to the principle that every English class deserved a well-qualified teacher.

25

THE HIGH SCHOOL ENGLISH CHAIRMAN LOOKS AT
THE HUMANITIES APPROACH FOR ALL STUDENTS

At the 1961 Convention of the National Council of Teachers of English it was my privilege to present a paper on "How Fare the Humanities in High School?"[1] I ventured to predict that the next few years would see a strengthening of the position of the humanities because of: the paperback revolution; the thematic approach in literature instruction; the more dynamic roles of school libraries; the contributions of music and art; increasing use of field trips to dramatic, art and music centers; the potentialities of the mass media; improvement of teaching techniques and methodology; improvement of administration.

Today the signs are even more encouraging. The National Council of Teachers of English has held two highly successful conferences on the humanities, and important papers on aspects of the humanities have appeared in various publications.[2] On the weekend of November 1, 2, 3, 1968, a regional conference sponsored by SCOPE—Suffolk County Educational Center—was held at Montauk Point, New York. Rarely has an affiliate of the N. C. T. E. held an annual meeting in recent years without devoting one or more sessions to a discussion of the humanities. The same is true for almost every annual N. C. T. E. convention since 1961. Certainly there has been much discussion of philosophy, procedures and successes or failures of local approaches. The fact that hundreds of applicants to the two N. C. T. E. conferences on the humanities had to be turned away is eloquent testimony to the great interest in the humanities way.

Another measure of the growth of interest in the humanities on the high school level is the increase of publications telling interested teachers just how they can build courses of studies in various aspects of the humanities. For example, the New York State Education Department in 1966 published *The Humanities: A Planning Guide for Teachers*[3] which is a treasury of successful units preceded by discussions of the meaning of the humanities and the best methods of incorporating this approach into the high school curriculum or program of studies.

In 1968 two additional bulletins were prepared by the same agency which are landmarks in their respective fields: *An Invitation to the Dance*[4] and *Performing Arts Education.*[5]

In addition to the publications produced by curriculum divisions associated with state education agencies or local education agencies, such books as Leon C. Karel's *Avenues to the Arts* have appeared.[6] This is, I believe, the first textbook on the related arts written for high school students, and it merits a place in every high school library.

Finally, there is the increasing number of articles in the professional journals dealing with the humanities. New York State Education Department's *The Humanities* lists seventy-five articles published up to 1966 alone.

What does all this mean for the further growth of the program? I believe that the humanities approach to all education will be given wider currency in the years to come, and teachers will find it a more rewarding experience than they have had utilizing other approaches.

I intend to devote the remainder of this chapter to a discussion of what a supervisor of an English Department can do to inspire his teachers to adopt the humanities approach by referring to actual experiences and situations during my tenure of thirty years in two large metropolitan high schools. While these suggestions are based on long experience, I well realize that other supervisors have had success with other methods and that it would be provincial, in my judgment, to say this is the only way to do it. There are many good ways, and each of us who has followed this way has probably been inspired by a different person, book, experience or emotion.

For the sake of organization let us speak of four ways in which the supervisor may help: procedures; approaches; content; readings.

To illustrate what I mean I will indicate how I recently introduced a literature anthology to my new eleventh-grade class. After years of teaching adolescents, I learned that to many of them the author of their textbook had no particular significance. Even on the college level, after spending months with a textbook and giving a test on its contents, I would get a chorus of groans when a question appeared on the names of its editors or of its publishers. Why, the students would ask, is it important to know who edited or who published our textbooks? I would then explain that a book does not make itself, that years of planning often go into the compilation of an anthology, that there are strict laws about copyright. When all these explanations were over, which go back historically in time to learning the meanings of such terms as *folio* (especially the First Folio), *quarto, colophon, end-paper,* the students began to grasp something about a book as the "precious life-blood of a master spirit embalmed and treasured up on purpose to a life beyond life." Even this quotation takes on dimensions when I ask where in New York City it is inscribed over the entrance to the main reading room of a large library.

Just as the great anatomist Louis Agassiz used to challenge his students to note what they saw in a preserved fish over a period of days to test their limits of observation, I ask my students to turn to the title-page of their newly-issued anthologies and list a dozen important facts. Most will list the obvious. Many will not know the difference between an author and an editor. Many will not know the meaning of the inscription, or such vignettes as Houghton Mifflin's *tout bien ou rien* or never will have noticed them before, mainly because no teacher ever took the trouble to point them out. When we are finished we are agreed that for the first time we noticed valuable information.

But this is only the beginning: our anthology is called the Laureate Edition. First, I elicit the meaning of *Laureate*. Why should an honored writer be termed *Laureate?*

Then we discover this word has a long and distinguished history going back to classical times, that at one time college graduates in rhetoric and poetry were presented with the laurel wreath. I seize this opportunity to suggest that the editors or publishers of such a series must have had some classical background, especially in view of the fact that two earlier editions of this literature series had borne the name Olympic and Mercury, and that the newest edition is called the Classic.

My purpose in this discussion of a single word is not to make classical scholars of these eleventh-graders but to widen their horizons and to enable them to get more out of the printed page and hence out of life itself. Without telling them specifically how or why, I emphasize that such curiosity leading to an understanding of words and concepts will enable them to understand better what they read and to develop greater sensitivities. The following day I brought in a copy of A. E. Housman's *A Shropshire Lad* and read to them "To An Athlete Dying Young," first urging them to be on the lookout for any words that were discussed the preceding day. Every student noticed:

> And early though the laurel grows
> It withers quicker than the rose.

and

> And round the early-laurelled head
> Will flock to gaze the strengthless dead.

There was a certain feeling of satisfaction as they realized how something learned the day before enabled them to appreciate more fully a subsequent poem. But the lesson on *Laurel* did not end here. Since I had mentioned that crowning a winner with the laurel wreath goes back to classical times, I asked whether anyone would look into this matter in a reference book and report to the class the next day. One student asked who was the first poet laureate (a good teacher could have anticipated such a question and been prepared with suggestions). Rather than supply that information, I referred the questioner to William Rose Benet's *The Readers' Encyclopedia*,[7] where the earliest poets laureate are listed. This provided the first opportunity of the new term to inform the students that there were sources of information other than *The Encyclopaedia Britannica* or the *World Almanac*. All through the term as needs arise other reference books would be mentioned or, much better, brought in.

One final stirring of curiosity. Although most students have heard of etymology and have on occasion looked up the etymology of this or that word, I try to make them go one step further—to interest them in that greatest of all English dictionaries, the *Oxford English Dictionary*—by asking them where they would look for the first appearance in print of the expression poet laureate. Few would know where, at the eleventh-grade level, and thus an opportunity presents itself to mention something about the enormous amount of information in that treasure house of linguistic information. Usually one or two students will volunteer to look this entry up, (i.e., poet laureate), and report on their findings the next day. Am I attempting to make lexicographers out of these sixteen-year olds? Obviously not. What I hope to do is begin a practice that goes on almost every day to arouse their interest in words, their origin, their changes in meaning, and their lives and deaths. I would be the first to admit that not every student becomes a passionate lover of etymologies or linguistics as a result of my own interest, but I do try to make them see that the person with the greater background is the one who lives the richer life, whether it be the reader of poetry or the listener to serious music. What I have tried to do is to humanize the study of literature and language.

KEEPING CURIOSITY ALIVE

Child psychologists agree that the growing child has a curiosity about almost everything. His most frequent word is why? In his earliest years in school he maintains that curiosity, but now he must learn to satisfy that curiosity by referring to books or to other printed materials. By the time the student is in the eleventh grade his sense of curiosity has been blunted. I consider it the function of the teacher using the humanities approach to rekindle it with such a word as laureate, with a picture, or with a passage from such tonal expressions as a great symphony, a movement from chamber music, an aria, or with any of the programs found on television which subscribe to serious music and ideas. The teacher of humanities will make use of various materials in his classroom activities, drawing from the lively arts as well as from literature and the mass media. He is ever on the alert for such materials and has a file for immediate exploitation when the occasion arises from the give and take of the classroom situation. One day it may be a story in the newspapers about a musical version of *The Canterbury Tales.* A second day it may be an item about an exhibit of interest to the class. The alert teacher hardly can read his daily newspaper these days without noting one or more items which can be fitted into his humanities-oriented course.

THE ROLE OF THE CHAIRMAN

Where does the chairman fit into the picture? As the curriculum director for his department, he can work with his teachers in helping them incorporate some of these concepts into the department's course of study, an ongoing concern. When he visits his teachers as part of his supervisory responsibilities, he can praise such approaches when he encounters them, or he can suggest them in the post-observation conference or in his written reports. He can spend time in his departmental conferences or draw the department membership's attention to certain aspects of the humanities program, or he may invite experts from the various branches of the humanities to discuss ways in which these may be incorporated into the department's scope and sequence. If he is sincere in his convictions and successful in his persuasive endeavors, some of his enthusiasm undoubtedly will rub off. Even if only one or two members are willing to try the humanities way at first, a beginning has been made. The supervisor must be careful to avoid dictation of this or of any other approach, for one cannot force any philosophy of instruction down the throat of the modern teacher! Besides, teachers are better missionaries in the ultimate analysis than their supervisors.

PROCEDURES AND APPROACHES

A study of typical humanities programs reveals that the procedures vary. For a single teacher to be acquainted with several of the arts and with their historical development is asking much. Here and there we may be blessed with a teacher with such a background in our department, but we cannot depend upon this. A far better way might be for a team of teachers, elected from among specialists in literature, the social sciences, music and the arts with, if we are lucky, one or two who have made a special study of philosophy and linguistics (linguistics is one of the humanities) to cooperate in such a teaching venture.[8] Joint planning sessions permit discussion of immediate and practical problems and elicit possible solutions to the problems which inevitably will arise. For example, will the concept under scrutiny be developed best by a lecture given by an expert teacher, by listening to a recording and conducting a follow-up discussion, or by an amalgam of methods? As any teacher knows, a constant diet of a single classroom procedure would eventually defeat our purposes.

Let us illustrate by a concrete example. The English teacher happens to have taken work in Middle English literature and wishes to give his students some idea of what life was like in Chaucer's time, 1340–1400. The English literature anthology has the "Prologue" to *The Canterbury Tales* and usually one of the tales such as "The Pardoner" or "The Nun's Priest's Tale." First he must plan with his colleagues to see what is available in the school itself to contribute to an understanding of life in Medieval England. We would like our students to know something of the art, the architecture, the music, the education, the modes of dress, the roles of the sexes, the working conditions, and any other aspects of the human condition prevailing in Medieval Europe that the team of teachers deem worthy of drawing to the attention of their students.

The English teacher has many sources of information with which to enrich his contribution to the project. There is *Chaucer's World* compiled by the medievalist, Edith Rickert and edited as a memorial to her by Clair C. Olson and Martin M. Crow.[9] An equally rewarding volume is G. G. Coulton's *Medieval Panorama*,[10] or there is Roger Sherman Loomis' more recent *A Mirror of Chaucer's World*,[11] useful for its detailed illustrations of actual situations found in Chaucer's poetry. Each phrase of Middle English literature has an extensive literature which is fully delineated in such books as John Edwin Wells' *A Manual of The Writings in Middle English*.[12]

The art specialist has any number of volumes about medieval art and architecture. *The Horizon Book of the Middle Ages*[13] is a most valuable reference work. There are numerous color slides which may be borrowed from such sources as the New

York Metropolitan Museum of Art and other municipal museums. A visit to the Cloisters would be most rewarding for the insights it would lend to our study if the unit were being done in the New York area. Most school libraries are equipped to provide rich illustrative materials from their vertical files and from the texts assembled dealing with Medieval times. Books of costumes through the ages would give students not only some ideas of what the clothes of the time were like but also would serve as valuable reference to the teacher interested in a dramatics approach to the era.

Several kinds of listening experiences can be provided. I always have found that students are interested in how Middle English sounded, and have used the Folkways recordings of *The Canterbury Tales* to gratify this curiosity.[14] Another reading of Chaucer by John C. Pope is contained in the Lexington Record Company's *Beowulf and Chaucer.*[15]

Music of the medieval period can be discussed by the music expert on the team and examples of medieval English ballads can be played. Because most music teachers insist that a humanities course should include manipulation of instruments and experience in the making of music, they may introduce recorders, tambours and other medieval instruments and invite some of the class membership to make music —to beat time, to create melody, to finger the instruments and assay their timbers. One interesting collection read and sung by Anthony Quayle is "The Ballad of Robin Hood" (Caedmon).[16] The lute accompaniment, a thing beautiful in itself, is by Desmond Dupre. Schwann's *Catalog of Longplaying Recordings and Cassettes*[17] is very useful to the teacher.

Another approach is through great themes. Whereas in the Culture Epoch approach a single period was studied in depth, in the Great Themes approach, students cover considerable ground by ignoring time and place; they pursue an idea wherever it leads. In one course students follow Euripides' *Electra* with Robert Penn Warren's *All the King's Men,* then Donne's "Meditation," Stevenson's "El Dorado" and O'Neill's *Emperor Jones,* because all draw attention to a similar aspect of the human condition. Looking into the theme "Man as a Creature with Potential for Growth," students read Helen Keller's essay "Three Days to See" and then viewed Flaherty's *Nanook of the North* as well as devoting time to the art and music which reveals man's potential, possibly such items as Beethoven's *Eroica* and Michaelangelo's "David."

A third approach, called for want of a better name, the Multimedia approach is concerned less with the products of aesthetic expression and more with the manner and method of the artist, or his point of view. Such a course is typified by the allied arts course taught in a number of secondary schools in Missouri.

In one New England school students studied Picasso's "Guernica," Wilder's *Skin of Our Teeth* and paid visits to the Metropolitan Museum of Art, the Yale Gallery and the Shakespeare Playhouse at Stratford, Connecticut. In Nassau County on Long Island, Hofstra University has a Shakespearean Playhouse modeled after the Globe, visited by many students and teachers.

To get an idea of how some great works of art were conceived and realized, students in another form of this multimedia approach read the diaries, autobiographies, letters and journals of such creative minds as Charles Darwin, Vincent Van Gogh,

Benvenuto Cellini, and then examined their accomplished works, whether in the form of paintings, conjectures upon the nature of nature, a poem, a sonata, or even a new approach of cosmology. Thus the students gradually became aware of the nature of the creative process.

A fourth variety of humanistic studies is based entirely upon the Great Books and goes back many years in the history of instruction in English. Such a course provides students with a wide range of selections from many countries and epochs. Students in such a course must be well read to begin with and, obviously, no teacher should undertake instruction in such a course who has not a strong and varied background or who has not the time and intellectual energies to pursue constantly more revealing insights. Although some English specialists would contend such courses are not related to the humanities but are simply "beefed up" literature courses, the points of departure in the humanities course are quite different. Mere coverage is not the main goal of the teacher and his students. The humanistic way comes out in the emphasis on the ideals and values of human conduct, moral, spiritual and aesthetic, expressed in the individual works, in their concern with the artist and how he expresses, perceives and celebrates human experiences, and in their concentration upon the felicities of expression. As long as the teacher of such courses does not want his students to become Tom Folios, as in Addison's charming essay, but instead more enlightened and sensitized human beings, such courses are excellent.

CONTENT

Concerning the content of a humanities course, we have already implied much. It may consist of a series of literary texts such as in the Great Books approach. Here, specially, the portability and availability of the paperback has proved to be a great boon. Any number of books can now be found in comparatively inexpensive editions.

Such a course, however, usually consists of more than one medium. I have found the following books immensely helpful for the lively arts other than literature. After consulting these and similar books, the teacher or team of teachers may work out in the dialogue of pre-teaching conferences the ultimate content of a meaningful and humanizing course for their students.

It should be noted that long before humanities courses were thought of for high schools, they were used on the college level. One of the earliest textbooks was *The Humanities* by Louise Dudley and Austin Faricy, originally published in 1940, revised in 1951 and again in 1960.[18] Raymond S. Stites in his *The Arts and Man* has written a scholarly and fascinating volume that will provide the English teacher or the teacher of a humanities course with many gratifying insights.[19] A cooperative effort was done by members of the faculties of Michigan State College in *An Introduction to Literature and the Fine Arts*.[20] Donald J. McGinn and George Howerton have produced an unusual volume in *Literature As a Fine Art*.[21] Here the authors' purpose has been to provide literary selections representing the main artistic trends from the Renaissance to the Mid-twentieth century, namely Mannerism, Baroque, Rococo, Romanticism, Realism, Impressionism and Expressionism. Examples from the fine arts of the period are cited. It is an excellent source book for the Cultural Epochs approach.

As one reads these and similar volumes, one can grasp the existing inter-relationships among the arts and at the same time gain insights into the way courses and their content in the humanities may be organized. All approaches when sensitively utilized can be seen to stress the centrality of Man in the human condition. All the aforementioned books were written for the college student. In recent high school literature, however, a selection on the fine arts has been added. This is true of the Classic Edition of the *Adventures in Literature* series published by Harcourt Brace Jovanovich.[22] Teachers' manuals to accompany each volume of the six-book Harcourt Brace Jovanovich series contain valuable suggestions on how to integrate the fine arts program into the regular scope and sequence of literary studies. I predict that in time almost all series of anthologized literature will seek to incorporate fine arts sections in their respective volumes. For those teachers or English departments interested in embarking upon a humanities program, a careful perusal of *The Humanities,* a planning guide prepared by the New York State Education Department, is useful. In the New York State Guide thirteen units are described in three main approaches: functions, elements and chronology. The contents in all the allied arts are listed, thus enabling the beginning humanities teacher to save untold hours of research for materials. Intensive analyses are given of John Steinbeck's "The Leader of the People," Rembrandt's "Christ Crucified between the Two Thieves," and Anton Dvorak's "Symphony No. 5 in E Minor" (from The New World). My point is that it is not necessary for the new teacher of humanities to start from scratch. Many protagonists of the humanities way already have demonstrated the hows and the whys of such a technique on both the college and secondary levels.

26

SOLUTIONS TO SOME PERSISTENT PROBLEMS

Writing about Longfellow's attitude toward his administrative duties while he was professor of Romance Languages in Harvard University, Newton Arvin makes this comment, which might well serve as the text for this chapter:

Lecturing was only a part of Longfellow's duties as Smith Professor; supervising a department made up of four instructors, visiting their classes at stated intervals and sometimes even when an instructor was lacking, taking over the teaching of elementary sections—these responsibilities were also involved; and the irksomeness of this uncongenial administrative work, as well as the tedium of elementary teaching, worried and wearied him all along. His letters and journals abound in expressions of rebellion—rebellion against the routine of his work itself and against its frustration of his true work, writing.[1]

From years of serving as an English department chairman, I shall try to cover as many aspects of our fascinating profession as possible. I shall discuss the problems of the English Department Chairman as they relate to five aspects.

THE CHAIRMAN'S RELATIONSHIP WITH HIS DEPARTMENT

I have found, after supervising thousands of English teachers that the basic cause for problems with our teachers is that we have failed to treat each as an individual, deserving of respect for that individuality and justifiably suspicious of our efforts whenever we forget or minimize it. No treatise on administration and supervision, with the 101 rules on how to administer and supervise a department, can take the place of the simple rule I have enunciated above. How that works out in practice, I shall now demonstrate. There are five areas in which the English department chairman serves his teachers—and I use the term *serves* advisedly. For, unless we conceive of our profession as one that serves all of our teachers in order to bring out the best elements from each teacher, then our purpose is wasteful. We serve them in these areas:

Preparing programs for each teacher
Making available suitable instructional materials
Observing and evaluating each teacher
Assisting our teachers with disciplinary matters
Developing an interest in each teacher as a person and as a human being

In my school, each department chairman makes out the programs for the new term. We are given the list of classes, and we use our best judgment in assigning classes to teachers in which they will be most effective. Right here is where many problems arise. Who will teach the difficult classes: the newly appointed teachers, the substitutes or the experienced teachers? What if the experienced teachers feel they already have served their time with the difficult students and cannot stand the strain? That is a reasonable request. But shall we entrust difficult students to inexperienced teachers even though they may have greater stamina? Will their inexperience not contribute to the lack of achievement already shown by many students?

Who will teach the gifted students? Should it be the experienced teachers just because they are experienced, even though they may be unpopular? Should it be the most popular teachers even though they may not have the scholarly equipment and training? When do we start giving gifted classes to our young teachers? Should we pass over the experienced teacher for a young teacher who has shown much promise? Can we as chairmen run the risk of censure from any segment of our department? How does one solve this ever-present problem?

I have tried to solve this in several ways. First, there is a policy of rotation which is required by the Union Contract. All other conditions being equal, teachers must be rotated when it comes to distributing the difficult and the more interesting classes. The Union will not force me to give an Honors class to a teacher from whom I have received many complaints about the behavior of our students and against whom I have received many complaints from both students and parents because of poor preparation, a sharp tongue, or harshness in attitude. Secondly, I submit to each teacher (by the way, this is a school practice) a form at the end of each term in which he suggests the program he would like. To the best of my ability, I try to fullfil each teacher's desire. When I cannot do so, I call the teacher in to my office and explain the reason why I could not comply. Furthermore, at the beginning of each term, at my first department conference, I permit each teacher to examine the entire department program and see whether any improvement can be made. If two teachers agree to a program change that makes their work easier, why should I object? My teachers know by this time that it is impossible to give to twenty five or thirty teachers exactly the program which each has requested, and that one can only do one's best. Furthermore, I can promise that if a teacher's program is difficult one term, I will attempt to make it easier the next.

To give teachers the best programs in the world and not supply them with instructional materials is of little value. We constantly must strive to supply each teacher with the books he or she needs, the film strips, the recordings and other instructional materials that are so necessary for a relevant English program. Of course, there never will be enough. We simply cannot stock all the books or all the other materials. We therefore must work out some sort of a rotation system so that each teacher will have sets of books for certain stated periods and then make them available for other teachers of the same grade. Fortunately, I had been granted a book room coordinator who was relieved of one building assignment and his homeroom to take care of our book needs. The teachers like him and know he has their best interests at heart. He also is in charge of reproducing materials and has trained a student staff who duplicate thousands of sheets of tests, lesson plans, bibliographies every term. The audio-visual aids, for want of a better place, are all lodged in the English Office, and I have had the responsibility of making lists of materials that are available and being on hand to supply the materials to teachers. Such work is very time-consuming, but until we have our own audio-visual room with personnel to operate it, I must assume this additional burden. We occasionally use some time from our monthly departmental conference to demonstrate how to use a particular machine or to discuss the value of new materials. By constantly keeping the staff informed of what is available and helping them to utilize these materials, we insure greater and greater utilization.

Whenever observation of the work of one professional by another takes place, there is tension and often difficulty. Most professionals do not like to be observed on the job unless it is a situation in which the professional is acting as a teacher, as in the case of a ward physician showing young doctors how to treat ward patients or a professor in dental school showing students how to fill cavities. Teachers who must be observed on the job are, in most cases, under tension, and the supervisor has to exercise the utmost tact and discretion in the way he handles the situation. What requires even more patience and tact is the interview which follows the observation and finally the writing of the observation report which becomes part of the teacher's written record and goes into his permanent file. There are various ways of solving the problem associated with regular visits. In the first place, experienced teachers need not be observed often. In the school in which I served, they were observed only once a year, hardly the cause of any emotional trauma. Secondly, I have always arranged with my teachers to let me know when not to come in because a test was being given, a composition was being written, or because the teacher did not feel the lesson was a fair indication of his or her work. Any teacher had the privilege of telling me when I came in to observe that it would have been better to come some other time.

The tension during the interview could sometimes be relieved by having it in the cafeteria while we both were having lunch or coffee and cake. Instead of beginning with all the faults that seemed to be in the lesson, one can ask: "How do you think the lesson went?" or "If you were to do it again, would you do it the same way?" or "How would you improve it?" I have found that in most cases the honest teacher would see more faults than I did and not hesitate to reveal them. I always made it a policy to commend the teacher for all the good points of the lesson, and one can find good points in any lesson. In fact in my written notes I had two columns in addition to the running summary of the lesson. One was marked Commendations, the other Recommendations. This is much better than "Good Points" and "Bad Points" or some similar designations.

Finally, in my written report, being aware that this was going to be part of the teacher's permanent record, I tried to be as fair as possible. After a narration of the lesson which would permit the principal to get a good picture of what took place, I followed with a section on Commendations and another on Recommendations. Since the teacher had to read and approve my report, he or she would have an opportunity to object to anything that seemed unfair or to point out something which I had undervalued. In that case, I would not hesitate to rewrite my report to make it acceptable to both of us. The best kind of criticism is not what comes from the supervisor but that which the teacher makes of his or her own work. Under conditions of frankness and mutual respect, the teacher will know far better how to improve the work than the supervisor.

I always made it a policy to permit the teacher to invite me anytime she or he had a special lesson I should observe. Some terms, I would be invited even though I already had paid my required visits. Such mutual confidence is not developed in a term or even a year. There is a natural suspicion on the part of teachers when a new supervisor comes into the department and only time will erode that suspicion. Eventually the observations will become the pleasant professional experiences they always should be.

The teacher in the classroom should be responsible for discipline. Sometimes, however, disruptions take place. There is always the problem of how the department chairman should handle this matter. When a refractory student is sent to the English Office by the teacher, the chairman has the responsibility of being fair both to the teacher and the student. Sometimes it may be just a question of hearing out the student, in a sympathetic way. Teachers sometimes are misunderstood by students when they are under pressure and may say the wrong thing. I never made a judgment against a teacher before any student. Rather, I would say that I would speak to the teacher and get her side of the story. Then, when I had listened to both sides, I promised to make a judgment. Sometimes it helped to ask the refractory student to assist me in the office, to send him around with a departmental notice, or show in some way that I respected him or her as a person. If I could not handle the situation after repeated efforts, my next resource was the Dean of Boys or the Dean of Girls. Sometimes I might send for the parent, but the Deans would prefer to handle that situation. For the teacher, it meant I was trying to assist her in teaching most effectively without any disruption. Of course, when a teacher kept sending students to me several times a day and several days in a row, I discussed the matter with her and offered some concrete suggestions. Sometimes, especially with inexperienced teachers, it might become necessary for me to step into the room. I tried to do this as inconspicuously as possible and not in a way to humiliate or lower the status of the teacher.

A teacher is more than an individual who has to teach five periods a day, manage a building assignment and a homeroom. She may have personal problems that will affect her work. She may become ill suddenly and will have to be driven home. Many a time the spouse of a teacher has been taken ill in the middle of the day, and someone else has had to be found to take over extra classes and transportation has had to be supplied to her home. There are happy occasions as well as sad occasions in the lives of teachers, and the department chairman must be aware of them. Marriages, births and deaths happen to teachers as they happen to everyone else. They appreciate it when their chairman is aware of them and takes appropriate action. Whether it is attendance at a wedding or paying a condolence call after the death of a teacher's parent, the action is remembered and appreciated for a long time. This interest is not confined to the extra-school associations of the teacher. A compliment about a new dress or hairdo, the daily greeting in the hallway, the sharing of coffee during a free period or a lift on the way home are some of the ways in which to demonstrate that you appreciate your teachers as persons. There is a subtle chemistry in human relationships, and one of the most important elements is respect and admiration for what one is.

THE CHAIRMEN'S RELATIONSHIP WITH THE SCHOOL ADMINISTRATION

The principal is the head of the school and all department chairmen must follow his directions. After all, he has both the professional and legal responsibility. There are times when the principal and the chairman will not see eye to eye. Some principals think a great deal of the English program. Others think that anyone can teach English, or that remedial reading is a waste of time, or that the classics should be taught in favor of the moderns. There are a hundred different ways in which problems may arise between principals and chairmen. Obviously we must work harmoniously. Just as the chairman must rate his teachers, the principal rates his chairmen. At first, it may be for tenure, but a chairman is being observed and rated all the time whether a written record is kept or not. Differences will always be there when two strong personalities exist in a daily confrontation. How can this problem be solved? Here are a few suggestions:

1. Keep your principal informed at all times of what is going on in your department. Often misunderstanding arises only because the lines of communication are poor.
2. Do not hesitate to discuss your differences with him or her. Frequently such discussion will clear the air of controversy.
3. Examine your own procedures to be certain that you are not in the wrong. Be certain that you are following the by-laws and regulations of the Board of Education.
4. Don't feel you know all the answers just because you happen to be the chairman of your department. The principal must see the whole school situation and may have a better perspective than you.
5. Don't hesitate to admit error and promise to try another approach.

The department chairman also has to deal with the assistant principals in various matters, such as rooms for English classes, funds for equipment such as filing cabinets and reproducing machines, out-of-license classes and who should teach them. He likewise has to deal with the program committee. We may wish to offer certain courses and not enough students enroll. Should we offer a course when only fifteen students want it and thus increase the register of other teachers? How many remedial classes should we have? At what point do we cut off students from honor classes? A hundred different problems may arise because of program difficulties, and in all instances the chairman must work with the program chairman to iron them out. Sometimes you have to decide against your department for the benefit of the school as a whole, with the understanding that on some other occasion, you will benefit.

The guidance department is another source of difficulties. Guidance counselors theoretically are functioning to help students find themselves, personally, educationally and emotionally. They frequently may take actions which will seem to undermine your own authority. For example, they will take students out of one class and place them in another without your approval. If this is the practice of the guidance department, you must learn to live with it. I have found, however, that talking the matter over with the head of the guidance department frequently helped to lessen the friction. After all, we both are working for the interest of the student. I will settle for being informed by the guidance counselor and do not feel that my integrity or authority has been undermined simply because I was not consulted before the fact.

THE CHAIRMAN'S RELATIONSHIP WITH STUDENTS

If the chairman's office is always open to any student who wants to discuss a problem with him, many problems with students can be averted.

I already have mentioned the procedures I have followed with respect to student discipline. Believing that there are usually two sides to a dispute, I try to permit any student sent to me to give his side of the story. In most cases, they have admitted their errors, and I have given them a second or third chance. For those students who insist on disrupting classes, we have the respective deans who are better qualified to handle discipline and have the time for it.

Every term, at the beginning, most of my time was taken up with changes of students' programs. In many cases errors have been made by the program committee, many of whom are students. In many instances, students should be in one class and were given another. Sometimes students have been failed by a teacher and do not wish to have that teacher a second time. In some instances, they have had differences of opinion, and a change of class would be mutually desirable. I had to listen to each case patiently and tried to do the best I can. This took many extra hours of my time, because I had to neglect all other work and attend to these students' complaints, but I always have felt that a human being has priority over a report and have acted accordingly.

Not all student contacts are on the complaining side. Students should be encouraged to participate in extracurricular activities related to English, and the chairman should be informed of such activities and bring such information to the attention of his teachers. I have tried to get in touch with students who have done outstanding work in English and commend them either orally or in writing. I have written letters to their parents, which they have universally appreciated. I made it a policy to stand in the doorway of my office at change of classes and greet as many students as I knew. At the same time, I have prevented many an argument just before it got started. Students hesitate to scream and run around the halls if they see a supervisor whom they respect. Thus an ounce of prevention is worth more than a pound of cure.

THE CHAIRMAN'S RELATIONSHIP WITH OTHER CHAIRMEN

In a school like mine, with over four thousand students, there were many department chairmen. We had fifteen. Each one, theoretically, was doing for his teachers what I have described I was doing for mine. Sometimes there was friction, although I believe that in our school this was reduced to a minimum. The reason for this harmony was that all of us realized the interests of any one department had to be subordinated to the interests of the entire school.

In all the years that I was a chairman, I never found enough money for all the instructional materials we needed. Some years certain departments had to have more money. It is foolish to bewail the fact that this is so. The principal apparently knows what he is doing when he gives a certain sum to one department and a smaller sum to another. Before jumping to the conclusion that favoritism is responsible, it is better to get the facts. In most instances the facts will prove that another chairman's needs were greater than your own.

Seldom is it possible to arrange the department program so that every English teacher has only English classes. Sometimes he must have a class in social studies, or foreign languages, or in art. Likewise, a social studies teacher may have to pick up a class or two of English. There are many possibilities of argument in this situation, but it cannot be helped. The chairmen must get together and try to make the situation as pleasant as possible. For example, it is not fair, in my opinion, to give a difficult class to an out-of-license teacher, because teaching a regular English class is enough of a problem. No chairman likes to exchange such classes, and a friendly realization of that fact will help avoid arguments.

Frequently chairmen of other departments will borrow sets of dictionaries, audio-visual equipment and other materials from the English department. Why not? We don't hold any monopoly on the child. On some other occasion we may wish to borrow materials or request a favor from another chairman.

In a large school such as ours, the time ran from 7:50 a.m. to 4:30 p.m. or even later. Few chairmen like the late session, because they do not want to get home too late. Yet some chairmen must be around for the late session, which always has a large proportion of younger students whose discipline needs improvement. What can we do? If we left it to the volunteers, we would never have chairmen for the late session. We therefore all agreed to accept a number of late session days (about eleven a semester), and thus we covered the late session every day. If, for some reason, a chairman could not cover a certain day, there always was a colleague who would exchange dates with him. All of us made a slight sacrifice for the benefit of the entire group.

The relationship with the library also may be a subject for friction if one is not understanding. There are limits to the time that the librarians can give to library classes either in the library or in English classes. Arrangements were made by means of a schedule, whereby all first and third terms students were given library sessions at the beginning of the term. Toward the end of their senior year, arrangements also were made for seniors to have review lessons in the library. For special classes, certain books were set aside on separate shelves for individual research. Books were recommended by the chairman for purchase. Students and English teachers were encouraged to utilize the library through supplementary reading assignments, thus increasing the circulation in the library. In many instances the library and its staff have assisted in enriching the English program. Once again, all this is possible when the English chairman realizes the importance of the library and cooperates with the staff.

THE CHAIRMAN'S RELATIONSHIP WITH PARENTS

Just as my door was always open for any teacher, chairman or student, so it was open for any parent. They may have a complaint because of a grade that is too low, because their child could not get into a certain class, or because a difference had arisen between their child and the English teacher. One must give each parent as much time as is needed. One must be patient in listening to the complaint or the request, and one must act for the best interest of the child. Not many parents come in, however, because either the guidance counselor or the dean of guidance already has remedied the situation. In our school we had a parents' night and a parents' afternoon every term. Although only a small percentage of parents came, it was an excellent way in which to meet with parents. They should know who their children's teachers are and what they look like and what they sound like. Students carry back strange notions to their parents.

Since we have a Parent Teacher Association, it is advisable for each teacher to join it and to attend as many meetings as possible. I have found that parents are most appreciative when teachers come to their meetings. I have been asked occasionally to write for their newspaper, describing our courses, or some innovations, or some remedial procedures. They are entitled to know about these matters.

Finally, parents should be used in the instructional program when they have special skills or expertise. They enjoy the experience, and the students show more interest sometimes than they do in their regular work. One of the ways in which I have learned about my parents' expertise was in interviews with them on parents' nights. They have been among the most worthwhile interviews in my entire teaching career.

I have by no means included all the problems of the English department chairman or the solutions. I have confined myself to a few. I should like to close with a quotation from Sydney J. Harris in his column, "Strictly Personal" in the *Miami Herald* for February 3, 1972:

Our fascination for "growth" has obscured the miracle of creation for most modern people; but, as Donne said in one of his sermons more than three centuries ago: "The distance from nothing to a little is ten thousand times more than from it to the highest degree in this life."

NOTES AND BIBLIOGRAPHY

CHAPTER 1: THE EMERGING CURRICULUM IN ENGLISH

Notes

1. James Fleming Hosic, *Reorganization of English in Secondary Schools* (Washington: U. S. Department of the Interior, Bureau of Education, 1917).
2. W. Wilbur Hatfield, ed., *An Experience Curriculum in English* (New York: Appleton-Century-Crofts, Inc. 1935).
3. National Association of Secondary School Principals, "The Emerging Curriculum in English in the Secondary School," *Bulletin of the National Association of Secondary School Principals,* XXX (February, 1946).
4. National Council of Teachers of English, Commission on the English Curriculum, *The English Language Arts,* NCTE Curriculum Series, Vol. 1 (New York: Appleton-Century-Crofts, Inc. 1952).
5. National Council of Teachers of English, Commission on the English Curriculum, *The English Language Arts in the Secondary School,* NCTE Curriculum Series, Vol. III (New York: Appleton-Century Crofts, Inc. 1956).
6. Arno Jewett, *English Language Arts in American High Schools,* Bulletin 1958, No. 13 (Washington: U. S. Department of Health, Education and Welfare, 1958), Chapter II, pp. 6-16.
7. James Moffatt, *A Child-Centered Language Arts Curriculum K-13* (Boston: Houghton Mifflin, 1968).
8. Joseph Mersand, "Project English: A Report to the Profession," *Scholastic Teacher,* LIII (September 20, 1963) pp. 16-16T. "Project English and College Teachers of English," *English Record,* XIV (October, 1963) pp. 36-40.
9. Richard Braddock, Richard Lloyd-Jones, and Lowell Schoer, *Research in Written Composition* (Champaign: National Council of Teachers of English, 1963). See also Richard Corbin, *The Teaching of Writing in Our Schools* (New York: Macmillan, 1966).
10. Arno Jewett, "Eclectic, Experimental Programs in Composition," *Bulletin of the National Association of Secondary School Principals,* XLVIII (February, 1964) pp. 18-52.
11. Arno Jewett, Joseph Mersand, Doris V. Gunderson, *Developing Language Skills among the Culturally Different* (Washington: Government Printing Office, 1964).
12. Excerpts from W. Nelson Francis, "Linguistics and Composition: The Teacher's Theoretical Training," *The Phi Delta Kappan* XLI (May, 1960) pp. 336-341.
13. Committee on National Interest, *The National Interest and the Continuing Education of Teachers of English.* (Champaign: National Council of Teachers of English, 1964). See also James R. Squire and Robert F. Hogan, "A Five Point Program for Improving the

Continuing Education of Teachers of English," *Bulletin* of the N. A. S. S. P., XLVIII (February, 1964) pp. 1-17.
14. *NEA Journal*, March, 1961, p. 4.

Bibliography

Books

Bennett, R. A. "The English Curriculum: Out of the Past into the Future," in Hipple, Theodore W. ed., *Readings for Teaching English in Secondary School.* New York: Macmillan, 1973, pp. 22-29.

Bernstein, Abraham. *Teaching English in High School.* New York: Random House, 1961, pp. 7-40.

Commission on the English Curriculum. *The English Language Arts in the Secondary School.* New York: Appleton-Century-Crofts, 1956, pp. 3-28.

Commission on the English Curriculum. *The English Language Arts.* New York: Appleton-Century-Crofts, 1952, pp. 3-78.

Committee on the Objectives of a General Education in a Free Society. *General Education in a Free Society.* Cambridge: Harvard University Press, 1945.

Conant, James B. *The American High School Today.* New York: McGraw-Hill, 1959.

Fowler, Mary Elizabeth. *Teaching Language, Composition and Literature.* New York: McGraw-Hill, 1965, pp. 1-46.

Gill, Kent. "Whither an English Curriculum for the Seventies?" in Hipple, Theodore W. ed. *Readings for Teaching English in Secondary School.* New York: Macmillan, 1973, pp. 22-29.

Guth, Hans P. *English Today and Tomorrow.* Englewood Cliffs, N. J.: Prentice-Hall, 1964, pp. 297-340.

Hipple, Theodore W. *Teaching English in Secondary Schools.* New York: Macmillan, 1973, pp. 27-38.

Hook, J. N. *The Teaching of High School English.* 4th ed. New York: Ronald Press, 1972, pp. 3-76.

Lewis, John S. and Sisk, Jean C. *Teaching English 7-12.* New York: American Book Company, 1963, pp. 35-68.

Morsey, Royal J. *Improving English Instruction.* 2nd ed. Boston: Allyn and Bacon, 1969, pp. 1-21.

Pilgrim, Geneva Hanna. *Learning and Teaching Practices in English.* New York: The Center for Applied Research in Education, 1966, pp. 1-15.

Rockefeller Brothers Fund. *The Pursuit of Excellence: Education and the Future of America.* Garden City, N. Y.: Doubleday, 1958.

Squire, James R. and Applebee, Roger N. *High School English Instruction Today.* New York: Appleton-Century-Crofts, 1968.

Whitehead, Alfred North. *The Aims of Education.* London, Eng.: Norgate, 1936.

Zahner, Louis C. "What Kinds of Language Teaching?" in Gordon, Edward J. and Noyes, Edward S eds. *Essays on the Teaching in English.* New York: Appleton-Century-Crofts, 1960, pp. 3-17.

Pamphlets and Periodicals

Educational Policies Commission of the National Education Association. *The Central Purpose of American Education.* Washington, D. C.: National Education Association, 1961.

Evans, William H. and Walker, Jerry L. *New Trends in the Teaching of English in Secondary Schools.* Chicago, Ill.: Rand, McNally and Company, 1966.

Haugh, Oscar M. *Revisiting Basic Issues in English Education.* Champaign, Ill.: National Council of Teachers of English, 1968.

Hook, J. N. "Trends in the Teaching of English," *Wisconsin English Journal.* October 1959. Reprinted in M. Jerry Weiss. *An English Teacher's Reader.* New York: The Odyssey Press, 1962, pp. 22-30.

Jewett, Arno. *English Language Arts in American High Schools.* Bulletin, 1958, No. 13. Washington, D. C.: U. S. Department of Health, Education and Welfare.

Jewett, Arno, "National Trends in Teaching High School English." *English Journal,* September, 1957, pp. 326-329.

Jewett, Arno, "National Trends in Teaching High School English." *English Journal,* March, 1958,

Mackintosh, Helen K. "The World of the English Teacher." *English Journal,* March, 1958, pp. 111-117.

Neville, Mark. "The Art of Plain English." *English Journal,* February, 1950. pp. 72-76.

Pooley, Robert C. "These Things Shall Not Pass." *English Journal,* February, 1946, pp. 76-82.

Reeves, Ruth B. "Planning a Literature Program for the Junior High School." *English Journal,* October, 1959, pp. 374-381, 392.

Rinker, Floyd B. "Priorities in the English Curriculum." *English Journal,* May, 1962, pp. 309-312.

Smith, Dora V. "Basic Considerations in Curriculum-making in the Language Arts." *English Journal,* March, 1948, pp. 115-126.

Smith, Dora V. "Reestablishing Guidelines for the English Curriculum." *English Journal,* September, 1958, pp. 317-326, 338.

Strickland, Ruth G. "Some Basic Issues in the Teaching of English." *Phi Delta Kappan,* May, 1960. Reprinted in M. Jerry Weiss ed. *An English Teacher's Reader.* New York: Odyssey Press, 1962, pp. 15-22.

Suhor, Charles, Mayher, Sawyer, John and D'Angelo, Frank J. *The Growing Edges of Secondary English.* Champaign, Ill.: National Council of Teachers of English, 1968. See section I: Emerging Structures for the Curriculum, pp. 3-64.

CHAPTER 2: THE AIMS OF ENGLISH INSTRUCTION

Notes

1. James F. Hosic, *Reorganization of English in Secondary Schools,* (Washington, D. C.: U. S. Department of the Interior, Bureau of Education, 1917).
2. Ibid., p. 26.
3. Dora V. Smith, chairman, *Basic Aims for English Instruction,* Pamphlet Publication of the N. C. T. E., No. 3. This was originally published in 1942 and may be obtained in education libraries.
4. Issued as Communication No. 7 of the Commission on the English Curriculum.
5. Each of these goals is explained in considerable detail in *The English Language Arts* (New York: Appleton-Century-Crofts, 1952).
6. These seventeen aims were originally formulated when the author was working on the English-Speech-Language Arts Project of the Bureau of Curriculum Research of the N. Y. C. Board of Education and are used with the permission of Dr. William H. Bristow, Director, and the late Dr. A. Barnett Langdale, Project Coordinator.
7. Educational Policies Commission, *The Purposes of Education in American Democracy,* (Washington, D. C.: National Education Association, 1938) p. 47.
8. Arno Jewett, *English Language Arts in American High Schools,* Bulletin 1958, No. 13 (Washington, D. C.: U. S. Department of Health, Education, and Welfare, 1959). p. 2.
9. Dora V. Smith, *Instruction in English,* Bulletin 1932, No. 17 (Washington, D. C.: U. S. Department of the Interior, 1933).
10. See for example the Manitowic, Wisconsin course of study for grade as reproduced in Jewett, op. cit., p. 23.
11. Jewett, op. cit., 27.

Bibliography

Books

Aikin, Wilford M. *The Story of the Eight-Year Study.* New York: Harper and Brothers, 1942.

Broening, Angela M. ed. *Conducting Experiences in English.* New York: Appleton-Century-Crofts, 1939.

Commission on the English Curriculum. *The English Language Arts.* New York: Appleton-Century-Crofts, 1952, pp. 41-54.

DeBoer, John J. ed. *The Subject Fields in General Education.* New York: Appleton-Century-Crofts, 1941.

Hatfield, W. Wilbur. ed. *An Experience Curriculum in English*. New York: Appleton-Century-Crofts, 1936.

Pooley, Robert C. and Williams, Robert D. *The Teaching of English in Wisconsin*. Madison: University of Wisconsin Press, 1948.

Roberts, Holland D., Kaulfers, Walter V., and Kefauver, Grayson N. eds. *English for Social Living*. New York: McGraw-Hill Company, 1943.

Weeks, Ruth Mary. ed. *A Correlated Curriculum*. New York: Appleton-Century-Crofts, 1940.

Pamphlets and Periodicals

Bulletin of the National Association of Secondary School Principals. *The Emerging Curriculum in English*. February, 1946. Entire issue is devoted to this topic.

Broening, Angela M. "Trends in Secondary School English: Developing Attitudes Favorable to Good Reading." *National Education Association Journal*, December, 1949, pp. 666-667.

Carlsen, G. Robert. "English and the Liberal Arts Tradition in the High School." *English Journal*, September, 1955, pp. 323-329.

Dixon, John. *Growth Through English*. National Association for the Teaching of English, 1967.

Educational Policies Commission. *Education for all American Youth*. Washington, D. C.: National Education Association, 1944.

Educational Policies Commission. *The Purpose of Education in American Democracy*. Washington, D. C.: National Education Association, 1938, p. 47.

Erickson, Frances. "What Are We Trying to Do in High School English?" *English Journal*, September, 1959, pp. 304-308, 314.

Hosic, James F. ed. *Reorganization of English in Secondary Schools*. Washington, D. C.: U. S. Department of the Interior, Bureau of Education, 1917.

Jewett, Arno. *English Language Arts in American High Schools*. Bulletin 1958, No. 13. Washington, D. C.: U. S. Department of Health, Education and Welfare, 1959.

Jewett, Arno. "National Trends in Teaching High School English." *English Journal*, September, 1957, p. 326-329.

LaBrant, Lou. "As of Now." *English Journal*, September, 1959, pp. 295-303.

Muller, Herbert J. *The Uses of English*. New York: Holt, Rinehart and Winston, 1967.

Neville, Mark A., Mason, James H. and Blaney, Charles D. *Suggestions for Thinking About the Teaching of English*. Terre Haute: Indiana Council of Teachers of English, 1966.

Smith, Dora V. ed. *Basic Aims for English Instruction*. Pamphlet Publication of the National Council of Teachers of English, No. 3. This was originally published in 1942 and may be found in education libraries.

Smith, Dora V. "The Basic Aims of English Instruction." *English Journal*, January, 1942, pp. 40-55.

Smith, Dora V. *Instruction in English*. Bulletin, 1932, No. 17. Washington, D. C.: U. S. Department of the Interior, 1933.

Smith, Dora V. "A Curriculum in the Language Arts for Life Today." *English Journal*, February, 1951, pp. 79-85.

Squire, James R. ed. *A Common Purpose*. Champaign, Illinois: National Council of Teachers of English, 1966, pp. 3-25.

CHAPTER 3: INDIVIDUALIZING INSTRUCTION IN ENGLISH IN LARGE AND SMALL CLASSES

Notes

1. Will Durant, *The Story of Philosophy* (New York: Simon and Schuster, 1927) p. 34.
2. Elwood P. Cubberley, *The History of Education* (Boston: Houghton Mifflin, 1920) p. 532.
3. Frank A. Butler, *Improvement of Teaching in Secondary School*. 3d ed. (Chicago: University of Chicago Press, 1953) p. 268.

Bibliography

Books

Appy, Nellie. ed. *Pupils Are People.* New York: Appleton-Century-Crofts, 1941.

Bentley, John E. *Superior Children.* New York: W.W. Norton, 1937.

Birch, Jane W. and McWilliams, Earl M. *Challenging Gifted Children.* Bloomington, Illinois: Public School Publishing Company, 1955.

Gold, Milton J. *Education of the Intellectually Gifted.* Columbus: Charles E. Merrill Books, 1965.

Gray, William S. ed. *Adjusting Reading to Individuals.* Supplementary Educational Monographs, No. 52. Chicago: University of Chicago Press, 1941.

Jenkinson, A. J. *What Do Boys and Girls Read?* London: Methuen, 1946.

LaBrant, Lou. *We Teach English.* New York: Harcourt, Brace, 1951, pp. 176-184; 246-299.

Norvell, George W. *The Reading Interests of Young People.* Boston: D. C. Heath, 1950.

Raushenbush, Esther. *Literature for Individual Education.* Sarah Lawrence College Publications, No. I. New York: Columbia University Press, 1942.

Smith, Dora V. "Guiding Individual Reading": *Reading in School and College.* The 47th Yearbook of the National Society for the Study of Education, Part II. Chicago: University of Chicago Press, 1948, pp. 194-205.

Stephens, Stephen. *Individual Instruction in English Composition.* Cambridge: Harvard University Press, 1928.

Strickland, Ruth G. *The Language Arts in the Elementary School.* 3rd ed. Boston: D. C. Heath, 1969, pp. 203-227.

Veatch, Jeannette. *Individualizing Your Reading Program.* New York: G. P. Putnam's Sons, 1959.

Pamphlets and Periodicals

American Council on Education. *Exploring Individual Differences.* American Council on Education Studies, Series I: Reports of Committees and Conferences, Vol. 12, No. 32, October, 1948. Washington D. C.: American Council on Education, 1948.

Bennett, Paul L. "A Reading and Writing Program for the Talented Student." *English Journal,* September, 1955, pp. 335-339.

Board of Education of the City of New York. "Developing Children's Power of Self-Expression Through Writing." *Curriculum Bulletin,* 1952–1953 Series, No. 2. New York: Bureau of Publication of the New York City Board of Education.

Booth, Miriam. "A Literature Program Designed for High School." *English Journal,* September, 1948, pp. 347-352.

Cathell, Dorothy. "Honors English: Break For Bright Students." *Clearing House,* February, 1955, pp. 331-337.

Evans, Dean H. "Individualized Reading—Myths and Facts." *Elementary English,* October, 1962, pp. 580-583.

Gordon, Edward J. "Levels of Teaching and Testing." *English Journal,* September, 1955, pp. 330-334.

Handlan, Bertha. "Group Discussion of Individual Reading." *English Journal,* February, 1943, pp. 67-74.

Jewett, Arno. "What Does Research Tell About the Reading Interests of Junior High Pupils?" in *Improving Reading in Junior High School.* Education Office Bulletin 1957, No. 10. Washington, D. C.: Department of Health, Education and Welfare, 1957.

Kiley, Frederick S. "Fate's Midnight: A Teaching Guide for Macbeth." *English Journal,* November, 1960, pp. 589-592.

King, Carlyle. "Conrad for the Classroom." *English Journal,* May, 1958, pp. 259-262.

Kraus, Silvy. "Grouping For the Teaching of Composition." *English Journal,* October, 1959, pp. 404-406.

Niles, Olive S. and Early, Margaret J. "Adjusting to Individual Differences in English" *Journal of Education,* Boston University School of Education, December, 1955.

Norvell, George W. "Some Results of a Twelve-Year Study of Children's Reading Interests." *English Journal,* December, 1946, pp. 535-556.

Reeves, Ruth. "The Gifted Student in the Literature Class." *English Journal,* November, 1956, pp. 462-469.

Sheppard, Anna G. "Teaching the Gifted in the Regular Classroom." *Educational Leadership,* January, 1956, pp. 220-224.

Squire, James K. "Individualizing the Teaching of Literature." *English Journal,* September, 1956, pp. 314-319.

Strang, Ruth. "Reading Interests." *English Journal,* November, 1946, pp. 477-482.

Thornton, Helen. "English for Technical Students." *English Journal,* September, 1955, pp. 343-346.

CHAPTER 4: THE ROLE OF THE DEPARTMENT HEAD IN PROVIDING FOR INDIVIDUALIZATION OF INSTRUCTION

Notes

1. Marchette Chute, *Geoffrey Chaucer of England,* (New York: E. P. Dutton, 1946) p. 38. Cf. Lynn Thorndike in *Speculum,* Volume XV (1940), pp. 400-408.
2. Bulletin, 1932, No. 17, National Survey of Secondary Education, Monograph No. 13, p. 9.
3. Appleton-Century-Crofts.
4. *Journal of Education,* Volume 138 (December, 1955) Number 2.
5. See William Featherstone, *Teaching the Slow Learners* (Bureau of Publications. Teachers College, Revised Edition, 1951).
6. In her volume *Fire under the Andes* (New York: Alfred A. Knopf, Inc., 1927).
7. New Brunswick: Rutgers University Press, 1946.
8. New York: Alfred A. Knopf, Inc., 1950.
9. Obtainable from the New York State Education Department, Albany, New York
10. Write to A. S. C. D., 1201 Sixteenth, S. W., Washington, D. C.
11. *English-Speech-Language Arts for Senior High Schools,* Bureau of Publication, New York City Board of Education, 1957.
12. Also obtainable at the Bureau of Publications, New York City Board of Education.
13. See "Fostering Personal Growth through Literature" in *Bulletin* of the National Association of Secondary School Principals, Volume XLII No. 241 (November, 1958) pp. 162-168.
14. See "Effective Supervisory and Administrative Bulletins," *Bulletin* of the National Association of Secondary School Principals. Volume XLI, No. 233 (December, 1957) pp. 97-118.
15. See "Using Audio-Visual Aids in English," *Audio-Visual Guide,* May, 1956.
16. See "Discovering the Individual in Large Classes," *English Journal,* October, 1957, pp. 406-409.
17. See *Principles and Practices of Guidance in English Classes,* Long Island City High School, N. Y. C., 1952.
    Successful Practices in Remedial English Classes. Long Island City High School, N. Y. C., 1953.

Bibliography

Books

Briggs, Thomas H. and Justman, Joseph. *Improving Instruction Through Supervision.* New York: Macmillan, 1952, pp. 16-17, 86, 89, 157, 166, 234.

Marks, James, Stoops, Emery and King-Stoops, Joyce, *Handbook of Educational Supervision.* Boston: Allyn and Bacon, 1973.

Rivlin, Harry N. *Educating For Adjustment:* Chapters 5 and 6. New York: Appleton-Century-Crofts, 1936.

Uhl, Willis L. *The Supervision of Secondary Subjects.* New York: D. Appleton, 1929, pp. 248-304.

Wiles, Kimball. *Teaching for Better Schools.* New York: Prentice-Hall, 1952, pp. 241-286.

Pamphlets and Periodicals

Aseltine, John. "The Duties of the Department Head in a Large City High School." *School Review,* April, 1931, pp. 272-279.

Association for Supervision and Curriculum Development, National Education Association. *The Department Head and Instructional Improvement.* Washington, D. C.: National Education Association, 1948.

Engleman, F. E. "Meeting the Problems of Individual Differences." *Educational Method,* November, 1936, pp. 63-66.

Friedman, Sherwood. "Notes on Classroom Observation." *High Points,* November, 1948, pp. 42-45.

Noyes, Louise. "All in Line of Duty." *Educational Leadership.* January, 1945, pp. 157-158.

CHAPTER 5: ENGLISH FOR THE BRIGHT STUDENT

Notes

1. Willard Abraham, *Common Sense About Gifted Children* (New York: Harper and Brothers, 1958) p. 17.
2. Cf. Merle R. Sumption and Evelyn M. Luecking, *Education of the Gifted* (New York: Ronald Press, 1960) pp. 21-39.
3. For a bibliography of teaching gifted students in English see Joseph Mersand, *Practices in Teaching Gifted Students in English* (New York: Jamaica High School, 1960) pp. 31-33.
4. *Education for the Age of Science* (Washington, D. C.: The White House, May 24, 1959) p. 17.
5. Peter F. Drucker, "The Importance of Language," *Toward the Liberally Educated Executive* (White Plains, N. Y.: The Fund for Adult Education, 1957) p. 49.
6. *Teaching Rapid and Slow Learners,* (Bulletin 1954, No. 5) (Washington, D. C.: U. S. Department of Health, Education and Welfare, 1954) p. 16.
7. Arno Jewett, editor, *English for the Academically Talented Student in the Secondary School* (Washington, D. C.: National Education Association Project on the Academically Talented Student and Champaign, Illinois: National Council of Teachers of English, 1960) pp. 14-35.
8. Many other useful booklists are available and should be either in the school library or in the classroom library.
9. A. J. Beeler, "English for Superior Students," *Kentucky English Bulletin,* VI, No. 3 (Spring, 1957) pp. 3-5.
10. Ibid., p. 9.
11. Many organizations publish reviews such as *The Catholic Film Newsletter.*
12. Miss Paula Silberstein, who is in charge of this project, issues a periodical newsletter, *Invitations,* which is sent to all the schools, informing them of the many facilities in New York City that may be used to enrich the school program. Write to her at 131 Livingston Street, Brooklyn, New York, 11201, for details of this program.
13. See the *New York Times* for March 22, 1962 which describes the exciting visit of Marianne Moore to Eastern District High School in New York City.
14. Each January the Young Adult Section of the New York Public Library issues *Books for the Teen Age,* a most useful list of annotated books of especial interest to the gifted student who already has developed a love for reading. The Enoch Pratt Free Library in Baltimore, to encourage summer reading, issues *Go Places With Books* and distributes it to the public schools. Many other public libraries issue similar compilations.
15. Arno Jewett, *English for the Academically Talented,* p. 63.

16. See Grace I. Armstrong, Herbert Egelko, and Helen E. Hansen, *The Very Superior Pupil, a Handbook for the Junior High School Teacher* (Long Beach, California: Long Beach Public Schools, Division of Instruction, 1955).

17. For the major arguments for or against ability grouping see Arno Jewett, *English for the Academically Talented Student,* pp. 82-83. See also Willard Abraham, *Common Sense About Gifted Children,* pp. 69-72 for another list of arguments pro and con.

18. For a summary of the highlights of these courses see Jewett, *English for the Academically Talented Student* pp. 68-70. For a description of 56 practices for the gifted in New York State, see *56 Practices for the Gifted from Secondary Schools of New York State* (Albany: State Education Department, 1958). For a description of special courses for the gifted in Jamaica (N. Y.) High School, see *Practices in Teaching Gifted Students in English* (Jamaica, N. Y.: Jamaica High School, 1960).

19. See *Reading List for the Theme Center* "The Individual's Quest for Universal Values" (New York: The Bureau of Curriculum Research, 1959).

20. *56 Practices for the Gifted,* p. 70.

21. A. J. Beeler, op. cit. p. 6. See also William Fidone, "An Above Average Class Studies *Hamlet.*" *English Journal* XLV (November, 1956) pp. 470-476.

22. Ruth Reeves, "The Gifted Student in the Literature Class," *English Journal* XLV (November, 1956), pp. 462-469.

23. A. J. Beeler, op. cit., p. 6.

24. Jewett, *English for the Academically Talented Student,* p. 79.

25. A. J. Beeler, op. cit., p. 7.

26. Nelson B. Henry, *Education for the Gifted,* The 57th Yearbook of the National Society for the Study of Education (Chicago: University of Chicago Press, 1958) pp. 280-281.

27. *56 Practices for the Gifted,* pp. 70-71.

28. Joseph Mersand, editor, *Practices in Teaching Gifted Students in English* (New York: English Department, Jamaica High School, 1960) p. 25.

29. A. J. Beeler, op. cit., p. 4. See also: *Challenging the Gifted Student in English: Composition.* Bulletin 56 CNMI (Houston, Texas: Houston Independent School District, 1956). Ruth Reeves, "The Gifted Student in the Composition Class," *Bulletin of the National Association of Secondary School Principals,* XLI (September, 1957) pp. 50-60. Helen Streubing, "Stimulating Creative Writing in the Junior High School," *English Journal,* XXXV (October, 1956) pp. 445-7.

30. Commission on the English Curriculum, *The English Language Arts in the Secondary School* (New York: Appleton-Century-Crofts, Inc., 1956) pp. 346-348.

31. Irna Rideout, "Clinic Solved Our Punctuation Problem," *Elementary English,* XXX (October, 1953) pp. 341-342.

Bibliography

Books

Abraham, Willard. *Common Sense about Gifted Children.* New York: Harper and Brothers, 1958, p. 17.

Commission on the English Curriculum. *The English Language Arts in the Secondary School.* New York: Appleton-Century-Crofts, 1956, pp. 346-348.

Gold, Milton J. *Education of the Intellectually Gifted.* Columbus: Charles E. Merrill Books, 1965, pp. 207-236.

Havighurst, Robert James, Strivers, Eugene and DeHaan, Robert F. *A Survey of the Education of Gifted Children.* Chicago: University of Chicago Press, 1955.

Henry, Nelson B. ed. *Education For the Gifted.* The 57th Yearbook of the National Society for the Study of Education. Chicago: University of Chicago Press, 1958, pp. 280-281.

Levine, Bert D. *Provisions and Practices to Serve the Exceptional Child in Texas Secondary Schools.* Texas Study of Secondary Education, Research Study No. 17. Austin, Texas: The Study, 1955.

Long Beach Public Schools. *The Very Superior Pupil: A Handbook for the Junior High School Teacher.* Long Beach, California: Division of Instruction, 1955.

Long Beach Public Schools. *The Very Superior Pupil: A Handbook for the Senior High School Teacher.* Long Beach, California: Division of Instruction, 1955.

Palo Alto Public Schools. *Meeting Individual Differences: The Gifted Child: A Handbook for Teachers and Administrators.* Palo Alto, California: The Schools, 1955.
Poley, Irvin C. *Speaking of Teaching.* Germantown, Pa.: Germantown Friends School, 1957.
Portland Public Schools. *The Gifted Child in Portland.* A Report of Five Years Experience in Developing a Program for Children of Exceptional Endowment. Portland, Oregon: The Schools, 1959.
Scheifele, Marian. *The Gifted Child in the Regular Classroom: Practical Suggestions For Teaching, No. 12.* New York: Teachers College, Columbia University, 1953.
Southworth, Mabel D., Leavens, Dolores and Schukart, Janice. *English and Literature Classes For the Exceptionally Endowed Students in the High Schools of Portland, Oregon.* Curriculum Publication GC-5, Portland, Oregon: Public Schools, 1957.
Sumption, Merle R. and Luecking, Evelyn M. *Education of the Gifted.* New York: Ronald Press, 1960, pp. 21-39.
Wilmington Public Schools. *An Introduction to the Education of the Able Student in the Wilmington Public Schools.* Instructional Bulletin Part I, Vol. I, No. I. Wilmington, Delaware: The Schools, 1958.
Witty, Paul. *The Gifted Child.* Boston: D. C. Heath, 1951.

Pamphlets and Periodicals

Beeler, A. J. "English For Superior Students." *Kentucky English Bulletin,* Spring, 1959, pp. 3-5.
Bureau of Secondary Curriculum Development. *Fifty-Six Practices For the Gifted From Secondary Schools of New York State.* Albany, New York: State Education Department, 1958.
Cathell, Dorothy. "Honors English: Break For Bright Students." *Clearing House,* February, 1955, pp. 331-337.
"Challenging the Gifted Student in English Composition." Bulletin 56 CNMI, Houston, Texas: Houston Independent School District, 1956.
Corbin, Richard. *Research Essay Project.* Schenectady, New York: New York State English Council, 1950.
Drucker, Peter F. *The Importance of Language: Toward the Liberally Educated Executive.* White Plains, N. Y.: The Fund for Adult Education, 1957, p. 49.
Educational Policies Commission. *Education of the Gifted.* Washington, D. C.: National Education Association, 1950.
Fidone, William. "An Above Average Class Studies *Hamlet.*" *English Journal,* 1956, pp. 470-476.
Gordon, Edward J. "Levels of Teaching and Testing." *English Journal,* September, 1955, pp. 330-334.
Hull, J. Dan and Jewett, Arno., compilers. *Teaching Rapid and Slow Learners.* Bulletin 1954, No. 5. Washington, D. C.: U. S. Department of Health, Education and Welfare, 1954, p. 16.
Jewett, Arno. ed. *English For the Academically Talented.* Washington, D. C.: National Education Association, 1961.
Mersand, Joseph. ed. *Practices in Teaching Gifted Students in English.* New York: Jamaica, New York, High School, 1960, pp. 31-33.
Peacock, Phyllis. "Highlights of Senior English For Superior Students." *North Carolina Teacher,* October, 1959, pp. 3-6.
Reeves, Ruth. "The Gifted Student in the Literature Class." *English Journal,* November, 1956, pp. 462-469.
Reeves, Ruth. "The Gifted Student in the Composition Class." *Bulletin of the National Association of Secondary School Principals,* September, 1957, pp. 50-60.
Research Division, N. E. A. *High School Methods With Superior Students. N. E. A. Research Bulletin,* Vol. XIX, September, 1941, No. 4. Washington, D. C.: Research Division, N. E. A.
Sheppard, Anna G. "Teaching the Gifted in the Regular Classroom." *Educational Leadership,* January, 1956, pp. 220-224.
Streubing, Helen. "Stimulating Creative Writing in the Junior High School." *English Journal,* October, 1946, pp. 445-447.
Witty, Paul. *Helping the Gifted Child.* Better Living Booklets, Chicago: Science Research Associates, 1952.

Wrightstone, J. Wayne. *What Tests Can Tell Us About Children.* Better Living Booklets, Chicago: Science Research Associates, 1954.

CHAPTER 6: ENGLISH FOR THE SLOW LEARNER

Notes

1.   See *Encyclopedia of Educational Research,* 3rd ed., (New York: Macmillan, 1960) p. 1280.
2.   Abraham H. Lass and Frank A. Smerling, "The English Teacher and the Slow Pupil," *High Points,* XXIX (February, 1947) pp. 5-12. Reprinted by permission.
3.   Curriculum Office and Division of Pupil Personnel and Counseling, Philadelphia Public Schools, 1958.
4.   Curriculum Office, Philadelphia Public Schools, 1959.
5.   "English for Slow Learners," *Kentucky English Bulletin* Volume VII, No. 1 (Fall, 1957-1958) pp. 15-24.
6.   *Teacher's Notebook in English,* Spring, 1962, New York, Harcourt, Brace, Jovanovich.
7.   Arno Jewett in his *Teaching Rapid and Slow Learners in High Schools* indicated that in 1954 special classes or ability groups were present in almost half of the schools surveyed. U. S. Office of Education, 1954, No. 5.
8.   W. B. Featherstone, *Teaching the Slow Learner* (Bureau of Publications, Teachers College, Columbia University; Revised and Enlarged Edition, 1951) p. 114. See also, Amy A. Allen, *Let Us Teach Slow-Learning Children,* Division of Special Education, Department of Education, State of Ohio, n. d. pp. 7-10.
9.   Teachers of slow learners should have the following books on hand to guide further reading: Ruth Strang, Ethlyn Phelps, Dorothy Withrow, *Gateways to Readable Books* (New York: H. W. Wilson, 4th ed., 1966). Anita E. Dunn, Mabel E. Jackman, Bernice C. Bush, J. Roy Newton, *Fare for the Reluctant Reader,* 3rd edition. (Albany, New York: New York State College for Teachers, 1964). George Spache, *Good Reading for Poor Readers* (Champaign: Garrard Pub. 1966). *Annotated Bibliography of Selected Books with High Interest and Low Vocabulary Level,* (Indianapolis Public Schools, Curriculum Bulletin No. 22 1C-Ns, 1954).
10.   Yarborough, op. cit., p. 4.
11.   Paul Kozelka, editor, *Fifteen One-Act Plays* (New York: Washington Square Press, 1961). M. Jerry Weiss, editor, *10 Short Plays* (New York: Dell Publishing Co, 1963). Morris Sweetkind, editor, *Ten Great One-Act Plays* (New York: Bantam Books, Inc., 1968). Richard H. Goldstone and Abraham H. Lass, editors, *The Mentor Book of Short Plays* (New York: New American Library, 1969). John Gassner and Mollie Gassner, editors, *15 International One-Act Plays* (New York: Washington Square Press, 1969).
12.   Op.cit, pp. 94-99.
13.   Indiana University Film Library at Bloomington, Indiana has an extensive collection.
14.   For many excellent suggestions on teaching writing to slow learners, consult the following: *Practices in Experimental Core Classes,* Curriculum Bulletin Number 8, 1953-1954 Series, Board of Education of the City of New York, 1954; *Developing a Core Program in the Junior High School Grades,* Curriculum Bulletin, No. 12, 1957-1958 Series, Board of Education of The City of New York, 1958; *Teaching Composition*—Grades 7, 8, and 9, Curriculum Bulletin, No. 5, 1961-1962 Series, Board of Education of the City of New York, 1962.
15.   Marie A. Toser, *Library Manual* Sixth Edition (New York: The H. W. Wilson Company, 1964). See also Maxwell Desser, *Using the Library* (New York: College-Entrance Book Company, 1956).
16.   Published by the H. W. Wilson Company, 950 University Avenue, New York 10052.
17.   To be obtained from the G. & C. Merriam Co., Springfield, Mass.
18.   Yarborough, op. cit., p. 6. See also *A Guide to the Teaching of English—An Adapted Course,* Philadelphia Public Schools, 1960, pp. 14-16; 25; 27-28.

Bibliography

Books

Allen, Amy A. *Let Us Teach Slow Learning Children*. Columbus, Ohio: Division of Special Education, Department of Education, n. d. pp. 7-10.

Brogden, J. D. *Developing Communication Skills in Non-Committed Learners*. West Nyack, New York: Parker Publishing Co., 1970.

Corbin, Richard and Crosby, Muriel, eds. *Language Programs For the Disadvantaged*. Champaign, Illinois: National Council of Teachers of English, 1965.

Crow, Lester D., Murray, Walter I., and Smythe, Hugh H. *Educating the Culturally Disadvantaged Child*. New York: David McKay Company, 1966.

Davis, Allison, *Social Class Influences on Learning*. Cambridge: Harvard University Press, 1955.

Karlin, Muriel S., and Berger, Regina. *Successful Methods for Teaching Slow Learners*. West Nyack, New York: Parker Publishing Co., 1969.

Kephart, Newell C. *The Slow Learner in the Classroom*. 2nd ed. Columbus: Charles E. Merrill, 1971.

Kohl, Herbert R. *Teaching the Unteachable*. New York: The New York Review, 1967.

Schonell, Fred Joyce. *Backwardness in the Basic Subjects*. London: Oliver and Boyd, 1949. See especially Chapters 17 and 18.

Strang, Ruth, Phelps, Ethlyn and Withrow, Dorothy. *Gateways to Readable Books*. 4th ed. New York: H. W. Wilson, 1965.

Strom, Robert D. ed. *The Inner-City Classroom: Teacher Behaviors*. Columbus: Charles E. Merrill, 1966.

Pamphlets and Periodicals

Aids for Selecting Books for Slow Readers. Chicago: American Library Association, 1959.

Annotated Bibliography of Selected Books with High Interest and Low Vocabulary Level. Curriculum Bulletin No. 22-1C-Ns. Indianapolis: Board of Education, 1954.

English - S (Communication Skills). Publication 2 - 106 TXT, Second Printing, August, 1962. Division for Improvement of Instruction, Department of Language Education, Detroit Public Schools (Experimental Work Copy).

A Guide to the Teaching of English—an Adapted Course, Grades 10-12 (Tentative). Philadelphia: Curriculum Office, Philadelphia Public Schools, 1960.

An Inquiry into the Nature and Needs of Slow Learners at the Senior High School Level. Philadelphia: Curriculum Office, Philadelphia Public Schools, 1958.

The Key to Teaching Slow Learners in the High School. Philadelphia: Curriculum Office, Philadelphia Public Schools, 1959.

Beeler, A. J. "English for Slow Learners." *Kentucky English Bulletin*, Fall, 1957–1958, pp. 15-24.

Bureau of Curriculum Research. *Teaching Composition—Grades 7-8-9*. Curriculum Bulletin, 1961–1962 Series No. 5. New York: Board of Education, 1962.

Bureau of Curriculum Research. *Developing a Core Program in the Junior High School Grades*. Curriculum Bulletin, 1957–1958 Series No. 12. New York: Board of Education, 1958.

Bureau of Curriculum Development. *Resource Units in Language Arts for General Course Students*. Curriculum Bulletin, 1966–1967 Series No. 13. New York: Board of Education, 1967.

Calitri, Charles. "*Macbeth* and the Reluctant Reader." *English Journal*, May, 1959, pp. 254-261.

Dunn, Anita, Jackman, Mabel E., Bush, Bernice C., Newton, J. Roy. *Fare for the Reluctant Reader*. 3rd ed. Albany, N. Y.: New York State College for Teachers, 1964.

Dutton, Joseph F. "The Slow Learner—Give Him Something New." *English Journal*, April, 1964, pp. 266-272.

Featherstone, W. B. *Teaching the Slow Learner*, Revised and enlarged edition. New York: Bureau of Publications, Teachers College, Columbia University, 1951, p. 114.

Finder, Morris. "Teaching English to Slum-Dwelling Pupils." *English Journal,* April, 1955, pp. 199-204.

Hull, J. Dan and Jewett, Arno. compilers. *Teaching Rapid and Slow Learners in High Schools.* Bulletin 1952, No. 5. Washington, D. C.: U. S. Office of Education, 1954.

Jewett, Arno, Mersand, Joseph and Gunderson, Doris V. *Improving English Skills of Culturally Different Youth in Large Cities.* Bulletin, 1964 No. 5 of the Office of Education. Washington: U. S. Government Printing Office, 1965.

Lutz, Una Dell. "Books for Severely Retarded Junior High School Readers." *English Journal,* October, 1950, pp. 439, 447.

Maertens, Grace Daly. "Organizing the Class to Care for Individual Needs." *English Journal,* October, 1958, p. 421.

Mersand, Joseph. "Individualizing Instruction in English in Large and Small Classes." *Bulletin of the National Association of Secondary School Principals,* March, 1960, pp. 111-123.

Rickert, Mary O. "Motivation for Slow Learners." *English Journal,* January, 1949, pp. 43-44.

Robinson, Esther Agnew. "Reclaiming the Slow Learning Boys and Girls." *English Journal,* March, 1947, pp. 134-137.

Spache, George. *Good Books for Poor Readers.* Champaign, Illinois: Garrard Publishing Co., 1966.

Sprague, Lois. "Non-Fiction Books for Retarded Readers in the Upper Grades." *English Journal,* January, 1951, pp. 28-34.

Sullivan, Helen Blair and Tolman, Lorraine E. *High-Interest-Low Vocabulary Reading Materials, a Selected Booklist. Journal of Education,* December, 1956. The entire issue is devoted to this list.

Teaching English for Higher Horizons. New York: Board of Education, 1965 (Tenth Grade).

Yarborough, Betty H. *Teaching English to Slow Learners.* Teacher's Notebook in English, Spring, 1962. New York: Harcourt, Brace and World, 1962.

Zink, Priscilla M. *"Hamlet*—Caviare to the Generals." *English Journal,* January, 1955, pp. 37-38.

CHAPTER 7: READING FOR THE SUPERIOR STUDENT IN A COMPREHENSIVE HIGH SCHOOL

Notes

1. Bureau of Secondary Curriculum Development, New York State Education Department, Albany, New York, 1958, 1960.
2. Published by Washington Square Press, 630 Fifth Avenue, New York City, 10020.
3. Published by R. R. Bowker Company, 1180 Avenue of the Americas, New York City, 10036, and available on subscription.
4. Obtainable from the Reading Clinic of Syracuse University, Syracuse, New York, and the National Council of Teachers of English, 1111 Kenyon Road, Urbana, Ill. 61801.
5. Obtainable from the Bureau of Independent Publishers and Distributors, 10 West 40th Street, New York City, 10036.
6. Prepared by Mrs. Irma G. Rhodes, former teacher of English, Jamaica High School, New York City.
7. Holt, Rinehart and Winston, 1959, pp. 212-216.
8. Harcourt, Brace, Jovanovich, 1961.
9. *Index to Plays* published by the Scarecrow Press, Metuchen, New Jersey.
10. New York: Holt, Rinehart and Winston, 1960 (4th ed.); New York: W. W. Norton, 1962 (Rev. ed.); New York: Holt, Rinehart and Winston, 1960 (3rd ed.).
11. An examination of *Paperbound Books in Print* will reveal several such compilations, all of which have some merit.
12. For inquiries about materials for the slow learner, write to Mrs. Theresa Carlucci, Jamaica High School, 168th Street and Gothic Drive, Jamaica, New York City, 11432.

Bibliography

Books

Bentley, John E. *Superior Children*. New York: W. W. Norton, 1937.

Cutts, Norma E., and Moseley, Nicholas. *Teaching the Bright and Gifted*. Englewood Cliffs, N. J.: Prentice-Hall, 1957.

De Haan, Robert F., and Havighurst, Robert J. *Educating Gifted Children*. Chicago: University of Chicago Press, 1957.

Gold, Milton J. *Education of the Intellectually Gifted*. Columbus: Charles E. Merrill, 1965.

Gray, William S. ed. *Adjusting Reading to Individuals*. Supplementary Educational Monographs No. 52. Chicago: University of Chicago Press, 1941.

Hall, Theodore. *Gifted Children: The Cleveland Story*. Cleveland: World Publishing Company, 1956.

Robinson, Helen M. ed. *Promoting Maximal Reading Growth among Able Learners*. Chicago: University of Chicago Press, 1954.

Veatch, Jeanette. *Individualizing Your Reading Program*. New York: G. P. Putnam's Sons, 1959.

Pamphlets and Periodicals

Arlington County School Board. *Suggestions for Working with the Gifted, Grades One Through Twelve*. Arlington, Virginia: The Board, 1956.

Baltimore County Public Schools. *Language Arts, Grades 1-12, for Superior and Gifted Students*. Towson, Maryland: The Schools, 1959.

Bennett, Paul L. "A Reading and Writing Program for the Talented Student." *English Journal*, September, 1955, pp. 335-339.

Barbe, Walter B. "A Study of the Reading of Gifted High-School Students." *Educational Administration and Supervision*, March, 1952, pp. 148-154.

Birch, Jack W., and McWilliams, Earl M. *Challenging Gifted Children*. Bloomington, Illinois: Public School Publishing Co., 1955.

Bureau of Curriculum Research. *Reading List for 9th Year; The Self-Reliant Individual*. Brooklyn, N. Y.: Bureau of Publications, N. Y. C. Board of Education, 1957.

Bureau of Curriculum Research. *Reading List for 10th Year; The Individual as a Member of the Group*. Brooklyn, N. Y.: Bureau of Publications, N. Y. C. Board of Education, 1957.

Bureau of Curriculum Research. *Reading List for 11th Year; The Individual and His American Heritage*. Brooklyn, N. Y.: Bureau of Publications, N. Y. C. Board of Education, 1958.

Bureau of Curriculum Research. *Reading List for the 12th Year; The Individual's Quest for Universal Values*. Brooklyn, N. Y.: Bureau of Publications, N. Y. C. Board of Education, 1958.

Bureau of Secondary Curriculum Development. *Fiction for Superior Students*. Albany, N. Y.: State Education Department, 1960.

Bureau of Secondary Curriculum Development. *More Books for High School Students of Superior Ability*. Albany, N. Y.: State Education Department, 1959.

Bureau of Secondary Curriculum Development. *Fiction for High School Students of Superior Ability*. Albany, N. Y.: State Education Department, 1958.

California State Committee on Developmental Reading. "Teaching Reading for the Gifted in the Secondary Schools." *Bulletin of the National Association of Secondary School Principals*, October, 1955, pp. 5-72.

Clark, E. Kathryn. "American School Libraries Provide for the Gifted." *American Library Association Bulletin*, February, 1958, pp. 97-100.

Clayton Public Schools. *An Enriched Curriculum in English for the Junior High*. Clayton, Mo.: Curriculum Committee, 1958.

Clayton Public Schools. *An Enriched Curriculum in English, Grade XII* Clayton, Mo.: School District of Clayton, 1959.

Clayton Public Schools. *Enrichment in Reading for Seventh and Eighth Grades.* Clayton, Mo.: School District of Clayton, 1959.

College Entrance Examination Board. *Advanced Placement Program.* New York: The Board, 1958–1959.

Connecticut State Department of Education. *Education for Gifted Children and Youth. A Guide to Planning Programs.* Bulletin No. 77. Hartford: The State Department of Education, 1957.

Estes, Helen J. "College Level English in High School." *English Journal,* September, 1959, pp. 332-334.

Friedman, Albert B. "The Literary Experience of High School Seniors and College Freshman." *English Journal,* December, 1955, pp. 521-524.

Gill, Naomi B. "Depth Reading." *English Journal,* September, 1953, pp. 311-315.

Huettner, O. F., and Hosmanck, J. J. "Reading Program for the Superior Student." Bulletin of the National Association of Secondary School Principals, March, 1957, pp. 65-68.

Houston Public Schools. *Challenging the Gifted Student in English: Literature.* Houston, Texas: Houston Independent School District, 1956.

Lazarus, Arnold Leslie. "English XL." *English Journal,* February, 1954, pp. 71-74.

Levine, Bert D. *Provisions and Practices to Serve the Exceptional Child in Texas Secondary Schools* Texas Study of Secondary Education, Research Study No. 17. Austin, Texas: The Study, 1955.

Long Beach Public Schools: *The Very Superior Pupil: A Handbook for the Junior High School Teacher.* Long Beach, Calif.: Division of Instruction, 1955.

Long Beach Public Schools. *The Very Superior Pupil: A Handbook for the Senior High School Teacher.* Long Beach, Calif.: Division of Instruction, 1955.

Palo Alto Public Schools, *Meeting Individual Differences. The Gifted Child: A Handbook for Teachers and Administrators.* Palo Alto, Calif.: The Schools, 1955.

Peacock, Phyllis. "Highlights of Senior English for Superior Students." *North Carolina Teacher,* October, 1959, pp. 3-6.

Portland Public Schools. *The Gifted Child in Portland. A Report of Five Years of Experience in Developing a Program for Children of Exceptional Endowment.* Portland, Oregon: The Schools, 1959.

Research Division, N. E. A. *High School Methods with Superior Students. N. E. A. Research Bulletin,* Vol. XIX No. 4, September, 1941, Washington, D. C.: Research Division, N. E. A.

Ryan, Eunice G. "Reading for Gifted Children." *Clearing House,* January, 1957, pp. 287-288.

Scheifele, Marian. *The Gifted Child in the Regular Classroom.* Practical Suggestions for Teaching, No. 12. New York: Teachers College, Columbia University, 1953.

Sheldon, William D. "Place of the Classroom Teacher in Handling Individual Differences in Reading." Conference on Reading. University of Pittsburgh, 1953, pp. 25-33.

Sheridan, Marion C. "Teaching English to Superior Students." *N. E. A. Journal,* December, 1952, pp. 566-567.

Southworth, Mabel D., Leavens, L. Dolores, and Schukart, Janice. *English and Literature Classes For Exceptionally Endowed Students in the High Schools of Portland, Oregon.* Curriculum Publication GC-5. Portland, Oregon: Public Schools, 1957.

Squire, James R. "Individualizing the Teaching of Literature." *English Journal,* September, 1956, pp. 314-319.

Wilmington Public Schools. *An Introduction to the Education of the Able Student in the Wilmington Public Schools.* Instructional Bulletin Part I, Vol. 1, No. 1. Wilmington, Delaware: The Schools, 1958.

CHAPTER 8: THE PAPERBACK IN THE HIGH SCHOOL

Notes

1. William D. Boutwell, "The Paperback Boom!" *Studies in The Mass Media* (December 1961). p. 9
2. Letter to the writer, dated December 19, 1961.

3. Letter to the writer, dated January 26, 1962.
4. M. Jerry Weiss, editor, *The Use of Paperbound Books.* (Urbana, Illinois: National Council of Teachers of English, 1959) pp. 19-20.
5. Ibid, pp. 18-19.
6. Letter to the writer, dated January 9, 1962. For a detailed description of the "Buffalo Plan" see the article by its originator, Austin Mc C. Fox, "The Buffalo Paperbook Project—More Than a Paper Moon," *Studies in the Mass Media* (November, 1961) pp. 18-20. See also "Buffalo's Program of In-Service Paperback Stores," *Publishers' Weekly,* November 21, 1960, pp. 14-17.
7. Sister M. Clarencia, "I Sing of the Paperback," *The Catholic Educator,* XXXI (March 1961) p. 541.
8. Albert Nissman, "Potpourri on Paperbacks," *Studies in the Mass Media* (December 1961) pp. 6-8.
9. Letter to the writer, dated January 10, 1962.
10. Letter to the writer, dated January 24, 1962. See his *Paperbound Books in America* (New York: New York Public Library, 1952).
11. Letter to the writer, dated January 10, 1962.
12. James W. Saunders, S. J., "Soft Covered Culture," *Catholic Educator,* XXIX (November 1959). For a bibliography of over one hundred articles on using paperbacks, consult Alexander Butman, Donald Reis and David Sohn, *Paperbacks in the Schools* (New York: Bantam Books, 1963) pp. 139-152.

Bibliography

Books

Butman, Alexander, Reis, Donald, and Sohn, David. eds. *Paperbacks in The Schools.* New York: Bantam Books, 1963.
Schick, Frank L. *The Paperbound Book in America.* New York: R. R. Bowker, 1958.

Pamphlets and Periodicals

Anderson, Vivienne. ed. *Paperbacks in Education.* New York: Teachers College Press, Teachers College, Columbia University, 1966.
Bogart, Max. ed. *Paperbound Books in New Jersey Public Schools.* Trenton, New Jersey: State Education Department, 1965.
Bruell, E. "Paperback Comes to Bremen High." *English Journal,* January, 1962, pp. 33-38.
Cooper, R. "Experiment with Paperbound Books in J. H. S. 217, N. Y. C." *Library Journal,* April 15, 1958.
Evans, William. "Teaching *The Pearl.*" *School Paperback Journal,* January, 1965, pp. 12-15.
Falke, M. H. "High School Students Like Paperbacks." *Wilson Library Bulletin,* November, 1960, pp. 248-249.
Guzie, T. W. "Paperbacks: A New Trend in High School Literature." *Catholic School Journal,* November, 1960, pp. 32-35.
Johnston, Gordon. "Teaching *To Kill A Mockingbird.*" *School Paperback Journal,* January, 1965, pp. 24-26.
Koneff, Donald. "Teaching *Lost Horizon.*" *School Paperback Journal,* January, 1965, pp. 16-18.
Lee, Norman. "Paperback Books for Senior High School English." *Studies in the Mass Media,* December, 1961, pp. 11-18.
Lewis, N. B. "Paperbounds: Valuable Source of Good Reading." *The Clearing House,* May, 1955, pp. 528-530.
Maher, K. U. "Try Pocket-Sized Books to Stimulate Reading." *English Journal,* October, 1958, pp. 421-422.
Marcus, Fred H. "Structure and the Short Story." *Studies in the Mass Media,* February, 1962, pp. 16-18.

McLaughlin, Frank. *"The Old Man and the Sea* Comes Home." *School Paperback Journal,* February, 1965, pp. 22-23.
McLaughlin, Frank, "Teaching *Ethan Frome." School Paperback Journal,* January, 1965, pp. 20-23.
Mirrielees, Edith R. "Pocketbooks Move Foreword." *English Journal,* May, 1956, pp. 223-230.
Moscow, David H. "Paperbacks: A Planned Program for Southfield High School." *Studies in the Mass Media,* January, 1963, pp. 13-16.
Newton, David E. "Teaching Research Techniques with Paperbacks." *School Paperback Journal,* February, 1965, pp. 10-12.
Rouse, John J. "Paperbacks and English Programs in High School." *Studies in the Mass Media,* January, 1963, pp. 10-12.
Sister M. Clarencia. "I Sing of the Paperback." *The Catholic Educator,* March, 1961, pp. 541-545.
Sister Mary Harriet. "Let's Use the Paperbacks." *English Journal,* April, 1957, pp. 202-204.
Tyre, Richard. "Teaching *Lord of the Flies." School Paperback Journal,* January, 1965, pp. 9-11.
Vedro, Alfred S. "Shades of Jules Verne and H. G. Wells." *School Paperback Journal,* February, 1965, pp. 18-19.
Warner, J. F. "Anthologies in the High School Classroom?" *English Journal,* October, 1959, pp. 382-386.
Zamchick, David. "Problems in Paperback Publishing." *English Journal,* December, 1958, pp. 562-565.

CHAPTER 9: HOW TO TEACH LIBRARY SKILLS

Notes

1. Thomas C. Blaisdell, *Ways to Teach English* (New York: Doubleday, Doran, 1930) p. 488.
2. John J. DeBoer, Walter V. Kaulfers, and Helen Rand Miller, *Teaching Secondary English* (New York: McGraw-Hill, 1951) p. 186. See also Jean Key Gates, *A Guide to the Use of Books and Libraries* (New York: McGraw-Hill, 1962) and Jessie Boyd, *Books, Libraries and You* (New York: Charles Scribner's Sons, 1941). Marie A. Toser, *Library Manual: A Study Work Manual on the Use of Books and Libraries.* Sixth Edition. (New York: H. W. Wilson, 1964) has been a useful volume for many years.
3. *Syllabus in English for Secondary Schools* (Albany: New York State Department, 1935) p. 230.

Bibliography

Books

Boyd, Jessie et al. *Books, Libraries and You.* New York: Charles Scribner's Sons, 1941.
Commission on the English Curriculum. *The English Language Arts.* New York: Appleton-Century-Crofts, 1952, pp. 233-245.
Cross, E. A., and Carney, Elizabeth. *Teaching English in High Schools.* New York: The Macmillan Company, 1950, pp. 352-369.
Cleary, Florence Damon. *Discovering Books and Libraries.* New York: H. W. Wilson Company, 1967.
Dakin, Dorothy. *Talks to Beginning Teachers of English.* Boston: D. C. Heath and Company, 1937, pp. 163-166.
Gates, Jean Kay. *A Guide to the Use of Books and Libraries.* New York: McGraw-Hill, 1962.
Hook, J. N. *The Teaching of High School English.* 4th ed. New York: The Donald Press, 1972, passim.

Lewis, John S., and Sisk, Jean C. *Teaching English 7-12.* New York: American Book Company, 1963, pp. 163-165; 185-186.
Mirrielees, Lucia B. *Teaching Composition and Literature.* Revised Edition. New York: Harcourt, Brace and Company, 1952, pp. 23-24; 211-217; 357-358.

Pamphlets and Periodicals

How to Use the Reader's Guide to Periodical Literature and Other Indexes. New York: H. W. Wilson Company, n. d.
How to Use Webster's New International Dictionary; Workbook for Use with Webster's New International Dictionary. Springfield, Mass: G. & C. Merriam Company, n. d.
Fargo, Lucile F. *The Library in the School.* Chicago: American Library Association, 1935.
Perkins, Flossie L. *Book and Non-Book Media.* Urbana: National Council of Teachers of English, 1972.
Toser, Marie A. *Library Manual: A Study-Work Manual on the Use of Books and Libraries.* 5th ed. New York: The H. W. Wilson Company, 1964.

CHAPTER 10: CONTEMPORARY PLAYS FOR THE ENGLISH CLASSROOM

Notes

1. Published by Charles Scribner's Sons, 1926.
2. Published by Charles Scribner's Sons, 1926.
3. Published by Charles Scribner's Sons, 1969.
4. Published by Harcourt, Brace, 1947.
5. Published by Globe Book Company, 1954.
6. Reprinted by permission of *Today's Speech* and its editor, Manuel H. Prosser.
7. Metuchen, N. J.: Scarecrow Press, 1966, Second Edition.
8. Urbana, Illinois: National Council of Teachers of English, 1965.
9. Metuchen, N. J.: Scarecrow Press, 1971, Fifth Edition.
10. Metuchen, N. J.: Scarecrow Press, 1966.
11. Garden City, N. Y.: Doubleday and Company.

Bibliography

Books

Austell, Jan. *What's in a Play?* New York: Harcourt, Brace, Jovanovich, 1968.
Chicorel, Marietta. ed. *Chicorel Theatre Index to Plays in Anthologies, Periodicals, Discs and Tapes.* Volume 1. New York: Chicorel Library Publishing, 1970. Volume 2, 1971.
Coleman, Arthur, and Tyler, Gary. *Drama Criticism.* Volume 1. A Checklist of Interpretations Since 1940 of English and American Plays. Chicago: Swallow, 1966. Volume 2. A Checklist of Interpretations Since 1940 of Classical and Continental Plays. 1971.
Esslin, Martin. *Reflections: Essays on the Modern Theatre.* Garden City, N. Y.: Doubleday, 1971.
Fowler, Mary Elizabeth. *Teaching Language, Composition, and Literature.* New York: McGraw-Hill, 1965, pp. 284-307.
Guernsey, Otis L., Jr. ed. and compiler. *Directory of the American Theatre, 1894-1971.* New York: Dodd, Mead, 1971.
Hatlen, Theodore W. *Orientation to the Theatre.* New York: Appleton-Century-Crofts, 1962.
Hook, J. N. *The Teaching of High School English.* 4th ed. New York: Ronald Press, 1972, pp. 165-208.

Ireland, Norma Olin. *Index to Full Length Plays, 1944–1964.* Boston: F. W. Faxon, 1965.
Johnson, Albert, and Johnson, Bertha. *Drama for Classroom and Stage.* Cranbury, N. J.: A. S. Barnes, 1969.
Loban, Walter, Ryan, Margaret, and Squire, James R. *Teaching Language and Literature.* New York: Harcourt, Brace, Jovanovich, 1961, pp. 323-377.
Lovell, John, Jr. *Digests of Great American Plays.* New York: Thomas Y. Crowell, 1961.
Mersand, Joseph. *Index to Plays, with Suggestions for Teaching.* Metuchen, N. J.: Scarecrow Press, 1966.
———, editor, *Guide to Play Selection.* 3rd ed. New York: R. R. Bowker and Champaign, Ill.: N. C. T. E., 1975.
Morsey, Royal J. *Improving English Instruction.* 2nd ed. Boston: Allyn and Bacon, 1969, pp. 92-95.
Ottemiller, John H. *Index to Plays in Collections.* 4th ed. Metuchen, N. J.: Scarecrow Press, 1964.
Salem, James M. ed. *Drury's Guide to Best Plays.* 2nd ed. Metuchen, N. J.: Scarecrow Press, 1969.
Salem, James M. *American Drama from O'Neill to Albee.* Metuchen, N. J.: Scarecrow Press, 1966.
———*The Musical Team: Rodgers-and-Hart to Lerner-and-Loewe.* Metuchen, N. J.: Scarecrow Press, 1967.
———*British and Continental Drama from Ibsen to Pinter.* Metuchen, N. J.: Scarecrow Press, 1968.
Shank, Theodore J. ed. *A Digest of 500 Plays.* New York: Crowell-Collier, 1963.
Shipley, Joseph T. *Guide to Great Plays.* Washington, D. C.: Public Affairs Press, 1956.
Sobel, Bernard ed. *The New Theatre Handbook and Digest of Plays.* New York: Crown, 1959.
Sprinchorn, Evert. ed. *20th Century Plays in Synopsis.* New York: Thomas Y. Crowell, 1965.
Wellwarth, George E. *The Theatre of Protest.* New York: New York University Press, 1965.

Pamphlets and Periodicals

Bureau of Curriculum Research. *Resource Units in Language Arts for Senior High Schools Literature.* Curriculum Bulletin, 1962–1963 Series, No. 36. New York: Board of Education, 1963, pp. 43-50. This is a unit on teaching the Drama.
Hoetker, James. *Dramatics and the Teaching of English.* Urbana: National Council of Teachers of English, 1969.
———*Students as Audiences.* Urbana: National Council of Teachers of English, 1971.
Hundhausen, David. "How to Succeed in Producing without Really Spending." *Wisconsin English Journal,* January, 1970, pp. 31-36.
For specific articles in the *English Journal* dealing with specific plays, consult the following issues:
Arthur Miller's *The Crucible,* March, 1961, pp. 183 ff.
Arthur Koestler's *Darkness at Noon,* September, 1961, pp. 416 ff.
Henrik Ibsen's *An Enemy of the People,* December, 1965, pp. 626 ff.
Tennessee Williams' *The Glass Menagerie,* February, 1968, pp. 100 ff.
Robert Bolt's *A Man for All Seasons,* November, 1966, pp. 1006 ff.

CHAPTER 11: HOW CAN WE HELP STUDENTS ENJOY LITERATURE?

Notes

1. Robert Morss Lovett, editor, *Marmion* (New York: Longman's Green, 1896) p. XXXI.
2. B. A. Hinsdale, *Teaching the Language-Arts* (New York: D. Appleton, 1896) p. 142.
3. See Appendix I: Textbooks on English Methodology, *Illinois English Bulletin,* XLVII, No. 1 (October, 1959) pp. 12-13.
4. W. S. Gray, "Is Yours an Effective Reading Program?" *University of Kansas Bulletin of Education* (February, 1958) p. 47.

 5. Hinsdale, op. cit., p. 136.
 6. Lester Walker, "Boom in Good Books," *Saturday Review of Literature*, February 8, 1958, p. 38.
 7. See Appendix III: Books on Reading Improvement for College Students, *Illinois English Bulletin*, op. cit., p. 115.
 8. Dora V. Smith, "How Literature is Taught in the Secondary Schools of Today," *Journal of the N. E. A.*, (April, 1951) p. 286.
 9. Obtainable from the Bureau of Publications of the Board of Education of New York City, 110 Livingston Street, Brooklyn, N. Y. C. 11201.
10. Commission on the English Curriculum of the National Council of Teachers of English, *The English Language Arts*, N. C. T. E. Curriculum Series Vol. 1 (New York: Appleton-Century-Crofts, 1952) pp. 246-273. See also *The English Language Arts in Secondary School*, N. C. T. E. Curriculum Series Vol. III (New York: Appleton-Century-Crofts, 1956) pp. 123-159.
11. Arthur H. Parsons, "The Teacher's Need to Read," *Journal of the N. E. A.* (March, 1958) pp. 168-169. See Appendix IV: Lists of Recommended Books, *Illinois English Bulletin*, op. cit., pp. 15-16.
12. Lou LaBrant, *We Teach English* (New York: Harcourt, Brace, 1951) pp. 242-248.
13. Dora V. Smith, op. cit., p. 285.
14. "Reading Trends for Year Ending June 30, 1957 (Washington, D. C.: Public Library, 1957) p. 12.
15. David Dempsey, "Young Readers Made to Order," *New York Times Book Review*, Children's Book Section, November 2, 1958, p. 3.

Bibliography

Books

Broening, Angela M. ed. *Conducting Experiences in English*. Monograph No. 8, National Council of Teachers of English. New York: Appleton-Century-Crofts, 1939, pp. 13-107.

Burton, Dwight L. *Literature Study in the High Schools*. Revised Edition. New York: Holt, Rinehart, and Winston, 1964.

Burton, Dwight L., and Simmons, John S. *Teaching English in Today's High Schools*. New York: Holt, Rinehart, and Winston, 1965.

Carlsen, G. Robert. *Books and the Teen-Age Reader*. New York: Bantam, 1967.

Cooper, Charles W. *Preface to Poetry*. New York: Harcourt, Brace, 1949.

DeBoer, John J., Kaulfers, Walter V., and Miller, Helen Rand. "Literature for Human Needs," in *Teaching Secondary English*. New York: McGraw-Hill, 1951, pp. 204-230.

Diltz, B. C. *Patterns of Surmise*. Toronto: Clarke, Irwin, and Company, Ltd., 1962.

Diltz, B. C. *The Sense of Wonder*. Toronto: McClelland and Stewart, Ltd., 1953.

Fader, Daniel N., and McNeil, Elton B. *Hooked on Books*. New York: Berkeley Publishing Corp., 1968.

Fagan, Edward R. *Field: A Process for Teaching Literature*. University Park: Pennsylvania State University Press, 1964.

Fowler, Mary Elizabeth. *Teaching Language, Composition, and Literature*. New York: McGraw-Hill, 1965, Chapters 9-14, pp. 217-353.

Hook, J. N. *The Teaching of High School English*. 4th ed. New York: Ronald Press, 1972, Chapters 4-7, pp. 77-260.

Jelinek, James J. *Experience Through Literature*. New York: Exposition Press, 1948.

LaBrant, Lou. *We Teach English*. New York: Harcourt, Brace, 1951, pp. 264-311.

Lewis, John S., and Sisk, Jean C. *Teaching English 7-12*. New York: American Book Company, 1963, Chapters 8-10, pp. 188-310.

Loban, Walter, Ryan, Margaret, and Squire, James, R. *Teaching Language and Literature*. New York: Harcourt, Brace and World, 1961, Chapters 6, 7, 12.

Lund, Thomas A. *The Modern Practical Approach to Teaching English*. West Nyack: Parker Publishing Co., 1971, Chapter 6, pp. 137-167.

Marx, Milton. *Enjoyment of Drama*. New York: F. S. Crofts, 1940.

Morsey, Royal J. *Improving English Instruction.* 2nd ed. Boston: Allyn and Bacon, 1969, Chapters 4-5, pp. 66-105.

National Council of Teachers of English, Commission on the English Curriculum. *The English Language Arts.* N. C. T. E. Curriculum Series, Vol. I. New York: Appleton-Century-Crofts, 1952, pp. 374-396.

National Council of Teachers of English, Commission on the English Curriculum. *The English Language Arts in Secondary Schools.* N. C. T. E. Curriculum Series, Vol. III. New York: Appleton-Century-Crofts, 1956, pp. 123-159.

Rosenblatt, Louise M. *Literature as Exploration.* New York: Appleton-Century-Crofts, 1938.

Ryan, Margaret. *Teaching the Novel in Paperback.* New York: Macmillan, 1963.

Smith, Dora V. *Communication, the Miracle of Shared Living.* New York: Macmillan, 1955, pp. 62-78.

Smith, James Harvey. *The Reading of Poetry.* Boston: Houghton Mifflin, 1939.

Smith, Reed. *The Teaching of Literature in the High School.* New York: American Book Company, 1935.

Sprau, George. *The Meaning of Literature.* New York: Charles Scribner's Sons, 1925.

Pamphlets and Periodicals

Barnes, Douglas. ed. *Drama in the English Classroom.* Champaign, Illinois: National Council of Teachers of English, 1968.

Broening, Angela M. "Development of Taste in Literature in the Senior High School." *English Journal,* April, 1963, pp. 273-287.

Bureau of Curriculum Research. *Resource Units in Language Arts for Senior High Schools.* Curriculum Bulletin, 1962–1963 Series No. 3. New York: Board of Education, 1963.

Burton, Dwight L. "Literature on the Topical Unit." *English Journal,* December, 1953, pp. 497-501.

Carlin, Jerome. "This I Believe—About the Essay." *English Journal,* September, 1962, pp. 403-411.

Ciardi, John. "Robert Frost—The Way to a Poem." *Saturday Review,* April 12, 1958, pp. 13-15, 65.

Denver Public Schools. *Literature Guide for Use in Junior High School.* Denver Public Schools, 1951.

Dunning, Stephen. *Scholarly Appraisals of Literary Works Taught in High Schools.* Champaign, Illinois: National Council of Teachers of English, 1965.

Early, Margaret J. "Stages of Growth in Literary Appreciation." *English Journal,* March, 1960, pp. 161-167.

Friedrich, Gerhard. "A Teaching Approach to Poetry." *English Journal,* February, 1960, pp. 75-81.

Gordon, Edward J. "Teaching Students to Read Verse." *English Journal,* March, 1950, pp. 149-154.

Hoetker, James. *Students as Audiences: An Experimental Study of the Relationship Between Classroom Study of Drama and Attendance at the Theatre.* Research Report Number 11. Urbana: National Council of Teachers of English, 1971.

Hunt, Kellogg W. "Getting into the Novel." *English Journal,* December, 1961, pp. 601-606.

Joll, Leonard W. "Developing Taste in Literature in the Junior High School." *Elementary English,* February, 1963, pp. 183-188.

Leary Lewis. ed. *The Teacher and American Literature.* Champaign, Illinois: National Council of Teachers of English, 1965.

Loban, Walter. "Teaching Literature: A Multiple Approach." *English Journal,* February, 1956, pp. 75-78.

MacLeish, Archibald. "Why Do We Teach Poetry?" *Atlantic Monthly,* March, 1956, pp. 48-53.

Ojala, William T. "Thematic Categories as an Approach to Sequence." *English Journal,* March, 1963, pp. 178-185.

Perrine, Laurence. "The Nature of Proof in the Interpretation of Poetry." *English Journal,* September, 1962, pp. 393-398.

———*The Range of English.* Champaign, Illinois: National Council of Teachers of English, 1968. See especially Dwight L. Burton's "The Centrality of Literature in the English Curriculum."

Rose, Elizabeth. "Teaching Poetry in the Junior High School." *English Journal,* December, 1957, pp. 540-550.

Rosenbatt, Louise. "The Acid Test for Literature Teaching." *English Journal,* February, 1956, pp. 66-74.

Sheridan, Marion C. "Teaching a Novel." *English Journal,* January, 1952, pp. 8-14.

Squire, James R. ed. *Response to Literature.* Champaign, Illinois: National Council of Teachers of English, 1968.

Thomas, Cleveland, A., chairman, Secondary Section Committee, N. C. T. E. *They Will Read Literature,* a Portfolio of Tested Secondary School Procedures. Champaign, Illinois: National Council of Teachers of English, 1955.

CHAPTER 12: SELECTION OF ADULT BOOKS FOR SCHOOL-AGE READERS

Notes

1. Joseph Mersand, "The Teaching of Literature in American High Schools, 1865–1900," in Robert C. Pooley ed. *Perspectives on English* (New York: Appleton-Century-Crofts, 1960) pp. 269-302.
2. Elinor Walker and Others eds. *Doors to More Mature Reading* (Chicago: American Library Association, 1964).
3. Richard S. Alm ed., *Books for You* (New York: Washington Square Press, 1964).
4. Lois R. Markey, compiler, *Senior Book List* (Boston: National Association of Independent Schools, 1967).
5. Lois R. Markey, compiler, *Junior Book List* (Boston: National Association of Independent Schools, 1967).
6. Young Adult Services, *Books for the Teen Age* (New York: New York Public Library). Published annually in January.
7. Geneva R. Hanna, and Mariana K. McAllister, *Books, Young People and Reading Guidance* (New York: Harper, 1960).
8. National Association of Independent Schools, *3000 Books for Secondary School Libraries* (New York: Bowker, 1961).
9. Elinor Walker ed., *Book Bait:* Detailed Notes on Adult Books Popular with Young People (Chicago: American Library Association, 1957).
10. George W. Norvell, *The Reading Interests of Young People* (Boston: D. C. Heath, 1950).
11. George W. Norvell, *What Boys and Girls Like to Read* (New York: Silver, Burdett, 1958).
12. Helen Wilmott, "YASD Asks the Young Adult," *Top of the News, 21* (January, 1965) pp. 143-147.
13. Robert G. Carlsen, *Books and the Teen-Age Reader* (New York: Harper, 1967).
14. Robert G. Carlsen, "For Everything There Is A Season," *Top of the News, 21* (January, 1965) pp. 103-110.
15. Joseph Mersand, *The Play's the Thing.* (New York: Modern Chapbooks, 1948) pp. 23-39.
16. Lois R. Markey, compiler, *Junior Book List* (Boston: National Association of Independent Schools, 1968).

Bibliography

Books

American Association for the Advancement of Science. *A. A. A. S. Science Book List.* 3rd ed. Washington, D. C.: American Association for the Advancement of Science, 1970.

American Association for the Advancement of Science. *A. A. A. S. Science Book List for Children.* Washington, D. C.: American Association for the Advancement of Science, 1963.

American Library Association. *African Encounter.* Chicago: American Library Association, 1963.

——— *Best Books for Young Adults*. Annual since 1931. Chicago: American Library Association.

——— *Books for Children:* 1960–1965 and Supplements. Chicago: American Library Association, 1966. Annual Supplements.

Baker, Augusta, compiler. *Books about Negro Life for Children*. New York: New York Public Library, 1970.

Brown, Ralph A., and Brown, Marion R. *American History Booklist for High Schools*. Washington, D. C.: National Council for Social Studies, 1969.

Carlsen, G. Robert. *Books and the Teen-Age Reader*. New York: Harper and Row, 1967; New York: Bantam, 1967, paperback edition.

Colwell, C. Carter. *A Student's Guide to Literature*. New York: Washington Square Press, 1968.

Deason, Hilary J. compiler and ed. *A Guide to Science Reading*. 2nd ed. New York: New American Library, 1966.

Duff, Annie. *Bequest of Wings: A Family's Pleasure with Books*. New York: Viking, 1954.

Embree, Ainslee T. ed. *Asia: A Guide to Paperbacks*. Revised Edition. New York: The Asia Society, 1968.

Fader, Daniel N., and McNeil, Elton B. *Hooked on Books: Program and Proof*. New York: Berkley Publishing Co., 1968.

Guilfoyle, Elizabeth. ed. *Adventuring with Books*. A Book List for Elementary Schools. New York: New American Library, 1966.

Hornstein, Lillian. ed. *The Reader's Companion to World Literature*. New York: New American Library, 1956.

Lueders, Edward. ed. *The College and Adult Reading List of Books in Literature and the Fine Arts*. New York: Washington Square Press, 1962.

Metzner, Seymour. *American History in Juvenile Books*. New York: H. W. Wilson, 1966.

New York Public Library. *Books for the Teen Age*. New York: New York Public Library. Published every January.

Noonan, Eileen F. compiler. *Basic Book Collection for High School*. 7th ed. Chicago: American Library Association, 1963.

Pilgrim, Geneva H., and McAllister, Mariana K. *Books, Young People and Reading Guidance*. 2nd ed. New York: Harper and Row, 1968.

Titowsky, Bernard. *American History*. Brooklawn, N. J.: McKinley Publishing Co., 1964.

Walker, Elinor. compiler. *Book Bait*. Detailed Notes on Adult Books Popular with Young Adults. 2nd ed. Chicago: American Library Association, 1969.

Weber, J. Sherwood. ed. *Good Reading*. 21st ed. New York: New American Library, 1964.

Willard, Charles B. ed. *Your Reading*. A Book List for Junior High Schools. New York: New American Library, 1966.

Wilson, Jean A. ed. *Books for You*. A Reading List for Senior High School Students. New York: Washington Square Press, 1971.

CHAPTER 13: WHAT HAS HAPPENED TO WRITTEN COMPOSITION IN THE PAST FIFTY YEARS?

Notes

1. *Tampa Times*, October 24, 1960.
2. Percival Chubb, *The Teaching of English* (New York: Macmillan, 1902) p. 106.
3. Sterling Andrus Leonard, *English Composition as a Social Problem* (Boston: Houghton Mifflin, 1917) p. *v*.
4. Joseph Mersand, *Attitudes Toward English Teaching* (Champaign: NCTE, 1959) p. 142.
5. Chubb, op. cit., p. 324.
6. James Fleming Hosic, compiler. *Reorganization of English in Secondary Schools* (Washington: Government Printing Office, 1917) p. 7. Cf. also p. 23.
7. Letter from Charles W. Eliot to an unknown inquirer included in Claude M. Fuess, *Selected Letters* (Boston: Houghton Mifflin, 1914) pp. 105-106.
8. B. A. Hinsdale *Teaching the Language-Arts* (New York: D. Appleton, 1896) p. 117.

9. Chubb, op. cit., p. 317.
10. Hosic, op. cit., p. 55. Cf. Leonard, op. cit., p. *vi*.
11. Leonard, op. cit., p. *viii*.
12. Leonard, op. cit., p. *vii*.
13. Hinsdale, op. cit., p. 114.
14. Samuel Thurber, "Five Axioms of Composition Teaching," *School Review,* January, 1897; quoted by Carpenter, Baker & Scott, *The Teaching of English* (New York: Longmans, Green, 1903) p. 230.
15. Joseph Mersand, ed. *Writing—Everybody's Job:* for teachers, for principals, for administrators (New London, Conn.: Croft, 1959).
16. Chubb, op. cit., p. 354.
17. Published by D. C. Heath.
18. Published by L. W. Singer.
19. Published by Row, Peterson.
20. Published by McGraw-Hill.
21. Published by Scott, Foresman.
22. *The English Journal,* November, 1960, p. 517.
23. Holt Service Bulletin number 7. Now out of print, but available in some curriculum libraries.
24. Hughes Mearns, *Creative Youth* (New York: Doubleday, 1925); *Creative Power,* Second Revised Edition (New York: Dover, 1958).
25. Carpenter, Baker & Scott, op. cit., p. 241.
26. *Journal of Education,* CXXXVII (December, 1955). Cf. also "Individualizing Instruction in Large and Small Classes," *Bulletin of National Association of Secondary School Principals,* XLIV (March, 1960), pp. 111-123.

Bibliography

Books

App, Astin. *Way to Creative Writing.* Milwaukee: Bruce Publishing Co., 1954.

Applegate, Mauree. *Helping Children Write.* New York: International Textbook Company, 1948.

Bernstein, Abraham. *Teaching English in High School.* New York: Random House, 1961, pp. 82-120.

Brown, Ivor John Carnegie. *No Idle Words* and *Having the Last Word.* New York: E. P. Dutton and Co., 1951.

Carpenter, Charles R., Baker, Franklin T., and Scott, Fred N. *The Teaching of English in the Elementary and the Secondary School.* New York: Longmans, Green, 1903.

Chubb, Percival. *The Teaching of English in the Elementary and Secondary Schools.* New York: Macmillan, 1902.

Cousins, Norman. ed. *Writing for Love or Money.* Thirty-five essays reprinted from *The Saturday Review of Literature.* New York: Longmans, Green and Company, 1949.

Fowler, Mary Elizabeth. *Teaching Language, Composition, and Literature.* New York: McGraw-Hill, 1965, pp. 129-162.

Fries, Charles Carpenter. *The Structure of English: An Introduction to the Construction of English Sentences.* New York: Harcourt, Brace, 1952.

Garrison, Roger H. *A Creative Approach to Writing.* New York: Holt, Rinehart and Winston, 1951.

Gordon, Edward J. and Noyes, Edward S. eds. *Essays on the Teaching of English.* New York: Appleton-Century-Crofts, 1960. Part II deals with "The Teaching of Writing."

Gurrey, Percival. *Teaching of Written English.* New York: Longmans, Green, 1951.

Hayakawa, S. I., in consultation with Basil H. Pillard. *Language in Thought and Action.* New York: Harcourt, Brace, 1949.

Hinsdale, B. A. *Teaching the Language Arts.* New York: D. Appleton, 1896.

Hipple, Theodore W. *Teaching English in Secondary Schools.* New York: Macmillan, 1973, pp. 142-184.

Hitchcock, Alfred H. *Bread Loaf Talks on Teaching Composition.* New York: Holt, 1927.

Hook, J. N. *The Teaching of High School English*. 4th ed. New York: Ronald Press, 1972, pp. 261-328.

LaBrant, Lou. *We Teach English*. New York: Harcourt, Brace, 1951, pp. 143-170.

Leacock, Stephen. *How to Write*. New York: Dodd, Mead, 1943.

Leonard, Sterling Andrus. *English Composition as a Social Problem*. Boston: Houghton, Mifflin, 1917.

Lewis, John S., and Sisk, Jean C. *Teaching English 7-12*. New York: American Book Co., 1963, pp. 311-462.

Loban, Walter, Ryan, Margaret, and Squire, James R. *Teaching Language and Literature*. 2nd ed. New York: Harcourt, Brace and World, 1969, pp. 319-377.

Lubbock, Percy. *The Craft of Fiction*. New York: Scribner, 1921.

Mearns, Hughes. *Creative Power*. 2nd ed. New York: Dover, 1958.

Mearns, Hughes. *Creative Youth*. New York: Doubleday, 1925.

Mersand, Joseph. *Attitudes toward English Teaching*. Philadelphia: Chilton, 1961.

Mirrielees, Edith. *Story Writing*. Boston: The Writer, Inc. 1947.

Mirrielees, Lucia B. *Teaching Composition and Literautre in High School;* Revised Edition. New York: Harcourt, Brace, 1952, Chapters I-X.

Munson, Gorham Burt. *Writer's Workshop Companion*. New York: Farrar, Straus and Cudahy, 1951.

———*The Written Word: How to Write Readable Prose*. New York: Creative Age Press, 1941.

National Council of Teachers of English, Commission on the English Curriculum. *The English Language Arts in the Secondary School*. N. C. T. E. Curriculum Series, Vol. 3. New York: Appleton-Century-Crofts, 1956, pp. 293-403.

———*The English Language Arts*. N. C. T. E. Curriculum Series, Vol. 1. New York: Appleton-Century-Crofts, 1952, pp. 302-327.

Palmer, Osmond E., and Diederich, Paul B. *Critical Thinking in Reading and Writing*. New York: Henry Holt, 1955.

Piercy, J. K., ed. *Modern Writers at Work*. New York: Macmillan, 1930.

Quiller-Couch, Sir Arthur. *On the Art of Writing*. New York: Putnam, 1916, pp. 1-51.

Sauer, Edwin. *English in the Secondary School*. Holt, Rinehart and Winston, 1960. Chapter 6 deals with writing.

Smith, Dora V. *Communication, The Miracle of Shared Living*. New York: Macmillan, 1955, pp. 78-94.

Wharton, Edith. *The Writing of Fiction*. New York: Scribner, 1925.

Pamphlets and Periodicals

California State Department of Education. *Practices in the Teaching of Composition in the California Public High Schools*. Bulletin of the California State Department of Education, No. 5, Volume 27, June, 1958. Sacramento: California State Department of Education, 1958.

Cook. Louella B. "Fundamentals in the Teaching of Composition." *English Journal,* May, 1941, pp. 360-370.

Godshalk, Fred I., Swineford, Frances, Coffman, William E. *The Measurement of Writing Ability*. Princeton, N. J.: College Entrance Examination Board, 1966.

Hach, Clarence W. "Needed: A Sequential Program in Composition." *English Journal,* November, 1960, pp. 536-547.

Hosic, James Fleming. ed. *Reorganization of English in Secondary Schools*. Bulletin, 1917, No. 2. Washington, D. C.: Bureau of Education, 1917.

Johnson, Eric W. "Stimulating and Improving Writing in the Junior High School." *English Journal,* February, 1958, pp. 68-71, 91.

Kraus, Silvy. "Grouping for the Teaching of Composition." *English Journal,* October, 1959, pp. 402-404.

LaBrant, Lou. "Inducing Students to Write." *English Journal,* February, 1955, pp. 70-74.

——— "Writing and Structure." *Education,* April, 1956, pp. 468-471.

Leavitt, Hart Day and Sohn, David. *Stop, Look and Write*. New York: Bantam Books, 1964.

McCarthy, A. "Teaching Slow Learners to Write." *Bulletin of the National Association of Secondary School Principals,* September, 1955, pp. 106-110.

New York City Board of Education. *Developing Children's Power of Self-Expression through Writing.* New York: The Board, 1953.

Sheridan, Marion C. "Can We Teach Our Students to Write?" *English Journal,* June, 1951, pp. 320-324.

Sister M. Judine, ed. *A Guide for Evaluating Student Composition.* Urbana, Illinois: National Council of Teachers of English, 1965.

Smith, Eugene H. *Teacher Preparation in Composition.* Champaign, Illinois: National Council of Teachers of English, 1969.

CHAPTER 14: WHY TEACH LISTENING?

Notes

1. Wendell Johnson, "Do You Know How to Listen?" *ETC,* VI, No. 4 (Autumn, 1949), p. 9.
2. Alan S. Downer, *The British Drama* (New York: Appleton-Century-Crofts, 1950) p. 72.

Bibliography

Books

Anderson, Harold A. "Teaching the Art of Listening." *Perspectives on English.* Edited by Robert C. Pooley. New York: Appleton-Century-Crofts, 1960, Chapter 8, pp. 89-106.

Barbara, Dominick A. *The Art of Listening.* Springfield, Illinois: Charles C. Thomas, 1958.

Duker, Sam. compiler. *Listening: Readings.* Metuchen, N. J.: The Scarecrow Press, 1966.

———*Listening: Readings,* Volume 2. Metuchen, N. J.: The Scarecrow Press, 1971.

———*Listening: Bibliography.* 2nd ed. Metuchen, N. J.: The Scarecrow Press, 1968.

Nichols, Ralph G. and Stevens, Leonard A. *Are You Listening?* New York: McGraw-Hill, 1957.

Roach, Helen. *Spoken Records.* 2nd ed. Metuchen, N. J.: The Scarecrow Press, 1966.

Pamphlets and Periodicals

Adams, Harlen M. "Learning to Be Discriminating." *English Journal,* January, 1947, pp. 11-15.

Adams, Harlen M. "Learning to Listen." *Clearing House,* March, 1946, pp. 401-403.

Adler, Mortimer J. "Listening Called Most Important Factor in Art of Communicating." *National Underwriter,* July 29, 1961, pp. 4-5.

Anderson, Rhea, Minshall, Lucille, and Comfort, Iris. *How to Teach Better Listening.* N. E. A. Elementary Instruction Service Leaflet. Washington: National Education Association, 1962.

Bird, Donald E. "Are You Listening?" *Office Executive,* April, 1955, pp. 18-19.

Bird, Donald E. "Listening." *N. E. A. Journal,* November, 1960, pp. 31-33.

Bois, J. S. A. *The Art of Listening. The Clarkson Letter.* Potsdam, New York: Clarkson Institute of Technology, May-June, 1952.

Brown, Charles T., and Keller, Paul W. "A Modest Proposal for Listening Training." *Quarterly Journal of Speech,* December, 1962, pp. 395-399.

Brown, James I. "Why Not Teach Listening?" *School and Society,* February 12, 1949, pp. 113-116.

Carlson, Evelyn F. "Effective Listening." *Chicago Schools Journal,* March 4, 1949, pp. 187-191.

Hatfield, W. Wilbur. "Advances in the Teaching of English." *N. E. A. Journal,* February, 1956, pp. 90-92.

Hood, Leon C. "Learning to Listen to English." *Bulletin of the National Association of Secondary School Principals,* September, 1955, pp. 79-81.

Macrorie, Ken. "Teach Listening?" *College English,* January, 1951, pp. 220-223.

Moore, Eva A. "Listening is a Skill." *English Journal,* October, 1953, pp. 378-381.

Murphy, George. "We Also Learn by Listening." *Elementary English,* March, 1949, pp. 127-128, 157.

Nichols, Ralph G. "Listening Instruction in the Secondary School." *Bulletin of the National Association of Secondary School Principals,* May, 1952, pp. 158-174.

Nichols, Ralph G. "The Teaching of Listening." *Chicago Schools Journal,* June, 1949, pp. 273-278.

Rankin, Paul T. "The Importance of Listening Ability." *English Journal* (College Edition), October, 1928, pp. 623-630.

Schreiber, Morris. compiler and ed. *An Annotated List of Recordings in the Language Arts* With Supplement by Robert Wolk. Urbana, Illinois: National Council of Teachers of English, 1971.

Wilt, Miriam E. *Let's Teach Listening.* Creative Ways of Teaching The Language Arts. Leaflet 4. Champaign, Illinois: National Council of Teachers of English, 1957.

CHAPTER 15: DEVELOPING COMPETENCE IN LISTENING IN SECONDARY SCHOOLS

Notes

1. Ralph G. Nichols, "Needed Research in Listening," *The Journal of Communication,* I (May, 1951) pp. 48-49.
2. Kenneth O. Johnson, "The Effect of Classroom Training Upon Listening Comprehension," *The Journal of Communication,* I (May, 1951) pp. 57-62.
3. James I. Brown, "Why Not Teach Listening?" *School and Society,* LXIX (February 12, 1949) pp. 113-116.
4. Lou LaBrant, *We Teach English* (New York: Harcourt, Brace, 1950) p. 193.
5. J. C. Tressler, *English in Action,* Fifth Edition, Course Four (Boston: D. C. Heath, 1950) p. 96.
6. J. N. Hook, *The Teaching of High School English,* Second Edition (New York: Ronald Press, 1959) p. 238.
7. A. Craig Baird and Franklin H. Knower, *General Speech* (New York: McGraw-Hill, 1949) pp. 281-282. Cf. Karl F. Robinson, *Teaching Speech in the Secondary School* (New York: Longmans Green, 1951) p. 219; Ralph G. Nichols,"Listening: Questions and Problems," *Quarterly Journal of Speech,* XXXIII (February, 1947) p. 84; J. C. Tressler, op. cit., Course Two, pp. 44-45.
8. Robinson, op. cit., pp. 220-221, 258.
9. Harlen M. Adams, "Learning To Be Discriminating Listeners," *English Journal,* XXXVI (January, 1947) pp. 11-15.
10. W. W. Hatfield, "Parallels in Teaching Students to Listen and Read," *English Journal,* XXXV (December, 1946) pp. 553-558.
11. Hook, op. cit., p. 240-249.
12. Tressler, op. cit., Course Two, p. 46 gives a clear statement of the variation of mental activity required of the different types of listening.
13. Jessie Mercer, "Listening in the Speech Class," *Bulletin of the National Association of Secondary School Principals,* XXXII, No. 151 (January, 1948) pp. 102-107. Robinson, op. cit., pp. 224-228, gives a copious extract of this article.
14. LaBrant, op. cit., pp. 197-198.
15. Harlen M. Adams, "Learning To Be Discriminating Listeners," *English Journal,* XXXVI (January, 1947) p. 11. Cf. his other excellent pioneer articles on listening: ——— "Listening," *Quarterly Journal of Speech,* XXXV (April, 1938) pp. 209-211;———"Teaching The Art of Listening," *The Nation's Schools,* XXXIV (November, 1944) pp. 51-54. ——— "Learning to Listen: An English and Social Studies Plan," *The Clearing House,* XX (March, 1946) pp. 401-403.
16. Hook, op. cit., p. 240.
17. Lucile Lohnas "Listening vs. Talking," *English Journal,* XXVI (June, 1937) p. 480.

18. Tressler, J. C., op. cit., Course I, pp. 222, 224.
19. Edna L. Sterling, Helen F. Olsen, and Harold Huseby, *English Language Series,* Senior Book II (New York: Henry Holt, 1950) p. 93; Senior Book III, p. 92.
20. Martha Gray and Clarence W. Hach, *English for Today,* Revised Edition, Grade 11 (Philadelphia: J. B. Lippincott, 1955) pp. 55-57, 67-69, 74.
21. Andrew T. Weaver and Gladys L. Borchers, *Speech* (New York: Harcourt, Brace, 1946).
22. Wilhelmina G. Hedde and William Norwood Brigance, *American Speech* (Philadelphia: J. B. Lippincott, 1950). See also John S. Lewis and Jean C. Sisk, *Teaching English 7-12* (New York: American Book Company, 1963) pp. 472-481; Mary Elizabeth Fowler, *Teaching Language, Composition, and Literature* (New York: McGraw-Hill, 1965) pp. 73-98; Royal J. Morsey, *Improving English Instruction,* Second Edition (Boston: Allyn and Bacon, 1969) pp. 131-142; J. N. Hook, *The Teaching of High School English,* Fourth Edition, (New York: Ronald, 1972) pp. 479-500; Thomas A. Lund, *The Modern Practical Approach to Teaching English* (West Nyack, N. Y.: Parker, 1971) pp. 78-101; Roger L. Cayer, Jerome Green, Elmer Baker, Jr., *Listening and Speaking: A Collection of Readings.* (New York: Macmillan, 1971).
23. Ibid. These are reprinted by Gray and Hach, *English For Today,* Grade 10 (1950) pp. 189-190.
24. Tressler, J. C., op. cit., Course One, p. 223.
25. Sterling, Olsen, and Huseby, op. cit., Senior Book II, p. 93.
26. W. W. Hatfield "Parallels in Teaching Students to Listen and to Read," *English Journal,* XXXV (December, 1946) pp. 553-558.
27. Hook, op. cit., p. 242; see his Fourth Edition (1972) p. 482.
28. Sterling, Olsen, and Huseby, op. cit., Senior Book II, p. 93
29. Tressler, op. cit., Course One, p. 223.
30. Bernice Freeman, "Listening Experiences in the Language Arts," *English Journal,* XXXVIII (December, 1949) pp. 272-276.
31. J. N. Hook, op. cit., pp. 484-486.
32. Weaver and Borchers, op. cit., p. 171.
33. Sterling Olsen, and Huseby, op. cit., Senior Book I, pp. 95-98, Senior Book III, pp. 59-69; Senior Book IV, pp. 67-68.
34. Gray and Hach, op. cit., Grade 10, pp. 191-192.
35. Samuel Smith and Arthur W. Littlefield, *Best Methods of Study* (New York: Noble and Noble, 1938) pp. 21-25.
36. Irvin C. Poley, "Teaching Obliquely and Testing Directly," *English Journal,* XXXIV (December, 1945) p. 540.
37. Hook, op. cit., p. 242.
38. Tressler, J. C., op. cit., Course One, p. 222; Course Two, pp. 48-49; Course Three, pp. 83-84.
39. Ibid., Course Three, p. 83.
40. Hook, op. cit., p. 243.
41. Tressler, op. cit., Course One, pp. 223; Course Two, p. 39; Course Three, p. 84; Course Four, p. 97.
42. Ollie Stratton, "Techniques for Literate Listening," *English Journal,* XXXVII (December, 1948) pp. 542-544.
43. Doris De Lap, Phoenix Union High School, Phoenix, Arizona.
44. Earl J. Dias, "Three Levels of Listening," *English Journal,* XXXVI (May, 1947) p. 252.
45. Harlen M. Adams, "Listening," *Quarterly Journal of Speech,* XXXIV (April, 1938) p. 209.
46. W. H. Ewing, "Finding A Speaking-Listening Index," *Quarterly Journal of Speech,* XXXI (October, 1945) p. 368. Cf. Robert W. Frederick, Clarence E. Ragsdale, and Rachel Salisbury, *Directing Learning* (New York: D. Appleton-Century, 1938) pp. 373-378.
47. Hook, op. cit., pp. 243-244.
48. Sterling, Olsen, and Huseby, Senior Book III, p. 93; Senior Book II, p. 94.
49. Edgar Dale, "Propaganda Analysis and Radio," in Max J. Herzberg, editor, *Radio and the Teaching of English* (New York: D. Appleton-Century, 1941) pp. 26-35. Cf. Dale's "Learning by Listening," *The News Letter,* XVI (November, 1950), No. 2
50. Wendell Johnson, "Do You Know How to Listen?" *ETC: A Review of General Semantics,* VII (Autumn, 1949) pp. 9-17.
51. S. I. Hayakawa, "How to Attend A Conference," *ETC,* II (Autumn, 1955) p. 509.
52. Lou LaBrant, op. cit., pp. 192-201.

53. Ibid., p. 195.
54. Alice P. Sterner, Katherine M. Saunders, and Milton A. Kaplan, *Skills in Listening* (Chicago: National Council of Teachers of English, 1942).
55. Max J. Herzberg, editor, *Radio and English Teaching*, (New York: D. Appleton-Century, 1941).
56. Alice P. Sterner, *A Course in Radio and Television Appreciation* (New Jersey: Audio-Visual Guide, 1950).
57. See *Syllabus in Communication Arts* (Jamaica, N. Y. C.: Jamaica High School English Department, 1964).
58. Lou LaBrant, op. cit., p. 196.
59. Ibid., pp. 196-197.
60. Wendell Johnson, op. cit., p. 3.
61. Lou LaBrant, op. cit., pp. 192-193.
62. Henry W. Wells, "Literature and the Phonograph," *Quarterly Journal of Speech,* (February, 1943) p. 68.
63. Harlen M. Adams, *Speak, Listen, and Learn,* (Chicago: National Council of Teachers of English, 1942).
64. Cf. Sterner, Saunders, and Kaplan, op. cit.
65. *Recordings for Classroom and Discussion Groups* (New York: New Tools for Learning, 1943).
66. David J. Goodman, editor, *Columbia Educational Catalogue* (New York: Columbia Records, 1950). Cf. Warren S. Freeman, editor, *Annotated List of Phonograph Recordings* (New York: Children's Reading Service, 1951).
67. "School Use of Magnetic Tape Recorders," *Nineteenth Yearbook of the Institute for Education by Radio* (May, 1949).
68. Norman Woelfel and Keith I. Tyler, *Radio and the School* (Yonkers: World Book Company, 1945) p. 206. Cf. Edgar Dale, *Audio-Visual Methods in Teaching* (New York: Dryden Press, 1946) pp. 265-266.
69. De Boer, Kaulfers, and Miller, op. cit., p. 81.
70. Robinson, op. cit, p. 222.
71. Sterling, Olsen, and Huseby, op. cit., Senior Book III, pp. 97-98; Senior Book IV, pp. 69-82.
72. Harold A. Anderson, "Teaching the Art of Listening," *School Review,* LVII (February, 1949) pp. 63-67.
73. Ollie Stratton, op. cit., pp. 542-544.

Bibliography

Books

Ace, Goodman. *The Book of Little Knowledge.* New York: Simon and Schuster, 1955.
Baird, A. Craig and Knower, Franklin H. *General Speech.* New York: McGraw-Hill Company, 1949, pp. 281-282.
Commission on the English Curriculum. *The English Language Arts.* N. C. T. E. Commission Series Volume I. New York: Appleton-Century-Crofts, 1952, pp. 328-373.
Commission on the English Curriculum. *The English Language Arts in the Secondary School.* N. C. T. E. Commission Series, Volume III. New York: Appleton-Century-Crofts, 1956, pp. 251-291.
Dale, Edgar. *Audio-Visual Methods in Teaching.* New York: Dryden Press, 1946, pp. 265-266.
Frederick, Robert W., Ragsdale, Clarence E., and Salisbury, Rachel. *Directing Learning.* New York: D. Appleton-Century, 1938, pp. 373-378.
Gray, Martha, and Hach, Clarence W. *English for Today.* Philadelphia: J. B. Lippincott, 1950.
Hazard, Patrick D. ed. *TV As Art.* Champaign, Illinois: National Council of Teachers of English, 1966.
Hedde, Wilhelmina G., and Brigance, William Norwood. *American Speech.* Philadelphia: J. B. Lippincott, 1950.
Herzberg, Max J. ed. *Radio and English Teaching.* New York: Appleton-Century-Crofts, 1941, pp. 26-35.

Hook, J. N. *The Teaching of High School English.* 4th ed. New York: The Ronald Press
  Company, 1972, pp. 479-500.
LaBrant, Lou. *We Teach English.* New York: Harcourt, Brace, 1950, pp. 187-201.
National Society for the Study of Education. *Mass Media in Education.* The 53rd Yearbook,
  Part II. Chicago: University of Chicago Press, 1954. Chapters IV, X, XI, XII.
Nichols, Ralph G., and Lewis, Thomas R. *Listening and Speaking.* Dubuque, Iowa: William C.
  Brown, Co., 1954.
Robinson, Karl F. *Teaching Speech in the Secondary School.* New York: Longmans, Green
  and Company, 1951.
Smith, Samuel, and Littlefield, Arthur W. *Best Methods of Study.* New York: Barnes and Noble,
  1938, pp. 21-25.
Sterling, Edna L., Olsen, Helen F., and Huseby, Harold. *English Language Series.* New York:
  Henry Holt and Company, 1950.
Tressler, J. C. *English in Action,* Fifth Edition. Boston: D. C. Heath and Company, 1950,
  Course Four.
Weaver, Andrew T., and Borchers, Gladys L. *Speech.* New York: Harcourt, Brace, and World,
  1946.
Woelfel, Norman, and Tyler, I. Keith. *Radio and The School.* Yonkers: World Book Company,
  1945.

Pamphlets and Periodicals

Adams, Harlen M. "Learning to Listen: an English and Social Studies Plan." *The Clearing House,*
  March, 1946, pp. 401-403.
Adams, Harlen M. "Teaching the Art of Listening." *The Nation's Schools,* November, 1944,
  pp. 51-54.
Adams, Harlen M. "Listening." *Quarterly Journal of Speech,* April, 1938, pp. 209-211.
Adams, Harlen M. "Learning to Be Discriminating Listeners." *English Journal,* January, 1947,
  pp. 11-15.
Adams, Harlen M. ed. *Speak, Look and Listen.* Champaign, Illinois: National Council of Teach-
  ers of English, 1942.
American Educational Research Association. "Review of Educational Research," Volume XXV,
  No. 2 (April, 1955) pp. 121-138.
Anderson, Harold A. "Teaching the Art of Listening." *School Review,* February, 1949, pp. 63-
  67.
Brown, Don. "Teaching Aural English." *English Journal,* March, 1950, pp. 128-138.
Brown, James I. "Why Not Teach Listening." *School and Society,* February 12, 1949, pp. 113-
  116.
Brown, James. "Construction of a Diagnostic Test of Listening Comprehension." *Journal of
  Experimental Education,* December, 1949, pp. 139-146.
Dale, Edgar. "Learn by Listening." *The News Letter,* November, 1950.
DeBoer, John J. ed. *Education and the Mass Media of Communication.* Champaign, Illinois:
  National Council of Teachers of English, 1950.
Dias, Earl J. "Three Levels of Listening." *English Journal,* May, 1947, pp. 252-254.
Education, January, 1955, Listening Number.
Education, March, 1952, Communications Skills Number.
Ewing, W. H. "Finding a Speaking-Listening Index." *Quarterly Journal of Speech,* October,
  1945, pp. 368-370.
Freeman, Bernice. "Listening Experiences in the Language Arts." *English Journal,* December,
  1949, pp. 572-576.
Freeman, Warren S. ed. *Annotated List of Phonograph Recordings.* New York: Children's
  Reading Service, 1951.
Goodman, David J. ed. *Columbia Records Educational Catalogue.* New York: Columbia Records.
Hatfield, Wilbur W. "Parallels in Teaching Students to Listen and Read." *English Journal,* Decem-
  ber, 1946, pp. 553-558.
Hayakawa, S. I. "The Task of the Listener." *ETC,* Autumn, 1949, pp. 9-17.
Johnson, Kenneth C. "The Effect of Classroom Training Upon Listening Comprehension."
  The Journal of Communication, May, 1951, pp. 57-62.

Johnson, Wendell. "Do You Know How to Listen?" *ETC,* Autumn, 1949, pp. 3-9.

Lohnas, Lucile. "Listening vs. Talking." *English Journal,* June, 1937, pp. 479-480.

Mercer, Jessie. "Listening in the Speech Class." *Bulletin of the National Association of Secondary School Principals,* January, 1948, pp. 192-107.

Nichols, Ralph G. "Listening Instruction in the Secondary School." *Bulletin of the National Association of Secondary School Principals,* May, 1952, pp. 158-174.

Nichols, Ralph G. "Listening: Questions and Problems." *Quarterly Journal of Speech,* February, 1947, p. 84.

Nichols, Ralph G. "Needed Research in Listening." *The Journal of Communication,* May, 1951, pp. 48-49.

"Nineteenth Yearbook Institute for Education by Radio." May, 1949, pp. 257-260.

Poley, Irvin C. "Teaching Obliquely and Testing Directly." *English Journal,* December, 1945, pp. 540-545.

Sterner, Alice P., Saunders, Katherine M., and Kaplan, Milton A. *Skills in Listening.* Champaign, Illinois: National Council of Teachers of English, 1942.

Stratton, Ollie. "Techniques for Literate Listening." *English Journal,* December, 1948, pp. 542-544.

Wells, Henry W. "Literature and the Phonograph." *Quarterly Journal of Speech,* February, 1943, pp. 68-73.

Wilson, C. E., and Frazier, Alexander. "Learning Through Listening–to Each Other." *English Journal,* September, 1950, pp. 367-373.

CHAPTER 16: TEACHING THE USE OF TELEVISION

Notes

1. Theodore W. Hipple, *Teaching English in Secondary Schools* (New York: Macmillan, 1973) p. 238.
2. Neil Postman, *Television and the Teaching of English* (New York: Appleton-Century-Crofts, 1961).
3. Ibid., p. 138.
4. Patrick D. Hazard, editor, *TV as Art* (Champaign, Illinois: National Council of Teachers of English, 1966).
5. Thomas R. Giblin, editor, *Popular Media and the Teachers of English* (Pacific Palisades, California: Goodyear Publishing Company, 1972).
6. *Teachers Guide to Television* can be obtained from P. O. Box 564 Lenox Hill Station, New York, New York 10021.
7. Television Information Office, 745 Fifth Avenue, New York, N. Y. 10022.
8. *TV Guide* is published by Triangle Publications, Inc. Radnor, Pennsylvania, 19088.
9. *Media and Methods* is published at 134 North 13th Street, Philadelphia, Pennsylvania, 19107.
10. *Scholastic Magazines,* editorial offices are at 50 West 44th St., New York, New York 10036
11. The address of *Education USA* is 1201 Sixteenth Street, N. W., Washington, D. C., 20016.
12. J. N. Hook, *The Teaching of High School English.* Fourth Edition. (New York: Ronald Press, 1972) pp. 492-496.
13. Postman, op. cit., pp. 82-87.
14. Ibid., pp. 88-91.
15. Ibid., pp. 92-104.
16. Ibid., pp. 105-114.
17. Theodore W. Hipple, op. cit., pp. 238-243.
18. The author wishes to acknowledge his indebtedness to Dr. Samuel Beckoff for many valuable suggestions in the list of activities by semesters.

Bibliography

Books

Bernstein, Abraham. *Teaching English in High School.* New York: Random House, 1961, pp. 298-305.

Bogart, Leo. *The Age of Television.* New York: Frederick Unger, 1956.

Boutwell, William D. ed. *Using Mass Media in the Schools.* New York: Appleton-Century-Crofts, 1962.

Commission on the English Curriculum. *The English Language Arts in the Secondary School.* New York: Appleton-Century-Crofts, 1956, pp. 251-291.

Deer, Irving. "Mass Media and the English Teacher," in Gary Tate. ed. *Reflections on High School English.* Tulsa, Oklahoma: University of Tulsa Press, 1966, pp. 38-45.

Fowler, Mary Elizabeth. *Teaching Language, Composition, and Literature.* New York: McGraw-Hill, 1965, pp. 333-339.

Giblin, Thomas R. ed. *Popular Media and the Teachers of English.* Pacific Palisades, California: Goodyear Publishing Co., 1972.

Hipple, Theodore W. *Teaching English in Secondary Schools.* New York: Macmillan, 1973, pp. 225-227.

Hook, J. N. *The Teaching of High School English.* 4th ed. New York: Ronald Press, 1972, pp. 479-500.

Loban, Walter, Ryan, Margaret, and Squire, James R. *Teaching Language and Literature, Grades 7-12.* 2nd ed. New York: Harcourt, Brace, Jovanovich, 1969, pp. 242-267.

McLuhan, Marshall. "Environment as Programmed Happening," in Walter J. Ong. ed. *Knowledge and the Future of Man.* New York: Holt, Rinehart and Winston, 1968, pp. 113-124.

Postman, Neil. *Television and the Teaching of English.* New York: Appleton-Century-Crofts, 1961.

Schramm, Wilber. ed. *The Impact of Educational Television.* Urbana, Illinois: University of Illinois Press, 1960.

Schramm, Wilbur, Lyle, Jack, and Parker, Edwin B. *Television in the Lives of Our Children.* Stanford, California: Stanford University Press, 1961.

Wertham, Frederick. *Seduction of the Innocent.* New York: Holt, Rinehart and Winston, 1954.

Pamphlets and Periodicals

Farrell, Edmund, J. *English Education and the Electronic Revolution.* Urbana, Illinois: National Council of Teachers of English, 1966.

Fillion, Bryant, P. "Turning on the Selling of the Present, 1970." *English Journal,* March, 1971, pp. 333-338.

Hazard, Patrick D. ed. *TV as Art.* Urbana, Illinois: National Council of Teachers of English, 1966.

MacNeil, Robert. "The News on TV and How It Is Unmade." *Harper's Magazine,* October, 1968, pp. 72-80.

Meadows, Robert. "Get Smart: Let TV Work For You." *English Journal,* January, 1967, pp. 121-124.

Niles, Olive S., and Early, Margaret J. "Listening." *Journal of Education,* December, 1955, Vol. 138, No. 3.

Smith, Rodney. "Learning with Television Commercials." *Teachers Guides to Television,* Fall, 1970, pp . 11-12.

Steinberg, Charles S. "Television and the Teacher." *English Journal,* December, 1968, pp. 1326-1329.

Tincher, Ethel. "The Detroit Public Schools Present English on Television." *English Journal,* April, 1967, pp. 596-602.

Witty, Paul. *Studies in Listening.* Urbana, Illinois: National Council of Teachers of English, 1959.

CHAPTER 17: HOW TO PLAN A LESSON

Notes

1. Percival Chubb, *The Teaching of English* (New York: Macmillan, 1902) p. 362.
2. George R. Carpenter, Franklin T. Baker and Fred N. Scott, *The Teaching of English in the Elementary and the Secondary School* (New York: Longmans Green, 1903) p. 180.
3. Dorothy Dakin, *How to Teach High School English* (Boston: D. C. Heath, 1947) pp. 359-361.
4. Virginia J. Craig, *The Teaching of High School English* (New York: Longmans Green, 1930) pp. 329, 341-342.
5. Clarence Stratton, *The Teaching of English in the High School* (New York: Harcourt–Brace, 1923) p. 195.
6. J. N. Hook, *The Teaching of High School English.* Fourth Edition. (New York: The Ronald Press, 1972) pp. 50-72.
7. Walter Loban, Margaret Ryan, and James R. Squire, *Teaching Language and Literature* (New York: Harcourt, Brace and World, 1961) p. 675.
8. Mary Elizabeth Fowler, *Teaching Language, Literature, and Composition* (New York: McGraw-Hill, 1965) pp. 395-401.
9. Chubb, op. cit., p. 363.
10. For the most detailed treatment of this subject in the English field, see Elizabeth Berry, *Guiding Students in the English Class* (New York: Appleton-Century-Crofts, 1957).
11. Chubb, op. cit., p. 366.
12. For a very complete analysis of the skills in reading for information and appreciation in the Junior High School, see *Reading–Grades 7, 8, 9: A Teacher's Guide to Curriculum Planning* (New York: Board of Education of the City of New York, 1959).
13. For additional treatments, see Olive S. Niles and Margaret J. Early, *Adjusting to Individual Differences in English, Journal of Education,* Vol. 138, No. 2 (December, 1955). A. J. Beeler, "Providing for Individual Differences in English," *Kentucky English Bulletin,* Vol. 6, No. 2 (Winter, 1959) pp. 24-32; –––"English for Superior Students," *Kentucky English Bulletin,* Vol. 6, No. 3 (Spring, 1957) pp. 3-10; ––– "English for Slow Learners," *Kentucky English Bulletin,* Vol. 7, No. 1 (Fall 1957–1958) pp. 15-24.
14. Craig, op. cit., p. 341.
15. Hook, op. cit., p. 50.
16. Dakin, op. cit., p. 359.

Bibliography

Books

Bernstein, Abraham. *Teaching English in High School.* New York: Random House, 1961, pp. 406-424.

Carpenter, George R., Baker, Franklin T., and Scott, Fred Newton. *The Teaching of English in the Elementary and the Secondary School.* New York: Longmans, Green, 1903, p. 180.

Chubb, Percival. *The Teaching of English in the Elementary and Secondary Schools.* New York: Macmillan, 1902, p. 362.

Commission on the English Curriculum. *The English Language Arts in the Secondary School.* New York: Appleton-Century-Crofts, 1956, pp. 44-45.

Craig, Virginia J. *The Teaching of High School English.* New York: Longmans, Green, 1930, pp. 329, 341-342.

Dakin, Dorothy. *How to Teach High School English.* Boston: D. C. Heath, 1947, pp. 359-361.

Fowler, Mary Elizabeth. *Teaching Language, Composition and Literature.* New York: McGraw-Hill, 1965, pp. 395-401.

Guth, Hans P. *English Today and Tomorrow.* Englewood Cliffs, N. J.: Prentice-Hall, 1964, pp. 381-383.

Hipple, Theodore H. *Teaching English in Secondary Schools.* New York: Macmillan, 1973, pp. 39-52.

Hook, J. N. *The Teaching of High School English*. 4th ed. Ronald Press, 1972, pp. 50-76.
Lewis, John S., and Sisk, Jean C. *Teaching English 7-12*. New York: American Book Company, 1963, pp. 65-67.
Loban, Walter, Ryan, Margaret, and Squire, James R. *Teaching Language and Literature*. 2nd ed. New York: Harcourt, Brace and World, 1969, pp. 676-720.
Lund, Thomas A. *The Modern Practical Approach to Teaching English*. West Nyack, N. Y.: Parker Publishing Company, 1971, pp. 17-39.
Morsey, Royal J. *Improving English Instruction*. 2nd ed. Boston: Allyn and Bacon, 1969, pp. 51-65.
Stratton, Clarence. *The Teaching of English in the High School*. New York: Harcourt, Brace, 1923, p. 195.

Pamphlets and Periodicals

Beeler, A. J. "Providing for Individual Differences In English." *Kentucky English Bulletin*, Winter, 1957, pp. 24-32.
––– "English for Superior Students." *Kentucky English Bulletin*, Spring, 1957, pp. 3-10.
–––"English for Slow Learners." *Kentucky English Bulletin*, Fall, 1957–1958, pp. 15-24.
Bureau of Curriculum Research. *Reading–Grades 7, 8, 9*. New York: Board of Education, 1959.
Niles, Olive S., and Early, Margaret J. *Adjusting to Individual Differences in English. Journal of Education*, December, 1955. Entire issue.
Sanders, Norris. *Classroom Questions*. New York: Harper and Row, 1966.

CHAPTER 18: HOW TO TEACH BY THE UNIT METHOD

Notes

1. Dora V. Smith, *Instruction in English*, Office of Education Bulletin 1932, No. 17. Monograph No. 20, (Washington, D. C.: U. S. Government Printing Office) p. 59-60.
2. Dorothy Dakin, *How to Teach High School English* (Boston: D. C. Heath, 1947) p. 357.
3. J. N. Hook, *The Teaching of High School English*. Fourth Edition (New York: The Ronald Press, 1972) p. 51.
4. *The English Language Arts in Secondary Schools* (New York: Appleton-Century-Crofts, 1956) p. 69.
5. Walter Loban, Margaret Ryan, James R. Squire, *Teaching Language and Literature*. Revised Edition. (New York: Harcourt, Brace and World, 1969) p. 221-223.
6. Bureau of Secondary Curriculum Development, *Syllabus in English for Secondary Schools* (Albany: New York State Education Department, 1960) pp. 91-93.
7. Ibid., pp. 158-160.
8. Loban, Ryan, Squire, op. cit., pp. 600-608.
9. Dwight L. Burton, *Literature Study in the High Schools*. Revised Edition. (New York: Holt, Rinehart and Winston, 1964) pp. 248-251.
10. Ibid., pp. 167-170.
11. Ibid., pp. 192-194.
12. Lucia B. Mirrielees, *Teaching Composition and Literature*. Revised Edition. (New York: Harcourt, Brace, 1952) p. 604. Cf. Roger Hyndman, "The First Poem," *English Journal*, XLVI (March, 1957) p. 158.
13. Mirrieless, op. cit., pp. 510-511.
14. *Reading List for the Theme Center*, "The Self-Reliant Individual" (New York: Bureau of Publications of the N. Y. C. Board of Education, 1957) pp. 38-57.
15. *Tall Tales and Tunes*, A Resource Unit for Junior High Schools (Albany, N. Y.: Bureau of Curriculum Development, New York State Education Department, 1959). Cf. also *High Adventures*, from the same source, p. 196.
16. Burton, op. cit., p. 41-44.

17. Mirrielees, op. cit., pp. 422-428.
18. *Practices in Experimental Core Classes,* Curriculum Bulletin 1953-1954 Series Number 8 (New York: Bureau of Publications of the Board of Education of the City of New York, 1954) pp. 14-19; 23-27. Cf. also *Developing a Core Program in the Junior High School Grades* (N. Y.: Bureau of Publications of the Board of Education of the City of New York, 1958).
19. *English-Speech Language Arts for Senior High Schools,* Curriculum Bulletin, 1955-56 Series, Number 12, (New York: Bureau of Publications of the Board of Education of the City of New York, 1956) pp. 61-63.
20. Conducted by the Speech Chairman of the Scarsdale, New York, High School.
21. *The Unit in Curriculum Development and Instruction* (New York: Bureau of Publications of the Board of Education of the City of New York, 1956) pp. 18-19.
22. *The English Language Arts in Secondary Schools,* op. cit., p. 112.

Bibliography

Books

Alberty, Harold. *Reorganizing the High School Curriculum.* New York: Macmillan, 1953, pp. 421-517.

Appy, Nellie. ed. *Pupils Are People.* Report of the Committee on Individual Differences. Monograph No. 13, National Council of Teachers of English. New York: Appleton-Century-Crofts, 1941, pp. 131-140, 193-206.

Broening, Angela M. ed. *Conducting Experiences in English.* Monograph No. 8, National Council of Teachers of English. New York: Appleton-Century-Crofts, 1939. See Index under secondary school units.

Burton, Dwight L. *Literature Study in the High Schools.* Revised Edition. New York: Holt, Rinehart, and Winston, 1964, pp. 263-267.

Burton, William H. *The Guidance of Learning Activities.* New York: Appleton-Century-Crofts, 1952, pp. 388-457.

Commission on the English Curriculum. *The English Language Arts in the Secondary School.* New York: Appleton-Century-Crofts, 1956, pp. 67-118.

Dakin, Dorothy. *How to Teach High School English.* Boston: D. C. Heath, 1947, p. 357.

Fowler, Mary Elizabeth. *Teaching Language, Composition and Literature.* New York: McGraw-Hill, 1965, pp. 387-395.

Hipple, Theodore W. *Teaching English in Secondary Schools.* New York: Macmillan, 1973, pp. 34-38.

Hook, J. N. *The Teaching of High School English.* 4th ed. New York: The Ronald Press, 1972, pp. 51-54.

Lewis, John S., and Sisk, Jean C. *Teaching English 7-12.* New York: American Book Co., 1963, pp. 48-50, 52-63, 179-186, 288-294, 295-302, 303-309, 439-443.

Loban, Walter, Ryan, Margaret, and Squire, James R. *Teaching Language and Literature.* 2nd ed. New York: Harcourt, Brace and World, 1972. Unit on "Oil" pp. 221-240; Unit on *Macbeth,* pp. 600-608; Unit on "Meeting a Crisis," pp. 427-434; Unit on "The Consequences of Character," pp. 659-675; Unit on "Humanities for the Seventies," pp. 609-623.

Mirrielees, Lucia B. *Teaching Composition and Literature.* Revised edition. New York: Harcourt, Brace, 1952, p. 604.

Morsey, Royal J. *Improving English Instruction.* Revised edition. Boston: Allyn and Bacon, 1969, pp. 60-65.

Pilgrim, Geneva Hanna. *Learning and Teaching Practices in English.* New York: The Center for Applied Research in Education, 1966, pp. 28-33.

Risk, Thomas M. *Principles and Practices of Teaching in Secondary Schools.* New York: American Book Co., 1958, pp. 151-174.

Smith, Dora V. *Communication, the Miracle of Shared Living.* New York: Macmillan, 1955, pp. 62-78.

Pamphlets and Periodicals

Alm, Richard S. "What Is a Good Unit in English?" *English Journal,* September, 1960, pp. 395-399.
Alwin, Virginia. "Planning a Year of Units." *English Journal,* September, 1956, pp. 334-340.
Andrews, Katherine. "A 3B Class Studies the Newspaper." *English Journal,* November, 1946, pp. 497-500.
Beeler, A. J., and Emery, Donald W., eds. *Classroom Practices in Teaching English.* Champaign, Illinois: National Council of Teachers of English, 1968.
Berry, Elizabeth. "The Unit Process." *The Educational Forum,* March, 1963, pp. 357-366.
Billet, Roy O. "The Unit on the Reading of Newspapers." *English Journal,* January, 1942, pp. 15-31.
Bureau of Curriculum Research. *The Unit in Curriculum Development and Instruction.* New York: Board of Education, 1956, pp. 18-19.
Bureau of Curriculum Research. *English-Speech Language Arts for Senior High Schools.* Curriculum Bulletin, 1955–1956 Series, No. 12. New York: Board of Education, 1956, pp. 61-63.
Bureau of Curriculum Research. *Practices in Experimental Core Classes.* Curriculum Bulletin, 1953–1954 Series, No. 8. New York: Board of Education, 1954, pp. 14-19; 23-27.
Bureau of Curriculum Research. *Developing a Core Program in the Junior High School Grades.* New York: Board of Education, 1958.
Bureau of Curriculum Research. *Reading List for the Theme Center,* "The Self-Reliant Individual." New York: Board of Education, 1957, pp. 38-57.
Bureau of Secondary Curriculum Development. *Tall Tales and Tunes, a Resource Unit for Junior High Schools.* Albany, N. Y.: State Education Department, 1959.
Bureau of Secondary Curriculum Development. *Syllabus in English for Secondary Schools.* Albany, N. Y.: State Education Department, 1960, pp. 91-93.
Burton, Dwight L. "Literature in the Topical Unit." *English Journal,* December, 1953, pp. 497-501.
Callahan, G. N. "Plan for a Year's Work in Ninth-Grade English." *Journal of Education,* April, 1954, pp. 206-209.
Carpenter, Robert H. "A Unit in Poetry." *English Journal,* November, 1932, pp. 744-748.
Finder, Morris. "Units Aplenty." *English Journal,* September, 1953, pp. 324-329.
Freeman, Bernice. "Teaching Short Stories." *English Journal,* May, 1955, pp. 284-287.
Graham, Helen. "A Plan for Teaching the Biography." *English Journal,* March, 1941, pp. 238-241.
Gregory, Margaret, and McLaughlin, W. J. "Teaching the Newspaper in Junior High School." *The English Journal,* January, 1951, pp. 23-28.
Harvey, C. C. "A Unit of Work on the Newspaper." *Bulletin of the National Association of Secondary School Principals.* January, 1949, pp. 65-75.
Hach, Clarence W. "Planning a Year's Program in Literature." *English Journal,* September, 1950, pp. 334-338.
Hyndman, Roger. "The First Poem." *English Journal,* March, 1957, pp. 158 ff.
McCrea, Mary. "A Unit on the Letter of Application." *English Journal,* June, 1941, pp. 497-499.
McCutchan, Mary. "The American Dream: a Unit in Junior English." *English Journal,* March, 1942, pp. 200-219.
Meade, Richard A. "Organization of Literature for Juniors and Seniors." *English Journal,* September, 1947, pp. 381-387.
Pettit, O. J. "Peoples of the Modern World—Unit in Literature." *English Journal,* October, 1948, pp. 404-408.
Reeves, Ruth E. ed. *Ideas for Teaching English: Grades 7-8-9.* Champaign, Illinois: National Council of Teachers of English, 1966.
Rider, Virginia. "Modern Drama Educates for Tolerance." *English Journal,* January, 1947, pp. 16-22.
Roody, Sarah I. "From Bridey Murphy to the Magic Casement." *English Journal,* February, 1947, pp. 100-103.
Rose, Elizabeth Lamar and Davis, Mary Houston. "An English Unit on Aviation." *English Journal,* March, 1943, pp. 126-132.

Ryerson, Edward. "Juluis Caesar Once Again." *English Journal,* January, 1958. pp. 574-577.

Scott, Richard E. "Shakespeare for Beginners." *English Journal,* December, 1953, pp. 504-506.

Sheridan, Marion D. "Teaching a Novel." *English Journal,* January, 1952, pp. 8-14.

Simmons, Josephine. "A Semester of Current Literature." *English Journal,* January, 1941, pp. 47-53.

Smith, Dora V. *Instruction in English.* Bulletin 1932, No. 17, Monograph No. 20. Washington, D. C.: Office of Education, 1932, pp. 59-60.

Stolper, B. J. R. "English Literature in the High School—a Project in World Literature." The 36th Yearbook of the National Society for the Study of Education, Part II, pp. 63-70.

Zollinger, Marian. "Five Units and How They Grew." *English Journal,* October, 1950, pp. 423-429.

CHAPTER 19: HOW TO TEST AND EVALUATE

Notes

1. Joint Committee on Testing, American Association of School Administrators, Council of Chief State School Officers, National Association of Secondary-School Principals, *Testing, Testing, Testing* (Washington, D. C.: National Education Association, 1962) p. 8.

2. Commission on the English Curriculum of the National Council of Teachers of English, *The English Language Arts* N. C. T. E. Curriculum Series, No. 1 (New York: Appleton-Century-Crofts, 1952) p. 417.

3. Dora V. Smith, *Evaluating Instruction in English,* English Monograph No. 11 (Chicago: National Council of Teachers of English, 1941).

4. Helen Heffernan, "Evaluation—More Than Testing," in the reprint *Testing and Evaluation* from the *N. E. A. Journal* (May, 1958) p. 9.

5. John J. DeBoer, Walter F. Kaulfers, Helen Rand Miller, *Teaching Secondary English* (New York: McGraw-Hill, 1951) pp. 405-413.

6. *Guideposts to the English Language Arts* (Seattle: Seattle Public Schools, 1962) p. 174.

7. Ibid., p. 174.

8. *The English Language Arts,* p. 417.

9. Dorothy Dakin, *How to Teach High School English,* (Boston: D. C. Heath, 1947) p. 370.

10. *Improving the Classroom Test,* (Albany: State Education Department, 1956) p. 7.

11. Ibid., p. 9.

12. Ibid.

13. "Evaluating a Theme," *Newsletter* of the Michigan Council of Teachers of English, X, No. 6 (Spring, 1958) p. 16.

14. *Suggestions on the Rating of Regents Examination Papers in English* (Albany: State Education Department, 1960) pp. 11-17.

15. *Guideposts to the English Language Arts of Seattle Public Schools,* op. cit., pp. 119-177.

16. For cautions to be observed, consult *Improving the Classroom Test,* op. cit., pp. 28-40.

17. For cautions to be observed consult *Improving the Classroom Test,* op. cit., 40-43.

18. See Louis A. Schuker, *Testing is One Form of Evaluation,* (Jamaica, N. Y.: Jamaica High School). Mr. Schuker was Principal from 1955–1971.

19. *The English Language Arts,* op. cit., pp. 417-440.

20. Commission on the English Curriculum of the National Council of Teachers of English, *The English Language Arts in Secondary Schools* N. C. T. E. Curriculum Series No. 3 (New York: Appleton-Century-Crofts, 1956). See articles under "Evaluation" in Index.

21. *The Reading Teacher,* XV. No. 5 (March, 1962).

22. Chester W. Harris, editor, *The Encyclopedia of Educational Research,* Third Edition (New York: Macmillan, 1960).

23. Louella B. Cook, "The Search for Standards," *English Journal* XLIX, No. 5 (May, 1960) pp. 321-328.

Bibliography

Books

Commission on The English Curriculum. *The English Language Arts.* New York: Appleton-Century-Crofts, 1952, Part IV, Chapter 18, "Methods of Evaluating Instruction."

Commission on The English Curriculum. *The English Language Arts in the Secondary School.* New York: Appleton-Century-Crofts, 1956, pp. 309, 313; 431-436.

Dakin, Dorothy. *How to Teach High School English.* Boston: D. C. Heath, 1947, p. 370.

De Boer, John, Kaulfers, Walter V., and Miller, Helen Rand. *Teaching Secondary English.* New York: McGraw-Hill, 1951, pp. 405-413.

Fowler, Mary Elizabeth. *Teaching Language, Composition, and Literature.* New York: McGraw-Hill, 1965, pp. 19, 105, 156, 206, 252, 407-408, 207, 206, 235-237, 251, 276.

Greene, Edward B. *Measurement of Human Behavior.* New York: The Odyssey Press, 1941.

Greene, Harry A., et al. *Measurement and Evaluation in the Secondary School.* New York: Longmans, Green and Co., 1943.

Guth, Hans P. *English Today and Tomorrow.* Englewood Cliffs, New Jersey, 1964, pp. 373-377.

Harris, Chester W. ed. *The Encyclopedia of Educational Research.* 3rd ed. New York: Macmillan, 1960. See sections on Evaluation, Testing, Examinations.

Hook, J. N. *The Teaching of High School English.* 4th ed. New York: Ronald Press, 1972, pp. 58-64.

Kaulfers, Walter V. *Modern Languages for Modern Schools.* Chapter 13. New York: McGraw-Hill Book Company, 1942.

Lewis, John S., and Sisk, Jean C. *Teaching English 7-12.* New York: American Book, 1963, pp. 15-16, 123-131, 121-122, 478, 216-217, 396-397, 375, 379, 120-123, 281-283, 368.

Morsey, Royal J. *Improving English Instruction.* 2nd ed. Boston: Allyn and Bacon, 1969, pp. 185-197.

Murray, Thomas R. *Judging Student Progress.* New York: Longmans, Green, 1954.

Odell, C. W. *How to Improve Classroom Testing.* Dubuque, Iowa: Willaim C. Brown Company, 1953.

Remmers, Herman H., and Gage, N. L. *Educational Measurement and Evaluation.* New York: Harper and Brothers, 1943.

Ross, Clay C. *Measurement in Today's Schools.* New York: Prentice-Hall, Inc., 1947.

Smith, Eugene R., et al. *Appraising and Recording Student Progress.* New York: Harper and Brothers, 1942.

Pamphlets and Periodicals

Carruthers, Robert B. "The Unit Test: A Test for Teachers." *English Journal,* September, 1958, pp. 339-343.

Cook, Louella B. "The Search for Standards." *English Journal,* May, 1960, pp. 321-328.

The Reading Teacher. March, 1962 is devoted entirely to the subject of Evaluation.

Gross, Lois M., Miller, Dorothy, and Steinberg, Erwin. *Suggestions for Evaluating Junior High School Writing.* Pittsburgh: Association of English Teachers of Western Pennsylvania n. d. Available from N. C. T. E. Urbana, Illinois.

Guideposts to the English Language Arts. Seattle: Seattle Public Schools, 1962, p. 174.

Joint Committee on Testing, American Association of School Administrators, Council of Chief State School Officers, National Association of Secondary School Principals. *Testing, Testing, Testing.* Washington, D. C.: National Education Association, 1962.

Loban, Walter. "Evaluating Growth in the Study of Literature." *English Journal,* June, 1948, pp. 277-283.

Principles and Standards in Composition for Kentucky High Schools and Colleges. Kentucky English Bulletin, Fall, 1956-1957.

Testing and Evaluation. Reprinted from the May 1958 issue of the *Journal of the National Education Association.*

Smith, Dora V. *Evaluating Instruction in English.* Champaign, Illinois: National Council of Teachers of English, 1941.

Evaluating a Theme. Newsletter of the Michigan Council of Teachers of English, Spring, 1958. Ann Arbor: University of Michigan.

Suggestions on the Rating of Regents Examination Papers in English. Albany, N. Y.: State Education Department, 1960.

Tinkelman, Sherman N. *Improving the Classroom Test.* Albany, N. Y.: State Education Department, 1957.

Traxler, Arthur E. *The Use of Test Results in Diagnosis and Instruction.* New York: Educational Records Bureau, 1937.

Weitzman, Ellis, and McNamara, Walter J. *Constructing Classroom Examinations.* Chicago: Science Research Associates, 1949.

Zollinger, Marion, and Dawson, Mildred A. "Evaluation of Oral Communication." *English Journal,* November, 1958, pp. 500-544.

CHAPTER 20: HOW TO PLAN A CURRICULUM

Notes

1. See *English-Speech-Language Arts in Senior High Schools,* Board of Education of the City of New York, 1956. Also "How an English Language Arts Course of Study Evolved," *Bulletin of the National Association of Secondary School Principals,* September, 1957, pp. 75-82.
2. See Commission on the English Curriculum, *The English Language Arts* (New York: Appleton-Century-Crofts, Inc., 1952) p. 56. Also *The English Language Arts in the Secondary School* (New York: Appleton-Century-Crofts, Inc., 1956) p. 56.
3. *The English Language Arts in the Secondary School,* p. 32.
4. Ibid., pp. 35-37.
5. Ibid., p. 37.
6. Ibid., p. 38.
7. Ibid., p. 39.
8. Ibid., p. 39.
9. See Joseph Mersand, "How an English Language Arts Course of Study Evolved, *Bulletin* of the National Association of Secondary School Principals, September, 1957, pp. 75-82.
10. John J. De Boer, Walter V. Kaulfers and Helen Rand Miller, *Teaching Secondary English,* (New York: McGraw-Hill Book Company, Inc., 1951) p. 399.
11. Bulletin No. 2, 1917, of the Bureau of Education, Department of the Interior, Washington, D. C.
12. James B. Conant, *The American High School Today* (New York: McGraw-Hill, 1959).
13. See Joseph Mersand, *Attitudes Toward English Teaching* (Philadelphia: Chilton Book Company, 1961) for comments from 1250 representatives of education, business, government about English Instruction.
14. *The English Language Arts,* pp. 70-76.
15. *The English Language Arts in the Secondary School,* p. 45.
16. Ibid., p. 47.
17. De Boer, Kaulfers, Miller, op. cit., p. 387.
18. For a listing of many courses of study published since 1932, see Arno Jewett, *English Language Arts in American High Schools* (Washington, D. C.: U. S. Office of Education, 1959). Each year the Association for Supervision and Curriculum Development publishes a list of *Curriculum Materials,* among which are the newly published courses of study in English. Write to A. S. C. D., 1201 Sixteenth Street, N. W. Washington, D. C. for the most recent compilation.
19. This and much of the ensuing discussion is an adaptation from *The English Language Arts in the Secondary School,* pp. 29-60.
20. A fascinating study of students' reaction to their high school education is found in Class of 1938, Ohio State University School, *Were We Guinea Pigs?* (New York: Henry Holt and Company, 1938).

21. *The English Language Arts in the Secondary School,* pp. 50-51.
22. Ibid., p. 53.
23. De Boer, Kaulfers and Miller, op. cit., pp. 391-393 cite an egregious example of a course of study that was obviously dictated by the literature anthology employed.
24. For example, the four resource units that accompany the 1957 *English-Speech-Language Arts Course of Study in Senior High Schools* of New York City contain hundreds of books on the grade levels that fit the four themes of the school years. Published by the Bureau of Publications of the Board of Education of the City of New York, 110 Livingston Street, Brooklyn, N. Y. 10021.
25. *English Language Arts in the Secondary School,* p. 54.
26. Ibid., p. 55.
27. Ibid., p. 56-58 gives instances of such all-school cooperation in Baltimore, the Latin School of Chicago, Minneapolis, and Seattle. De Boer, Kaulfers and Miller, op. cit. make an eloquent plea for this cooperation.
28. Published in 1951.
29. *The English Language Arts in the Secondary School,* p. 61.

Bibliography

Books

Class of 1938, Ohio State University School. *Were We Guinea Pigs?* New York: Henry Holt, 1938.

Commission on the English Curriculum. *The English Language Arts.* New York: Appleton-Century-Crofts, 1952, Part III, Chapter 8, "Planning Minimum Essentials, and Relative Emphasis on Aspects of the Program."

Conant, James B. *The American High School Today.* New York: McGraw-Hill, 1959.

DeBoer, John J. ed. *The Subject Fields in General Education.* New York: Appleton-Century-Crofts, Inc. 1941.

DeBoer, John J., Kaulfers, Walter V., and Miller, Helen Rand. *Teaching Secondary English.* New York: McGraw-Hill, 1951, pp. 67-77. Contains an outline of four years of functional grammar.

Fowler, Mary Elizabeth. *Teaching Language, Composition, and Literature.* New York: McGraw-Hill, 1965, pp. 384-399.

Giles, H. H., McCutcheon, S. P., and Zechiel, A. N. *Exploring the Curriculum.* New York: Harper & Brothers, 1942.

Gray, William S. *Reading in an Age of Mass Communication.* Chapter 6. New York: Appleton-Century-Crofts, 1949.

Hipple, Theodore W. *Teaching English in Secondary Schools.* New York: Macmillan, 1973, pp. 27-38.

Hook, J. N. *The Teaching of High School English.* 4th ed. New York: Ronald Press, 1972, pp. 548-564.

Lewis, John S., and Sisk, Jean C. *Teaching English 7-12.* New York: American Book, 1963, pp. 37-52, 64-65.

Loban, Walter, Ryan, Margaret, and Squire, James R. *Teaching Language and Literature.* Revised edition. New York: Harcourt, Brace and World, 1969, pp. 676-688.

Mersand, Joseph. *Attitudes toward English Teaching.* Philadelphia: Chilton Book Co., 1961.

Morsey, Royal C. *Improving English Instruction.* 2nd ed. Boston: Allyn and Bacon, 1969, pp. 15-17, 41, 43, 93-94.

Parrish, Louise, and Waskin, Yvonne. *Teacher-Pupil Planning.* New York: Harper & Brothers, 1958.

Pamphlets and Periodicals

English Language Arts in California Public High Schools. Bulletin No. 26, September, 1957. Sacramento: California State Department of Education, 1957.

Bureau of Curriculum Research. *English-Speech-Language Arts in Senior High Schools.* New York: Board of Education, 1956.

Educational Policies Commission. *The Purposes of Education in American Democracy.* Washington, D. C.: National Education Association, 1938.

Florida State Department of Education. *Planning Instruction. English in Secondary Schools,* Bulletin 35A. Tallahassee, Florida: Florida State Department of Education, 1962.

Hook, J. N. "If a Curriculum Is to Be Sequential." *English Journal,* February, 1962, pp. 79-84.

Hosic, James Fleming. ed. *The Reorganization of English in Secondary Schools.* Bulletin 1917, No. 2. Washington, D. C.: U. S. Bureau of Education, Department of the Interior, 1917.

Jewett, Ida A."Gathering Forces in the High School English Curriculum." *Teachers College Record,* December, 1947, pp. 143-153.

Jewett, Arno. *English Language Arts in American High Schools.* Washington, D. C.: U. S. Office of Education, 1959.

Johns, Kingston, and Smith, Donald E. "A Drama Course: Planned, Used, Evaluated." *English Journal,* December, 1950, pp. 571-574.

Pooley, Robert C. "Basic Principles in English Curriculum Making." *English Journal,* November, 1941, pp. 709-712.

CHAPTER 21: ARTICULATING OUR EFFORTS IN THE TEACHING OF ENGLISH

Notes

1. John Brubacher, *A History of the Problems in Education* (New York: McGraw-Hill, 1947) pp. 438-441. See also Chester W. Harris, editor, *Encyclopedia of Educational Research,* 3rd Edition (New York: The Macmillan Company, 1960) pp. 87-92.

2. James Fleming Hosic, compiler, *Reorganization of English in Secondary Schools,* Bulletin, 1917, No. 2 (Washington: Bureau of Education, 1917) pp. 123-128; especially p. 123.

3. Ibid., pp. 126-127.

4. Charles Swain Thomas, *The Teaching of English in the Secondary School* (Boston: Houghton Mifflin, 1917) pp. 21-33. See also his second edition, 1927, pp. 58-83.

5. Ibid., pp. 25-26.

6. Ibid., pp. 25-26.

7. Ibid., p. 26.

8. Ibid., pp. 27-28. In the revised edition of 1927, these topics are listed on pp. 64-66.

9. Ibid., p. 28.

10. Ibid., pp. 29-30. In the revised edition of 1927, this appears on pp. 67-68.

11. Ibid., pp. 31-32. In the revised edition of 1927, see pp. 70-73, which has a more amplified discussion of the merits of the junior high school.

12. Ibid., p. 32. In the revised edition of 1927, see pp. 79-80.

13. These three wastes were indicated in the so-called Andover Study. See Allan R. Blackmer, chairman, *General Education in School and College* (Cambridge: Harvard University Press, 1952).

14. *Encyclopedia of Educational Research,* Third Edition (1960) p. 89.

15. *Freshman English at the Ohio State University* (Columbus: Department of English, 1957) p. 6. See also Otto F. Drauschaar, "Articulation—Our Common Concern," *Baltimore Bulletin of Education,* Volume XXXV No. 2 (March, 1958) pp. 1-5.

16. Dora V. Smith, *Evaluating Instruction in Secondary English,* English Monograph No. 11 (Champaign, Illinois: N. C. T. E., 1941) p. 12.

17. *English Language Arts in the Secondary School* (New York: Appleton-Century-Crofts, 1956) p. 440.

18. Copies may be obtained from the Department of English of any of the cooperating institutions.

19. Copies may be obtained from the Department of English, Ohio State University, Columbus, Ohio.

20. See Otto F. Draushaar, op. cit. (Footnote 15 of this chapter).

21. Copies may be obtained from Royal J. Morsey, Ball State Teachers College, Muncie, Indiana.
22. *University of Illinois Bulletin,* Volume LIII, No. 46, February, 1956.
23. Ibid., p. 1.
24. *Basic Issues in the Teaching of English* (Champaign, Illinois: N. C. T. E., 1959).
25. *The English Language Arts in the Secondary School.* op. cit., pp. 52-53. See also the somewhat similar procedure described by Charles Swain Thomas, op. cit., 1917, pp. 29-30.
26. For information about this program, consult Erwin Steinberg, Dean, Mary Morrison College, Carnegie Institute of Technology, Pittsburgh, Pa.
27. See Footnote 2.
28. See Footnote 4.
29. Thomas, op. cit., 1917, p. 32.
30. *The National Interest and the Teaching of English* (Champaign, Illinois: N. C. T. E, 1961) p. 5.
31. *Guideposts to the English Language Arts,* a Course of Study for Teaching the English Language Arts in Elementary, Junior High and Senior High Schools. (Seattle: Seattle Public Schools, 1962) pp. vi-x.
32. Available from the A. S. C. D., 1201 Sixteenth Street, N. W., Washington, D. C. 20006.
33. Edwin A. Juckett, "A Pleasant Bridge in the Hyde Park Schools, " *The Clearing House,* Volume XXIX (1954) pp. 81-83. Marion W. Hodge, "Articulation of Secondary and Elementary Schools," *California Journal of Secondary Education,* Volume XXXI (1956) pp. 322-325. *English Language Arts* op. cit., p. 11.
34. *They Went to College Early* (New York: Fund for the Advancement of Education, 1957).
35. *College Admission with Advanced Standing* (School and College Study of Admission with Advanced Standing, 1956).
36. *Encyclopedia of Educational Research,* p. 90.
37. *Advanced Placement Program* (New York: College Entrance Examination Board, 1956). There are later studies.
38. See the Advanced Placement Program brochure issued by the State Education Department, Albany, New York.
39. *Evaluating Instruction in Secondary School English,* op. cit., pp. 109-119.
40. *The English Language Arts,* op. cit., pp. 39-40.

Bibliography

Books

General Education in School and College. A Committee Report by Members of the faculties of Andover, Exeter, Lawrenceville, Harvard, Princeton, and Yale. Cambridge: Harvard University Press, 1953.

They Went to College Early. New York: Fund for the Advancement of Education, 1957.

Blackmer, Allan R. ed. *General Education in School and College.* Cambridge: Harvard University Press, 1952.

Brubacher, John S. *A History of the Problems of Education.* New York: McGraw-Hill, 1947, pp. 438-441.

Commission on the English Curriculum. *English Language Arts in the Secondary School.* New York: Appleton-Century-Crofts, 1956, pp. 52-53, 440.

Harris, Chester W. ed. *Encyclopedia of Educational Research.* 3rd ed. New York: Macmillan, 1960, pp. 87-92.

Thomas, Charles Swain. *The Teaching of English in the Secondary School.* Boston: Houghton Mifflin, 1917, pp. 21-23. See also his second edition, 1927, pp. 58-83.

Pamphlets and Periodicals

College Entrance Examination Board. *Advanced Placement Program.* New York: College Entrance Examination Board, 1956.

Committee on the Basic Issues. *Basic Issues in the Teaching of English.* Champaign: National Council of the Teachers of English, 1959.

Committee on the National Interest. *The National Interest and the Teaching of English.* Champaign: N. C. T. E., 1961, p. 5.

Department of English at Ohio State University. *Freshman English at the Ohio State University.* Columbus: Department of English, Ohio State University, 1957, p. 6.

Fund for the Advancement of Education. *Bridging the Gap between School and College.* Evaluation Report No. 1. New York: Fund for the Advancement of Education, 1953.

Guideposts to the English Language Arts, a Course of Study for Teaching the English Language Arts in Elementary, Junior High, and Senior High School. Seattle: Seattle Public Schools, 1962, pp. vi-x.

Hodge, Marion E. "Articulation of Secondary and Elementary Schools." *California Journal of Secondary Education,* October, 1956, pp. 322-325.

Hosic, James Fleming. ed. *Reorganization of English in Secondary Schools.* Bulletin, 1917, No. 2. Washington, D. C.: Bureau of Education, 1917, pp. 123-128.

Juckett, Edwin A. "A Pleasant Bridge in the Hyde Park Schools." *The Clearing House,* October, 1954, pp. 81-83.

Kraushaar, Otto F. "Articulation—Our Common Concern." Baltimore Bulletin of Education, March, 1958, pp. 1-5.

Mersand, Joseph. "Articulating Our Efforts in the Teaching of English." *The English Review,* May, 1963, pp. 8-17.

———"Effective Supervisory and Administrative Bulletins." *Bulletin of the National Association of Secondary School Principals,* December, 1957, pp. 97-118.

———"The Role of the Department Head in Providing for Individualization of Instruction." *High School Journal,* April, 1959, pp. 278-284.

———"Creative Supervision in Secondary Schools." *Bulletin of the National Association of Secondary School Principals,* December, 1959, pp. 23-27.

——— "The Junior High School Principal Works with His Faculty for Continuous Professional Growth." *Bulletin of the National Association of Secondary School Principals,* October, 1956, pp. 109-112.

Morsey, Royal J. ed. *A College Seminar to Develop and Evaluate an Improved High School English Program.* Muncie, Indiana: Ball State Teachers College, 1959.

Smith, Dora V. *Evaluating Instruction in Secondary English.* English Monograph No. 11. Champaign, Illinois: National Council of Teachers of English, 1941.

CHAPTER 22: CORRELATION AND INTEGRATION IN ENGLISH

Notes

1. Curriculum Commission of the National Council of Teachers of English, *An Experience Curriculum in English* (New York: D. Appleton-Century, 1935) p. 10.
2. Ibid., p. 10.
3. Ibid., p. 10.
4. For early references to this type of correlation between English and history in the early textbooks on teaching English, refer to: George R. Carpenter, Franklin T. Baker, Fred N. Scott, *The Teaching of English in the Elementary and the Secondary School* (New York: Longmans, Green and Co., 1903) pp. 136-137; Percival Chubb, *The Teaching of English in the Elementary and the Secondary School* (New York: The Macmillan Company, 1902) pp. 254-255.
5. *An Experience for Curriculum in English,* p. 11. For a historical treatment of the values of correlation, consult N. Thut and J. Raymond Gerberich, *Foundations of Method for Secondary Schools* (New York: McGraw-Hill, 1949) pp. 196-201. See also Carpenter, Baker and Scott, op. cit., p. 136.

6. These were published by Methuen & Co., Ltd., London, 1928.
7. Edwin Carr, *Guide to Reading for Social Studies Teachers* (Washington, D. C.: National Council of Social Studies, 1951).
8. Published by the Council, Washington, D. C.
9. Chubb, op. cit., p. 79. Cf. Also, Carpenter, Baker and Scott, op. cit., pp. 177-178.
10. The syllabus was published by Teachers College, Columbia University in 1932.
11. Angela M. Broening, editor, *Conducting Experiences in English* (New York: D. Appleton Company, 1939) pp. 243-248.
12. Lucia B. Mirrielees, *Teaching Composition and Literature in Junior and Senior High School.* Revised Edition. (New York: Harcourt, Brace and Company, 1952) p. 16. For a complete discussion of this experiment, consult Frank L. Cummings, "Practices in Fusion of Subject Matter in Various Courses" *California Quarterly of Secondary Education,* X (1934), pp. 13-18.
13. The Commission on the English Curriculum, *The English Language Arts in the Secondary School* (New York: Appleton-Century-Crofts, Inc., 1956) pp. 422-442. For a complete description, see Grace D. Broening, "Integrating English and Social Studies," *Baltimore Bulletin of Education,* XXV (December, 1947) pp. 112-114, 143, 151.
14. Mirrielees, op. cit., pp. 134-214.
15. Lou LaBrant, *English in Common Learnings* (Champaign, Illinois: National Council of Teachers of English, 1951) p. 4.
16. Roland C. Faunce and Nelson L. Bossing, *Developing the Core Curriculum.* Second Edition. (Englewood Cliffs, N. J.: Prentice Hall, 1958) See also Harold Alberty, *Preparing Core Teachers for the Secondary Schools* (Columbus, Ohio: Ohio State University, 1949).
17. For descriptions of the core programs in the junior and senior high schools of New York City where they have been in existence for almost fifteen years consult: *Suggestions to Teachers of Experimental Core Classes,* Curriculum Bulletin No. 2, 1950–1951 Series (N. Y. C.: Board of Education of the City of New York, 1952); *Practices in Experimental Core Classes,* Curriculum Bulletin No. 8, 1953–54 Series (N. Y. C.: Board of Education of the City of New York); *Developing a Core Program in the Junior High School Grades,* Curriculum Bulletin No. 12, 1957–58 Series (N. Y. C.: Board of Education of the City of New York, 1958).
18. *Progress Report–Experimental Core Programs in New York City Schools,* (N. Y. C.: Bureau of Curriculum Research, 1952) p. 6.
19. Dwight L. Burton, *Literature Study in the High Schools.* Revised Edition (New York: Holt, Rinehart, and Winston, 1964) p. 59-77.

Bibliography

Books

Bernstein, Abraham. *Teaching English in High School.* New York: Random House, 1961, pp. 398-405.

Broening, Angela M. ed. *Conducting Experiences in English.* New York: D. Appleton Company, 1939, pp. 243-248.

Burton, Dwight L. *Literature Study in the High Schools.* Revised edition. New York: Holt, Rinehart, and Winston, 1964, pp. 59-77.

Carpenter, George R., Baker, Franklin T., and Scott, Fred Newton. *The Teaching of English in the Elementary and the Secondary School.* New York: Longmans, Green, 1903, pp. 136-137.

Chubb, Percival. *The Teaching of English in the Elementary and the Secondary Schools.* New York: Macmillan, 1902, pp. 254-255.

Commission on the English Curriculum. *The English Language Arts in the Secondary School.* New York: Appleton-Century-Crofts, 1956, pp. 422-442.

Faunce, Roland C., and Bossing, Nelson L. *Developing The Core Curriculum.* 2nd ed. Englewood Cliffs, New Jersey: Prentice-Hall, 1958.

Fowler, Mary Elizabeth. *Teaching Language, Composition, and, Literature.* New York: McGraw-Hill, 1965, pp. 9, 13, 11, 77, 238.

Hatfield, W. Wilbur. ed. *An Experience Curriculum in English.* New York: D. Appleton-Century, 1935, p. 10.

Mirrielees, Lucia B. *Teaching Composition and Literature in Junior and Senior High School.* Revised edition. New York: Harcourt, Brace, 1952, p. 16.

Morsey, Royal J. *Improving English Instruction.* Revised edition. Boston: Allyn and Bacon, 1969, pp. 42-44.

Thut, N., and Gerberich, J. Raymond. *Foundations of Method for Secondary Schools.* New York: McGraw-Hill, 1949, pp. 196-201.

Tidyman, Willard, Smith, Charlene Weddle, and Butterfield, Marguerite. *Teaching the Language Arts.* 3rd ed. New York: McGraw-Hill, 1969, pp. 433-460.

Pamphlets and Periodicals

Alberty, Harold. *Preparing Core Teachers for the Secondary Schools.* Columbus: Ohio State University, 1949.

Bennett, Robert. "Integrated Programs in Secondary Education." *High School Journal,* April, 1948, pp. 22-26.

Bragdon, Henry W. "Teaching Writing through History." *Atlantic,* November, 1959, pp. 118-120.

Broening, Grace D. "Integrating English and Social Studies." *Baltimore Bulletin of Education,* December, 1947, pp. 112-114, 143, 151.

Bureau of Curriculum Research. *Suggestions to Teachers of Experimental Core Classes.* Curriculum Bulletin, 1950-1951, Series No. 2. New York: Board of Education, 1952.

———*Developing a Core Program in the Junior High School Grades.* Curriculum Bulletin, 1957-1958, Series, No. 12. New York: Board of Education, 1958.

———*Progress Report—Experimental Core Programs in New York City Schools.* New York: Bureau of Curriculum Research, 1952.

Carr, Edwin R. *Guide to Reading for Social Studies Teachers.* Washington, D. C.: National Council of Social Studies, 1951.

Coan, Otis W., and Lillard, Richard G. *America in Fiction: An Annotated List of Novels That Interpret Aspects of Life in the United States.* Stanford: Stanford University Press, 1956.

Cummings, Frank L. "Practices in Fusion of Subject Matter in Various Courses." *California Quarterly of Secondary Education,* October, 1934, pp. 13-18.

Greene, Jay C. "Teachers of English, Social Studies, and Speech Coordinate Efforts." *English Journal,* October, 1950, pp. 451-452.

Karwand, Elwood C. "Teaching Literature of the Orient." *English Journal,* April, 1960, pp. 261-264.

Kegler, Stanley B., and Simmons, John S. "Images of the Hero—Two Teaching Units." *English Journal,* September, 1960, pp. 417.

LaBrant, Lou. *English in Common Learnings.* Champaign: National Council of Teachers of English, 1951, p. 4.

Lewis, Charles Stephen. "The Orient-Blind Spot in High School Literature." *English Journal,* January, 1956, pp. 26-29.

Lowry, Lorraine. "Windows on the World." *English Journal,* February, 1960, pp. 115-117.

McHarry, Liesette. "A Plan for Correlation." *English Journal,* April, 1932, pp. 408-413.

Neville, Mark. "English as a Positive Factor in Correlation." *English Journal,* January, 1938, pp. 44-49.

Stegall, Carrie. "Now They Are Real Buddies." *English Journal,* February, 1959, pp. 78-81.

CHAPTER 23: CREATIVE SUPERVISION IN THE SECONDARY SCHOOL

Notes

1. Charles A. Wagner, *Common Sense in Supervision* (Milwaukee: Bruce Publishing Company, 1921) p. 7.
2. John A. Bartky, *Supervision As Human Relations,* (Boston: D. C. Heath, 1953) p. 14.
3. See Chapter 26.

4. Witter Bynner, *The Way of Life According to Lao-tzu, an American Version* (New York: The John Day Company, 1944) pp. 34-35.

Bibliography

Books

Adams, Harold P., and Dickey, Frank G. *Basic Principles of Supervision.* New York: American Book Co., 1953.

Anderson, C. J., Barr, A. S., and Bush, Maybell G. *Visiting the Teacher at Work.* New York: D. Appleton-Century, 1925.

Ayer, Fred C. *Fundamentals of Instructional Supervision.* New York: Harper and Brothers, 1954.

Barr, A. S., and Burton, William H. *The Supervision of Instruction.* New York: D. Appleton-and Co., 1926.

Barr, A. S., Burton, William H., and Brueckner, Leo J. *Supervision: Principles and Practices in the Improvement of Instruction.* New York: D. Appleton-Century, 1938.

Barr, A. S., Burton, William H., and Brueckner, Leo J. *Supervision: Democratic Leadership in the Improvement of Learning,* 2nd ed. New York: Appleton-Century-Crofts, 1947.

Bartky, John A. *Supervision as Human Relations.* Boston: D. C. Heath, 1953.

Boardman, Charles W., Douglass Harl, R. and Bent, Rudyard K. *Democratic Supervision in Secondary Schools.* Boston: Houghton Mifflin and Co., 1953.

Briggs, Thomas H. *Improving Instruction.* New York: The Macmillan Co., 1938.

Briggs, Thomas H., and Justman, Joseph. *Improving Instruction Through Supervision.* New York: The Macmillan Co., 1952.

Burton, William H., and Brueckner, Leo J. *Supervision: A Social Process.* 3rd ed. New York: Appleton-Century-Crofts, 1955.

Chapple, Eliot D., and Wright, Edmond F. *How to Supervise People in Industry.* New London: National Foremen's Institute, 1946.

Commission on English. *12,000 Students and Their English Teachers.* Princeton, New Jersey: College Entrance Examination Board, 1968.

Douglass, Harl R., and Boardman, Charles W. *Supervision in Secondary Schools.* Boston: Houghton Mifflin and Co., 1934.

Hammock, Robert C., and Owings, Ralph S. *Supervising Instruction in Secondary Schools.* New York: McGraw-Hill Book Co., 1955.

Lateiner, Alfred R. *The Techniques of Supervision.* New London, Conn.: National Foremen's Institute, 1954.

MacKenzie, Gordon N., and Corey, Stephen M. *Instructional Leadership.* New York: Bureau of Publications, Teachers College, Columbia University, 1954.

Marks, James, Stoops, Emory, and King-Stoops, Joyce. *Handbook of Educational Supervision.* Boston: Allyn and Bacon, 1973.

McNerney, Chester T. *Educational Supervision.* New York: McGraw-Hill Book Co., 1951.

Melby, Ernest O. *Organization and Administration of Supervision.* Bloomington, Illinois: Public School Publishing Co., 1929.

Melchior, William T. *Instructional Supervision.* Boston: D. C. Heath and Co., 1959.

Mitchum, Paul M. *The High School Principal and Staff Plan for Program Improvement.* New York: Bureau of Publications, Teachers College, Columbia University, 1958.

Parody, Ovid F. *The High School Principal and Staff Deal with Discipline.* New York: Bureau of Publications, Teachers College, Columbia University, 1958.

Schmidt, Warren H., and Buchanan, Paul C. *Techniques That Produce Teamwork.* New London, Conn: Arthur C. Croft, 1954.

Spears, Harold. *Improving the Supervision of Instruction.* Englewood Cliffs, New Jersey: Prentice-Hall, 1953.

Uhl, Willis L. *The Supervision of Secondary Subjects.* New York: D. Appleton and Co., 1929.

Wiles, Kimball. *Supervision for Better Schools.* Englewood Cliffs, New Jersey: Prentice-Hall, 1950.

Yauch, Wilbur A. *Helping Teachers Understand Principals.* New York: Appleton-Century-Crofts, 1957.

Yauch, Wilbur A. *Improving Human Relations in School Administration.* New York: Harper and Brothers, 1949.

Pamphlets and Periodicals

Brett, Sue M. ed. *Supervision of English Grades K-12*. A Resource Book for State and Local School Systems. Champaign, Illinois: National Council of Teachers of English, 1964.
Committee on National Interest. *The National Interest and the Continuing Education of Teachers of English*. Champaign, Illinois: National Council of Teachers of English, 1964, pp. 151-164.
Jenkinson, Edward., and Daghlian, Philip B. eds. *Books for Teachers of English*. Bloomington: Indiana University Press, 1968.
Squire, James R. *High School Departments of English: Their Organization, Administration, and Supervision*. Champaign, Illinois: National Council of Teachers of English, 1965.

CHAPTER 24: THE PRINCIPAL AND HIS INFLUENCE ON THE ENGLISH PROGRAM

Notes

1. Quoted by John F. Schereschewsky, Director, Rumsey Hall School, at the 33rd Annual Meeting of the Secondary Education Board, Hotel Statler, New York City, March 6, 1959, and reprinted with his and Dr. Watson's permission.
2. Joseph Mersand, *Attitudes Toward English Teaching* (Philadelphia: Chilton, 1961).
3. Howard C. Zimmerman, "Structural Linguistics and High School Grammar," *Curriculum Bulletin*, No. 223, Vol. XVIII (May, 1962) School of Education, University of Oregon.
4. Committee on National Interest, *The National Interest and the Teaching of English* (Champaign, Illinois: National Council of Teachers of English, 1961). See also Committee on National Interest, *The National Interest and the Continuing Education of Teachers of English* (Champaign, Illinois: National Council of Teachers of English, 1964) pp. 151-164.

Bibliography

Books

Association for Supervision and Curriculum Development, National Education Association. *Action for Curriculum Improvement*. Chapters III, IV. Washington, D. C.: A. S. C. D., 1951.
――― *Leadership Through Supervision*. Washington, D. C.: A. S. C. D., 1949.
――― *Role of the Supervisor and Curriculum Director in a Climate of Change*. Washington, D. C.: A. S. C. D., 1965.
Jacobson, P. B., and Reavis, W. C. *Duties of School Principals*. New York: Prentice-Hall, 1941, pp. 379-417.
Kyte, George C. *The Principal at Work*. Revised edition. Boston: Ginn, 1952, Chapter XIX, pp. 333-354.
Marks, James, Stoops, Emory, and King-Stoops, Joyce. *Handbook of Educational Supervision*. Boston: Allyn and Bacon, 1973.
Mitchum, Paul M. *The High School Principal and Staff Plan for Program Improvement*. New York: Bureau of Publications, Teachers College, Columbia University, 1958.

Pamphlets and Periodicals

Bureau of Curriculum Development, Board of Education of the City of New York. *Curriculum Development in the Elementary Schools*. Curriculum Bulletin, 1955–56 Series, No. 1. New York: Board of Education, 1955, pp. 16-19.
Bureau of Curriculum Research, Board of Education of the City of New York. *Guide to Curriculum Improvement in Grades 7-8-9*. Curriculum Bulletin, 1955–56 Series, No. 10. New York: Board of Education, 1957, pp. 47-52.

A Guide to Curriculum Improvement in the Junior High Schools. New York: Board of Education, 1946.

Committee of the Northwest Association for Supervision and Curriculum Development, *Helping the New Teacher.* Washington, D. C.: A. S. C. D., 1956.

Educational Leadership. April, 1948. The entire issue is devoted to Administration's concern with School Programs.

CHAPTER 25: THE HIGH SCHOOL ENGLISH CHAIRMAN LOOKS AT THE HUMANITIES APPROACH FOR ALL STUDENTS

Notes

1. Joseph Mersand, "How Fare the Humanities in High School?" *English Journal* (November, 1962) pp. 552-559.
2. Louise M. Berman, editor, *The Humanities and the Curriculum.* Papers from a Conference Sponsored by the ASCD Commission on Current Curriculum Developments (Washington, D. C.: A. S. C. D., 1965).
3. Vivienne Anderson, editor, *The Humanities: a Planning Guide* (Albany: State Education Department, 1966).
4. ———, *An Invitation to the Dance* (Albany: State Education Department, 1968).
5. ———, *Performing Arts Education* (Albany: State Education Department, 1968).
6. Leon C. Karel, *Avenues to the Arts.* Second Edition. (Kirksville, Mo.: Simpson Publishing Co., 1969).
7. William Rose Benét, editor, *The Reader's Encyclopedia* (New York: Thomas Y. Crowell, Co., 1948).
8. Bernard S. Miller, *The Humanities Approach to the Modern Secondary Curriculum* (New York: The Center for Applied Research in Education, 1972). Contains much valuable information on various approaches.
9. Edith Rickert, compiler, Clair C. Olson and Martin W. Crow, editors, *Chaucer's World* (New York: Columbia University Press, 1948).
10. G. G. Coulton, *Medieval Panorama* (New York: Macmillan, 1938).
11. Roger Sherman Loomis, *A Mirror of Chaucer's World* (Princeton: Princeton University Press, 1965).
12. John Edwin Wells, *A Manual of the Writings in Middle English* (New Haven: Yale University Press, 1916 and several later supplements).
13. Morris Bishop, editor, *The Horizon Book of the Middle Ages* (New York: American Heritage Publishing Co., 1968).
14. Victor Kaplan, reader, *Readings from the Canterbury Tales* (New York: Folkways, Fl. 9859). Theodore Morrison has provided a modern English translation of "The Pardoner's Tale" and "The Miller's Tale," read by Michael MacLiammoir and Stanley Holloway (New York: Caedmon Records, No. TC 1130).
15. John C. Pope, reader, *Beowulf and Chaucer* (Pleasantville, New York: Lexington Records, No. L E 5505).
16. Anthony Quayle, reader, *The Ballad of Robin Hood* (New York: Caedmon Records, No. TC 1177).
17. ———, *Schwann Record & Tape Guide* (Boston: W. Schwann, Inc.). Appears monthly.
18. Louise Dudley and Austin Faricy. Third Edition. *The Humanities* (New York: McGraw-Hill, 1960).
19. Raymond S. Stites, *The Arts and Man* (New York: Macmillan, 1940).
20. ———, *An Introduction to Literature and the Fine Arts* (East Lansing: Michigan State College Press, 1950).
21. Donald J. McGinn and George Howerton, *Literature as a Fine Art* (Staten Island, New York: Gordian Press, 1967).
22. Various authors, *Adventures in Literature,* Six Volumes (New York: Harcourt, Brace Jovanovich, 1968).

Bibliography

Books

An Introduction to Literature and the Fine Arts. East Lansing: Michigan State College Press, 1950.

Angoff, Charles. ed. *Humanities in the Age of Science.* Teaneck, New Jersey: Fairleigh-Dickinson University Press, 1968.

Asheim, Lester. ed. *Humanities and the Library: Problems, Interpretations, Evaluation, and Use of Library Materials.* Chicago: American Library Association, 1957.

Beardsley, Monroe C. ed. *Humanities and the Understanding of Reality.* Lexington, Kentucky: University of Kentucky Press, 1966.

Bishop, Morris. *The Horizon Book of the Middle Ages.* New York: American Heritage Publishing Company, 1968.

Dunkel, Harold Baker. *General Education in the Humanities.* Washington, D. C.: American Council on Education, 1947.

Dudley, Louise, and Faricy, A. *Humanities.* 3rd ed. New York: McGraw-Hill, 1961.

Fenton, E. B. *Humanities in the Social Settings.* New York: Holt, Rinehart and Winston, 1968.

Karel, Leon C. *Avenues to the Arts.* 2nd ed. Kirksville, Mo.: Simpson Publishing Co., 1969.

Miller, Bernard S. *The Humanities Approach to the Modern Secondary School Curriculum.* New York: The Center for Applied Research in Education, 1972.

Satin, Joseph. *Humanities Handbook.* New York: Holt, Rinehart and Winston, 1970.

Stites, Raymond S. *The Arts and Man.* New York: Macmillan, 1940.

Van Ess, Donald H. ed. *The Commonwealth of Arts and Man.* New York: Thomas Y. Crowell Co., 1973.

Pamphlets and Periodicals

For an extensive bibliography of articles on the teaching of the Humanities, consult:

Anderson, Vivienne. ed. *The Humanities: A Planning Guide.* Albany: State Education Department, 1966. This lists seventy-five articles published up to 1966; ———, ed. *Forum on the Humanities.* Albany: State Education Department, 1968; ———, ed. *Humanities. . . .* Albany: State Education Department, 1969; ———, ed. *An Invitation to the Dance.* Albany: State Education Department, 1968; ———, ed. *Performing Arts Education.* Albany: State Education Department, 1968.

Berman, Louise M. ed. *The Humanities in the Curriculum.* Washington, D. C.: A. S. C. D., 1967.

Lape, James T. ed. *The English Leaflet. New England Association of Teachers of English,* 1964. The entire Fall, 1964 issue is devoted to the Humanities.

Markwardt, Albert H. ed. *Literature in Humanities Programs.* Papers delivered at the N. C. T. E. Humanities Conference, Fall, 1966. Champaign, Illinois: National Council of Teachers of English, 1967.

Taylor, Harold. ed. *The Humanities in the Schools.* New York: Citation Press, 1968.

Weinstein, Gerald and Fantini, Mario D. eds. *Toward Humanistic Education: A Curriculum of Affect.* New York: Praeger Publishers, 1970.

CHAPTER 26: SOLUTIONS TO SOME PERSISTENT PROBLEMS

Notes

1. Newton Arvin, *Longfellow* (Boston: Little, Brown, 1963) p. 47.

Bibliography

Books

Benne, Kenneth D., and Bozidan, Muntyan. *Human Relations in Curriculum Change.* New York: Dryden Press, 1951.

Commission on English. *Speaking about Teaching.* Papers from the 1965 Summer Session of the Commission on English. Princeton, N. J.: College Entrance Examination Board, 1967.

Corey, Stephen M. *Action Research to Improve School Practices.* New York: Bureau of Publications, Teachers College, Columbia University, 1953.

Gromman, Alfred H. ed. *The Education of Teachers of English.* New York: Appleton-Century-Crofts, 1963, pp. 367-461.

Hook, J. N. *The Teaching of High School English.* 4th ed. New York: Ronald Press, 1972, pp. 548-564.

National Society for the Study of Education. *In-Service Education.* The 56th Yearbook, Part I. Chicago: University of Chicago Press, 1957.

Rubin, Louis J. *Improving In-Service Education.* Boston: Allyn and Bacon, 1972.

Schmidt, Warren H., and Buchanan, Paul C. *Techniques That Produce Teamwork.* New London, Conn.: A. C. Croft Publications, 1954.

Spears, Harold. *Curriculum Planning Through In-Service Programs.* Englewood Cliffs, N. J.: Prentice-Hall, 1957.

Pamphlets and Periodicals

Brett, Sue M. ed. *Supervision of English, Grades K-12:* A Resource Book for State and Local School Systems. Urbana: National Council of Teachers of English, 1965.

Committee on National Interest. *The National Interest and the Continuing Education of Teachers of English.* Urbana: National Council of Teachers of English, 1964.

Hartley, Helene. "The Continuing Education of Teachers of English" in *Perspectives in English.* ed. by Robert C. Pooley. New York: Appleton-Century-Crofts, 1960, pp. 303-313.

Lacampagne, Robert J. ed. *High School Departments of English: Their Organization, Administration, and Supervision.* Urbana: National Council of Teachers of English, 1965.

Strom, Robert D. *The Preface Plan, a New Concept of In-Service Training for Teachers Newly Assigned to Urban Neighborhoods of Low Income.* Columbus: Ohio State University, 1967.

INDEX